Once upon a time there lived a little Princess with Hair black as ebony, Lips red as a Rose = and Skin white as Snow.

THE FAIREST ONE of ALL

J.B. KAUFMAN

To little Joan and little Gretchen,
who watched *Snow White*
three times in one day
in 1938

Aurum *e*
entertainment

CONTENTS

FOREWORD

I have to believe that 1933 was one of the most important years in my father's life. Technicolor had developed a three-color process for film that was still not perfected for live-action photography, but could be used for cartoons. Dad persuaded the company to grant him exclusive rights to use the process for two years, and he used it in the Silly Symphony *Flowers and Trees*, which was released in July of 1932. It created a sensation. The previous year, he had arranged with Nelbert Chouinard to have his artists attend night classes in her art institute because the kind of training they needed for what he wanted to do wasn't taught in the art schools of that time. In November of 1932, he received his first Academy Award—the first award for a cartoon, for *Flowers and Trees*, and a special award for the creation of Mickey Mouse. There was great triumph that year, but also great disappointment. Mother had suffered the second of two miscarriages, and my dad was profoundly disappointed.

Three Little Pigs was a huge hit when it opened in 1933. The silly, simple little song became wildly popular, with the Wolf representing the Depression of that time. It earned Dad another Oscar. My mother was with child again, throughout this year. Dad was scheduled to receive an award from *Parents* magazine on December 18, and it was early that morning when Mother became aware that the child she carried was ready to be born. The rest has never really been explained to me, but I assume Dad must have taken her to the hospital and been assured by her doctor that it would be some time before the baby arrived. He went on to the award banquet but was called away after it had begun. News articles from that time indicate that the audience was baffled by his hurried exit until, some time later, the chairman of the event, Dr. Rufus B. Von Kleinsmid, rose and announced, "I'd like to propose a toast to Miss Diane Marie Disney!" I like to think that this event, near the end of an exciting, busy, successful year, was the grand finale.

It was during this year that Dad became convinced that his staff was ready and able to undertake a feature-length cartoon, and that audiences would be eager to receive one. Dad had selected the story of Snow White and the Seven Dwarfs, and he presented it to his men on the studio sound stage one evening. He acted out all the parts of the story, and his audience became very engaged in it and were very excited about it. Some of them, however, were dubious. They were makers of shorts. But by the end of 1934, work had begun on the story and development of characters.

During the summer of 1935, Uncle Roy, sensing that Dad needed a break from the pressure he'd put himself under, proposed that they take a trip to Europe. They did, the four of them: Mother, Dad, Roy, and Edna. Dad was received with great interest and acclaim wherever they went, and, while in Paris, he took note of a movie theater that ran nothing but Mickey Mouse cartoons all day long.

My first experience with the film wasn't auspicious at all. I still have vivid memories of it. It was being screened in the sound stage. I was there with my mother—maybe Dad was sitting with us, but I don't remember. When the Queen began turning into the Witch I became terrified and can remember screaming repeatedly in fear. I was rushed outside; I don't know by whose hands, but I remember being left outside those big doors of the sound stage, from the darkness into the bright sun, and a man I'd never seen before was looking down at me. I don't recall if I was returned to the theater or who might have retrieved me if I was retrieved. I would have been about three-and-a-half years old. As far as I know, Dad didn't cut anything out of that sequence because of my reaction. But it is interesting that one of my favorite games when I was four or five was "Old Witch." When Bill Cottrell and my Aunt Hazel came to our home, I would demand that Bill chase Sharon and me through our house, being as witchlike as he could be.

So many of the artists, musicians, and writers who worked on *Snow White* remember it as a uniquely exciting creative experience. The studio was bursting at the seams, and satellite studio space was secured nearby in Hollywood. From *Flowers and Trees* in 1932 to *Snow White* a mere four years later, the improvement in the work of the animators was astonishing. This was the result of the school Dad established on his lot under the supervision of Don Graham with the fine instructors from the Chouinard Art Institute. Dad worked closely with Graham in developing the curriculum for the school, with action analysis, good draftsmanship, and knowledge of caricature stressed. Along with story there was still the need for "gags," as in the early cartoons.

When we interviewed Ward Kimball for our film *Walt: The Man Behind the Myth*, we of course asked him to talk about the Soup sequence, the sequence that he'd worked on for months, which Dad had to cut from the film. Ward admitted that "It kinda hurt," but in acknowledging Dad's decision, he said of the film, "I still think it's the best thing we ever did." Many of the others at the studio felt the same way about it.

Before undertaking this project, J.B. Kaufman's passion and field of study had been confined to silent films. He had collaborated with Russell Merritt, professor of film at UC Berkeley, on the book *Walt in Wonderland: The Silent Films of Walt Disney*, which was published in Italy by Le Giornate del Cinema Muto. Years later they followed with a volume on the Silly Symphonies. While writing the script for our museum, he proposed this book. We are proud to offer it in this year, the 75th anniversary of the film, as the definitive book on the making of *Snow White and the Seven Dwarfs*, and the first publication of the Walt Disney Family Foundation Press.

Diane Disney Miller

7

INTRODUCTION

Slave in the magic mirror,
Come from the farthest space!
Through wind and darkness I summon thee.
Speak! Let me see thy face!

With these words, spoken by a beautiful but cold and ruthless Queen, begins a classic motion picture. The slave appears in a blast of wind and lightning, and the Queen utters these lines:

Magic mirror on the wall,
Who is the fairest one of all?

—and we're drawn into the familiar story once again. The fairest one of all is, of course, the enslaved princess Snow White, and the ensuing film will tell us her story. But the figures on the screen are not live actors, the wind and lightning no ordinary special effects. Every image we will see for the next 83 minutes has been drawn, painted, or otherwise fashioned by hand. And not by the hand of a single artist, but by hundreds, brought together and coordinated by the guiding vision of one extraordinary filmmaker.

Walt Disney's *Snow White and the Seven Dwarfs* was first shown to a theatrical audience in December 1937 and brought overwhelming, joyous applause from a house full of hardened film-industry professionals. In subsequent months it would open around the world, happily acclaimed by audiences everywhere. The fresh, handcrafted and yet seemingly real world it depicted on the screen, its engaging characters, its profusion of delightful, witty details, and its tuneful musical score were a revelation. Viewers of every age returned to see it again and again. Critics hailed it as all ten of "the ten best pictures of 1938" and

"the happiest thing that has happened in this world since the Armistice."

If *Snow White* was appreciated as a phenomenal achievement even by the heightened standards of the 1930s, its stature seems astronomical today. From a later perspective, seeing *Snow White* as the flowering of an all-too-brief Golden Age of animation—not to mention what passes for entertainment in our own age—we can perhaps appreciate, even more than the audiences of 1938, the artistry of this remarkable film. Its craftsmanship, delightful at first glance, becomes more absorbing and impressive the more closely we look. In hindsight, too, it takes on additional dimensions as a document of its time, a time capsule in which the theatrical, musical, cinematic, and other popular arts of the early twentieth century are seamlessly absorbed. Other fantasy films may pale or tarnish with repetition; *Snow White* grows richer and more luminous with each viewing.

This level of artistic achievement doesn't happen by accident. Walt Disney and a staff of exceptionally talented artists labored over *Snow White* for four years, endlessly working and reworking their scenes to achieve an ever higher standard. In the studio "sweatboxes"—the small projection rooms where the artists' pencil animation was screened for critique—Walt and his directors and artists studied their work endlessly, criticizing, refining, polishing. *Snow White* was not so much animated as *re*animated; every scene, every frame, was subjected to a grueling process of analysis and refinement.

The result was a film not only for its own time, but for all time. Long since absorbed into our culture, endlessly exploited as a marketing tool for kiddie merchandise, *Snow White* remains undiminished. In the long view of history, in the world where *Intolerance* and *Citizen Kane* are recognized as great films, *Snow White and the Seven Dwarfs* is a great film—unique, cherished, and timeless. This is its story.

PART ONE

Before 1934

A Queen, beautiful but wicked and vain, learns from her magic mirror that her own stepdaughter, Snow White, is more beautiful than she. Summoning her Huntsman, the Queen sends him into the forest with Snow White, giving him instructions to kill the girl there. The Huntsman cannot bring himself to carry out this order, and Snow White runs away into the deep forest, where she finds refuge with seven dwarfs. Learning that Snow White is still alive, the Queen disguises herself and seeks out the dwarfs' cottage. She makes several attempts on the girl's life and finally tricks her into eating a poisoned apple. Snow White seems to have died, and the dwarfs mourn their beloved princess. But when a prince finds her still form and falls in love with her, it is revealed that Snow White did not die after all. She is revived and marries the prince.

THE BIRTH OF THE TALE

The Grimms' *Kinder- und Hausmärchen,* originally published as a scholarly anthology, found new popularity as a children's storybook.

[1] D.L. Ashliman points out that "Sneewittchen," meaning "Little Snow White," is a compound word derived from Low German, although the Grimms published the tale itself in High German. The High German translation of the heroine's name is "Schneeweißchen."

No one knows exactly where or when the story of "Snow White" originated. Today we tend to associate the story with the Brothers Grimm—but the Grimms were not creators so much as collectors. Their publication of "Sneewittchen" in 1812 was meant simply to preserve a traditional German folk tale for posterity. In truth, elements of the "Snow White" story had been deeply rooted in the Grimms' culture, and in many others, for centuries before that. One of the earliest written versions, "La schiavottella" ("The Young Slave") by Giambattista Basile, was published in Italy in the 1630s, predating the Grimms' version by nearly 200 years. "The Young Slave" is a heartrending tale of a lovely young orphaned girl whose life is apparently cut short by a fairy's curse. By a cruel twist of fate, she is freed from this artificial death only to be cast into a living hell at the hands of her bitterly jealous aunt, who beats her, enslaves her, and denies her any scrap of comfort or kindness. In despair, the girl is at the point of suicide when her plight finally comes to her uncle's attention. He rescues her and drives the aunt away, and the girl is finally restored to her rightful place. There is magic and enchantment in this story, but no seven dwarfs, and precious little happiness. Like many traditional fairy tales, it takes place in a very dark world.

Basile's story was not itself an original composition, but a story passed down through an already long-standing oral tradition. Similar tales abounded in other European cultures, and had done so for centuries, many of them probably generated independently of one another in a process that folklorists call *polygenesis*. Basile was simply one of the earliest writers to record these stories in written form. As time passed, other writers in Italy and elsewhere began to publish similar collections of folk tales. Later in the seventeenth century a literary fairy-tale tradition began to flourish in France, in the hands of such writers as Charles Perrault. Other cultures made contributions of their own, and soon the literary fairy tale was an established genre, preserving a wide variety of regional traditions for future generations, even as they influenced each other. By the time Jacob and Wilhelm Grimm came to record their stories in the early 1800s, they came as academics seeking to add their country's voice to a widespread and diverse institution.

The Grimms saw themselves as scholars charged with preserving the cultural history of their beloved native Germany, in part as a mild form of resistance against the current Napoleonic occupation. Their collection *Kinder- und Hausmärchen* (*Children's and Household Tales*), published in two volumes in 1812 and 1814 (the second volume dated 1815), was not a children's storybook but a scholarly anthology of traditional German folktales, complete with notes on distribution patterns and variant versions of the stories. The tale of "Sneewittchen,"[1] included in the first volume in 1812, was related to the Grimms by two sisters in Cassel. This cultural variant retained the same core element that had driven Basile's story—an older woman's murderous jealousy of the heroine's beauty—but added distinctive elements of its own. The Queen's mirror, a symbol of her vanity, became also the oracle that informed her of the still greater beauty of Snow White. The deep forest into which Snow White escaped was a natural feature of Germany's topography, and the dwarfs with whom she sought refuge were cousins to the dwarfs who appeared in other German stories collected by the Grimms. That there were seven of them was also characteristic: the number seven, symbolizing fullness or completeness, was a significant number that cropped up elsewhere in the Grimms' tales—as here, where the disguised queen travels "beyond the seven hills" to reach the dwarfs' cottage.[2] The poisoned apple in this version was not actually ingested by Snow White. Instead a piece of it lodged in her throat, and she *seemed* to have died; later, when the morsel was dislodged, she instantly recovered.

Intentionally or not, the Grimms' collection of stories became widely popular with family audiences and prompted a demand for further editions. Wilhelm Grimm, the younger of the two brothers, happily obliged. A natural storyteller in his own right, Grimm was quick to see that the published stories had found a large and unexpected audience and shrewd enough to adapt them to that audience. In his subsequent editions of the fairy tales, the scholarly notes were banished to a separate volume or eliminated altogether, and the stories themselves were increasingly retailored for children and their parents. In the original 1812 publication of "Sneewittchen," as in the oral version related to the Grimms, the jealous Queen who tries to kill Snow White is the girl's own mother! For the second edition in 1819, Grimm rewrote the beginning of the story so that the mother died, the father remarried, and the villainess became Snow White's stepmother. Other elements of the story were similarly softened as "Sneewittchen" worked its way through successive editions.

The popularity of "Sneewittchen" and the Grimms' other stories was not confined to Germany; translations quickly began to appear in other countries. An English translation, "Snow-Drop," was published in England as early as 1823; this was followed by a specifically British variant, "Snow-White," which retained much of the Grimms' basic plot but replaced the seven dwarfs with three robbers and ended with the wicked Queen roasted in a brick kiln. Many of the other cultural variants likewise used robbers in place of the dwarfs. In Italy, whose folklore seldom featured dwarfs, their place in the story was taken by robbers ("Bella Venezia" and "Maria, the Wicked Stepmother, and the Seven Robbers"), fairies ("The Crystal Casket" and "A Tuscan Snow-White"),

an ogre and his wife ("The Beautiful Anna"), or even the moon ("Giricoccola"), while in other versions the dwarfs had no counterpart at all. In at least one case, the dwarfs branched off into a grisly story of their own: the unnamed Snow White is merely a supporting character in the Swiss tale "Death of the Seven Dwarfs," which concentrates on a wicked peasant woman's visit to the dwarfs' cottage, their refusal to give up their fair visitor, and the woman's return with two henchmen who ruthlessly slaughter the dwarfs and burn their cottage to the ground! In other variations the stepmother became neither a peasant nor a queen, but an innkeeper or a schoolteacher. The Italian "Bella Venezia" and the Scottish "Gold-Tree and Silver-Tree," like the Grimms' original edition, cast the girl's own mother as the villainess, while in other stories like "Giricoccola" or the Greek "Myrsina, or Myrtle," the girl's life was sought by her jealous sisters. In two Celtic variants, "Gold-Tree and Silver-Tree" and "Lasair Gheug, the King of Ireland's Daughter," the Queen's magic mirror was replaced by a talking trout. All in all, by the end of the nineteenth century there were literally hundreds of published variants of the "Snow White" story, many of them no doubt enriched by cross-fertilization.

Nevertheless—despite the multitude of variant versions, despite the long oral tradition that preceded the Grimms, despite the considerable variations even within the Grimms' own versions of the story—the Brothers Grimm had established a proprietary hold on the story of "Snow White." Their version, or one of their versions, came to be regarded as the definitive standard. Something about their combination of themes touched a universal chord, underlying all the cultural variations, to give their "Snow White" a potent staying power; as Maria Tatar comments, "it has remained one of our most powerful cultural stories." In the Aarne-Thompson-Uther index *The Types of International Folktales*, universally accepted as the definitive index for students of folklore, "Snow White" was codified as tale type 709, with a list of motifs—the cruel stepmother, the compassionate executioner, the seven dwarfs, the poisoned apple, the glass coffin, and others—all of which were drawn from the Grimms' story, and any or all of which might be found, sometimes with variations, in any of the hundreds of other related stories in the same category.[3]

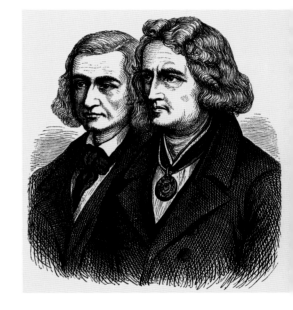

An engraving of the Brothers Grimm: Wilhelm (left) and Jacob (right).

[2] This is one of the devices retained in the Disney film: the magic mirror, queried by the Queen, tells her that "over the seven jeweled hills, beyond the seventh fall, in the cottage of the Seven Dwarfs," Snow White still lives.

[3] It's worth noting that "Snow White," as a spoken or written tale, has continued to maintain an active life of its own independently of stage and film adaptations. Maria Tatar, in *The Classic Fairy Tales*, cites variant analyses extending well into the late twentieth century, including such feminist interpretations as that of Sandra M. Gilbert and Susan Gubar in *The Madwoman in the Attic: The Woman Writer and the Nineteenth-Century Literary Imagination*, published by Yale University Press in 1979.

2

"SNOW WHITE" ON STAGE AND SCREEN

Carl August Görner, author of the 1856 stage adaptation of *Sneewittchen.*

The wide popularity of the "Snow White" story in oral and published form was a virtual guarantee that it would appear in other forms, including stage adaptations. To catalogue *all* the stage adaptations of "Snow White" might fill a book much longer than this one, but we can chart some of the major versions that have a significant bearing on our story. One important early dramatic version, if not actually the first, was mounted by one of the Grimms' countrymen in the 1850s. Not only was this production notable in its own right, it inaugurated a remarkable chain of adaptations that we can trace, almost directly, from Germany in the mid-nineteenth century to the Walt Disney studio in the 1930s.

SNEEWITTCHEN UND DIE ZWERGE (KINDER-THEATER, 1856)
This adaptation was written and produced by the prominent German playwright Carl August Görner (1806–1884). It was presented in 1856 at Görner's recently opened Kinder-Theater, its appearance corresponding loosely to publication of the seventh and final edition of the Grimms' *Kinder- und Hausmärchen* in 1857.

In this first major stage version of the story, Görner confronted the same challenge that would face subsequent adapters: fleshing out the Grimms' short story into a form that would provide a full evening's entertainment. Ideas and characters that can be quickly glossed over in a written or recited story assume tangible, specific form in their stage incarnations. Görner's play remains faithful to the basics of the Grimms' plot: the Queen's jealousy of Snow White; the Huntsman's

murderous mission and his mercy toward Snow White; the girl's refuge in the forest with the seven dwarfs; the Queen's consultation of the magic mirror; and her attempts to kill Snow White with two of the Grimms' devices, the poisoned comb and the poisoned apple. As in the Grimms' story, the piece of apple doesn't actually kill Snow White but simply lodges in her throat, so that she revives when it is dislodged (an event that takes place offstage in this version).

But in expanding the story into a five-act play, Görner also takes some creative liberties. Some are minor: the Queen orders the Huntsman to bring back Snow White's tongue, rather than her lungs and liver. The Huntsman, nameless in the story, becomes a more substantial character here and is named Berthold. But there are significant structural differences too: the Prince, who appears only at the end of the Grimms' tale, is here introduced in the first act (as the Prince of "Goldlande") searching for a bride. With his companion Otto, the Prince is traveling incognito, disguised as a poor knight so that he can discern the true character of those he meets. Not surprisingly, he gets a cold reception from the Queen, but is smitten with Snow White and inquires about her background. Learning that she is by rights a princess, the Prince departs to inform his father of his decision to marry her—thus removing him from the action of the following scenes, but preparing for his return at the end of the story. The Queen's mirror, a wall mirror in the Grimms' story, here becomes a hand mirror so that the Queen can carry it with her and consult it in the field—until, in a fit of temper, she

smashes it in the last act. At the end, as in the story, red-hot iron shoes are prepared for the Queen to dance in, but here Snow White intervenes and insists on showing her mercy instead.

Perhaps most important, the seven anonymous dwarfs of the Grimms' story become seven individuals here. Few strong characteristics are given them, but Görner gives them names: Blick, Pick, Knick, Dick, Rick, Strick, and Schick. Blick is the leader, mainly because he marches at the head of the line (the dwarfs' marching chant implies that he runs ahead of the group in order to be first). His opposite is Schick, who brings up the rear and is occasionally given a humorous line of dialogue for comic relief. Joyfully welcoming Snow White into their home, the dwarfs demonstrate their modest little tricks for her entertainment: Blick sings, Pick jumps, Strick stands on one leg, Dick turns around. On Snow White's apparent death, the dwarfs' despondency is manifest: all seven stand vigil over her glass shrine because no one has the heart to go back to work.

Viewed from our much later perspective, Görner's play may seem austere, even somber. It's important to remember that his play shared not only the Grimms' narrative, but also their cultural context; fairy tales were expected to contain elements of magic and enchantment but also commonly depicted a cold, forbidding, and dangerous world. Subsequent American versions of *Snow White* would add successively greater helpings of comedy and entertainment value, so that, entirely apart from the Disney film, our perceptions of *Snow White* and of fairy tales in general have become far sunnier and more comforting. In any case, Görner's *Sneewittchen* was a success in its time and was periodically revived. By the late 1890s, regular presentations with interpolated music had become a Christmas tradition in some locations.

SNOW-WHITE (CHILDREN'S EDUCATIONAL THEATRE, 1905)

In succeeding decades other *Snow Whites* would appear on the stage, including at least one operatic version, presented in England in 1899. But half a century after its first appearance in Germany, Görner's adaptation was itself adapted in America. When the Children's Educational Theatre opened its doors on New York's East Side in the autumn of 1905, its mission was to present plays for the educational betterment of children, both in the casts and in the audience. One of the plays in the Theatre's inaugural season was *Snow-White*, written by Marguerite Merington and based on Görner's play. In some ways this is a very close adaptation of Görner's script. The structure is roughly the same: the Prince of Goldland still appears with his companion Otto in the opening scene, searching incognito for a bride, and is smitten with Snow-White. The Huntsman retains the name Berthold (and is still charged with bringing back Snow-White's tongue), and the dwarfs too retain their individual names. The Queen, driven by jealousy, still pursues more or less the course of her predecessor in the Grimms' tale, but here again she carries her mirror as a hand mirror and smashes it in fury in the last act. And once again, at the end, the awful punishment of the red-hot iron shoes is averted by Snow-White's natural impulse of kindness.

These early storybook illustrations show two of the commonly recurring elements of the story. At left, the disguised Queen tempts Snow White with a poisoned comb.

In the Franz Jüttner illustration at right, Snow White, still in the glass coffin, revives when the piece of poisoned apple in her throat is jarred loose.

American theatrical impresario Winthrop Ames, who brought Snow White to Broadway.

But Merington's script is not simply a translation of Görner's; there are significant variations here, too. For one thing, events that are simply described verbally in the Görner play are here shown onstage. One is the meeting of Snow-White and the Prince, who not only meet in the first scene but enjoy a romantic formal dance together, each still unaware of the other's identity. The removal of the poisoned morsel from Snow-White's mouth and her revival, related by Blick to the other dwarfs in Görner's play, occurs onstage in the last act of Merington's version.

Too, the element of humor seems far more pronounced in Merington's adaptation—presumably on the theory that this will make the dark aspects of the story more palatable for American children. The Queen, without losing any of her evil nature, becomes a somewhat comic character in this version. Her violent temper comes in for ridicule: during her periodic outbursts, her crown slips over one eye and has to be adjusted for her. Whenever someone fails to understand what she's talking about, she spells it for them and invariably spells it wrong. Her leading trait, vanity, is also ridiculed. In one scene she calls for "a moment of silent contemplation of our beauty," then flies into a rage when her courtiers fail to understand that "our beauty" means *her* beauty.

The dwarfs provide their own strong undercurrent of comedy—in particular Schick, the last in line, the odd man out. In Görner's play Schick had been given an occasional funny line, but here he's full-fledged comedy relief, sounding off with mindless inappropriate remarks that invariably bring a reproving "Schick!" from the other dwarfs. When Snow-White, who has never baked a cake before, volunteers to bake one for the dwarfs, Schick eagerly rejoins: "I'll eat it! I'd give my very life for you!" The dwarfs as a group also get an occasional moment of comedy. In the last act, the Prince swears vengeance against the Queen and raises his sword high in a defiant gesture; Otto also raises his sword; the dwarfs manage to lift theirs "by united effort."

There's also a striking abundance of music in this version, more integral to the script than in Görner's play. The dwarfs, returning from a day at the mine, identify themselves in a marching song. When the

Queen appears in the third act disguised as a peddler, she sings an elaborate song to peddle her wares: "Here's thimbles and thread. Here's needles and pins./Here's finest of flax for my lady who spins./Here's buckles and brooches and garters. Gay laces,/And ribbons like rainbows to set off sweet faces . . ." Later, when she returns with her apples, she's heard offstage singing another song that reminds the homesick Snow-White of the apple peddlers at home.

In keeping with the lofty ideals of the Children's Educational Theatre, Merington's *Snow-White* includes numerous appeals to the better spiritual natures of her young audience. When Görner's Snow White was abandoned in the woods by Berthold, she offered up a prayer; here the prayer is expanded into an "Evening Hymn," which Snow-White later repeats with the dwarfs: "Father in Heaven, through the day/O may Thy love enlighten me./And when the sun goes down I pray/Let not the darkness frighten me . . ." The dwarfs, offering Snow-White their hospitality, apologetically point out that they are only dwarfs and their house only a hut. Snow-White replies: "Gentlemen, dear friends, your hearts are palaces, your souls reach clear to Heaven." In the last act, when Snow-White seems to have died and the Prince offers to help the dwarfs keep vigil, they repeat the same humble observation they had made to Snow-White—and the Prince responds with exactly the same words of affirmation.

The educational mission of the Theatre may also have dictated the pseudo-Shakespearean style of Merington's dialogue, which, to the modern ear, seems incongruous in a children's play. The first scene alone contains such lines as (Otto to Prince) "We've scarce arrived, I'd fain remark"; (Prince to Otto) "Aye, to horse. For shines a star in Heaven above"; (Queen to Snow-White) "I like not thy looks, my maid. Let that suffice." Later, when the Queen orders Berthold to kill Snow-White, he protests: "My babes would shrink from me with loathing an they read such shame upon my brow."

However this language may strike us today, it was evidently no deterrent for the children of New York in 1905. A. Minnie Herts, founder of the Children's Educational Theatre, singled out *Snow-White* two years later as the popular favorite of all the Theatre's produc-

Winthrop Ames's Little Theatre on West 44th Street at the time of its opening in 1912. In later years the building changed hands numerous times; at this writing, a full century after its opening, it is still in operation as the Helen Hayes Theatre.

tions to date. She quoted one young attendee who articulated her preference: "I like *Snow-White* because the wicked Queen is so cruel to Snow-White and tries so hard to kill her that I always have to cry . . . but the Queen *don't* kill her. Snow-White marries the Prince, so you get glad again in the end."

SNOW WHITE AND THE SEVEN DWARFS (WINTHROP AMES PRODUCTION, 1912)

Children's theater productions of *Snow White* were one thing, but a professional Broadway production was another matter. It was producer Winthrop Ames who took the story to this significant new level in 1912. The Broadway stage had shown an increasing interest in children's fare during the early years of the twentieth century: productions of *The Wizard of Oz* (1903), *The Little Princess* (1903), *Babes in Toyland* (1903), *Peter Pan* (1905), *Little Nemo* (1908), *The Blue Bird* (1910), and *Rebecca of Sunnybrook Farm* (1910) had all played to great success. Despite their childhood associations, some of these productions relied on their spectacular stage settings and/or their music to lure adult patrons. *Babes in Toyland* and *Little Nemo* both boasted original scores by Victor Herbert, while the stage *Wizard of Oz*, with its topical jokes, slapstick humor, and extended program of vaudeville numbers, was so slanted toward an adult audience that today's Oz enthusiast might be unable to recognize it.

Winthrop Ames had something different in mind for *Snow White*: a smaller, more intimate production that retained its orientation toward children. Earlier in 1912 Ames had opened the Little Theatre on West 44th Street in New York. As its name suggested, the Little Theatre had a seating capacity of fewer than 500 and was designed for small-scale or experimental drama. Without the need to attract large audiences and fill a huge hall, Ames could afford to stage a modest production of a children's story. He took a special interest in *Snow White* and wrote the script himself, adopting the feminine pseudonym of Jessie Braham White. (He also commissioned a full-fledged musical score from composer Edmond Rickett.)

Marguerite Clark as Snow White, with her "maids of honor," in the stage production.

[4] Merington wrote to Ames in August 1912 acknowledging "our agreement," a $500 payment for her assistance on his script: "I think your ideas as you read them to me charming. It will be a great pleasure to work with you."

Ames's version of *Snow White* was based on the Marguerite Merington script of 1905 and, in fact, he consulted with Merington as he was writing his version.[4] His script retains the same basic structure—introducing the Prince (here called Prince Florimond) at the beginning, returning to the palace at the end for a confrontation with the Queen—and, like Merington's, it is aimed primarily at children, though it includes a few subtle jokes for the benefit of adults in the audience. (One of Snow White's maids of honor, gossiping about the Queen's advanced age, declares: "She's thirty if she's a minute!" The Queen, before revealing the murderous mission she has in mind for the Huntsman, coaxes him with an inducement: "Suppose I promote you to be Lord High Admiral? As we have no navy, the duties will be light.") The Huntsman's name is still Berthold, and the names of the dwarfs are changed only slightly. Now the lineup is Blick (still the leader), Flick, Glick, Snick, Plick, Whick and—the odd man out—Quee.

This is only the beginning of the changes in Ames's version. For one thing, the high-flown Shakespearean language of the Merington play is gone, replaced by more natural-sounding speech, and Ames's script is noticeably less preachy. His dwarfs are messy house-keepers; whereas the Grimms, Görner, and Merington had portrayed the dwarfs as neat and tidy, the dwarfs in the Ames play are careless and their house cluttered, badly in need of a housekeeper. Quee, the youngest, is responsible for giving the others a quick swipe with a wet sponge each day, but has not himself been washed in fifty years. Quee himself is a far more developed character than Schick, the youngest dwarf in the previous versions. Here the dwarfs are introduced to us as they return from a day's work at the mine, but only six of them are present. Quee is late, and the dwarfs sadly speculate that he's out stealing again. When he returns, loaded down with his stolen goods, they eagerly gather around him for their share of the swag. In what is clearly a nightly ritual, the dwarfs scold Quee for his reprehensible practice of stealing—then place their orders for items they want him to pick up the following night. Quee accepts his disgrace without question and, we may note—apart from the line "Hip-hip-hurrah!", spoken twice for comic effect—never utters a word throughout the play.

Ames also introduced an element of magic and fantasy that far exceeded that of the earlier plays *or* the Grimms' version. In the Grimms' tale, the apparently dead Snow White is mourned by the birds; here Snow White, making her way through the forest to the dwarfs' house, is guided by a Brown Bird who returns as her companion in a later scene. Perhaps the most striking variation in Ames's version is the division of the Queen's evil nature into two separate characters. The Queen is now named Queen Brangomar; the witch is a bona fide witch who is, at that, less evil than the Queen herself. Witch Hex is, in fact, a comic character, simply an eccentric old lady (and therefore less potentially frightening to children in the audience) who exercises a certain power over the Queen because it's only her magic that maintains the Queen's beauty. Learning that Brangomar plans to have Snow White killed, Witch Hex is mildly disgusted but asks, since Snow White is to be dead anyway, if she can have the girl's heart—as an ingredient in a magic hair restorer. (The witch needs this solution because she's totally bald. When Berthold brings back a pig's heart instead, the witch adds it to the mixture and dips her head into the cauldron; instantly her scalp is covered with dozens of pigs' tails.)

One of Ames's most significant additions came from another traditional story: in this play Snow White became a kitchen drudge. This was a relatively new idea. Earlier versions of the story had sometimes reduced Snow White to servitude, but only on occasion, and it was rarely stressed. The Aarne-Thompson-Uther index, in its listing of essential elements in the variant versions of "Snow White," says nothing about the girl's being forced to work in the kitchen. The Merington play suggests that Snow-White has never set foot in a kitchen before; when she undertakes to bake a cake for the dwarfs, it's a new experience for her, and the dwarfs are nervous at the prospect of having to eat it. By contrast, in Ames's first scene Snow White must be summoned from her duties in the palace kitchen to meet her new maid of honor, and then only in secret, when the Queen isn't looking. When Snow White takes up residence in the dwarfs' house, her new hosts apologize for their messy housekeeping. "That's just how I could be useful!" Snow White exclaims, and immediately sets to work sweeping and cooking.

This is important because it suggests that another long-established fairy tale, "Cinderella," is being com-
bined with the story of Snow White. To be sure, the stories of the two characters had never been mutually exclusive. Maria Tatar points out that—the Aarne-Thompson-Uther index notwithstanding—these two persecuted heroines of folklore may well have been blended in some earlier, unrecorded tale. (We've already seen that in some cultural variants of "Snow White," the girl was victimized by her sisters, suggesting the cruel stepsisters of the traditional Cinderella story.) Nevertheless, we know that the traditional character of Cinderella, or Aschenputtel, *is* defined partly by her lowly status and forced kitchen labor; and we can see that Ames, unlike the Grimms, Görner, or Merington, is at pains to put Snow White in a similar role. In any case, the addition of this element to Snow White's story—the sight of the poor little princess in rags, reduced to menial labor—underscores Queen Brangomar's cruelty toward her and increases our sympathy for her. The idea of Snow White meeting the Prince early in the story, apparently introduced on a whim by Görner in 1856, also meshes nicely with the story of Cinderella, who likewise wins her Prince's heart before he learns her identity.[5] Ames's use of these devices was a significant turning point; it marked a subtle linking of the Snow White and Cinderella narratives in the popular imagination of the twentieth century. In succeeding years the two fairy-tale heroines would continue to appear in close proximity. As we'll see, their kinship would be impressed on Walt Disney at an early age. And as he grew to maturity, the link between them would be retained in his art—and, thanks to his growing influence, reinforced in American popular culture.

To play the role of Snow White, Ames cast Marguerite Clark, an actress under his management. The petite Clark was a natural choice for children's plays, having already appeared in *Babes in Toyland* and toured in *Peter Pan*. Her appearances in these roles drew upon a contemporary quirk of American popular culture. During the first two decades of the twentieth century, the cult of the child/woman—the heroine who synthesizes both childlike innocence and young womanhood—flourished in the popular arts. Mary Pickford remains the best remembered adult actress of these

A studio portrait of Marguerite Clark, who played Snow White on both stage and screen.

[5] The Brown Bird in Ames's play may be taken as yet another parallel with "Cinderella": it suggests the little bird that grants Cinderella's wishes in the Grimms' version of the story.

years who portrayed girls "standing with reluctant feet/ where the brook and river meet," and she continued to play little girls like Pollyanna and Little Annie Rooney well into her thirties. But she was not an isolated phenomenon; audiences eagerly embraced other actresses who played similar roles—including Marguerite Clark, whose stage and screen portrayals of *Snow White* were very much a part of the child/woman tradition. Whatever we may think of this spectacle today, it was an undeniable part of popular entertainment during the "age of innocence," and it lingered into the more sophisticated 1920s.

It's a measure of Clark's suitability for the role that Ames's production, although distinctly removed from the earlier children's-theater productions, was cast largely with children. Snow White's "maids of honor" actually were played by little girls around ten years of age (among them the Fairbanks twins, Madeleine and Marion, who had appeared in *The Blue Bird*). The dwarfs, too, underneath their stage beards, were played by children, including a couple of girls. Quee, the youngest, was a seven-year-old Brooklyn girl named Dorothy Farrier. Marguerite Clark, 25 years old at the time, engaged charmingly with these small thespians in their scenes together, as one critic noted: "She did not look in the least out of place among the children." (Another reviewer observed: "You'd never believe she wasn't a little girl, except that her legs look a lot more than seven.") Moreover, she used the occasion to display her acting versatility. *Snow White and the Seven Dwarfs* was presented at the Little Theatre only at matinees, while the evenings were given over to Schnitzler's sophisticated *The "Affairs" of Anatol*, starring John Barrymore and featuring a succession of his romantic partners—one of them portrayed by Marguerite Clark.

If Ames had had any doubts about the public's acceptance of his stage *Snow White*, they were dispelled when the play opened on 7 November 1912. Critics and young audiences alike welcomed it eagerly. The day before the opening, a special dress rehearsal was held for an invited audience of children. Ames noted that many of the youngsters in the audience were distressed at Scene VI, which depicted the dwarfs standing vigil over Snow White's glass coffin in the forest; the short scene

was quickly cut from the script, and *Snow White* was reduced from seven scenes to six. As the play's run continued, other changes were made, including the downsizing of Witch Hex's three cats (played by boys in costume) to one, and the improvisation of some comedy business for the remaining cat.[6] But the play was an immense hit, and continued an extended run in the New York area—still at matinee performances only—then went on a short tour. (The tour was cut even shorter than expected because the presence of so many children in the cast came into direct confrontation with some cities' child-labor laws.) Periodic revival performances were mounted for the next few years, continued sporadically during the 1920s, and resurfaced with fresh vigor in 1938, after the opening of the Disney film.

SNOW WHITE (PARAMOUNT, 1916)

Four years after its opening, the Ames play was adapted to film: the 1916 Paramount version of *Snow White*, again starring Marguerite Clark. It was here that destiny brought Walt Disney and Snow White together, for this was the film that the young Walt saw in Kansas City.

In 1914, after more than a decade on the stage, Marguerite Clark had contracted with Adolph Zukor's Famous Players Film Company. She had proceeded to star in fifteen feature films in the space of two years. Zukor's company had been formed in 1912, with the slogan "Famous Players in Famous Plays" and with the express purpose of featuring well-known stage stars in film versions of their theatrical successes. By 1914 Famous Players had become one of the two principal production companies that made up Paramount Pictures and had drifted away from its original mission; most of Clark's films were based on novels or original stories, not plays. Still, her petite size and winsome personality suited her for child-oriented stories. In 1915 she had starred in *The Goose Girl*, unofficially based on another Grimm Brothers tale; in 1916 she had appeared in *Little Lady Eileen*, an original story of fairies and magic. These films were well received and suggested her stage success *Snow White* as an obvious candidate for the movies. It was announced by Paramount in November 1916 as a special production to be released for the Christmas holiday.

[6] This particular change—from three cats (named Long Tail, Short Tail, and Lack Tail) to one (named Fiddle)—was made in January 1913 when the production moved to Maxine Elliott's Theatre on West 39th Street. Subsequent productions, as well as the 1913 published script and the 1916 Paramount film, retained the single cat. Interestingly, the Samuel French edition of the script, published in 1925 (see endnotes and bibliography), resurrected the three cats but added a note to the producer: "two of the Cats may be omitted if it is desired to shorten the cast."

Ames himself consulted with director J. Searle Dawley in adapting the story for the screen, and the interiors were filmed at Famous Players' New York studio. Nevertheless, the resulting film was anything but "filmed theater." The story, as successively adapted three times for the stage, was again modified for the film and new episodes were added, some of them taking full advantage of the magical effects offered by the movies. One was prompted by the planned Christmastime release: in a prologue, Santa Claus makes his nocturnal visit to one household and arranges a row of dolls on a table. The dolls come to life and become the characters in *Snow White*. The film's exteriors were filmed in the woods in Georgia, near Savannah, and the picturesque scenes of moss hanging from the trees occasioned much comment from critics. Aside from Marguerite Clark, none of the original stage cast appeared in the film, and some of the key players who did appear would go on to distinguished careers in the movies after 1916. (Creighton Hale, who played Prince Florimond, was just beginning what would become a prolific film career that lasted well into the 1950s. Today he is perhaps best remembered for his character roles in such silents as *The Cat and the Canary* and Griffith's *Way Down East*. The Australian actress Dorothy Cumming, who appeared as

Queen Brangomar, likewise went on to many other film roles, among them the malicious wife in MGM's 1928 production *The Wind*.)

Upon its Christmas 1916 release, *Snow White* was hailed as a delight. "Grown people will enjoy this play fully as much as the children," predicted *Motion Picture News*, "and we know the children will just rave about it." Other trade papers concurred, praising both the film and Marguerite Clark's performance in it. "*Snow White* is a remarkable picture," declared *Moving Picture World* in words that seem oddly prescient in hindsight, "remarkable for the way it establishes illusion, for the way it makes the unreal seem real, for its pictorial quality, and for its real drama, which will hold and move the adult as it will the child."

In the winter of 1916–17, when the film was released, Walt Disney was living with his family in Kansas City and had just celebrated his fifteenth birthday. *Snow White* opened in Kansas City on 26 December 1916 and enjoyed the usual first-run engagement at the Royal Theater, ending its run on New Year's Day 1917. But then it returned in a far more spectacular way. The *Kansas City Star*, the city's leading newspaper, announced early in January 1917 that it was sponsoring a "movie party" later in the month. The event would be

Scenes from the Paramount
film. At left: Snow White with
the Brown Bird. At right:
Snow White peers into the
dwarfs' cottage in a striking
pictorial composition. A
similar scene would later
appear in the Disney film; see
page 127.

held at the city's 12,000-seat Convention Hall, and no admission would be charged. Everyone in Kansas City was invited to attend. The film would be *Snow White*.

The *Star*'s movie party, held on the 27th and 28th of January 1917, was a remarkable occasion in its own right. To accommodate the crowds and to ensure that everyone in the house could see the picture, an elaborate four-sided screen was suspended in the center of the huge hall, level with the balcony seats. Four pairs of projectors, all at varying distances from their respective screens, projected *Snow White* simultaneously from the four corners of Convention Hall, and a makeshift bell system was installed so that the team of projectionists could coordinate their changeovers between reels. On a platform directly below the screens in the center of the hall, a 35-piece orchestra accompanied the film. (The musical score was compiled, and the orchestra conducted, by the Royal Theater's musical director Leo Forbstein, who would later become head of the Warner Bros. music department during the sound-film era. In addition, the *Snow White* event was coordinated by the manager of the Royal, Frank L. Newman—coincidentally the man for whom Walt Disney would produce his first series of theatrical films, the *Newman Laugh-O-grams*, just a few years later.)

By all accounts, the *Snow White* movie party was a huge success. THEY CAME IN THOUSANDS, exulted a headline in the *Star*. The nominal seating capacity of Convention Hall was 12,000, but many of the smaller children sat two to a seat, and adults availed themselves of standing room. At the close of the weekend, after five showings in the course of two days, the *Star* estimated that a combined audience of 67,000 had seen the film.

Word of this extraordinary exhibition reached the Paramount offices in New York before the weekend was out, and both Marguerite Clark and Adolph Zukor sent telegrams of congratulations and thanks. The singular nature of the event seems remarkable even today; no less an authority than Kevin Brownlow describes it as "one of the most astonishing presentations in silent film history."

Small wonder that *Snow White* had a strong impact on 15-year-old Walt! "My impression of the picture stayed with me through the years, and I know it played a big part in my selecting *Snow White* for my first feature production," he wrote in 1938 to Frank Newman. "From the spot where I viewed the picture I was able to watch two screens at the same time." When two of the projectors got slightly out of sync, "I could look at one screen and tell what was going to happen on the next. I remember the show very well, and I am sure it will remain a vivid reality with me the rest of my life."

But after its initial run, the Paramount *Snow White* was gradually forgotten, and by the end of the silent era it was apparently a lost film. We have no indication that the Disney staff had access to it even during their own *Snow White* story conferences in the 1930s. For decades the film's influence on Walt remained a tantalizing footnote in history; writers and historians were forced to rely on written accounts and their own speculation. Then, in 1992, a tinted and toned 35mm nitrate release print surfaced in the collection of the Nederlands Filmmuseum in Amsterdam. The film was sent to George Eastman House in Rochester, New York. There, in 1994, a team of restoration experts led by Ed Stratmann and Philip Carli worked to produce a preservation print, carefully preserving the color effects and reconstructing English titles from the Dutch titles in the Amsterdam print and from Ames's stage script. Finally, after eight decades, the Paramount *Snow White* was restored to view.

Seen from today's perspective, this *Snow White* is a paradoxical experience. A delightful film on its own terms, it seems at first to have nothing whatever in common with the Disney classic. The plots of the two films vary wildly, mainly because the Paramount film inherits most of its plot from the Ames play. Here the Queen and the Witch are still two separate characters, the disguised Queen still makes two attempts on Snow White's life, and the bite of poisoned apple still simply sticks in Snow White's throat, to be dislodged at the end.

When the film varies from the play, it wanders even farther from either Grimm or Disney territory. The Brown Bird (played here by a small parrot) assumes an expanded role, rescuing Snow White on several occasions in gratitude for having been set free. The Huntsman subplot, extended in the Ames play, is still further elaborated in the film: here Berthold's children (three of them this time) are introduced onscreen, and Snow White enjoys a friendly chat with them early in the film.[7] Later, after the Huntsman spares Snow White's life in the forest, the film devotes considerable footage to the imprisonment of both Berthold and his children in the Grey Tower and to their escape (with the help of the Brown Bird). In the closing reels the Prince and Berthold, both separately searching in the woods for Snow White, meet each other, discover the glass coffin, and march in force on the palace for a confrontation with the Queen.

Perhaps even more disorienting, in hindsight, is the character of Snow White herself. Marguerite Clark's performance in the film—and we can infer a similar stage characterization four years earlier—is nothing like we might have expected. To be sure, she fits easily into the child/woman mold, but this Snow White adds an extra dimension. She is, as Karen Merritt has written, "full of American spunk and can-do spirit, an orphan who answers hardships by rolling up her sleeves and going to work." When she and the Prince meet in the forest in the film's early scenes, each unaware of the other's identity, they seem to be the all-American boy and girl next door, casually enjoying a harmless teenage flirtation. Little, if anything, rattles this Snow White; each new challenge she faces is taken in stride with a smile. Alone in the forest

with the Huntsman, she discovers his murderous mission—and reacts with dismay for all of five seconds, quickly regaining her composure and teasingly cajoling him. Abandoned in the forest and facing danger (two interpolated shots of a lion sitting quietly in the foliage), she succumbs to a quick cry, then brushes aside her fears and presses on with self-assurance.

But as the film continues, we begin to see more and more elements—sometimes plot devices, sometimes simple visual motifs or influences—that may have stuck in Walt's mind, to be resurrected two decades later. The dwarfs are played in the film by adults, but they retain their stage names. Blick is still the leader, and although Quee's criminal activities are written out of the film, he's still the smallest dwarf, the last in line, and the one who lags behind the others in returning home from the mine. It's tempting to imagine the seed that was planted in young Walt's mind in January 1917 by this odd-man-out motif that would later be more fully developed in Dopey (as well as other Disney characters). Tempting, too, to note the dwarfs' group-washing ritual, and the scene in which the offending Quee is unceremoniously dumped into a barrel while the other dwarfs forcibly wash him, both retained in the film. There's even a short snippet of animation, as Witch Hex (Alice Washburn), after consulting with the Queen, is depicted as a silhouetted figure riding her broomstick through the sky back to her lair.

And so it goes: the more closely we look at the Paramount *Snow White*, the more points of contact we see with the Disney film. Snow White, arriving at the dwarfs' cottage, peers through a window and is photographed from inside, her face framed by the window opening—a striking device that will be repeated for her animated counterpart. The dwarfs, preparing to lay their gifts beside the sleeping Snow White, turn one by one and beckon their fellows forward, until the last dwarf in line finds himself gesturing to thin air, much as Dopey will do in 1937. When Snow White is threatened by the disguised Queen, news of her danger is conveyed by the Brown Bird to a rabbit, who creeps down the dwarfs' mine shaft to whisper the warning to them. This animal action, impossible on the stage, is made possible by the magic of the movies—but is still awkwardly staged with a live bird and rabbit. Two decades later, the still more lib-

[7] Note that the Huntsman's family grows successively smaller with each new adaptation. In the Merington play, he has nine children; in the Ames play, six; in the Paramount film, three. In the Disney film, of course, no mention is made of his family.

A LA CONQUÊTE DU MONDE
scène vécue
PATHÉ FRÈRES   1894-19...

Souvenir de l'OMNIA-PATHÉ

French film pioneers Charles and Emile Pathé, whose company produced an early version of *Snow White,* are caricatured in this circa 1906 poster.

[8] Later in life Walt would describe the Paramount *Snow White* as "probably one of my first big feature pictures I'd ever seen," but not necessarily *the* first.

[9] At this time Lubin was mainly in the business of motion-picture equipment sales, and *Snow White* and the other films were simply accessories offered with one of his projection outfits. The film was not copyrighted until nearly a year later.

erating magic of animation will replace those two creatures with a whole army of birds and animals and transform the scene into a rousing, extended action sequence.

If elements of the "Cinderella" story had found their way into the Ames stage version of *Snow White,* they became even stronger in the Paramount film. Here Snow White's work as a kitchen slave is not only described but shown. She is gradually revealed at our first introduction to her, half hidden inside a large pot as she scrubs it. Her kitchen duties are, again, treated whimsically: Snow White's new lady-in-waiting is brought with her companions to the kitchen, so that the princess in rags can receive her. Later, as in the play, Snow White enjoys a Cinderella-like romantic interlude with the Prince: slipping into a court ball in borrowed finery, she waltzes with the Prince, who still doesn't know her true identity.

In this connection, it's worth pointing out that Famous Players/Paramount had produced a film version of *Cinderella* two years earlier, starring Mary Pickford. It's more than likely that the 1914 *Cinderella* exercised a strong influence on the 1916 *Snow White* by inaugurating a policy of releasing fairy-tale films at Christmastime. It's also possible that the influence worked both ways: in the Paramount *Cinderella* the two stepsisters go to consult a "fortune-teller," who wears a traditional witch's garb and is surrounded by a gang of evil-looking dwarfs.

Without indulging too much in conjecture, we might take a further step and speculate that young Walt may well have seen the Paramount *Cinderella* during its Kansas City run, and that—although the showing was probably far less memorable than the later Convention Hall exhibition of *Snow White*—it may have left its own imprint on him, further reinforcing the Snow White-Cinderella connection in his mind.[8] Certainly it's possible to see parallels between the Paramount *Cinderella* and Walt's later work. Mary Pickford's shy, vulnerable Cinderella seems closer to both the Grimm and Disney conceptions of Snow White than does Marguerite Clark's resourceful, can-do heroine. *Cinderella* also included visual ideas (for example the garden setting, with vines growing along the stone walls) that would find echoes in

the Disney *Snow White.* And the connections don't end there: we know that Walt's fledgling Kansas City animation studio, Laugh-O-gram Films, would produce a one-reel cartoon version of *Cinderella* in 1922. Further, as we'll see in a later chapter, the Snow White and Cinderella stories—intertwined as early as 1912—would continue to be linked at the Disney studio in later years.

OTHER SILENT SNOW WHITES

The Paramount film was not Snow White's first screen incarnation in the silent era, and it would not be the last. As early as 1902, motion-picture pioneer Siegmund Lubin had advertised a version of *Snow White* as part of a selection of fairy-tale films.[9]

La petite Blancheneige (Pathé, 1910) One early film version of *Snow White* has survived in fragmentary form: the one-reel French production *La petite Blancheneige*, produced in 1910 by Pathé Frères. While it's unlikely that this film had any influence on either Winthrop Ames or Walt Disney, a viewing of the fragments provides an interesting sidelight on early twentieth-century versions of "Snow White." This film version shares some common elements with contemporary American stage versions of the story: the Queen's mirror is still a hand mirror; the dwarfs are children with stage beards; the denouement still finds the piece of poisoned apple stuck in Snow White's mouth. On the other hand, there are some significant differences too. The Queen in this version tries two different means to kill Snow White but, unlike her contemporaries, foregoes the poisoned comb. Instead she opts for a piece of lace—not the Grimms' staylaces, but literally a piece of lace with which she tries to throttle Snow White from behind. The element of magic is present here: the dwarfs, after interring Snow White in the glass coffin, vanish in a puff of smoke when they hear the Prince and his entourage approaching. Perhaps because the Pathé film is a one-reeler—the closest cinematic form to the Grimms' short story—there seems to have been no attempt made to differentiate the dwarfs. *La petite Blancheneige* was offered in 1910 with Pathé's distinctive hand-coloring effects. The English-language edition, *Little Snowdrop*, was simultaneously released in the U.S. by the company's American exchanges.

Snow-White (Regent/Educational, 1916) Upon the December 1916 release of the Paramount *Snow White*, a rival version cropped up almost simultaneously: an amateur production filmed in Cleveland with a cast composed largely of children. Starring as Snow-White was a young actress named Aimee Erlich who could boast some professional experience, having appeared on Broadway in 1908 in the musical stage production of *Little Nemo*. Apparently intended only for local exhibition in Cleveland, this four-reel *Snow-White* was picked up by Educational Films for national release in December 1916 in an attempt to compete with the Paramount picture.

This version of *Snow-White* survives today in an incomplete and jumbled print. Clearly inspired by either the Ames play, the Paramount film, or both, it shares with them the device of presenting the Queen and the witch as two separate characters. Aimee Erlich's Snow-White costume, too, seems similar to that worn by Marguerite Clark in the Paramount film. On the other hand, this film differs in some respects from *any* other known film version of the story. It devotes an inordinate amount of footage to the palace, apparently because the filmmakers were allowed to shoot on the grounds of a local estate. Snow-White's mother, here called "Queen Mary" and likewise played by Aimee Erlich, is seen in the opening scenes weeping because she has no child. In a rather charming scene, the fairies gather a bouquet of white flowers and place them in her lap, where they are magically transformed into a baby. The Queen's rival, here a princess named "Alice" and played by Ruth Richey, enlists the witch's help to strike the Queen dead on Snow-White's second birthday, and thereafter becomes the girl's persecutor. The dwarfs, again played by children (including one girl) with stage beards, return from a day at the mine to find Snow-White asleep in their home, and spend the night outside so as not to disturb her sleep. Some details of the film's continuity are unclear today because of missing footage, but in one extant scene, "Prince Paul" "begs the dwarfs to let him take Snow-White's body to his palace." This suggests such earlier literary versions of the story as the Italian "Bella Venezia" or "The Crystal Casket."

Upon release, this film was given surprisingly positive coverage by the trade press. The *Motion Picture News* reviewed it glowingly: "This picturization of Grimm's fairy tale enacted wholly by juveniles can take its place near the head of the list in the library of children's productions." A month later the *News* announced that, in Cleveland at least, the Paramount and Educational versions of *Snow White* would be pitched in direct competition with each other: "it will be interesting to note which film will be adjudged the best." But the Educational version was never really a serious rival to Paramount's feature. An ambitious and sometimes charming amateur effort, it was no match for a professional production. It survives today as a curio, an interesting footnote to film history.

Scenes from Pathé's *La petite Blancheneige* (1910), shown in America as *Little Snowdrop*.

Colorful film pioneer Pat Powers, who produced one of the early versions of *Snow White,* would later play a prominent role of his own in Disney history.

Snow White (Universal, 1913/1917) One silent *Snow White* of special interest is the three-reel version produced in 1913 by the Powers company. The February 1913 release date of this film suggests that it may have been inspired by the recent opening of the Ames play, but reviews indicate that the filmmakers scrupulously avoided one of Ames's major innovations: here there was no separate witch character, and all the villainy was in the hands of the Queen. In this version Snow White's father was still alive but simply happened to be away on a trip when the Queen committed her depredations. Elsie Alberts starred as Snow White, and once again the dwarfs were played by children.

Powers, the producer of this film, was one of the small production companies that released its films through Universal Pictures. In the spring of 1917, *Snow White* was reissued under a different Universal label, Rex, probably to cash in on the success of the Paramount feature. Here again, we have no way of knowing whether the young Walt Disney saw this film either in 1913 or in 1917—but if he did, it would be another striking coincidence in film history. For the Powers company had been founded by Pat Powers, the same Pat Powers who would remain in the film business and whose path would cross Walt's in 1928 during the historic production of *Steamboat Willie*. It was Powers's sound process, Powers Cinephone, that Walt would use to record his first soundtracks, and Powers's distribution network that would release the earliest Mickey Mouse cartoons to theaters.

Compounding the coincidence, we have two tantalizing scraps of evidence that young Walt *may* have seen and remembered the Powers *Snow White*. One is a scene described in one review as a "big field . . . where the seven little men come trooping over the knolls at the close of their day's work in the mines." This is a scene that doesn't occur in the Paramount feature, and today it suggests the memorable homeward march of the dwarfs that would later be created for the Disney feature. The other evidence is more compelling. In the Grimms' tale, Snow White had been revived when the morsel of poisoned apple, stuck in her throat, was accidentally dislodged. As we've seen, the Ames play, the Paramount film, and other contemporary film versions

had retained this idea. But according to written accounts, the Powers *Snow White* borrowed a different device from yet a third fairy-tale heroine, Briar Rose (Sleeping Beauty): the heroine—who *has* swallowed the apple—is awakened, instead, by the Prince's kiss.

SNOW WHITE (FLEISCHER/PARAMOUNT, 1933)

In March 1933, shortly before the Disney studio embarked on its groundbreaking feature, Paramount released another film titled *Snow White*—and an animated film, at that. But any resemblance to the future Disney classic ended there. This *Snow White* was a one-reel cartoon in the Fleischer studio's Betty Boop series, with Betty herself, the baby-faced flapper modeled after Helen Kane, in the role of Snow White.

Even in the surreally loony world of Fleischer cartoons, *Snow White* is recognized as a standout. The original "Snow White" story becomes, in this film, merely a springboard for a stream of bizarre, unrelated, dreamlike gags. This is a "Snow White" that finds roles not only for Betty Boop but also for KoKo the Clown and Bimbo the dog, a "Snow White" that thinks nothing of devoting a third of its short running time to Cab Calloway's graceful, bluesy rendition of the song "St. James Infirmary." The thread of the original story doesn't quite get lost in this hallucinatory world; the Queen still consults her mirror and orders her fair rival's execution, and the would-be executioners (Bimbo and KoKo) still take pity on Snow White (Betty) and let her go. The Seven Dwarfs make a brief appearance, skiing downhill as they carry Betty in a block of ice (a substitute for the glass coffin, the name "Snow White" apparently having inspired a wintertime setting). Although the Prince is nowhere in sight, the short ends happily with Betty somehow revived and united with Bimbo and KoKo. For devotees of this kind of wildly non-sequitur animation, the Fleischer *Snow White* is a classic in its own right, but it's related to the Disney *Snow White* by name only.

In fact—extending the Snow White–Cinderella connection still further—it wasn't until the following year, in a version of the "Cinderella" story, that the Fleischer studio more closely approached the Disney universe. *Poor Cinderella*, released in August 1934, once again featured Betty Boop in the title role, but it was a far

more ambitious production than its predecessor. It was produced in color, not Technicolor (in 1934 the Disney studio still held exclusive rights to three-strip Technicolor for animated cartoons) but the rival Cinecolor process, with a limited two-color palette.[10] Here, too, the Fleischers unveiled their new "setback" device for producing a three-dimensional effect in cartoon settings, a sort of precursor to Disney's later multiplane camera. The multiplane, shooting vertically through widely separated glass planes, would allow the Disney cameras to penetrate into a forest or other setting, producing a convincing illusion of depth. The Fleischer camera was instead mounted horizontally before a turntable on which were constructed miniature settings, allowing for convincing *lateral* movement. Characters and objects, such as Cinderella's coach, could travel across the screen in a pan shot while buildings and other background objects rotated, turning in perspective behind them.

Along with this unaccustomed production extravagance, the Fleischers took special care with the story. Gone are most of the wild, surreal gags;[11] this film is a more or less straight retelling of the Cinderella story, with a deliberate attempt to build sympathy for the heroine, and a lilting original title song. Clearly this short, which inaugurated a new series called Color Classics, was earmarked as something special—and it's not difficult to imagine the motivation behind it: the

Fleischers were attempting to re-create something of the charm and appeal that the Disney studio had built into the Silly Symphonies by 1934. *Poor Cinderella* is no Silly Symphony, but it does achieve a quaint charm of its own. With its deliberately unrealistic colors and its pen-and-ink characters moving against tiny dollhouse settings, it creates a fragile, artificial fairy-tale world, like a puppet theater come to life.

But by August 1934 the Disney artists had already embarked on something far more ambitious than this. And within a few short years, the result of their efforts would make history.

In the Fleischer version of *Snow White* (1933), the Queen consults her mirror. At right, after transforming herself into a dragon-like creature, she menaces Betty Boop and her friends.

[10] In this, her one appearance in a color film, it was revealed that Betty Boop was a redhead. So *that's* settled.

[11] Some typically crazy Fleischer gags did, inevitably, remain in the story. As Cinderella/Betty and her Prince dance at the court ball, they're serenaded by a singer who turns out to be a caricature of Rudy Vallee (but adopts some of Bing Crosby's musical trademarks). Later, as one of the stepsisters tries to cram her large foot into the glass slipper, her foot is shown in closeup. The big toe grows a little face, which turns and glares up at its owner.

PART TWO

The Making of *Snow White and the Seven Dwarfs*

3

A NEW CHALLENGE

"As far as I can say," Walt Disney later recalled, "the whole idea of making this feature crystallized in 1933."

In the spring of 1933, the effective center of the animation world was a small studio at Hyperion Avenue and Griffith Park Boulevard in Hollywood. There, in the course of a few short years, Walt Disney had gone a long way toward revolutionizing the animated cartoon, and in the process had become a world celebrity. Beginning with the success of Mickey Mouse in 1928–29 and continuing through the introduction of the Silly Symphonies—first in black and white, then in vibrant new Technicolor—he had produced a series of fresh, exciting, delightful animated cartoons that had caught the attention of the world. New innovations, it seemed, sprang from his imagination on a daily basis. His latest triumph was *Three Little Pigs,* released in May 1933, which quickly achieved a sensational popularity all its own.

It was around this time that Walt was approached by Mary Pickford with a proposal for a novel new project. Pickford was one of the biggest movie stars in the business as well as a founding partner in United Artists, the company that was then distributing Walt's cartoons. She was also a great admirer of his work, and now she proposed a feature-length production of *Alice in Wonderland,* a combination of live action and animation, with herself in the role of Alice and the inhabitants of Wonderland animated by the Disney studio. Walt corresponded with her, registering cautious enthusiasm for her idea, but ultimately backed away from the

project—which was thwarted anyway by Paramount's production of its own live-action version of *Alice.*

Still, it was a short leap from the Pickford *Alice* idea to the idea of a completely animated feature-length film, produced in its entirety by the Disney studio. This was just the kind of challenge that Walt thrived on. By late July 1933, a scant two months after abandoning the *Alice* project, he was in New York speaking publicly of his intention to produce a feature. "Disney has plans worked out for a feature-length cartoon picture," reported *Film Daily,* "but has been unable to find response from United Artists executives, he said."

But, a later publicity item explained, Walt "didn't call his staff together and announce, 'Boys, we're going to make a feature.' He introduced the idea by the method of slow infiltration. He dropped it on everyone individually in the midst of casual conversations."

The reaction was enthusiastic. The Walt Disney studio in the early 1930s was a bustling, exhilarating wellspring of creativity, and Walt's artists were as excited as he was about the new possibilities of animation and about this fresh challenge. As early as May 1933, studio artist Ferdinand Horvath was writing eagerly to his wife with the news. In November, animator Art Babbitt wrote to his friend Bill Tytla: "We're definitely going ahead with a feature-length cartoon in color—they're planning the building for it now . . . Walt has promised me a big hunk of the picture." (Heeding Babbitt's exhortations, Tytla would soon move to California and join the Disney staff, and would become one of the stellar artists behind

[12] Coincidentally, 1917 also saw the release of two separate cartoons, one produced by Pat Sullivan and the other by Paul Terry, both parodying the recent Universal feature *20,000 Leagues Under the Sea*. Although contemporary trade press drew attention to the extraordinary length (800 feet) of Terry's film, and both cartoons have been referred to in some sources as two-reel films, in reality each was only one reel in length and so did not qualify as a "feature" by any standard.

[13] All evidence indicates that Walt selected *Snow White* as his story from the very beginning, although as early as mid-1933 he had been encouraged to consider an alternative idea instead. The prominent director Sidney Franklin, fired with enthusiasm for Felix Salten's book *Bambi,* had already approached Walt with the proposition that Disney animation was the ideal medium to bring that story to the screen. From the beginning, however, Walt seems to have recognized that *Bambi* presented technical challenges surpassing even those of *Snow White*—challenges that would, in time, delay the production and completion of his version of *Bambi* until nearly a decade later. By October 1933 an associate could report: "Walt is growing cold on *Bambi* as he sees certain production difficulties looming, and it looks as if he prefers to make *Snow White*."

Snow White, as well as other Disney classics.)

Strictly speaking, of course, there had been other animated features before this one. From the beginnings of the animation industry, the sheer difficulty of producing *one* reel of animated cartoons had inspired ambitious filmmakers to consider the possibility of even longer subjects. One little-known animated feature had been produced in Argentina as early as 1917: *El apóstol,* a political satire by Quirino Cristiani. In the United States, during that same year, Essanay released the five-reel feature *The Dream Doll,* much of whose footage was given over to Howard Moss's stop-motion animated puppets.[12] Today the most famous animated feature of the silent period is probably Lotte Reiniger's silhouette-animated *The Adventures of Prince Achmed,* produced in Germany in 1926. And animation pioneer Max Fleischer, alongside his popular Out of the Inkwell series, produced two four-reel scientific subjects—*The Einstein Theory of Relativity* (1923) and *Evolution* (1925)—which used animated charts, diagrams, and illustrations to explain their concepts.

Clearly, however, while all these films technically could be described as a) feature-length and b) wholly or partly animated, none of them was anything like the picture Walt now had in mind. His vision involved more than the simple technical challenge of increasing the *length* of the film; an entirely different kind of story would be required. A little over a decade earlier, the great comedians of the silent screen had faced a similar challenge. Having established a standard form, the two-reel comedy, that provided a perfect showcase for sight-gag humor, they had confronted the task of adapting their method to feature films—retaining the slapstick gags that were their stock in trade, but integrating them into a story substantial enough to sustain a feature-length picture. This was an extremely difficult problem, and the first comedian to solve it successfully was Charlie Chaplin. His first feature, *The Kid* (1921), is a classic partly because it brilliantly combines visual comedy with a well-constructed and engaging plot. Similarly, Walt in 1933 had something more than a ten-reel Mickey Mouse in mind. The story would have to be unlike anything ever seen before in animation.

He chose *Snow White,*[13] he said, not only because of his childhood memory of the Paramount film but also for purely practical reasons: "*Snow White and the Seven Dwarfs* is known and beloved in practically every country in the world. The Seven Dwarfs, we knew, were 'naturals' for the medium of our animated pictures. In them we could instill humor, not only as to their physical appearances, but also in their mannerisms, individual personalities, voices, and actions. In addition, with most of the action taking place in and around the dwarfs' cottage in the woods, we realized that there were great opportunities for introducing appealing little birds and animals of the type with which we have had success in the past. The human characters, too, were fanciful enough to allow us a great deal of leeway in our treatment of them."

Those early casual conversations soon led to something more serious. By mid-1934 Walt had committed to his feature-length *Snow White,* and he formally announced it to the press in July. "And won't that be a welcome event on the screen!" commented Edwin Schallert in the *Los Angeles Times*. "The film will be made all in color with cartoon characters. It will not include the Big Bad Wolf, the Three Little Pigs, or even Mickey Mouse." This passage suggests how radical Walt's announcement must have seemed at the time, and how baffled Schallert and other observers must have been about just what kind of picture he might have in mind. Similar comments appeared in other newspapers around the country in July 1934, and for the next three and a half years, as *Snow White* worked its way toward completion, the press continued to regard it with occasional statements of curiosity, bemusement, and anticipation.

At this time, Walt and the writers adopted a wide-ranging approach, remaining open to any and every idea that might be suggested. One of the earliest story documents to survive today is an outline titled "Manuscript," dated 9 August 1934 and probably written by Dick Creedon, who had joined the Disney story department the previous year. In hindsight, the "Manuscript" makes eye-opening reading today. It's not clear how much of the content is Creedon's own and how much is a reflection of story conferences with Walt and other writers, but in any case, the "Snow White" suggested in the "Manuscript" is wildly unlike the finished film that we know today. A 21-page assortment of suggestions for characters and scenes, it manufactures elaborate episodes having nothing to do with the plot, including Snow White's journey through such settings

as Boogeyland, the Valley of the Dragons, and the Morass of Monsters. Few of the ideas in this remarkable document lasted very long.

October 1934 marked a significant turning point for the feature; in that month Walt began to hold weekly story meetings with a small group of writers. The meetings were documented only by brief, cursory notes—a far cry from the verbatim conference transcripts that started to appear soon afterward—but it's clear from reading those notes that something much closer to the familiar *Snow White* was beginning to emerge. The dwarfs' identities were already taking shape (Grumpy was an early arrival); key episodes in the story, such as the dwarfs' discovery of Snow White in their house, were under discussion. At the end of the month, on Tuesday, 30 October, an important event took place: Walt went beyond his small circle of writers and introduced the feature project to the studio at large. Assembling the staff on the sound stage at 7:30 that evening, Walt held court for three hours, telling his artists the story of *Snow White*.

It's one of the tantalizing unknowns of history that we have no direct record of that performance. The meeting is, again, represented by a short page of notes documenting the story suggestions offered by some of the attendees, but Walt's telling of the tale survived only in the memories of his audience. In their eyewitness accounts, his performance assumed legendary proportions. Ken Anderson, who had just been hired in September, claimed in numerous interviews to have been present: "We were spellbound . . . He would *become* the Queen. He would *become* the dwarfs. He was an

incredible actor, a born mime." It was the first of many times Walt would perform the story for audiences great and small. "I think I probably heard the entire story of *Snow White* three or four dozen times," Joe Grant told Richard Greene. "His idea was to go from room to room, tell sequences, and then whatever we would add would be put into his next routine discussion." In addition, there were further large-scale recitals; Ollie Johnston, who didn't start work at the studio until 1935, remembered a recital that he described in terms similar to Anderson's.

As if tackling a feature were not ambitious enough in itself, the Disney studio was continuing production of its bread-and-butter product, the Mickey Mouse and Silly Symphony shorts, at the same time—and not in a perfunctory way; the shorts flourished and became more elaborate and brilliant, even as work went ahead on *Snow White*. In late 1934, Walt had a relatively conservative idea of just how long it would take to produce his feature. "We are now working on our first Silly Symphony feature," he wrote to a theater manager in October, "which we expect to have finished in about a year." A review of the Silly Symphony *The Goddess of Spring,* released in November, made a similar claim: "'The Goddess of Spring' . . . is a preliminary study for the feature-length color cartoon, 'Snow White,' which [Walt] hopes to finish in a year or so."

In fact, however, rather than gearing up, work on *Snow White*—after a few months of conferences and outlines—slowed dramatically around this time. Walt was still committed to his feature, but at the end of 1934 and through the first half of 1935, preparation of the

Lotte Reiniger's silhouette film, *The Adventures of Prince Achmed* (1926), is probably the best-known animated feature predating *Snow White*.

Walt presides over a story meeting for the Silly Symphony *Grasshopper and the Ants*. Left to right: Webb Smith, Bill Cottrell, Ted Sears, Walt, Pinto Colvig, Harry Reeves, and Albert Hurter. This photo was taken in the autumn of 1933; every artist in this shot went on to work on *Snow White*.

Opposite: Walt's discovery of this all-Disney program at a Paris theater in 1935 helped reinforce his determination to produce a feature.

[14] New York's Bijou Theatre had opened in the autumn of 1934, featuring a steady diet of Disney cartoons but also including a ration of Fleischer and Lantz shorts.

story came to a virtual standstill while he reconsidered his production method. In the mid-1930s a standard system had evolved at the Disney studio: each cartoon short was supervised by a director who was in turn supervised by Walt. By 1935 Wilfred Jackson, Dave Hand, and Ben Sharpsteen had established themselves as the top Disney directors. Each of the three brought a personal touch to the films he directed—Jackson, for example, had a musical background that was manifested in brilliant musical gags in his cartoons—but none was a true *auteur* because all the films were subject to the personal stamp of Walt himself. In the case of *Snow White*, it was originally assumed that Walt would direct the feature personally.

Early in 1934, Walt assumed personal direction of one of the shorts: *The Golden Touch*, a Silly Symphony retelling the story of King Midas. Generally understood as a trial run for Walt's direction of the feature, *The Golden Touch* proceeded slowly through production for a good nine months, from June 1934 to February 1935. By that time it was painfully clear that this short—directed by Walt Disney himself, and animated by two of the best artists in the studio, Fred Moore and Norm Ferguson—was not a very good film. "With the best men and the best brain in the business . . ." said Dick Huemer to historian Joe Adamson, "the picture was not funny, it wasn't convincing, you weren't with it—it just wasn't there. And he had to admit it himself. Now, isn't

that a funny thing?" Seen today, *The Golden Touch*, like other perceived Disney "failures" of the time, is a much better film than its reputation would suggest. But it's clearly not one of the best Disney pictures of its time, and in 1935 it was regarded as an outright embarrassment. Under the circumstances—and considering the difficulty the animators were still having with convincing human movement, a difficulty we'll observe shortly—it's hardly surprising that Walt decided to pause and rethink his approach to the much more consequential production of *Snow White*.

The summer of 1935 brought another interruption: a vacation trip to Europe by Walt, his brother Roy (also the business manager of the studio), and their wives. For three months Walt simply wasn't at the studio, and while he made advance arrangements to keep production going on the shorts during his absence, production of *Snow White* was an uncharted process that would simply have to wait for his return. However, the European trip served to fortify Walt's plans in an unexpected way: in Paris he found a movie theater whose entire program was made up of Mickey Mouse and Silly Symphony shorts. "[They were] putting five or six of these things together and running them," Walt told interviewer Pete Martin in later years. This all-Disney program had been showing in Paris since the previous year and had already inspired at least one all-cartoon theater in the United States.[14] If Walt had entertained any doubts about *Snow White*, this

discovery of a full program of Disney animation dispelled them. "I made up my mind that I was going to make this feature," he told Martin. "I just felt sure if I made a feature it would go, you see?"

The Disneys returned to the United States in August 1935, and Walt, refreshed and brimming with enthusiasm, held court at a New York press conference. "We never tried [a feature] before because we didn't have enough confidence in ourselves," he told a reporter. "We had to be sure first. You know, it's a big thing . . . We've got it all worked out now. Yes, everything is all ready. We'll start at once."

Walt returned to the studio, ready to plunge back into the making of his feature. He was also newly suffused with European atmosphere. He had, he told the story department, brought back a selection of European storybooks with "very fascinating illustrations of little people, bees and small insects who live in mushrooms, pumpkins, etc. This quaint atmosphere fascinates me . . ." His memo was concerned with future short subjects, but *Snow White,* a story of European origin, was an obvious candidate for enriched atmospheric touches. By the time it was completed, many of these would be provided by Albert Hurter, a Swiss-born artist who had been working at the studio since 1931. Hurter's specialty was inspirational sketches, providing imaginative gags and ideas for the shorts, but he also had an unerring feeling for the atmospheric details that would be so pronounced in *Snow White.* In 1936, Walt placed him in a unique role on the feature, overseeing the backgrounds to be sure they maintained a quaint Old World atmosphere. "Albert [is] to be the supervisor of the keying of the picture," said Dave Hand to a group of layout artists, "[the] interior of the dwarfs' house and all exteriors—woods, sunlight, dark moonlight shots—Albert [is] to watch that closely. For that reason mainly it would be necessary for each layout man to work with Albert." The dark, cozy interior of the dwarfs' cottage, their inventively carved furniture and cuckoo clocks, and other evocative details owed much to Hurter's influence.

Another European artist, the Swedish Gustaf Tenggren, joined the studio staff in the spring of 1936. Despite his late arrival, his concept art would help influence the Old World look of *Snow White;* he would also create much of the publicity art that was seen by the public upon the film's release—most notably the classic poster design that theaters used in their advertising.

As for *Snow White*'s production setup, by the end of 1935 a system had evolved that was essentially an extension of the system already used on the shorts. The story was divided into *sequences*—thirty-one of them in the finished picture—each sequence produced as if it were a separate short. The sequence directors would report to a single supervising director, who in turn reported to Walt. The myriad details of producing the feature were delegated through many levels of an increasingly large staff, but Walt's control and attention to detail extended through every level and coordinated all these discrete sequences in a cohesive whole.

The supervising director was Dave Hand, one of the studio's top directors of short subjects, whose credits included the Academy Award winners of both 1935 and 1936 (*Three Orphan Kittens* and *The Country Cousin,* respectively). The other top directors, Wilfred Jackson and Ben Sharpsteen, each directed several sequences, as did Bill Cottrell, one of the best minds in the story department. Perce Pearce, a relative newcomer, ultimately directed more footage in the picture than any other director "because," said Hand, "he delegates to other people all work that is not essential for him to do. Offhand I don't know of any other director who will do that . . . Perce has turned out more work in a short time than others because he is smart."

Work on the *Snow White* story resumed in earnest in the final months of 1935. It's notable that Walt, in adapting his film story, included an element of "Cinderella"—the same element that had appeared in Winthrop Ames's play and in the Paramount film. Walt's Snow White, like Marguerite Clark, wears rags and is reduced to menial labor around the castle. Walt was conscious of this adaptation and even referred to it explicitly in some meetings: "She's got to be doing some Cinderella type of work, something dirty"; "Her dress here should be the Cinderella type."

Apart from this, Walt maintained a strong fidelity to the Grimms' "Snow White." He was acutely aware of the particulars of their story and frequently argued for restoring their ideas, changed in other films and plays: "So many people remember those old things from the fairy tale." In general, the trend of the writers' work was to tighten the plot, eliminating superfluous scenes and

dialogue. Some of the theatrical versions had padded the story with gratuitous characters and scenes having no connection with the plot; most of these disappeared from the Disney version. Even the Grimms' original continuity, spare as it was, was trimmed in this version: for a time Walt considered retaining two of the Witch's three attempts on Snow White's life—with both the poisoned comb *and* the poisoned apple—but finally decided to use only the apple.

One of the scenes in the 1934 "Manuscript" outline had suggested that the Queen, seeing the Prince's ardor for Snow White, would have him seized and imprisoned in a dungeon. There she would taunt him with the details of her plan to kill Snow White. This idea was not immediately scrapped, and versions of it appeared in subsequent outlines, including some in which skeletons of the Queen's earlier victims, still hanging by their chains, would perform a gruesome dance. Before leaving to dispatch Snow White, the Queen would open a valve that flooded the dungeon with water, threatening the Prince, helpless in his chains, with drowning. After her departure, the Prince would escape—with help from some friendly birds, in some outlines—and ride, too late, to save Snow White. Versions of this idea remained in the story as late as October 1936.

In the end, however, all these superfluous ideas—those generated within the studio as well as those imposed by earlier dramatists—were eliminated. The result, after endless months of analysis and discussion, was a tight, lean story line that mostly hewed to the essence of the Grimms' plot. Apart from the Prince's

final discovery of Snow White in the glass coffin, all the action in the Disney *Snow White* takes place in the space of three days. Surplus characters, such as the miscellaneous courtiers and ladies-in-waiting in the Winthrop Ames play, are nowhere to be seen. Here the Queen rules an unnamed land, but we never see any of her subjects except those necessary to the story: Snow White, the Huntsman, and the dwarfs.

The point of reducing the story to its essentials, of course, was to make the most of the essentials. If the finished film emerges as a colorful, overflowing banquet of animation art—and it does—it's because Walt and his artists, having refined the story down to a spare framework, proceeded to embroider each section of that framework with an inspired profusion of pictorial, dramatic, and comic ideas. Without unnecessary characters and incidents to clutter the story, the Disney *Snow White* can dwell on the inherent drama of the Queen's dialogue with her magic mirror, for example, or the stark terror of Snow White alone in the woods. Minor episodes that lend themselves to animation, such as the dwarfs' discovery of Snow White in their house, can legitimately be expanded into full-fledged comedy set-pieces. As we'll see, it's useless to speak of an "original" version of the Disney film story because the story was an endlessly shifting matrix of these ideas, constantly in flux, right up to the finish of production. As it continued to develop, none of the details could be changed without affecting others—and Walt, in his single-minded drive to finish the film, somehow managed to keep track of all of them in his head.

Two Ferdinand Horvath sketches of the Queen's dungeon, suffused with Gothic horror—as well as some unused story ideas.

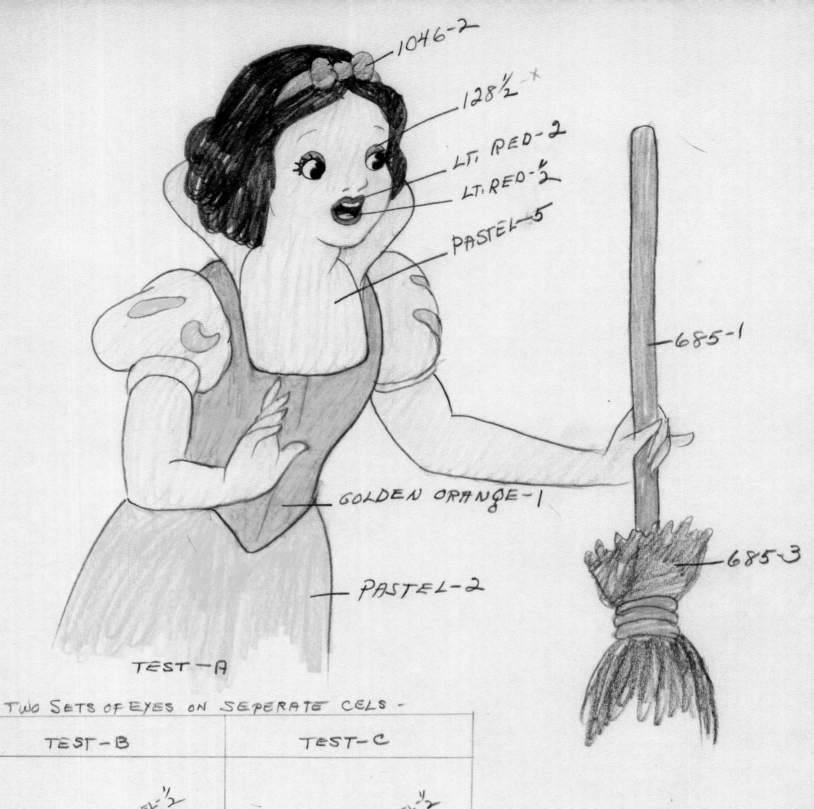

1046-2

128½-×

LT. RED-2

LT. RED-½

PASTEL-5

685-1

GOLDEN ORANGE-1

685-3

PASTEL-2

TEST-A

TWO SETS OF EYES ON SEPERATE CELS-

TEST-B	TEST-C
OR. YEL-½	OR. YEL-½
135-½	685-1
B	B
539-4-X	POWDER BLUE-½

TEST MODEL
SEQ-3C- SC26L

F.C. 60
(RETAKE)

4

CHARACTER DESIGN

SNOW WHITE

As if the very idea of a feature-length picture were not challenging enough, Walt's selection of the story of *Snow White* automatically compounded the difficulty of his project. The character at the center of the story, the character around whom most of the action would revolve, was not a simple, broadly caricatured, "cartoony" character, but a delicate, feminine creature. And she was a human being.

Human characters in animated cartoons were not a new phenomenon in the mid-1930s. On the contrary, in the early history of American animation, human characters outnumbered animal characters by a wide margin: pre-1920 audiences might see Krazy Kat at the movies, but they were also apt to see Col. Heeza Liar, Bobby Bumps[15], Dreamy Dud, Mutt and Jeff, Bud and Susie, the Katzenjammer Kids, and Silk Hat Harry—all of them human beings, more or less. The tremendous success of Felix the Cat in 1921–22 began to suggest the possibilities of "funny animal" characters as an ideal subject for animated cartoons, but Farmer Al Falfa continued to thrive alongside Felix in American animation of the 1920s—as did numerous other human characters, including quite a number in the Felix films themselves. For that matter, Walt Disney's own earliest animated cartoons abounded in human characters. His Laugh-O-gram Films, produced between 1921 and 1923 in Kansas City, were adaptations of fairy tales with a Jazz Age twist, including *Little Red Riding Hood*, *Jack and the Beanstalk*, *Cinderella*, and a *Puss in Boots* that

devoted more screen time to its human cast than to the title character.

It's important to remember, though, that the *craft* of animation was still relatively undeveloped at this time. For that reason, there was little need to distinguish between animal characters and humans, most of whom were broad caricatures like Mutt and Jeff anyway, "human" only in the loosest possible sense. If a character moved in short, jerky actions, calculated to get the figure from point A to point B with a minimum of effort, it didn't much matter whether the character was Krazy Kat or Silk Hat Harry. To be sure, some animators were far more conscientious than others, and some actually did invest their characters with a sense of lifelike movement. The best of these was the great Winsor McCay, who brought his baroque sensibility to a series of animated films between 1911 and 1921. Both human and animal characters moved through McCay's strange, dreamlike world in measured cadences, occasionally displaying a moment of evocative movement, observed from life. In *The Flying House* (1921), for example, a woman ascends a flight of stairs, her body slightly bent, her hand resting lightly at intervals along the banister as she goes. Moments like this conveyed sudden, vivid flashes of life, but they popped up sporadically, almost at random, in McCay's films.

Another animator of the silent era sought to put "lifelike" movement on the screen in a very different way. Max Fleischer, still on the threshold of his own

Opposite: Color was an important part of character design. The ink and paint department conducted experiments to determine the most effective color scheme for Snow White's costume, and even her eyes. This color callout was created for a test in October 1936.

[15] It's worth noting that Bobby Bumps, one of the characters in this list, was created in 1915 by an important pioneer in American animation: Earl Hurd. In later years Hurd continued to work in various capacities in the animation business, and by the mid-1930s he was a member of the Disney story department. He actively contributed to the making of *Snow White;* we'll meet him again in these pages.

animation career in 1915, patented an invention called the *rotoscope*. In an effort to improve the appearance of the animated figure *and* cut down on production time, Max made a live-action film of his brother Dave Fleischer cavorting in a clown suit. The rotoscope was a device that rear-projected the resulting film, frame by frame, onto a translucent screen, where Max simply traced the figures from individual frames onto animation paper. When his clown tracings were inked and photographed, they produced a figure that moved on the screen with a startling illusion of reality. To the *New York Times*, the resulting films were delightfully "smooth and graceful"; the clown "walks, dances and leaps as a human being, as a particularly easy-limbed human being might." Seen today in retrospect, from the far side of the Golden Age of animation, those early rotoscope films convey a disconcerting, almost disturbing effect. They represent a head-on collision between the simple, linear, weightless world of early animation and the world inhabited by human beings, subject to the law of gravity, restrictions of movement, and the normal tics of everyday life. The clown in those early experimental films became the leading character in Fleischer's Out of the Inkwell cartoon series (he was dubbed KoKo in 1924), and most of the early Inkwell films included some rotoscoped scenes, bursting into

the world of cartoons like some unnatural hybrid from another planet. A film like *The Clown's Little Brother* (1920) seems to revel in that discrepancy: the clown attempts some simple gymnastics and is trumped with contemptuous ease by his little brother. The clown's rotoscoped actions, with their uncanny echoes of recognizable human movement, make a clumsy contrast with the brother's simple, smooth, and wildly flexible action.

In 1920, of course, such discrepancies were perfectly acceptable in the still largely uncharted world of animated cartoons. By the mid-1930s, everything in that world had changed. Thanks to the Disney studio, the art of animation had been completely redefined, not only in terms of story, design, and technology, but also in the way the characters *moved*. Disney animators had gone beyond the simple, abrupt actions of early cartoons, analyzing the principles of movement in the real world, and then harnessing those principles for their own use. No viewer would mistake the Big Bad Wolf for a real wolf or Pluto the pup for a real dog; rather, the characters' actions were *based* on real life, translated into cartoon terms. How could this principle be applied to human-like characters?

Throughout the early 1930s, a variety of human beings appeared in the Silly Symphonies. Some of them, such as the roly-poly heroes of *Santa's Workshop* (1932)

Left and opposite:
Unsuccessful "human"
animation in *The Goddess of
Spring* (1934). Note
Persephone's rubbery arms
on the opposite page.
Black-and-white stills from a
color film.

and *Old King Cole* (1933), were the counterparts of Mutt and Jeff or Farmer Al Falfa in the silent era: so broadly cartoony that they presented no special problem and could be animated like other characters. When the studio attempted a human character with a greater degree of realism, the problems escalated. The title character in *The Pied Piper* (1933) was designed and animated as a more or less realistic human being, and the result was written off as a failure.[16] Most difficult of all were the pretty girls. Many of them appeared in the Disney cartoons, with varying degrees of success: the porcelain girl in *The Clock Store* (1931) who danced a dainty minuet with her partner; the similar character in the loose Technicolor remake, *The China Shop* (1933), who not only danced but was kidnapped by a lecherous satyr; the chorus of mermaids in *King Neptune* (1932); the beautiful fairy in *The Flying Mouse* (1934) who granted the title character a pair of wings. By the time of *The Flying Mouse,* Walt had definitely decided to produce *Snow White,* but the animators' difficulties in animating these girls must have given him pause. The porcelain dancers could be forgiven a certain stiffness, but the fairy in *The Flying Mouse* had no such excuse, and her movements seemed clumsy and awkward. If such a girl was to be the central character in a story, especially a feature-length story, her actions must be a

great improvement on this—but they could not be McCay's erratic flashes of genius, nor Fleischer's eerie ghosts of reality. A new technique must be found.

It had not been found by the time of *The Goddess of Spring,* another Silly Symphony released in November 1934. This short, a retelling of the myth of Pluto and Persephone, was the studio's boldest attempt yet to put human-like characters on the screen. This time the god and goddess were not supporting characters, but held center stage as the story unfolded. We have evidence that viewers and critics were greatly impressed with *The Goddess of Spring* in 1934, but within the studio it was regarded as an appalling embarrassment. Latter-day viewers, conditioned by hindsight, have been inclined to agree; in recent decades *The Goddess of Spring* has become a popular illustration of just how far the Disney animators still had to go. The scene most often held up to ridicule is Ham Luske's introductory scene of Persephone, executing what is meant to be a graceful dance. The dance is instead a parody of graceful move-ment: Persephone arches through the air like some ungainly bird, her arms undulating strands of spaghetti. Other scenes are less embarrassing, but Persephone remains a cardboard illustration moving stiffly through her scenes, with none of the cartoon life that empowers Disney's concurrent animal stars. Clearly, a girl like this

[16] Animator Izzy Klein quoted a letter that Ted Sears had written him in November 1933: "Having just completed *The Pied Piper*, we've come to the conclusion that . . . we haven't advanced far enough to handle humans properly and make them perform well enough to compete with real actors."

Above and opposite: Grim Natwick's exploratory sketches displayed charm and femininity but were still far more cartoony than the final version of Snow White.

[17] Harry Bailey's "Routine Procedure on Feature Production," undated but written in 1935, makes specific provision for "stage settings, sets, props, costumes . . . make-up men, camera men, electricians, [and] carpenters." Roy Disney, dealing with the ongoing problem of constant studio expansion, reported to Walt in August 1935 on the possible use of a vacant building across the street. The building, Roy wrote, had some structural weaknesses, but the second floor might be used for "the building of the *Snow White* sets."

[18] These sentiments became deep-rooted among the Disney animators. This writer can testify that, 50 years later, some of them still bristled with indignation at the very mention of the word "rotoscope."

could never have carried a feature-length story.

In November 1935, Walt issued a six-page memo naming the animators he had chosen to assign to the feature. He opened by announcing the artist he would entrust with the title character: "From now on, *Ham Luske* is definitely assigned to *Snow White*." Luske would be the first animator to start work, and he would work almost exclusively on Snow White herself. Walt outlined a long list of sequences assigned to him, as well as a corps of assistants to help him. Luske was the same artist who had animated the principal scenes of the Pied Piper as well as Persephone's dance, two perceived failures. But these were two isolated and unusually demanding cases; Luske also had a string of brilliantly animated characters to his credit. Moreover, he had the analytical capacity to learn from his experiences with Persephone and the Piper. Former coworkers remembered Luske as an artist with little natural facility, who struggled to achieve his results—but, in the end, those struggles paid off. His work on *Snow White* is an enduring testimony. During the two years following Walt's memo, Luske played a unique role in the making of *Snow White:* animating many key scenes himself, supervising a large unit of other animators, controlling virtually every appearance of Snow White as well as the animals and birds that surrounded her. Operating independently of the nominal sequence directors, Luske enjoyed an autonomy second only to that of Walt himself.

The first order of business, of course, was to design the character. By now it had been generally agreed that Persephone, the Flying Mouse's fairy, and the other preceding girl characters had suffered a common problem: they were designed according to the realistic proportions of adult human beings—proportions that did not lend themselves well to animation. In designing Snow White, Luske went to the opposite extreme. Frank Thomas and Ollie Johnston have reported that Luske suggested a Snow White who looked like an awkward, gangly teenage girl, a Snow White whose charm would be largely comic. Such a character would have been relatively easy to animate. Albert Hurter and other artists modified this concept, designing Snow Whites who were prettier and daintier but still largely cartoon-like. The Snow White who finally appeared in the film was a compromise: superficially conforming to the "pretty girl" pattern of her predecessors, but designed for animation, with a head much larger than normal and her other proportions similarly modified.

To create lifelike movements for this character, it was now conceded that the studio would have to fall back on live action. Studio documents indicate that live-action filming figured in the plans for *Snow White* at an early date, well before Walt's November 1935 memo.[17] Accordingly, Luske and his fellow artists resorted to the rotoscope—but not in the way Max Fleischer had used it in 1915. By the mid-1930s, in fact, traditional rotoscoping was scorned at the Disney studio. Immersed in the study of movement and proud of their increasing ability to represent it on the screen, the Disney artists were quick to take offense at any hint that they might use such a crutch as simple tracing.[18] But a different use was found for the rotoscope. An actress would be filmed

playing the role of Snow White, and the resulting film would be traced, frame by frame, just as Fleischer had traced his film two decades earlier. But these tracings were not for production. Instead they were given to the animator as a *guide* for production. The animator of the finished scene was under no obligation to reproduce every wrinkle in the girl's dress as she walked or danced, but he had an opportunity to analyze the *essence* of her movement—the swing of a leg, the turn of her head—and, at his discretion, incorporate those isolated actions into his animation. That extra layer of drawings between rotoscope and screen allowed the animator to retain all the advantages of live action, with none of the disadvan-

tages: recognizable human action could be applied *selectively* to a character designed for animation. At long last, the Disney artists had found a solution to the seemingly insurmountable problem of representing lifelike human action in an animated character.

The job of making those rotoscope tracings initially fell to Australian-born Kendall O'Connor. Soon enough O'Connor would become a respected layout artist, but in 1935 he was a relative newcomer to the studio, and now he found himself saddled with the rotoscope work for *Snow White*. He didn't relish the prospect. "You know," he explained, "you're in there eight hours a day in a black room, no light except what's

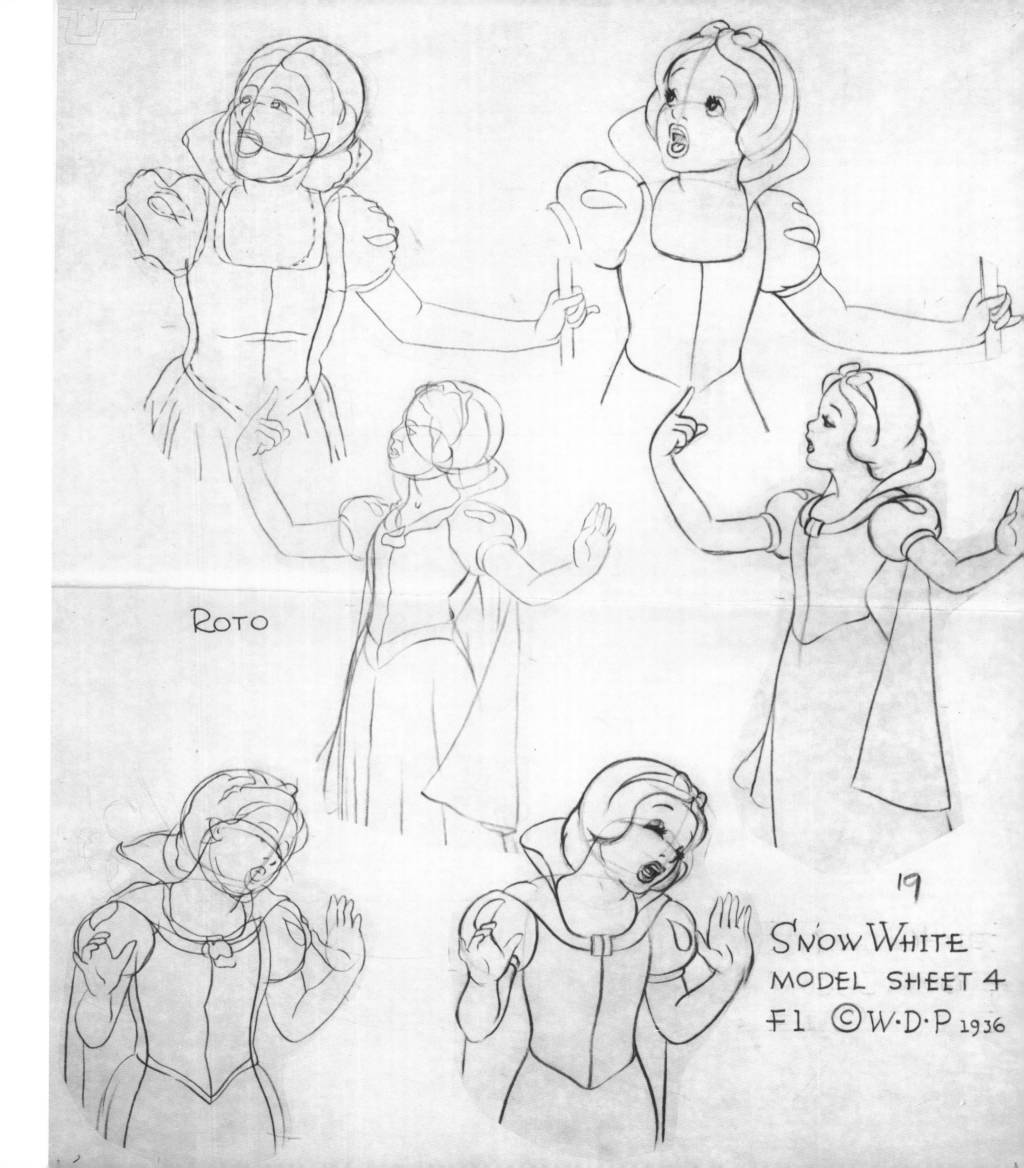

ROTO

19

SNOW WHITE
MODEL SHEET 4
F1 © W·D·P 1936

coming from the board—you don't see the sun except for half an hour for lunch. You don't see anybody else, there's nobody else in there, and you just turn out hundreds of tracings, you know. And this is where Walt sort of convinced me that he could sell anybody anything. Because I really hated that; I said, 'Here I'm a creative guy, what the hell am I doing in here just duplicating things?' And one day—I was about to quit, really. Walt came in unexpectedly to see what I was doing, and he looked over my shoulder and he says, 'Boy, you're lucky!' And I was just about to tell him how lucky I felt I was, and he launched into a big thing. He said, 'You know, we have classes called action analysis for the animators. We run stuff a frame at a time and stop it, you know, so they can analyze the action of animals or people and all that. But they only get an hour of it a week or something,' you know, because it was not production, it was education. He said, 'Here you get it coming at you all day long! Here's this girl, Snow White, and you can see precisely how this human action works and you can analyze it,' and God, you know, in a flash I saw that I'd been thinking entirely wrong. I should have been thinking the way he was saying and trying to get something out of it. Because human action is very fluid, and it has a whole lot of particular things about it that you should know in the animation business . . . So when he went out, I looked at those extra tracings I'd been making and I realized, 'Damn, I should have been worrying about what I was seeing, instead of just blindly tracing off drawing by drawing.' Because he was right, and I did learn quite a bit."

To play the role of Snow White in this live-action filming, the studio initially cast Virginia Davis, the girl who had played Alice in Walt's first silent Alice Comedies, more than a decade earlier. Ultimately, however, most of Snow White's action was performed by a girl with professional dance experience: Marjorie Belcher. Marjorie's father, Ernest Belcher, was the proprietor of a Hollywood dance school that the studio approached for talent. "They showed me storyboards and then they would say, you know, why don't you try doing this or that or the other thing," she later told John Canemaker. "That's all the guidance I had. By the time I'd been there two or three times, I felt really almost at home."[19] During her time at the studio, Marjorie met and eventually married animator Art Babbitt. The union was a short-lived one; later she would marry fellow dancer Gower Champion, and the two would go on to become famous as the dance team Marge and Gower Champion.

As supervisor of Snow White's action throughout the film, Ham Luske was in effect the director of Marjorie's live-action filming sessions. Initially, to simulate the exaggerated size of Snow White's head, the artists asked Marjorie to perform her actions while wearing a football helmet. "It was heavy, it was hot, the lights were very strong," she chuckled. "I nearly fainted under them, and I never fainted in my life. I was really very woozy under the lights. And then they poked holes in [the helmet] for a while . . . [but] it still didn't help because it constricted my action too much." The helmet was quickly dispensed with. For other scenes Luske and the crew improvised simple props. For the scenes of Snow White in the forest, fighting her way through the vines, "they hung a rope, like a clothesline, across the stage, and hung a lot of ropes from it so that I'd have something to push."

To create a human-like character who moved convincingly on the screen was, of course, only half the battle. Once that technical hurdle was surmounted, what kind of personality would Snow White project? Walt had already gone out of his way to recruit another specialized artist for his hand-picked crew of Snow White animators: Grim Natwick. Older than most of the Disney animators and with a solid background of artistic training, Natwick had earned a reputation in the industry as an artist with a special knack for animating feminine characters. At the Fleischer studio in New York, he had created Betty Boop, and had gone on to animate other girls at Ub Iwerks's California studio. Through hindsight this may seem a curious recommendation: Betty Boop is a long way from the design and personality eventually developed for Snow White. But in 1934, when Natwick first came to the Disney studio, Snow White was still in a formative stage, and Natwick's unusual ability to create a feminine form that moved with real grace was surely seen as an asset.

Above: A three-dimensional bust of Snow White.

Opposite: This model sheet demonstrates the difference between the rotoscope tracings and the proportions of the finished character.

[19] Live-action reference filming for *Snow White* was an extremely informal affair. Marjorie Belcher was not the only Snow White model for these sessions; her performance was supplemented by those of Virginia Davis and, on at least one occasion, vocalist Esther Campbell. Conversely, the influence of Marjorie's performance extended beyond Snow White herself; for the "entertainment sequence," Marjorie also donned loose, floppy clothing and danced for some of the dwarfs.

Snow White
Model Sheet #1
F1 © W·D·P 1936
19

Above and opposite: Snow White's head and face were designed so that she could be animated, yet still retain her "pretty girl" look.

"So I drove over after work one night," Natwick recalled, "and met Walt, and he was very nice. Apparently we were the only two in the studio. He showed me all through the rooms. I remember at that time Dick Huemer was one of these artists who—oh, his drawings were immaculate. You know, my drawings were always kind of sloppy. But that was the only animator room [we visited]. Walt knew I had known Dick Huemer out East, and so he said, 'This is Dick's room; let's see what he's working on.' And he had some of the most beautiful drawings I'd ever looked at on his drawing desk, and I thought, oh boy, if I have to draw like that, I don't know if I'll make it here! But we went from place to place, down to the sound stage, and then finally ended up in Walt's room. And I guess we probably spent an hour together, and talked about different things. And he finally said, 'Well, okay, if you want to come in—.' I think I went in there the next Monday, 'cause I'd already told Iwerks that I probably would go over there if he had a job." Natwick was promptly put to work in the Disney animation department. His first assignments included some feminine characters: the cookie girl in *The Cookie Carnival* and the blind doll in *Broken Toys* (both 1935). Clearly he was being groomed for *Snow White*.

As the animation hierarchy for the feature emerged, Ham Luske and Grim Natwick were established as the two principal animators of Snow White. As we've seen, Luske was the predominant force. He played the determining role in Snow White's design, and he presided over a large unit of artists, including several assistants

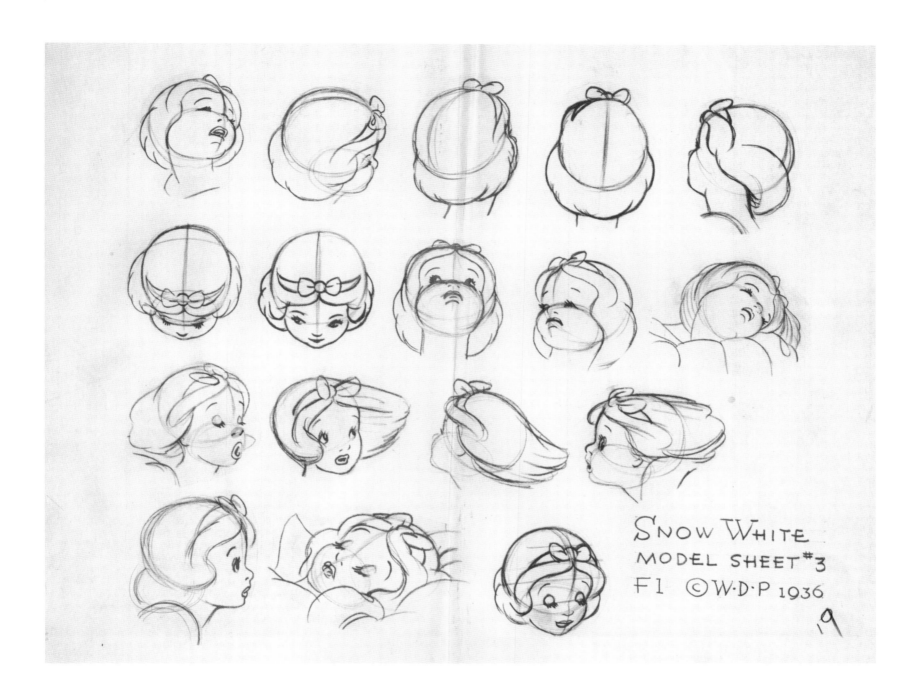

SNOW WHITE MODEL SHEET #3 F1 © W·D·P 1936

who were carefully coached to draw and animate Snow White exactly as Luske did. In turn, during nearly two years of production, some of these assistants (Jack Campbell in particular) graduated to full animation of key portions of the picture, their scenes virtually indistinguishable from those animated by Luske. But Natwick also headed a smaller unit, with his own group of assistants (including Marc Davis), likewise devoted to animation of Snow White.

In his masterful account of the film's animation, Michael Barrier has offered a useful analysis of Luske's and Natwick's differing approaches to the character of Snow White. Essentially, Luske, like Walt, saw her as a wide-eyed, innocent young girl, while Natwick tended to portray her as a somewhat more mature and knowing young woman. Some of Walt's comments early in production suggest that he intended Luske to animate the closeups that would express Snow White's personality, while Natwick's ability to animate the human form would be reserved for longer shots of Snow White in action.[20] In any case, since Luske was so firmly in control of the character—and since, sitting alongside Walt, he carefully reviewed all of Natwick's animation in sweatbox—one might assume that Natwick's interpretation of the character was entirely submerged. In fact, however, Natwick's unit did animate numerous closeups; and, in fact, there are unmistakably two distinct Snow Whites throughout the finished film. Almost every time the character appears on the screen, she is instantly recognizable as one or the other: the Luske

[20] "To help speed Ham up," Walt wrote in November 1935, "I intend that Natwick and [Eddie] Strickland shall handle certain action scenes in all of Ham's Snow White assignment. In other words, they will act in a way as assistants to Ham, handling these scenes under his direction, with Ham concentrating on personality entirely." Ultimately Strickland played a very minor role in the film, more or less along the lines Walt had suggested in this memo.

These two images of Snow White—a close shot by Ham Luske on the left, and a more distant view by Grim Natwick on the right—demonstrate the two artists' differing approaches to the character.

[21] "Almost" because, as we'll see, a third animator takes over the character briefly, during the late sequence in which she's threatened by the Witch. This third animator is Bob Stokes, and his version of Snow White falls somewhere between the Luske and Natwick extremes.

[22] In fairness, it should be noted that Caselotti's voice has also had its devotees. Upon release of the film, *Time* magazine described Snow White as having "a voice like a chime of bells."

unit's young innocent, or the Natwick unit's more mature young lady.[21]

An important factor in this tug-of-war was the casting of the actress who would provide Snow White's voice. Walt, not wanting his judgment to be swayed by a vocalist's appearance, listened by way of a speaker in his office while the various candidates auditioned on the studio sound stage. Several of those candidates can be heard in the finished film: Virginia Davis recorded some miscellaneous vocal tracks that were retained and used in the final cut, and Thelma Hubbard—a popular radio actress who would later portray Snow White and other Disney characters on the air—performed Snow White's screams in the forest sequence, and some of her little outbursts in other scenes. But the principal actress chosen to record Snow White's dialogue and songs was a teenager named Adriana Caselotti, daughter of a Hollywood vocal coach, who was short on experience but did have some operatic training. (Marge Champion remembered that some of the artists referred to Snow White's two component models, Marge Belcher and Adriana Caselotti, by a composite nickname: Margiana Belchalotti.)

Much has been made of Walt's rejection of Deanna Durbin for the role because she sounded "too mature." And, of course, much criticism has been leveled at his choice of Caselotti's high-pitched, childlike voice to represent Snow White. Even during production, several

of the artists had misgivings about Caselotti. "She is getting on my nerves," said Luske at one meeting, and even Walt admitted: "I do think the singing will irritate." In the decades since the film's release, Snow White's voice has remained perhaps the most controversial element of this universally loved picture; even some of *Snow White*'s most devoted admirers confess their distaste for Caselotti's shrill, piercing tones.[22]

In truth, however—whether by design or by instinct—Walt, as usual, knew exactly what he was doing. Intentionally or not, all these competing elements combine to give *Snow White* an important cultural dimension: they address an inconsistency in Snow White's character that goes back as far as the Brothers Grimm—the age of the heroine. The Grimms' Snow White is explicitly described as seven years old at the beginning of her adventures, but at the end of them—after a passage of time that is unspecified but seems relatively short—she marries the Prince. Over the years, commentators have offered various explanations for this awkward incongruity. In reality it's simply one of the charming inconsistencies of fairy tales, the kind of disconnect that can easily be overlooked in a short verbal story. D.L. Ashliman explains that such intervals of time in fairy tales "are symbolic expressions, not literal measurements of time." Illustrators, faced with the task of giving visual form to this discrepancy in Snow White's story, have tended to ignore it; as

Snow White's two alter egos.

Left: Marjorie Belcher in the costume she wore for filming.

Right: Adriana Caselotti, the voice of Snow White.

Maria Tatar reports, "Most illustrations for the story depict her as an adolescent or young adult approaching an age suitable for marriage."

When the story was transferred to the more tangible, literal world of stage and film, one might expect that the issue of Snow White's age would have become even more problematic. Instead, as we've seen, those earliest stage and film versions coincided with the cult of the child/woman in popular entertainment, and the issue became a non-issue. Playing to a 1916 audience that readily accepted adult actresses in child roles, Marguerite Clark could play Snow White as a wide-eyed innocent without upsetting expectations—but her love scenes with the Prince were not a problem either; she was, after all, a 29-year-old actress. Both sides of Snow White's character could be subsumed in her persona without difficulty. The vogue for the child/woman character flourished throughout the "age of innocence" and lingered into the more sophisticated 1920s. By the time of the hard-bitten, Depression-ridden 1930s, it had all but disappeared. But by that time, thanks to Marguerite Clark's performance, it had become an inextricable part of Snow White's cultural legacy.

That legacy, with all its accumulated layers of popular tradition, was at the core of the character Walt Disney brought to the screen. For viewers of the 1930s as for us today, those inherent contradictions are encapsulated in the Disney Snow White. The baby voice singing songs of mature romantic longing, the tension between the Luske little girl and the Natwick young woman, combine to give this Snow White a complexity that reflects *both* the aspects of her traditional character. It's a quality missing from later fairy-tale figures like the Disney Cinderella, who is unmistakably a young woman throughout her story, and therefore a far less interesting character. Somehow, on the screen, Snow White is made to contain both the disparate poles of her heritage, and they coalesce into a vibrant and compelling girl/woman—the sum of her literary antecedents, with the added dimension of a new and distinctly twentieth-century art.

Early gag sketches for the Dwarfs' search of their house, exploring their individual reactions to a crisis.

If Snow White represented one kind of challenge for the animators, the other title characters, the Seven Dwarfs, represented a challenge of a different kind.

The idea of casting the dwarfs as seven different personality types, identified by their names, was not a revelation that occurred in the course of production; it was embedded in Walt Disney's concept of the film from the very beginning. As we've seen, earlier stage and film adaptations of the story had sometimes included slight differentiation of *some* of the dwarfs. By contrast, the earliest surviving story outlines of the Disney version, from mid-1934, are based on the idea of differentiating *all* the dwarfs by strong personality types. This concept—sometimes criticized by folklore purists as if it were a flaw in the film—actually stemmed from the nature of character animation at the Disney studio during those peak years and was central to Walt's reasons for producing *Snow White* in the first place.

The wonderful explosion of creativity that emerged from the Disney studio in the 1930s has been rightly celebrated, but viewers, then and now, have often failed to understand the heart of Disney's breakthrough: *personality animation*. If the characters in Disney cartoons were suddenly reaching out and endearing themselves to audiences as no other animated characters had ever done, it was because they projected convincing, appealing personalities. This was no accident; it was the result of well-conceived story situations, the design of the characters, and—most important of all—the way the characters *moved*. The phenomenally popular *Three Little Pigs* (1933) gained much of its appeal from its chubby, jolly little pigs, bouncing around in vivid contrast to the movements of the stealthy, sly (but none-too-bright) Big Bad Wolf. *The Tortoise and the Hare* (1934) offered not only a compelling story but also a cocky Hare who zipped in circles around the lumbering, slow-witted, good-natured Tortoise. Pluto, the dog in the Mickey Mouse series, distinguished himself by his lanky, loose-limbed movement and by his facial expressions, which seemed to convey his laborious thought processes to the audience. This craft of personality animation was, in effect, a new art form, which would reach its zenith at the Disney studio during the 1930s and early 1940s. It was notoriously difficult to master, but certain artists—Fred Moore, Ham Luske, Norm Ferguson, Bill Tytla, Art Babbitt, and a few others—had shown a special facility for it and had become the new "stars" of the studio.

As characters, the Seven Dwarfs were tailor-made for this artistic environment. If ever there was a textbook exercise in personality animation, this was it: seven characters, all of similar height and appearance, who must be designed and animated so that they could instantly be distinguished from each other. And, since earlier versions of the story had rarely bothered to single out any of the individual dwarfs, the Disney artists were essentially starting from scratch. It was an inspiring challenge. "Just think," Dick Huemer commented to historian Joe Adamson, "taking each one of those dwarfs and making each one an entirely different personality. Seven of the little bastards! It was just unheard of!"[23] In a sense, the dwarfs are the key to the picture: integral to the Grimms' story, ideally suited to development in Disney's medium. It's in this perfect meshing of story and form that the Disney *Snow White* finds its focus.

One of the early challenges in designing these characters was to determine whether, and to what extent, the dwarfs should resemble real dwarfs. One of the earliest story meetings resulted in a warning directed to all the writers: "CALL THEM SEVEN LITTLE MEN, *NOT* DWARFS." (This policy was maintained throughout production; the word "dwarfs," inherited from the Grimms, remained in the film's title, but within the film itself the characters are usually referred to as "little men.") In 1936, several genuine dwarfs were brought to the studio and filmed in 16mm to see whether the animators could make use of their movements. Any suggestion of deformity would of course be a touchy issue with these characters, but Walt and the artists sought creative ways to suggest the characteristics of real dwarfs. What would be the proportions of their limbs? Would they walk in a manner that reflected the pelvic structure of dwarfs?[24] Some early dwarf sketches, particularly those of Albert Hurter, suggested a precarious balance between grotesqueness and charm, but the challenge of putting these ideas in motion—without

[23] For the record, Huemer was animating at the Disney studio during the time *Snow White* was in production, but he worked on only one section of the feature: sequence 11B, the Bed-Building sequence, which was subsequently cut from the picture.

[24] Dave Hand made a mildly tactless remark at one meeting: "I think a duck is an excellent basic thing to build from. As the duck walks along, he waddles from side to side."

GRUMPY

HAPPY

DEAFY

SLEEPY

BASHFUL

DOC

DOPEY

A wide range of design possibilities were suggested for the Dwarfs.

[25] Joe Twerp, real name Joe Boyes, was primarily a radio comic but also worked occasionally as a writer and performer in motion pictures. He died in 1980.

giving offense *or* distracting the audience from the story at hand—proved too daunting. Walt continued to hold out for some kind of distinctive traits; as late as December 1936 he was urging shorter arms and legs for Dopey—"one of these characters has to look like a dwarf." In the end, however, any troublesome characteristics were smoothed away, and the Seven Dwarfs remained, simply, seven little men.

A GALLERY OF DWARFS

Beginning in 1934, more than fifty names, with their corresponding character types, were suggested for the dwarfs. Many of these were quickly discarded; some were considered for a time and then dropped. It's fascinating to review some of the rejected dwarfs through hindsight, not least because some of their traits were developed, refined, and ultimately distilled into the personalities of the dwarfs that did remain in the picture.

Jumpy Sometimes also known as Hoppy, Jumpy was a nervous, easily excitable individual. As we'll see, many of the dwarfs were designed to be voiced by popular radio comedians—and, as we'll also see, several of them were inclined to get their words mixed up, a popular gimmick for radio comics in the 1930s. Jumpy was designed with comic Joe Twerp in mind, and like his role model would emit a high-speed stream of chatter, barely intelligible because of his constant spoonerisms.[25] His nervousness took a colorful form: he was constantly in fear of being goosed. "Whenever he hears a noise behind him or senses someone walking behind him," the 1934 "Manuscript" suggested, "he starts and his hand automatically protects his fanny. He is also exceedingly ticklish." Jumpy flourished briefly during 1934, his phobia surfacing in one treatment as the dwarfs search their house for an intruder: when the teakettle hisses behind him, "JUMPY leaps high into the air, with

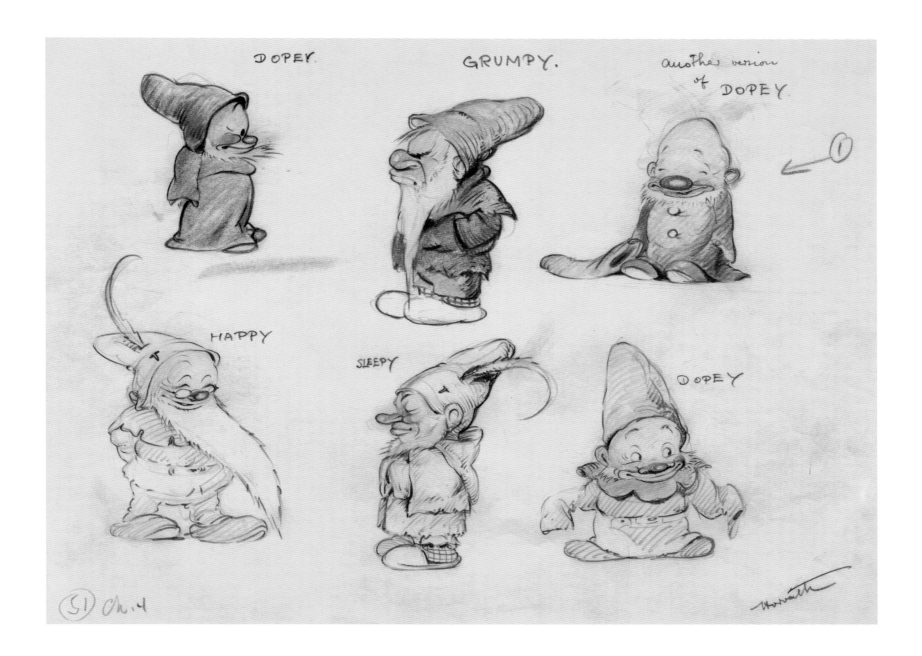

DOPEY.

GRUMPY.

another version of DOPEY.

HAPPY

SLEEPY

DOPEY

a scream!" By mid-November 1934 he had disappeared from the lineup. But it's worth noting that at least one small vestige of his character remained in the finished film. During the Entertainment sequence, as the dwarfs take turns singing their song, Grumpy sounds a loud warning chord on the organ—and Bashful does a quick, involuntary "goose take" as he launches into his verse.

Fatty Also known as Chubby, this dwarf was suggested very early in story development but didn't last long. One early document described him as "a fat little red-nosed dwarf with nice white whiskers, good natured, a twinkle in his eye. Every time he laughs his belly shakes." His pleasant disposition was merged into the character of Happy, as was his ample girth.

Biggy-Wiggy/Biggo-Ego This self-important dwarf was described as "a pompous, oily tongued, know-it-all." Constantly feigning an air of superiority, Biggo-Ego was actually a cowardly, lazy blowhard. The other dwarfs were never fooled in the slightest by his pretensions, but shouted him down and tolerated him only with difficulty. This character, too, was to be voiced by a radio comedian, in this case "Eddie Holden in his character of Hipplewater."[26] It was suggested that Biggo-Ego would eventually redeem himself by performing some act of self-sacrifice for Snow White, but this extremely unpleasant dwarf was not destined to remain in the story for long. Some of his pomposity would later be absorbed by the character of Doc.

Ferdinand Horvath suggests a distinctive basic model for the Dwarfs, and several alternate versions of Dopey.

[26] At this time Holden was already known at the studio, having just supplied the voice for Toby Tortoise in *The Tortoise and the Hare*.

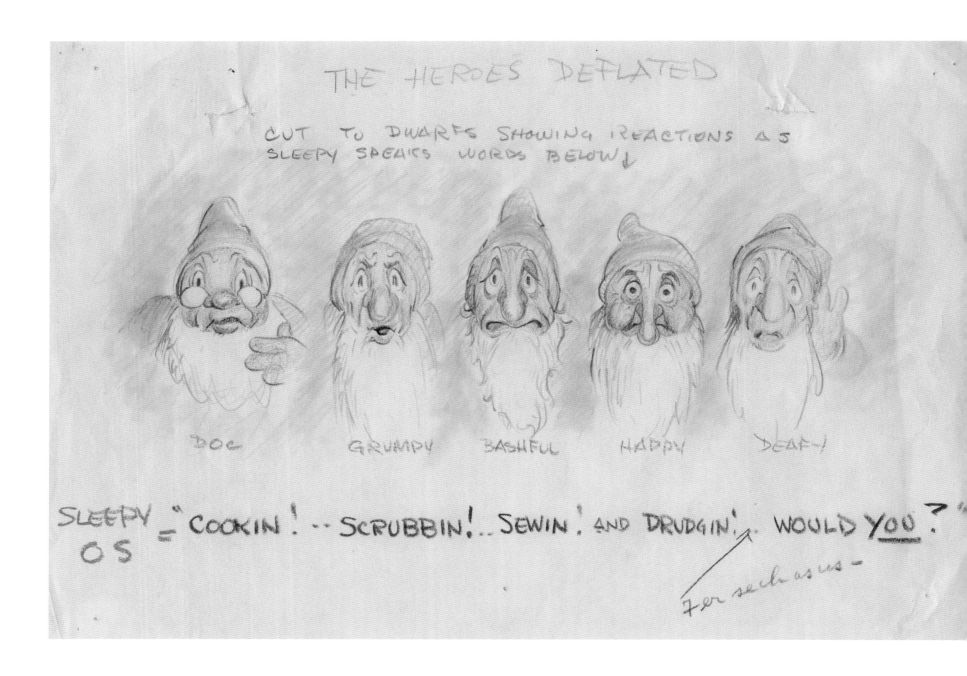

THE HEROES DEFLATED

CUT TO DWARFS SHOWING REACTIONS AS SLEEPY SPEAKS WORDS BELOW↓

DOC   GRUMPY   BASHFUL   HAPPY   DEAFY

SLEEPY "COOKIN! ·· SCRUBBIN!... SEWIN! AND DRUDGIN'. WOULD YOU?"
OS
                                                    For such as us -

Much of the story development took place while Deafy was still a member of the cast.

Awful One of the most interesting early candidates, Awful "steals and drinks and is very dirty. The other dwarfs have impressed on him that his is a soul beyond redemption." Accordingly, Awful was constantly being lectured on his shortcomings and treated with casual disdain by the other dwarfs. It's not difficult to see traces of Winthrop Ames's character Quee in this dwarf. Like Quee (the stage version), Awful was the acknowledged scapegoat of the group, and in fact some of the ideas suggested for Awful specifically recall Quee's scenes in the play. Ames had made Quee responsible for the other dwarfs' nightly washing ritual, while he himself was so dirty that the dwarfs had simply dumped him in the barrel. Now, in 1934, the "Manuscript" outline suggested a washing scene in which the other dwarfs would line up at the well and wash each other in turn, while Awful, being last in line and having no one to wash him,

would simply be tossed into the well. When Snow White protested, the other dwarfs would answer carelessly: "Don't worry. He always gets out all right!"

Clearly, Awful was seen at this point as the "odd man out," his role corresponding loosely to that of Quee in the play. But Disney character development would proceed along very different lines, and if any dwarf in the finished film qualified as the "odd man out," it would be Dopey—a character who had practically nothing in common with Awful. (To further complicate matters, the washing scene would be completely rewritten for Grumpy.) In the meantime, during his short imaginary life, Awful established himself as a unique individual with some traits shared by *none* of these other dwarfs, such as a special affinity for animals. Perhaps most remarkable was his attitude, accepting without complaint his lowly status in the group. Whenever punished or reprimanded for some infraction, whether he was actually guilty or not, his response invariably was a cheerful "I deserve it."

Stubby Another reprobate, Stubby, was proposed in mid-1934. "He has a peg leg, lazy, drawl humor, bad habit of always spitting, no matter where he is. Has another bad habit of telling big lies." But in the constantly changing mix of story ideas at this time, the name Stubby remained while the character changed radically. By early October, a dwarf named either Wheezy or Stubby was "Always behind or last in processions—fatter and shorter than the rest." Within two weeks, this character assumed a starring role in a sequence outline titled "The Dwarfs Find Snow White." In this version, "cherub-faced" Stubby was "determined, but futile, the baby and the goat of the gang"—the "goat" not because he was reprehensible, like Awful, but because he was helpless, smaller than the rest, and easily picked on, like a mistreated little brother. At this point he was probably a precursor of Dopey, although he spoke plenty of dialogue in this outline. But *all* the characters were in a state of flux at this time; a pencil note on the copy of the outline preserved in the Disney Archives reads "Note: Stubby is Bashful"!

Deafy Of all the dwarfs proposed but not used, the one who came nearest to appearing in the film was Deafy. Deafy was deaf—good-natured, cheerful, constantly whittling or engaged in some other activity, but forever missing or misunderstanding everyone else's words. "You know the type of dialogue," one outline noted, "'Going fishing?' 'NO! I'M GOING FISHING!' Naturally, he always shouts." At least two outlines were written late in 1934, describing the dwarfs' search of their house before meeting Snow White—this was the first section of the story to be developed in detail—and both outlines featured Deafy prominently. The dwarfs' terror, as they searched their home for an unknown intruder, was complicated by the constant need to explain everything to Deafy, more than once.

Many prospective dwarfs fell by the wayside before the end of 1934, but Deafy remained in place. As char-

acter development proceeded slowly near the end of 1935, a provisional lineup of seven dwarfs came into focus, and Deafy was one of the seven. Two developing sequences were discussed in story conferences during December 1935, and Deafy was pictured in both. By this time, like the other dwarfs, he had been carefully refined, and notes from one of those conferences reflect some of the thought that had gone into his character: "A horn was suggested for [Deafy], but Walt didn't approve of that since it would mean an additional prop and was a trite treatment to show deafness—get over his deafness by the turn of his head—don't overdo him too much—and don't have him misunderstand what is being said all the time, just at times when it adds comedy to the dialogue or business." Walt himself commented that Deafy "misinterprets other people's attitude toward him. He feels, lots of times, that they are saying something about him, or that they have made some remarks, which they haven't at all—he takes exception to some of the most ridiculous things." When the studio auditioned voice talent for the dwarfs in January 1936, one of the scheduled actors was John Qualen as Deafy.[27]

But Deafy disappeared from the film shortly after that, replaced by Sneezy. Why was he dropped? It's possible that the constant need to repeat dialogue for his benefit became a cumbersome device, slowing down the story. But Michael Barrier proposes another possible factor: "With Deafy gone, none of the dwarfs had a name that suggested a serious physical affliction."

Dozens of other names/traits were suggested for dwarfhood during the early stages of story development: Weepy, Dirty, Cranky, Hungry, Lazy, Thrifty, Nifty, Shifty, Woeful, Wistful, Soulful, Graceful, Blabby, Dippy, Nuertsy, Dizzy, Strutty, Chesty, Hotsy (?)—and many others besides. As the refining process continued, seven final choices were made, and seven complete characters took shape.

Overleaf: Comparative charts showing the relative proportions of the Dwarfs.

[27] John Qualen, an extremely prolific character actor, had appeared in the Fox film *Servants' Entrance* (1934), for which the Disney studio had created a special animated sequence. Of his scores of other Hollywood appearances, he is perhaps best remembered for two 1940 roles: the dispossessed farmer Muley in John Ford's *The Grapes of Wrath,* and the unlikely convicted killer Earl Williams in Howard Hawks's *His Girl Friday.*

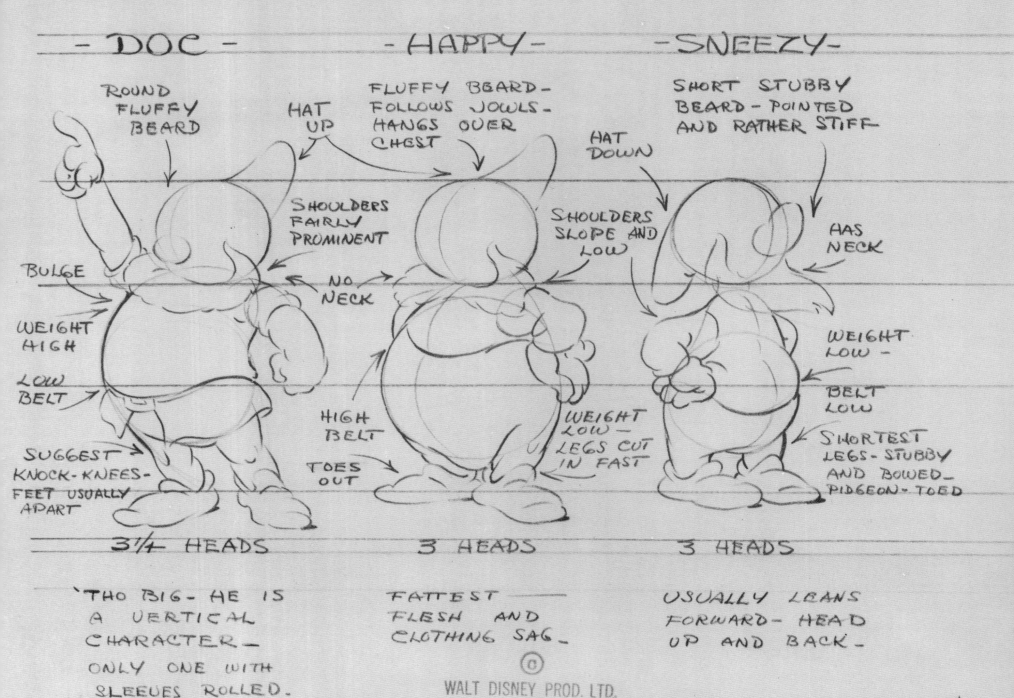

SUPPLEMENTARY CHART —
SHOWING RELATIVE PROPORTIONS.

N.B. THESE FIGURES ARE TRACED FROM REGULAR MODEL SHEETS

- DOC -   - HAPPY -   - SNEEZY -

ROUND FLUFFY BEARD

HAT UP

FLUFFY BEARD - FOLLOWS JOWLS - HANGS OVER CHEST

HAT DOWN

SHORT STUBBY BEARD - POINTED AND RATHER STIFF

SHOULDERS FAIRLY PROMINENT

SHOULDERS SLOPE AND LOW

HAS NECK

BULGE

NO NECK

WEIGHT HIGH

WEIGHT LOW -

LOW BELT

HIGH BELT

BELT LOW

WEIGHT LOW - LEGS CUT IN FAST

SUGGEST KNOCK-KNEES - FEET USUALLY APART

TOES OUT

SHORTEST LEGS - STUBBY AND BOWED - PIDGEON-TOED

3¼ HEADS   3 HEADS   3 HEADS

'THO BIG- HE IS A VERTICAL CHARACTER - ONLY ONE WITH SLEEVES ROLLED.

FATTEST — FLESH AND CLOTHING SAG -

USUALLY LEANS FORWARD - HEAD UP AND BACK -

WALT DISNEY PROD. LTD.
1937

SHEET #1

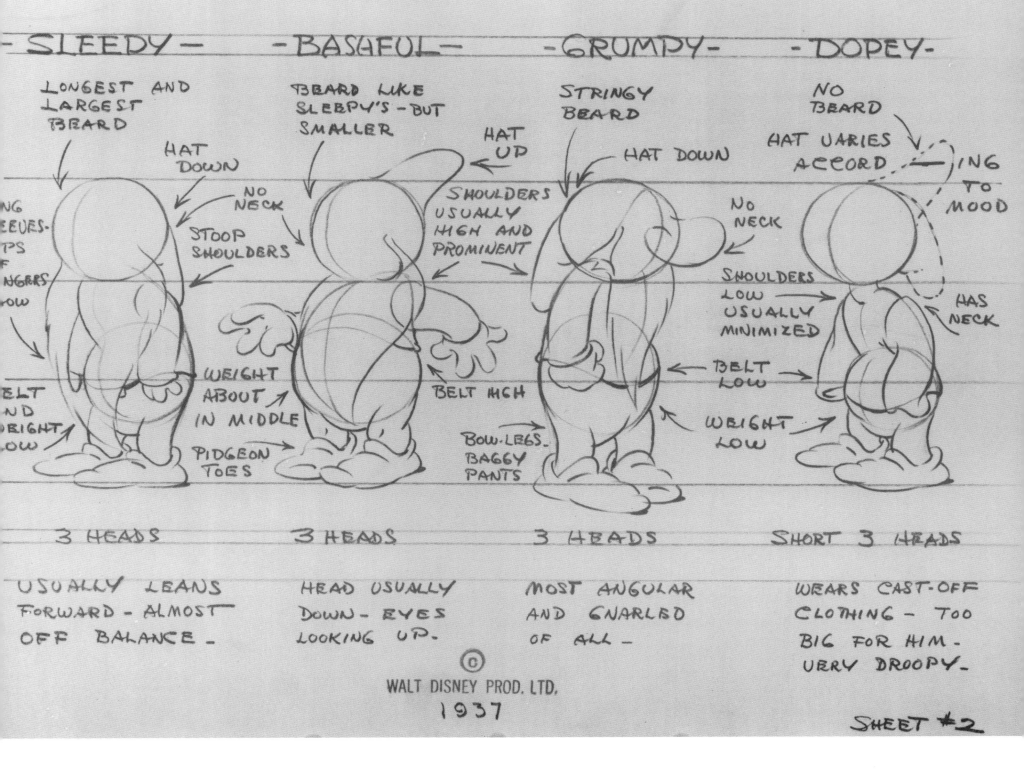

SUPPLEMENTARY CHART —
SHOWING RELATIVE PROPORTIONS —

N.B. THESE FIGURES ARE TRACED FROM REGULAR MODEL SHEETS

— SLEEPY —   — BASHFUL —   — GRUMPY —   — DOPEY —

LONGEST AND LARGEST BEARD

HAT DOWN

BEARD LIKE SLEEPY'S - BUT SMALLER

HAT UP

STRINGY BEARD

HAT DOWN

NO BEARD

HAT VARIES ACCORDING TO MOOD

NO NECK

STOOP SHOULDERS

NO NECK

SHOULDERS USUALLY HIGH AND PROMINENT

NO NECK

SHOULDERS LOW USUALLY MINIMIZED

HAS NECK

ING SLEEVES TIPS OF FINGERS LOW

WEIGHT ABOUT IN MIDDLE

BELT HIGH

BELT LOW

BELT AND UPRIGHT LOW

PIDGEON TOES

BOW-LEGS. BAGGY PANTS

WEIGHT LOW

3 HEADS   3 HEADS   3 HEADS   SHORT 3 HEADS

USUALLY LEANS FORWARD - ALMOST OFF BALANCE -

HEAD USUALLY DOWN - EYES LOOKING UP.

MOST ANGULAR AND GNARLED OF ALL -

WEARS CAST-OFF CLOTHING - TOO BIG FOR HIM - VERY DROOPY.

© WALT DISNEY PROD. LTD.
1937

SHEET #2

The final designs of the Dwarfs were established in September 1936, as seen in the model sheets on this and the following pages.

[28] In connection with the character Doc, we might mention two notable individuals in Walt's life whom he knew as "Doc." One was Doc Sherwood, a retired doctor who had befriended young Walter during his childhood years on the farm in Marceline, Missouri. Doc Sherwood was one of the first adults to encourage Walt's drawing ability, and to the end of his days, Walt retained fond memories of him. "Doc" was also Walt's nickname for Boris Morkovin, a USC professor who was concurrently a guest at the studio, having been engaged in 1934 to lecture the artists. For a time Walt stubbornly defended Morkovin's theories on the psychology of humor and his value to the story department, but most of the artists who worked with him regarded Morkovin with amused tolerance as a pompous pseudo-intellectual. It's tempting to speculate that his pomposity, and Walt's personal affection for both Docs, had some influence on the personality of their cartoon namesake. And, as we'll see on p. 225, production of Snow White would bring yet another important "Doc" into Walt's life.

[29] W.C. Fields, enjoying a peak of screen popularity in the 1930s, was frequently caricatured in animated cartoons, and inevitably his name came up in the Snow White story conferences: one writer suggested in 1934 that Doc might "talk as W.C. Fields would speak."

DOC

From the first stage adaptations of *Snow White,* one dwarf had been set apart as the leader of the group. In the Görner, Merington, and Ames plays and in the Paramount film, the leader was called Blick, and his leadership consisted of little more than marching at the head of the line. The leader of the Disney dwarfs, by his own volition, was Doc.[28]

The Disney character we know as Doc is really a composite of several different traits. One of the earliest story documents, in mid-1934, had suggested a dwarf called Doc who actually was a doctor. This idea persisted for several months: Doc examined Snow White when she was poisoned by the Witch, and in one outline "Doc's stethoscope tangles up with beard" as the dwarfs tried to revive her. At this point, nothing was said about his being the leader, although he was described as "The wise man of the family, fatherly type, practical and understanding." But by mid-October 1934 a change had taken place. The character called Doc had assumed leadership, as well as the basic personality he would

retain in the film: "The Leader and Spokesman of the dwarfs—Pompous, Wordy, Great Dignity—Feels His Superiority, But Is More or Less of a Windbag." In other words, he had lost his medical authority but inherited some of Biggo-Ego's pomposity—hopefully without the latter's unpleasant extremes.

Much of Doc's personality would hinge on his voice. Several actors, including Eddie Holden, were suggested for the role.[29] But in late 1934 and for more than a year thereafter, Billy Bletcher—the Hollywood character actor whose booming bass tones had already been used for the Big Bad Wolf and other Disney characters—was the candidate most often considered for the voice of Doc.

At the same time, there was general agreement that one of the dwarfs would have a habit of mixing up his words. This was a staple of radio comics in the 1930s. Jumpy, a dwarf proposed in 1934, had been modeled on the vocal delivery of one such comic, Joe Twerp, but when Jumpy was phased out of the lineup, Joe Twerp also disappeared from the film[30]. After this, the trait of garbled speech was passed around to other dwarfs. Happy was briefly saddled with a stutter, and even Dopey, before he became mute, tangled his words in one story outline. But here again, much depended on the voice actor. Because radio comics with trick dialogue were so plentiful in the 1930s, many of them distinguished themselves with unique specialties; malapropisms, spoonerisms, and a variety of other tics were available. Some gifted performers might offer more than one forte, as with the assortment of lisps and stammers that Mel Blanc provided for the Schlesinger/Warner Bros. characters. In the early months of 1936, the Disney studio settled on Doc as the dialogue-mangling dwarf by casting Roy Atwell as his voice.

Atwell's show-business career went back to the turn of the century. He had appeared on Broadway as early as 1901, generally in comedy roles, and had also tried his hand as a playwright, songwriter, and actor in silent films. But by the mid-1930s, he was known primarily as a radio performer. Atwell's specialty was the authoritative speaker who drones on in apparent seriousness, all the while garbling his dialogue by accidentally switching consonants, syllables, or entire words. He displayed this specialty on the screen, notably in a 1934 Warner Bros./Vitaphone short subject, an entry in their series *Rambling 'Round Radio Row*. In this short, Atwell is "interviewed" by a young journalist about his success as a radio star. He could hardly have asked for a better audition for the role of Doc. As the young actress struggles to keep a straight face, Atwell pontificates on the demands of a radio career, advising her that a successful announcer "must distinct talkly—er, squawk distinct—er . . ." and so on, never managing to navigate through a complete sentence. Atwell's style perfectly expressed Doc's ineffectual leadership: besides being funny in itself, his garbled delivery suggested both the character's pretensions to authority and his constant befuddlement.

Grounded by Atwell's vocal interpretation, the artists refined Doc's personality and visual design. Doc and Happy were the two heaviest dwarfs but were distinguished from each other by posture. "[Doc] is the pompous guy," said Fred Moore. "Even though he is big, he has to maintain a shape—sort of chesty—in order to distinguish him from Happy who is also large and fat. Happy is fatter and lets his weight slip and fall down, while Doc is holding his weight up with a pompous attitude." Bill Tytla summed up Doc's manner as "sort of a French Provincial Mayor's attitude." Walt's analysis went to fine points of the character's personality: "Doc is upset by the least little thing, the least little annoyance. [When interrupted] he doesn't know where he was, and somebody has to help him out . . . He can't remember things very long. He has this habit of getting mixed up, only when he is upset or when he is angered or when he meets Snow White. When he meets Snow White, he is like a fellow meeting a girl—gets awfully flustered—sort of an inferiority complex."

At these and other conferences, an unusual amount of attention was focused on Doc's hands. When Doc made one of his frequent verbal mistakes, he usually reacted with a combination of head shakes and nervous, fluttering movements of his hands—gestures which, to some extent, were inherited from Atwell. The animators analyzed these movements carefully, going so far as to shoot 16mm film of Atwell so that they could study his hands. When Doc's scenes began to appear in sweatbox, these actions were criticized more than any other aspect of his animation. Walt, correcting one of Art Babbitt's scenes, explained: "When Doc corrects himself, his action should not be broader than before, but more confined. His gestures on his correction should be small and confined; this is a Doc characteristic . . . He should have a tight little feeling of annoyance with himself for having got mixed up."

Along with the model sheets, jointed wooden models were made of some of the Dwarfs.

[30] In his more familiar medium of radio, Twerp did enjoy a further Disney connection. In 1938, when Walt decided that his schedule would not permit continued involvement in the *Mickey Mouse Theatre of the Air* radio program, Joe Twerp succeeded him as the voice of Mickey Mouse.

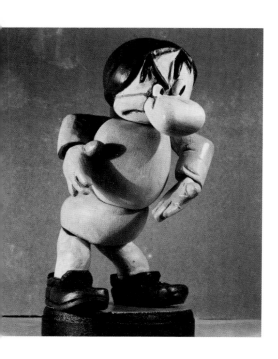

A jointed wooden model of Grumpy, showing his belligerent stance.

31 In the spring of 1923, while Walt was still living in Kansas City, Paramount Pictures had released a feature titled *Grumpy*, with veteran character actor Theodore Roberts in the title role of a retired lawyer whose gruff exterior barely concealed a heart of gold. In 1930, by which time Walt was well established in Hollywood, Paramount had remade *Grumpy* as a talking picture, this time with Cyril Maude in the role. We have no evidence that Walt or his writers had seen either of these films, but we certainly can't rule it out. It's also worth noting the Disney short *Woodland Café* (1937), a Silly Symphony produced concurrently with *Snow White*. This short featured a cast of insects, including a crotchety old bee who walked with a cane, unidentified by name onscreen but known as "Grumpy" to the artists who worked on him.

GRUMPY

Of all the dwarfs, Grumpy was arguably the strongest personality, "the easiest character to get a hold of," as Dave Hand noted at one meeting. While other dwarfs went through long periods of character development, Grumpy sprang to life virtually fully formed. One of Walt's earliest handwritten notes in mid-1934 read: "One skeptical & pessimistic dwarf always predicting trouble." The name "Grumpy" appeared by August 1934,[31] and by October various outlines were describing him as "Typical Dyspeptic and Grouch—Pessimist, Woman-hater—the Last to Make Friends with Snow White" and "a hold-out . . . crabby about everything until SNOWWHITE recovers from poison comb, then he weakens, but reverts to type again until her poison apple sequence, when he is as sorry as the rest." In other words, essentially the same character that would appear in the finished film three years later.

More than one of these early descriptions made reference to a character from a 1932 Silly Symphony, *Santa's Workshop*. In that holiday-themed short, one of the "gnomes" who help Santa Claus at his North Pole workshop is a wizened little secretary. As Santa sits reading the letters sent to him by children, the sour-faced secretary leafs through an enormous book to see whether the boy or girl in question has been good. One boy requests a long list of gifts, and the secretary objects in a croaking voice: "But Billy Brown, for seven years/ Hasn't washed behind his ears!" This little misanthrope proved to be an ideal model for Grumpy, and even spoke with the voice of the same actor who would provide Grumpy's voice: Pinto Colvig. Nominally a member of the story department, the irrepressible Colvig had already put his stamp on the Disney shorts with a variety of other talents, including his voice. By the time of *Snow White*, he was best known as the voice of Goofy but had also spoken for other characters, including the Practical Pig in *Three Little Pigs*. His crotchety, irritable voices for Santa's secretary and Practical Pig were not far from the voice he would provide for Grumpy.

Of the two leading dwarf animators, Fred Moore and Bill Tytla, it was Tytla who most strongly influenced the character of Grumpy. This is not to minimize Moore's contribution; like every character he touched, Grumpy benefited from Moore's instinctive flair for appealing drawings. To the junior artists, Moore offered practical insights into Grumpy's design: "Grumpy has sort of a Mickey body. He can get cocky, but be sure to shove the chest and fanny out."

But it was in Tytla's scenes that Grumpy crystallized, suddenly and vividly, into an extraordinarily strong personality among the dwarfs. Vladimir "Bill" Tytla has been stereotyped in animation history as an artist who specialized in large, villainous characters; in reality the scope of his talent was much broader than that. But it's fair to say that a dark, brooding forcefulness in Tytla's own personality projected itself into his animation, and that forcefulness erupted in Grumpy with ferocious intensity. It was Tytla who took the initiative, late in 1935, to shoot live-action film of Pinto Colvig performing some of Grumpy's actions, then to build on Colvig's foundation to create Grumpy's performance. The result would become one of the great bondings of animator and character. As Michael Barrier has written: "only Grumpy was an obvious vehicle for Tytla's animation; and it was through his animation of Grumpy that Tytla was giving shape to his distinctive ideas about cartoon acting."

As Grumpy's character developed, he came to occupy a central role in the film's plot. The more defiantly he opposed Snow White at the outset, the more poignant his gradual change of heart toward her would be. In Walt's mind, this became one of the most important threads of the story; wholly original, it became inextricably intertwined with the Grimms' traditional narrative. In one conference after another, Walt recounted the gradual stages by which Grumpy would succumb, however reluctantly, to Snow White's charms. By December 1936, when one writer suggested that Grumpy might show a slight weakening toward Snow White after the Entertainment sequence, the progression was so firmly established in Walt's mind that he could respond instantly: "We shouldn't have Grumpy fall for her at that point, I don't think, let's save that for in the morning—it is very definite that he falls for her in the morning."

Grumpy's model sheet includes some instantly recognizable poses from the washing sequence.

If special attention was being focused on Doc's hands, Grumpy's nose came in for equal notice. The most prominent of all the dwarfs' noses, Grumpy's snout was large, rubbery, vulnerable, and an obvious target for slapstick gags. "It's a gag license; come back on Grumpy getting the worst of it again," said Walt, pitching a gag at one story meeting. "It is that big nose that was smacked by Doc in the bedroom, the nose that bumped into the door, and the nose that is going into the knot hole." Clearly he was eager to heap further indignities on that nose. But of course Grumpy's proboscis was more than a slapstick prop; Walt had definite ideas about the character's appearance and warned at another meeting: "Watch Grumpy's nose that it doesn't get to looking like Barney Google's nose."

Although Bill Tytla is rightly celebrated for his animation of Grumpy, several other artists did work on the character, and it's worth singling out the contribution of Dick Lundy. Lundy, who had helped to define another irascible Disney character, Donald Duck, was called on for some of Grumpy's key scenes: playing the organ and then sulking in the corner in the Entertainment sequence, trying to sleep in the soup pot shortly afterward. In the Lodge Meeting sequence (see page 202), later cut from the picture, all the Grumpy animation was Lundy's work.

An early version of Happy.

HAPPY

Like Grumpy, Happy was one of the first names suggested for the dwarf ensemble. *Unlike* Grumpy, the dwarf Happy was conceived in unrecognizable terms before evolving into the character we know today. The earliest known mention of Happy, in mid-1934, describes him as "a little skinny fellow" with a stuttering problem, while Fatty/Chubby, whom we've already met, was the good-natured dwarf with "a twinkle in his eye." In the August 1934 "Manuscript" outline, Happy is described as having one tooth and as being voiced by "Professor Diddleton D. Wurtle, whose wild Ben Turpin eyes are reinforced by one of the funniest tricks of speech in radio." In this version, Happy's "funny trick of speech" was caused by a physical defect: his jaw habitually dislocated in mid-sentence! His elbows, knees, and other joints likewise periodically slipped out of their sockets and had to be reassembled by the other dwarfs. "It is funny to the eye," the outline claimed, "but especially funny because of the painful psychology behind it. Happy grins away and sputters gaily even as the beads of pain pour from his brow."

It's not clear how long this bizarre concept of Happy survived, but in any case it had been phased out by January 1936, when Otis Harlan was engaged to record his dialogue.

Part of *Snow White*'s power as a work of art comes from the actors who provide its voices. The combined wealth of cultural history represented in their careers is embedded in the film and functions on an almost subliminal level as a time capsule of American entertainment. Otis Harlan is one example of that golden legacy. His career extended well back into the nineteenth century; he had made his New York stage debut in 1887, fully a half-century before *Snow White*. He had gone on to star in numerous stage comedies, heading his own theatrical company for a time and appearing with the likes of Weber and Fields, Elsie Janis, and Anna Held. Beginning in 1915 he had played character roles in more than 100 films, among them Cap'n Andy in the first film version of *Show Boat*. By the mid-1930s, he was working steadily in films ranging from B Westerns to prestige productions such as Warner Bros.' *A Midsummer Night's Dream*. His performance in *Snow White* was a valedictory to a long, varied career in show business; it would prove to be one of his last professional engagements.

As character development continued, Harlan contributed not only Happy's voice but also much of his physical appearance. "Happy is a cartoon of Otis Harlan," Fred Moore stated flatly to a group of dwarf animators in November 1936. "I just watched Otis Harlan for about two or three days. When I came back, I was full of all his mannerisms." He added that Walt not only permitted this, but encouraged it: "Walt had a particular walk for Happy, an Otis Harlan walk, flat-footed with his feet out at the side. He has a definite rocking roll on the balls of his feet." This was only the beginning: the tilt of Harlan's head, his nervous hand

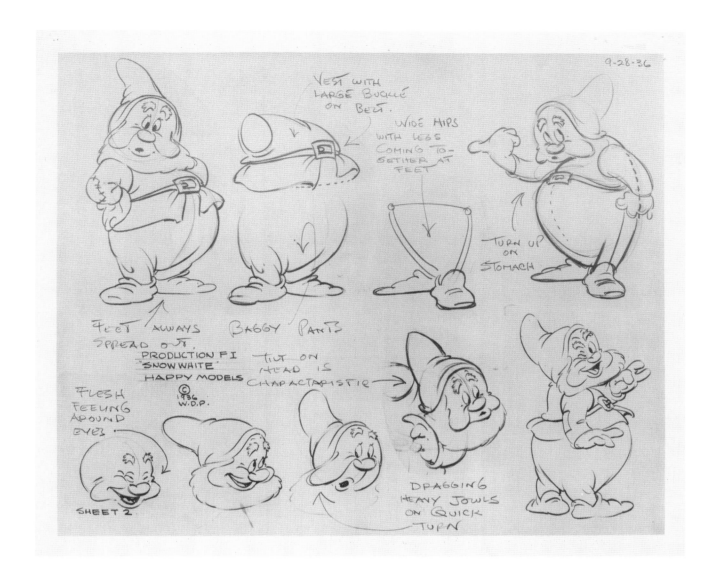

Happy's bulk, more ample than Doc's, was further accentuated by his posture.

gestures, and other characteristic movements all found their way into Happy's performance. In short, Harlan's movement resurfaced in Happy much as Marjorie Belcher's did in Snow White—not as a crutch, as in traditional rotoscoping, but selectively, as a translation of recognizable human traits from one medium into another.

As for Happy's personality, he emerges in the finished film as a perennially cheerful optimist and little more. During story development, he had been conceived as a more rounded character; Walt had taken pains to give each of the dwarfs more or less equal time on the screen. "You will find that Happy has an awful lot of personality that we have not got out of him yet," he commented at one story meeting. But as the story was continually refined and trimmed to its essentials, that balance of power shifted, and some dwarfs became more prominent while others receded into supporting positions. One by one, Happy's starring moments were eliminated from the film until he became one of the "supporting" dwarfs. As late as December 1936, when

Walt suggested a gag that would bring out the practical-joker side of Happy's personality, Dave Hand—supervising director of the feature—commented: "I never heard of that angle in his character." Fortunately, Happy's bubbling effervescence keeps him from getting lost in the background.

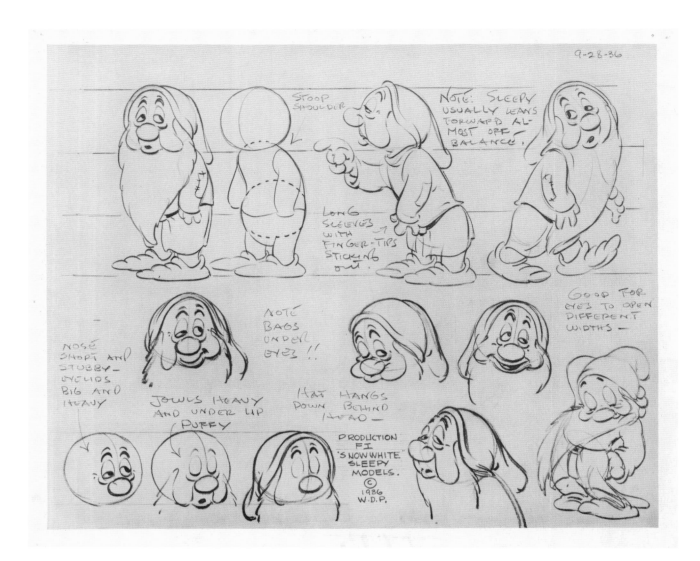

Details of Sleepy's facial features, especially the eyes, contribute to his perpetually drowsy appearance.

SLEEPY

Sleepy was another dwarf suggested in some of the very earliest outlines—*and* another dwarf whose early conception was utterly unlike the character we know in the finished film. For several months in late 1934, veteran stage actor Sterling Holloway, whose high, distinctive vocal tones had become a familiar fixture in sound films, was pictured as the voice of Sleepy. "Holloway's melodious and screwy singing voice will be an asset," claimed the "Manuscript" outline. For a time, Holloway seems to have influenced the concept of Sleepy as Otis Harlan influenced Happy; the "Manuscript" also suggested a lot of impossibly talky dialogue for the character, clearly written with Holloway's vocal delivery in mind. One description of Sleepy as the "long, lanky type"—surely a contradiction in terms for a dwarf—was probably based on Holloway's own physical type. Even after the Sterling Holloway idea was abandoned,[32] Sleepy was compared more than once to another long, lanky actor: the African-American character player Stepin Fetchit,

whose performances featured slow, sleepy movements and a lazy drawl.

In the end, of course, Sleepy became as compact as any of the other dwarfs, his sleepiness expressed by his posture and his sluggish walk and movement. "He drags along as though he had weights in his feet," Art Babbitt suggested, "and his arms would hang down in the same way." After Sterling Holloway was eliminated as Sleepy's voice, radio performer Johnny Gibson was suggested instead, and recorded some dialogue at a prerecording session in February 1936. In the end, however, the studio turned once again to Pinto Colvig to supply the character's voice. Colvig's voice for Sleepy was distinct from the vocal characterization he had adopted for Grumpy but roughly similar to his most famous Disney voice, that of Goofy.

The fly that plagues Sleepy throughout the picture also appeared very early in story development. One early document suggested that Sleepy would frequently

[32] Holloway would later make his Disney recording debut as the voice of the stork in *Dumbo* (1941), and would go on to record other voices for the studio.

Sleepy rides home.

Ferdinand Horvath proposes a lazy mode of transportation for Sleepy.

be bothered by flies and that, at the end of the film, "after Snow White has been taken out of the gold casket with the glass cover SLEEPY takes advantage of the opportunity to crawl into the casket to sleep, pulling the glass cover over him so the flies won't bother him." This slightly macabre idea persisted for some months, but by October 1934 the multiple flies had been replaced by one individual fly that habitually annoyed Sleepy. During the ensuing months of story development, so many Sleepy/fly gags were suggested that Perce Pearce warned against depending too much on the device: "You can't use the fly as a label for Sleepy. We have to build his character minus the fly." As viewers of *Snow White*, we know, of course, that numerous fly gags were retained in the finished picture, but just as many were discarded. (For example, during the Entertainment sequence, it was suggested that the fly might fly into Sleepy's mouth just before his clarinet solo, come shooting out of one of the instrument's air holes when Sleepy played a note, then dodge in and out of the other holes.)

As with the other dwarfs, Sleepy's personality was refined as the conferences continued. Some artists assumed that this perpetually drowsy dwarf would be depicted as a stupid character, but Walt was quick to assert otherwise. "Walt created this character as a very clever and ingenious type," Pearce pointed out at one meeting. "Only once in a while he rouses himself to the extent of making a remark. When he does, it is very intelligent. They all pick it up . . . He is the smartest character in the whole bunch, even when he is sleeping." As the film's continuity was polished in succeeding months, several sequences were cut, and this ingenious quality of Sleepy's personality was gradually lost. Only one of his insightful comments remains in the film: as the dwarfs try to understand the agitation of the animals and birds swarming around them at the mine, it's Sleepy who lazily suggests, "Maybe the old Queen's got Snow White."

When the dwarfs mount the backs of the deer and go racing back to their cottage to try to save Snow White from the Witch, one writer suggested that Sleepy might fall asleep on the back of his deer. Walt quickly put this trait in perspective: "Sleepy isn't sleepy all the time. When the opportunity presents itself he is always ready to relax, but he isn't always going around dead. I feel that it would be wrong to have him asleep on the deer."

BASHFUL

The dwarf we know as Bashful seems to have had his origins in a character called Baldy, proposed in mid-1934. "He is bashful," said an early outline, "blushes at everything, face becomes very red when he blushes." Throughout the remainder of 1934, various outlines identified this dwarf alternately as either Bashful or Baldy, and one actually referred to him as "Bashful Baldy." Moreover, these outlines gave him something to blush about: his skull came to a point on top. "Funny shaped head, goes clear up into the peak of his cap, and he is very sensitive about it, keeps his cap on in the house all the time. The other dwarfs like to kid BALDY, but Snow White sympathizes with him." Another outline referred to him as "the dwarf with the pyramid-like skull." For a time Bashful/Baldy was seen as the smallest one of the dwarfs, the one who served as a scapegoat for the others, until Dopey arrived to take over that position.

In the finished film, of course, Bashful is relieved of his embarrassing affliction (and *all* the dwarfs are bald, and *all* wear their caps inside the house). His bashfulness is simply an element of his personality. In the course of story development, Bashful—although often overshadowed by the other dwarfs—became one of the most interesting characters in *Snow White*. In the finished picture he's a true romantic, his bashfulness merely a manifestation of his sensitive nature. More openly than the other dwarfs, he falls in love with Snow White the instant he lays eyes on her. "He is not a sissy," Perce Pearce maintained. "His charm is in his very retiring and sentimental personality." Pearce also identified a characteristic Bashful pose: "when he looks at anything, he is holding his head down and looking up from under his eyebrows in a Will Rogers expression"— a comparison that was repeated more than once in later conferences. Walt, for his part, likened Bashful to Charles Ray, the silent-film star known for his shy country-boy roles, and to Stan Laurel. He also picked up on an earlier suggestion that "he would have music in his soul . . . I would like to see Bashful in the Entertainment sequence play a drum or some instrument, and when Snow White would look at him, he would have this coquettish look on his face, and express

this same thought in the playing of the instrument."

Just as Bill Tytla was the pace-setting animator for Grumpy and Fred Moore displayed a similar affinity for Dopey, Bashful likewise had a specialist on the animation staff. This was Marvin Woodward, one of the lesser-known Disney artists. To be sure, Bashful did pass through the hands of many other artists—and, for that matter, Woodward animated other characters in the course of production—but somehow his ability to capture Bashful's "blushing, hesitating, squirmy, giggly" nature was recognized from the start. Most of Bashful's key scenes in the picture are Woodward's work, even in sequences to which he was not otherwise assigned. In the Entertainment sequence, for example, Woodward makes what amounts to a guest appearance to animate Bashful's stumbling, blushing verse in the "Silly Song" and, later, his dance with Snow White.

Bashful's voice was provided by character actor Scotty Mattraw. The rotund Mattraw was a fixture in Hollywood during the 1920s and 1930s and had played minor roles in a variety of films, including Douglas Fairbanks's *The Thief of Bagdad* (1924) and the 1934 Laurel & Hardy version of *Babes in Toyland*.[33]

[33] In addition to this *Snow White* connection, the 1934 *Babes in Toyland* has a special interest for Disney enthusiasts because it reflects the influence Walt and his characters had on popular culture in the mid-1930s. In this version of *Babes*, produced by Hal Roach and released by MGM, the citizens of Toyland include the Three Little Pigs, clearly modeled on the Disney characters. The Pigs not only appear but play an active role in the plot, and their appearances are heralded on the soundtrack by the instrumental strains of Frank Churchill's "Who's Afraid of the Big Bad Wolf?", sandwiched in among the familiar Victor Herbert themes. There's also a monkey that causes general mischief during the action scenes, costumed and disguised to look like Mickey Mouse!

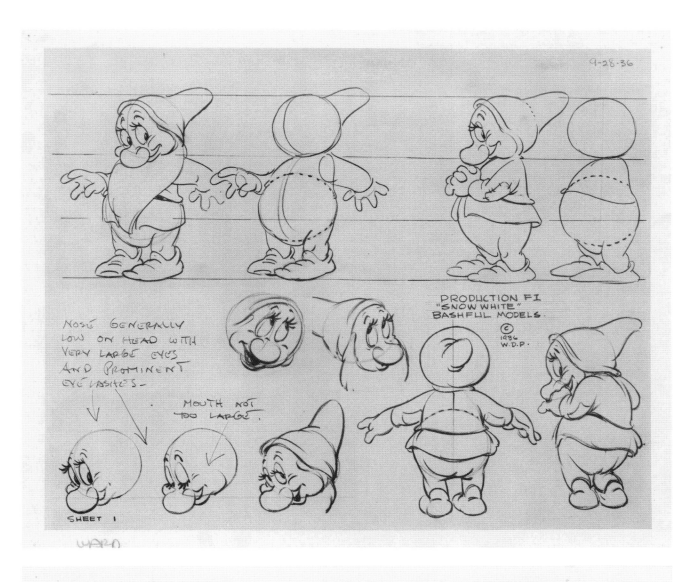

In his final incarnation, Bashful was not only bashful, but sensitive, romantic, and hopelessly smitten with Snow White.

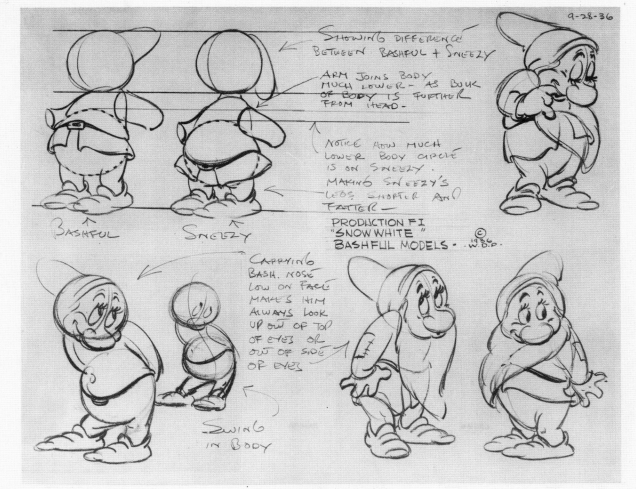

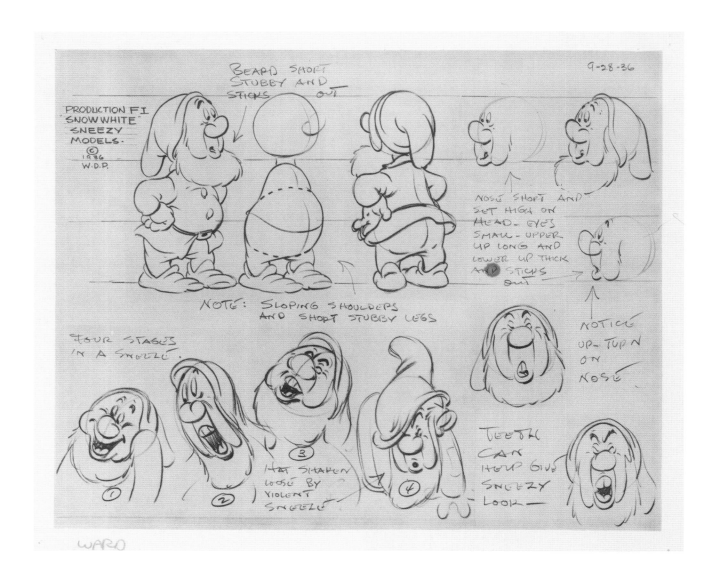

Not surprisingly for a character who suffered from perpetual hay fever, Sneezy's nose was an important feature of his design.

SNEEZY

Sneezy was the last dwarf to join the lineup, as Deafy's replacement early in 1936. A dwarf named Sneezy-Wheezy or Gaspy had actually been proposed very early in story development, in the "Manuscript" outline of August 1934. Described in this document as a character who was "Always sneezing or, perhaps, about to sneeze" and who "Talks like he had a cold in his head," he was also "Dapper—quick movements—nimble dancer." Walt apparently liked this suggestion; his copy of the outline, preserved today in the Walt Disney Archives, bears his handwritten "OK" next to the description of this character. But the idea was quickly forgotten, and nothing more was heard of it for more than a year.

Early in 1936, as Deafy was eased out of the picture, the sneezing dwarf returned to take his place. Sneezy's ailment, unlike Deafy's, could give no possible offense; sneezing was accepted as a comedy staple by audiences everywhere long before Sneezy arrived on the scene. As early as 1894, Edison's famous experimental film *Fred*

Ott's Sneeze had been received as "a topic inclined to incite a smile." Ten years later, Winsor McCay had built an entire comic strip around sneezing: *Little Sammy Sneeze* featured a little boy who, week after week, disrupted some gathering, endeavor, or event with a mighty sneeze. (The last panel almost invariably depicted Sammy being booted out of the premises, even though, as the title banner apologetically explained each week, "HE NEVER KNEW WHEN IT WAS COMING.") Subsequent artists and entertainers, including Walt himself, continued to play cataclysmic sneezes for laughs. Sneezy, inducted into the Seven Dwarfs in 1936, carried on the tradition.

At a story conference in January of that year, Wilfred Jackson suggested Sneezy as one of the dwarfs who might play a concertina in the party sequence. Walt saw him instead as a singer: "Sneezy has a funny voice." By now that funny voice was the key to Sneezy's character, for by now the character had been specifically designed

around Billy Gilbert's voice. Gilbert was one of the busiest character players in Hollywood; in the course of his career, he appeared in literally hundreds of short and feature-length films. Latter-day accounts of his work in *Snow White* tend to suggest that his entire act consisted of his sneezing routine, but in truth, Gilbert's expressive sneezes were only a small part of his repertoire. "People remember me as the comedian with the funny sneeze," he recalled late in his life. "Funny thing is that I didn't use it in more than five or six of all those films I made, but the way it sticks in people's memories you'd think that was all I ever did." Indeed, filmgoers of the 1930s could see Gilbert in dozens of Hal Roach comedy shorts featuring Laurel & Hardy, Our Gang, and Charley Chase—along with numerous feature films—without ever seeing his sneezing act at all.

But when he did perform his sneezing specialty, it was memorable. In the 1934 Roach short *Maid in Hollywood,* for example, Gilbert, as a visitor to a movie set, demonstrates a range of differentiated sneezes. This was an engaging novelty, like Donald Duck's voice, and here it became the premise of Sneezy's character: he was the dwarf afflicted with hay fever, forever haunted by the threat of a monumental sneeze. Sneezy sneezes five times in the course of *Snow White,* and most of those occasions are set apart as comedy set-pieces. Even during production, Walt noted, "Everybody seems to get a kick out of that sneeze."

In short, Sneezy's sneezes were a gimmick drawing on an American comedy tradition. Of all the dwarfs, he was the only one whose name denoted a physical condition rather than a personality type or trait. Still, as story development proceeded and Sneezy was further integrated into the picture, rudiments of a personality began to emerge from his respiratory affliction. "There is more to him than just the sneeze," Perce Pearce declared. "We are giving him lines in the Spook Sequence, for instance, where we show him as a dense or serious type of fellow who sort of fights his predicament—a type of guy that [has] always got a cold in his nose, and life is the prettiest thing. He hasn't much sense of humor, and is not a responsive type like Happy." From a physical standpoint, Fred Moore pointed out, Sneezy was short and squat but carried himself with an erect posture: "He looks over the top of his nose . . . His belt is fairly low. Shoulders are very low. He has the appearance of his nose holding his head up and everything else is dropping away." Pearce observed that "Sneezy carries that nose of his in the air as though he were balancing a teacup on it" and "is built very much with a long neck." "As though he had a serious outlook on life," added Frank Thomas.

As these conferences continued, Walt added another subtle observation: "We kind of pair Sneezy and Bashful, don't we, in our cuts? They agree with each other. They yes each other."

DOPEY

Even among the Seven Dwarfs, each one established as a distinct individual, it was a foregone conclusion that one dwarf would be set apart as the "odd man out." Chosen to fill this role was Dopey, by any measure the dwarf most widely beloved by audiences when *Snow White* was released. But Dopey was a long time evolving.

Earlier stage versions of *Snow White*, especially the Winthrop Ames version, had established the convention of one dwarf who was "different," and early character development of dwarfs for the Disney film was influenced by this idea. Stubby, "the baby and the goat of the gang" in an October 1934 outline written by Dick Creedon, clearly owes something to Quee, the youngest dwarf in the Ames play. Creedon's outline attempts to build sympathy for Stubby as, with "his short, kneeless legs," he tries to keep up with the other dwarfs in their march home from the mine. Reaching a clearing near their home, the dwarfs indulge in what is apparently a standard practice: crying "Last one home has to wash the dishes," they sprint for the door. Stubby, of course, with his short legs, has no hope of keeping up. Creedon describes him dissolving into tears: "It's always me! I've washed all the dirty dishes for the last three hundred years!"

In hindsight, it's not difficult to see Stubby as a precursor of Dopey—but, clearly, he had a long way to go. During the final months of 1934, the concept of the little/fall-guy dwarf appeared in a variety of forms. The name "Dopey" seems to have been applied to this character first in November 1934, in another outline about the dwarfs' meeting with Snow White. Here Dopey has (thankfully) lost Stubby's whining, self-pitying attitude, but he's still a long way from the Dopey who appears in the finished film. For one thing, he still has the power of speech—and, in fact, talks a blue streak, constantly making silly comments for which the others slap him down. (As the dwarfs speculate on what manner of intruder could be inside their house, Dopey pipes up: "Maybe it's Santa Claus!") And, just once, he gets his words mixed up—a trait that has yet to be applied to Doc.

During the next two years, Dopey endured a long refining process. Still the "baby" of the group, he ceased to be a mindless chatterbox and became a more precisely defined character. "He is not an imbecile," said Perce Pearce. "He is full of fun and life. Life is just a bowl of cherries to him and just a game . . . he is a little guy that hasn't grown up." To suggest that he was dressed in the cast-off clothing of the others, his clothes were floppy, loose-fitting, and much too large for him, his sleeves hanging far down over his hands.[34] Walt provided an important key to Dopey's character by comparing him repeatedly to silent-film comedian Harry Langdon. Langdon's screen persona was a peculiar one: living and functioning in the adult world, his pantomime and mannerisms were those of a small child. Similarly, Dopey, not truly a child, nevertheless behaved like one. "I see Dopey in kind of a way like Langdon," Walt said, "his kid mannerisms—the way he would rub his nose as though he didn't know how to use his hands—the little run he has, holding onto his hat . . . Don't you feel that he is eager—like a puppy waiting for someone to throw a ball—ready to go. Dopey is right with the other dwarfs all the time, following the conversation more or less. When he would run, he runs like a kid with little fast steps."

When the decision was made to take away Dopey's speech, he immediately brought to mind another, more contemporary comedian: Harpo Marx. This was another analogy made repeatedly in story conferences. It was a valid comparison that went beyond the simple lack of dialogue; Dopey displays Harpo's near-magical ability to bounce back from any situation. Bombarded with one slapstick gag after another, Dopey invariably prevails with a smile; utterly without guile or mean-spiritedness, he is simply impervious to attack. "At times there is great violence done him," said Pearce, "just like the Duck . . . whether he gets socked on the head or whatever it is, it never hurts him."

The idea of Dopey's speechlessness took hold gradually during this time. Late in 1935, Walt wrote: "He is unable to talk—no reason given for it, except that he just never tried." Yet, for months after this, Dopey continued to speak up occasionally in some story outlines. One writer suggested, with Walt's approval, that Dopey might be one of the yodelers in the Entertainment

[34] A similar effect had been used for Mickey Mouse in the classic 1935 short *The Band Concert:* Mickey had appeared in a bandleader's coat that was several sizes too large.

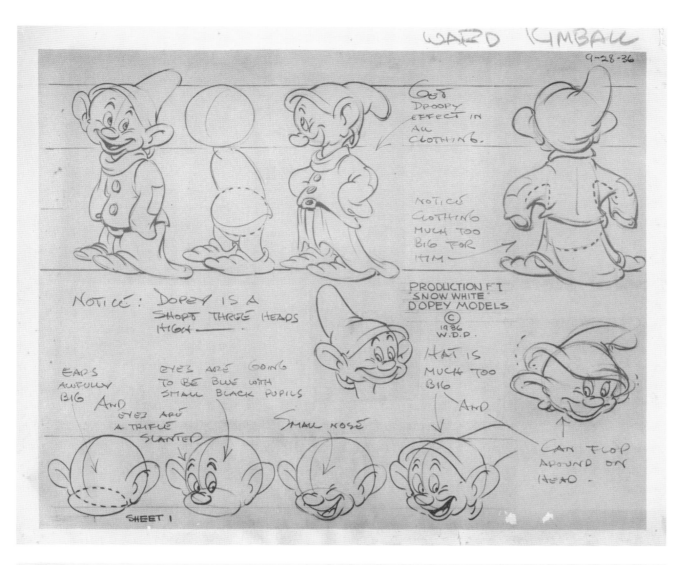

Dopey's too-large clothing helped to define his personality, suggesting a child trying to dress up like an adult.

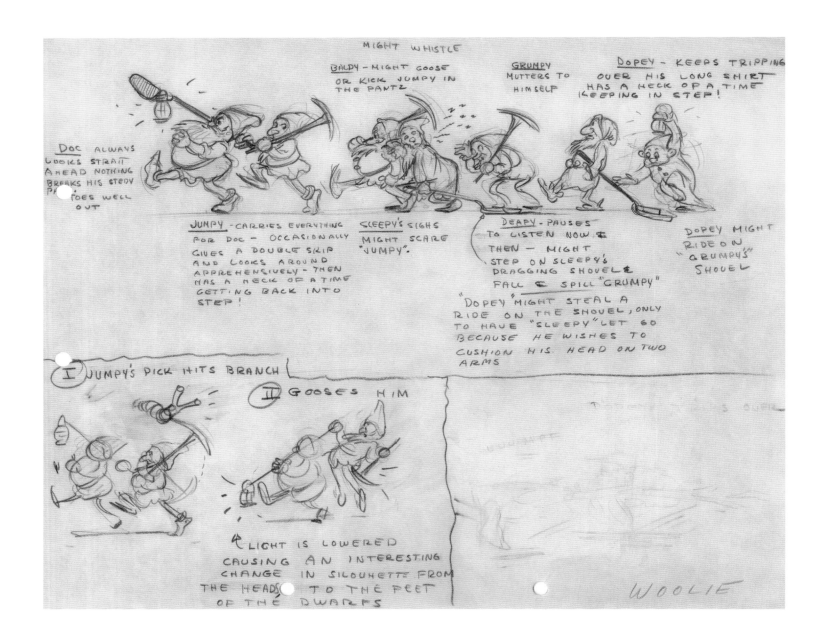

In this early sheet of gag suggestions by Woolie Reitherman, both Jumpy and Dopey have difficulty keeping in step.

[35] It's important to add that those February model sheets had been designed by Moore himself; the subsequent design changes were determined by Walt and by Moore's animation of Dopey's first scenes—that is, the process of transforming him from a static design into a moving, living character.

sequence: "He can't talk but he can yodel." As late as May 1936, references were made to Dopey's dialogue in a story conference. In the finished film, of course, Dopey does remain mute, with one exception. Sent upstairs to the bedroom by the other dwarfs, Dopey sees something stirring beneath the sheet, imagines it's a monster, and—just as in the earliest story outlines—lets out a yell of fright. Late in 1936, after all of his dialogue had been eliminated, one of the writers questioned this last remaining vestige of Dopey's vocal cords. Walt shrugged it off: "The explanation is that he just never tried to talk."

Although many hands contributed to Dopey's design, his final appearance was determined by Fred Moore. Moore has been enshrined in animation history as a specialist in "cute" characters, but to pigeonhole him in terms of "cuteness" is to trivialize his work. A strikingly direct, almost preternatural appeal was the

hallmark of Moore's animation, and his coworkers testified that that appeal seemed to flow effortlessly from his pencil onto the animation paper. He was the quintessential instinctive artist—short on analysis, long on native ability—and in the mid-1930s he was in his element at the studio, defining much of the look of classic Disney animation. In particular, during 1936, he and Bill Tytla were defining the dwarfs. Now Dopey, deprived of speech and required to project a maximum of appeal through his design and pantomime, became a special test case for Moore's talents. If Grumpy was Tytla's signature character, Dopey was Moore's. Michael Barrier has described the changes Moore wrought in the character during the course of 1936: Dopey, conceived in the February 1936 model sheets as a "bucktoothed imp," evolved into a far more appealing, baby-like character by the end of the year.[35]

Just as other dwarfs drew some of their characteristics from the actors who supplied their voices, so Dopey had a human role model: not Langdon or Marx, but a burlesque comedian named Eddie Collins, who was appearing regularly at the Follies Theater in Los Angeles. Onstage, Collins presented an empty-headed, childlike persona of his own, which suggested qualities that might be useful in animating Dopey. "Les Clark and I went down there to this burlesque theater to watch [Collins]," recalled Art Babbitt, "and I took movies of him with my Bell & Howell camera hidden under my coat. And some goon came and wanted to throw us out, and wanted to take my camera and all that, 'cause he thought we were photographing the girls." Added Babbitt, a notorious playboy: "Hell, I've never been interested in girls in my life! Who would ever think such a thing?"

Walt was impressed enough with Collins to bring him to the studio. As the artists filmed 16mm reference footage, Collins executed miscellaneous walks, dance steps, and other actions. Frank Thomas and Ollie Johnston, both of whom assisted Fred Moore during the production of Snow White, later wrote that Moore "ran the Collins film over and over on his Moviola, searching not so much for specifics as for the overall concept of a character. Then he sat down at his desk and animated a couple of scenes that fairly sparkled with fresh ideas."[36] Collins's Snow White connection later became a source of great pride for him, as well as a shot in the arm for his career.[37]

One of the most distinctive actions associated with Dopey was the hitch step. Frank Thomas, who was Fred Moore's assistant at the beginning of production, graduated to the position of full animator during 1936 and contributed some important animation of his own to Snow White. One of his first major assignments was the sequence in which Snow White sends the dwarfs outside to wash their hands before dinner. In later years, Thomas enjoyed telling the story of what happened next: noticing an unusual situation in the story drawings, he incorporated it into his animation. Dopey, marching to the door at the end of the single-file line of dwarfs, realized that he was out of step with the rest of the group and performed a little hitch step in order to synchronize his movements with theirs. According to Thomas's story, Walt saw this action in sweatbox and was so delighted with it that he decided to use it through-

out the picture. Soon a host of Dopey scenes, already animated, were recalled so their respective animators could add the hitch step. And, soon after that, those same animators made a point of dropping by Thomas's room to tell him just what they thought of him.

Actually, production papers reveal that Dopey was having trouble keeping in step with the other dwarfs months before those scenes were assigned to Thomas. The idea of a comedian being unable to keep in step with others was a time-honored tradition in American comedy long before the 1930s; most of the major film comedians, especially when placed in military settings, had shown their lack of conformity by their inability to stay in step with a troop of marching soldiers. A perfect example appeared on movie screens in 1935 in the Laurel & Hardy feature Bonnie Scotland. In this feature the pair unexpectedly found themselves serving in the British army. A running gag throughout the picture shows Stan Laurel marching out of step with other soldiers, and doing a little hitch step of his own to get back into his rhythm. In one of the film's comedy set-pieces, Laurel, marching with a company of soldiers, is constantly unable to match his steps with theirs. Soon he distracts the soldiers around him, who unwittingly fall into Laurel's rhythm instead of the correct one. The mistake spreads until, finally, the entire company is marching to Laurel's out-of-step step.

Bonnie Scotland was released in August 1935, during story development of Snow White, and soon Stan Laurel joined the list of live-action comedians who would influence Dopey.[38] By late 1936, variations on Laurel's hitch step were being suggested for Dopey at various points throughout the picture. "Dopey is waiting for the last," said Walt of the dwarfs preparing to march home from the mine. "When it is his turn he steps into it, but out of step and always trying to get in as they go off. I think you ought to do that all through the picture. He never can get into step. He does a skip when he gets in and he gets out again. When they send him out to wash it's the same thing." Others chimed in with their own suggestions, among them writer George Stallings: "Dopey is kind of pounding those steps trying to get in step. When he does get in step, he is all right, and then he trips—then right out of step again." Soon these and other ideas were so firmly established that Wilfred

[36] Coincidentally, in 1935, the studio's Roy Scott had interviewed several comedians about the possibility of filming their pantomime in 16mm as a training exercise for the artists, not directly related to Snow White. One of the comedians was Harry Langdon. Apparently nothing came of this idea.

[37] When his new visibility led him to a role in Twentieth Century-Fox's Down to Earth (title later changed to Always in Trouble), Collins proudly cited his association with Dopey in his announcements to the trade press. This role led to a contract with Fox and major roles in prestige productions, in particular the Shirley Temple remake of The Blue Bird. Collins seemed on the verge of a significant film career when he died suddenly of a heart attack at age 57 in 1940. His obituary in the Los Angeles Times credited Walt personally with bringing him to Fox's attention.

[38] Aside from the fact that Walt was an inveterate movie fan, we know he was specifically aware of Bonnie Scotland because he referred to it in connection with another scene. Discussing Dopey in the unfinished Bed-building sequence, Walt commented: "I see Dopey going around with the music with the scissors—he's kind of clever—kind of like Laurel & Hardy in Bonnie Scotland where they were cleaning up the yard." Moreover, in another conference—in April 1937, still preceding Thomas's hitch-step animation—Walt commented: "Try for effect of Dopey working hard to get in step, like Laurel business."

R.F. Outcault's pioneering comic character, the Yellow Kid, exerted an unmistakable influence on Dopey.

[39] These were the scenes of Dopey with the soap, and his subsequent hiccups, in the washing sequence.

Jackson referred to Dopey's efforts to keep in step as "this game of his."

Still, something about Thomas's animation of his scenes—in the late spring and early summer of 1937—does seem to have sparked a new interest in Dopey's hitch step. Perhaps Thomas's action was more exaggerated than earlier efforts; perhaps he found a new way to convey Dopey's personality as he concentrated on his uncooperative feet. Whatever the case, a comparison of sweatbox notes suggests that Walt, having gradually lost interest in the hitch step, became recommitted to it after seeing Thomas's scenes. Perhaps the most dramatic example is a series of Walt's notes to Bill Tytla about a scene in the washing sequence, showing Dopey trailing the rest of the dwarfs as they march toward a confrontation with Grumpy. In September 1936, Walt asked Tytla to redraw this already-animated scene so as to show Dopey out of step with the group. In February 1937 he changed his mind and, apparently to simplify the scene, asked Tytla to do the scene over with Dopey *in* step. Then, in July—following the appearance of Thomas's scenes in sweatbox—Walt returned the scene to Tytla yet again, asking him to *re*animate the scene with the addition of the hitch step! The action was similarly added or reinforced in other scenes and, of course, appears periodically throughout the finished film.

Without in any way minimizing the importance of Fred Moore's work, it should be mentioned that Dopey, like Grumpy, had a second "specialist" on the animation staff: Fred Spencer. To be sure, many hands animated Dopey in the course of production—and, conversely, Spencer was assigned some group scenes featuring *all* the dwarfs—but his animation of Dopey, in particular, was second in importance only to that of Moore himself. Dopey's pantomime description of the monster in the bedroom, Dopey sitting on the rafters after the "Silly Song," Dopey attempting to claim the pillow and left with a single feather—these and more are Spencer's work. Grim Natwick went so far as to recall: "Fred Spencer got almost all of the Dopey scenes . . . He had his little group of assistants, and most of the Dopey, I think, went through his hands." Indeed, in some cases Spencer was called on to rework Dopey scenes that had already been completed by other animators—including, in at least one instance, Moore himself.[39]

In this connection, and in light of the emphasis on Dopey as the "cute" dwarf, it's also worth noting that the Dopey we see in the finished film is more than simply a generic cuddly-sweet character. Vestiges of his earlier, more grotesque self remain: this is the dwarf who whimpers and stirs in his sleep like a dog, who is furiously clobbered by the other dwarfs (when they mistake him for the monster) and cheerfully bounces back for more, who swallows foreign objects like soap and then hiccups soap bubbles. Visually, too, for all his baby-like appeal, he bears an unmistakable resemblance to the jug-eared, idiotically grinning "Yellow Kid" of R.F. Outcault's historic comic strip. All these elements, blended in a particular way, comprise the Dopey that we see onscreen. Like the other dwarfs, he's not simply a "type" but a specific, unique individual.

Before moving on, we may note that casting of the dwarfs' voices was extremely flexible. The film's composite dialogue track is an amalgam of hundreds of bits and pieces, and in the process of assembling them, many miscellaneous voices found their way into the mix. If the sound editors found themselves in need of a grunt, gasp, or odd syllable from Doc or Happy, and the nominal voice actor was not immediately available, Jim Macdonald, Hal Rees, or another studio hand frequently filled in. Dopey's yell and hiccups became a popular studio pastime; Macdonald, Pinto Colvig, Dick Rickard, Clarence Nash, and others all dropped in at one time or another to try recording these sounds. Nash—remembered today as the voice of Donald Duck—is, in fact, all over the *Snow White* soundtrack: as one of the whistling birds, as an owl hooting at Snow White in the forest, joining in group exclamations by the dwarfs, providing the "old hag's cackle" when the Queen brews her potion. Even apart from these odds and ends, the dwarfs' *singing* voices were in a category of their own. Hollywood vocal director Freeman High provided a men's ensemble that took over for the dialogue actors when the dwarfs launched into "Dig Dig Dig" or "Heigh-Ho."

This model sheet helped the artists keep the Dwarfs in consistent proportion to Snow White and to each other.

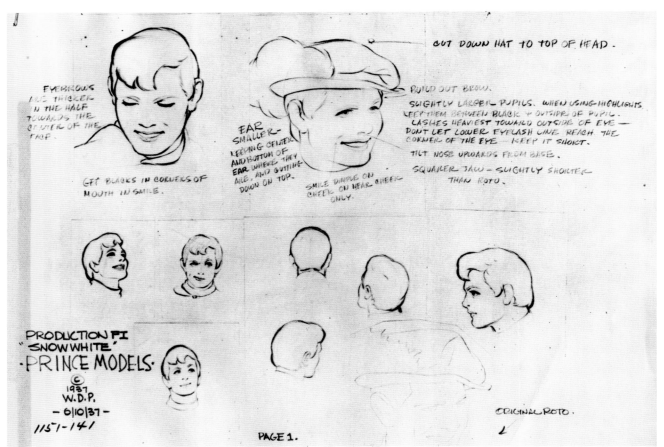

Model sheets for the Prince, the single most difficult character for the artists to animate, and details of his costume.

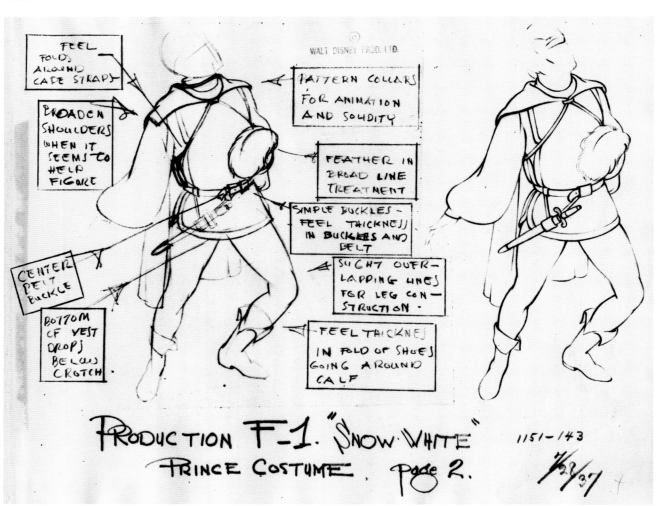

THE PRINCE

If animating Snow White was a difficult challenge for the Disney artists, animating the Prince was a nearly insurmountable one. Indeed, both Walt and the animators would come to regard the Prince as the single weakest element in the finished film. Here the problems of convincingly moving the human figure were compounded; any shortcomings in Snow White's movement could be smoothed over satisfactorily with the "cute," cuddly touches that the studio had used on other characters, but those touches were not an option with the Prince. In fact, maintaining the Prince's masculinity was apparently a touchy issue. The August 1934 "Manuscript" outline warned against making him a "romantic sap" and suggested "giving him a masculine sounding name, opportunity to be very brave and defiant under all conditions, and let him hack, fence, leap his way through the palace guards with tricks Doug Fairbanks would like to have thought of." "Get a decent pose here," said Walt during a story conference on the garden sequence, "something to give a masculine effect to him." When the pigeon delivers Snow White's kiss to him, "the Prince ought to be amused himself, so he won't be sissy-like."

As these comments suggest, there was some question as to exactly what kind of character the Prince should be. Walt considered a variety of approaches to the character. Late in 1935, when the extended musical-comedy garden sequence and the dungeon sequence were still planned as part of the picture, Walt indicated that he was thinking of assigning the Prince to Fred Moore: "I have in mind that . . . all the Prince animation would be done by Fred." This idea, and story sketches for what were then the current versions of those sequences, suggest a film very different from the *Snow White* we know today. As the story continued to develop and the Prince became less playful and demonstrative, Moore was assigned elsewhere. The elimination of the dungeon sequence, the dream version of "Some Day My Prince Will Come," and other proposed scenes had the effect of strengthening the *Snow White* story, but we can assume that some of the cuts were made partly to minimize animation of the problematic Prince.

In the end, much of the remaining Prince animation was assigned to Grim Natwick, the human-animation specialist. Decades later, Natwick looked back on his Prince animation with embarrassment: "Part of it, at least, was unfortunate . . . I was the least proud of those [scenes]." Natwick relied heavily on his assistant, Marc Davis, who would later come to specialize in human characters himself. Other isolated Prince scenes were tossed, like a hot potato, to artists from the Ham Luske unit: Clair Weeks, Hugh Fraser, and especially Jack Campbell. Unexpected assistance came from the young Milt Kahl, a junior artist who had nominally been assigned to the animals-and-birds unit. In years to come, Kahl's phenomenal drawing ability would make him one of the top Disney animators; here he demonstrated his gifts—first as a cleanup artist, then as a full animator—and rescued some of the Prince's most difficult scenes.

In short, unlike Snow White and some of the dwarfs, the Prince was not primarily brought to life by any single animator. His brief performance was assembled from the work of several different artists, all of them straining simply to simulate the mechanics of convincing movement.

To provide the Prince's voice, the studio briefly considered the well-known radio tenor Kenny Baker, who had sung in some of the Silly Symphonies. Other voices were also tested; finally the role was given to Harry Stockwell, a high baritone who had already launched a modest movie career.[40] To perform the Prince's action for live-action reference footage, the studio recruited Louis Hightower, one of Marjorie Belcher's fellow pupils at her father's dance school.

Ultimately, whether by accident or design, the Prince became one more element of the Disney *Snow White* that resurrected something of the Grimm Brothers' concept. Like the Princes in earlier stage and film versions, he appears at the beginning of the story—but here, by virtue of his tightly restricted appearances, he never becomes a fully developed character. Like the Grimms' anonymous prince, he remains simply an icon of romance.

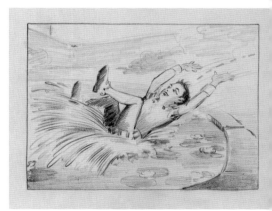

Early plans for an active, playful Prince were sharply scaled back in the finished film.

[40] In addition to appearing in some MGM musicals, Stockwell was announced for what later became Allan Jones's role in the Marx Brothers comedy *A Day at the Races*. He appeared onstage with the Marxes in the pre-filming tour for that picture, shortly before recording the voice of the Prince in *Snow White*. Today he's also remembered as the father of Guy and Dean Stockwell.

An early document compared the Queen's beauty to that of Benda masks: theatrical masks created by illustrator and designer Władysław T. Benda.

[41] Around this same time, when it was planned that the Queen would make two different attempts on Snow White's life, one of her disguises was to be that of "a fat bulging old woman peddler." Sketches of this character and of the Queen as "a fat, cartoon type" have sometimes been confused in later accounts.

[42] Some latter-day accounts have suggested that the Queen's design was based on Joan Crawford. Actually no such reference survives in the story files, and while it's true that Crawford was a well-known star by the mid-1930s, she had not yet acquired the cold, formidable quality that we may associate with her today. Contemporary reviewers found a different point of reference: one wrote that the Queen looked "something like Theda Bara fifteen years ago."

THE QUEEN

The Queen's role in the story could never be minimized; it was her vindictive jealousy of Snow White that motivated the plot. Here again the Disney *Snow White* returns to the essentials of the Grimms' tale: instead of separating the two characters of the Queen and the Witch, as Winthrop Ames and the Paramount film had done, the Disney film recombines them into one character—a beautiful queen, *disguised*, at story's end, as a witch.

As the third major human character in the story, the Queen represented yet another daunting animation challenge. "The Queen is stately, beautiful in the way of a Benda mask," said the early "Manuscript" outline. "Her face and voice are almost always expressionless. Even when angry, or torturing her victims, her voice is low, cool, serene . . . Her eyes are usually veiled by heavy, half-closed lids. Thus, when she opens them suddenly, there is dramatic value in the movement." Another early document, much quoted in latter-day accounts, described her as "a mixture of Lady Macbeth and the Big Bad Wolf—her beauty is sinister, mature, plenty of curves." Very early in story development, realizing the tremendous difficulty in animating such a character, the studio briefly considered a safer alternative. Notes from a meeting in October 1934 read: "Queen to be tried out as a fat, cartoon type; sort of vain—batty—self-satisfied, comedy type; and also as a high collar stately beautiful type. Sketches to be submitted and story constructed for either angle."[41] But the idea of the "fat, cartoon type" didn't last long. Clearly, to make credible her vanity and her quest to be the fairest one of all, the Queen must be the "high collar stately beautiful type." Rejecting the easy way out, the studio pressed on to create a coldly beautiful Queen.

This was no easy task; even before animation began, simply finalizing the design of the character was a prolonged undertaking. One concept after another was submitted, then rejected as not quite right. Some *Snow White* enthusiasts have long believed that the final design of the Queen's costume was influenced by the RKO adventure film *She* (1935). Helen Gahagan, in the title role of Hash-A-Mo-Tep, "She Who Must Be Obeyed," appears midway through *She* in a costume strikingly similar to that of the Queen in *Snow White*. Gahagan's manner, too, is cold and regal, her voice subdued except in moments of intense emotion. No references to this film seem to have survived in *Snow White* story files, but considering the many other contemporary films that influenced the production, it's certainly possible that *She*, released in July 1935, played a part. In any case, the Queen's design was not finalized until much later. As late as March 1937, in a story conference, Ham Luske criticized the current design and was told: "Joe [Grant] says it was for sinister effect; other designs are being worked out." At times the Queen was pictured as having live peacocks in the throne room, at other times a deadly pet panther. In the finished film none of these pets appeared, but her throne was given an elaborate peacock design.

The primary responsibility for animating the Queen was given to Art Babbitt—seemingly an odd assignment for an animator whose career highlights to date had been the development of Goofy and the mouse's drunk scene in *The Country Cousin*. But Babbitt had a passion for the analysis of movement and the way it reflected character, high priorities at the Disney studio during the 1930s. Although he struggled with the severe technical demands of creating the Queen's subtle, realistic movements, in the end Babbitt surmounted those difficulties and created the desired character—a Queen whose cold, hypnotic beauty was balanced by her forbidding and at times frightening nature.[42]

The Queen's alter ego, the Witch, was an entirely different matter. Although she was to be every bit as frightening as the Queen's beautiful self, it was recognized from the beginning that the rules of realistic human design and movement need not apply to the Witch. Because of her grotesque appearance, she was allowed a wide latitude of cartoon license. Her design, in the tradition of other witches in illustrated fairy tales, was made to order for cartoon animation. Norm Ferguson, another of the studio's leading animators, was assigned to bring her to life on the screen. His previous achievements included the development of Pluto and such other expressive characters as the Big Bad

Joe Grant's sketches of the Queen acknowledge her visual kinship with the Witch.

Wolf in *Three Little Pigs*. Ferguson took full advantage of the Witch's exaggerated design, animating her dark deeds with zest.[43]

The voices of both the Queen and the Witch were provided by the celebrated character actress Lucille La Verne. Of the several notable performers whose talents were woven into the fabric of *Snow White,* none had a career more distinguished than La Verne's. Her theatrical longevity rivaled Otis Harlan's; she had appeared on Broadway as early as 1888 in a bit part in *La Tosca* and had continued an active stage career for nearly five decades. One of her successes had been the 1923 mountaineer play *Sun-Up;* La Verne had appeared in it on the New York, London, and Los Angeles stages, then mounted her own vaudeville version and continued to play it as late as 1928. This was followed by a more radical venture: a London revival of Shakespeare's *The Merchant of Venice* in which La Verne played Shylock. In between all these stage roles, she found time to appear in dozens of silent and sound films, including MGM's 1925 adaptation of *Sun-Up.* She also appeared in several of D.W. Griffith's films; today she is perhaps best remembered as the hag, La Frochard, in Griffith's *Orphans of the Storm* (1921).

La Verne was a perfect type to provide the Witch's voice, but even with her distinguished record she was not an automatic shoo-in for the role of the Queen. As late as May 1937, after she and other actresses had recorded some tests, it was still undecided whether she would perform both roles. "It was the age of the voice," said Dave Hand at one meeting. "Some contended her voice was a little old for the Queen." At this time La Verne was 68 years of age. "The main point of argument," Hand added, "is really that La Verne knows how to deliver lines. We are willing to sacrifice a little to get that correct delivery, that punch we need." In the end this consideration carried the day; La Verne did perform both voices in *Snow White.* It would prove to be the last professional engagement of her career.

Bill Cottrell, who directed the various Queen and Witch sequences in the picture, was much in awe of La Verne. "She was just marvelous to work with," he recalled. "We'd been trying, oh, a dozen or two actresses, mostly from radio, to do the voice of the Queen and the Witch. And most of them came in, and they saw the drawings of the Queen and the Witch, so they all did that typical Witch that they were all kind of using in the old radio shows. You know, it was a very broad, cackling thing. Lucille La Verne was a stage actress, and she came in and glanced at the storyboard, took the script

[43] But see Frank Thomas's and Ollie Johnston's assessment in their book *Disney Animation.* While acknowledging the Witch's effectiveness onscreen, they attribute her design to Ferguson and claim: "Fergy's handling of her face was less of a typical formula than most Disney designs, with shapes that did not relate as well as they should for animation because of the Witch's illustrative quality. The mouth to cheek to eye and brow relationship, which is so important in animating expression changes, suffered from his concept in design."

PRODUCTION FI
"SNOW WHITE"
WITCH MODELS
© 1931
W.D.P.
FEB. 25 1937

SHEET 3
117-80

Joe Grant's model sheet captures both the Witch's exaggerated outlandishness and her very real menace.

Opposite: Comic versions of the Witch, which might have made the animators' job easier, were considered but quickly rejected in favor of a more frightening version.

and read it, and you could have recorded and used the dialogue as she read it, she was so great. I thought she was marvelous." He laughed at the memory. "She was a lot of fun to work with. She was a little bit like the Queen herself; she'd been a leading lady and now she was dealing with young people, and didn't tolerate a lot of monkey business! But you didn't have to fool around with her; she knew what to do. She was great." Cottrell was not alone in his appreciation of La Verne's talent; Walt, too, professed his admiration. When one of the writers suggested a change in the Witch's dialogue, Walt responded: "All the dialogue sounded bad to me until she read it."

Besides recording both voices, La Verne also performed in some live-action reference footage for the Witch. (For additional scenes the studio tried using another of Ernest Belcher's dance students, Paul Godkin,

but then replaced him with character actor Don Brodie, outfitted with a cloak and a large false nose.)

In the finished film, of course, both of La Verne's voices are not only adequate but richly evocative. (Cottrell recalled that she made the transition from Queen to Witch simply by taking out her teeth!) Her performance in both roles provides a benefit that may not have been foreseen. The Queen's two personae—her controlled, repressed movement as Queen on one hand, and the Witch's unrestrained, melodramatic performance on the other—may seem to be incompatible; but their voices, provided by the same actress, help to unify them. Lucille La Verne, besides enriching *Snow White* with the wealth of her theatrical experience, also reminds us that Queen and Witch are two facets of the same character.

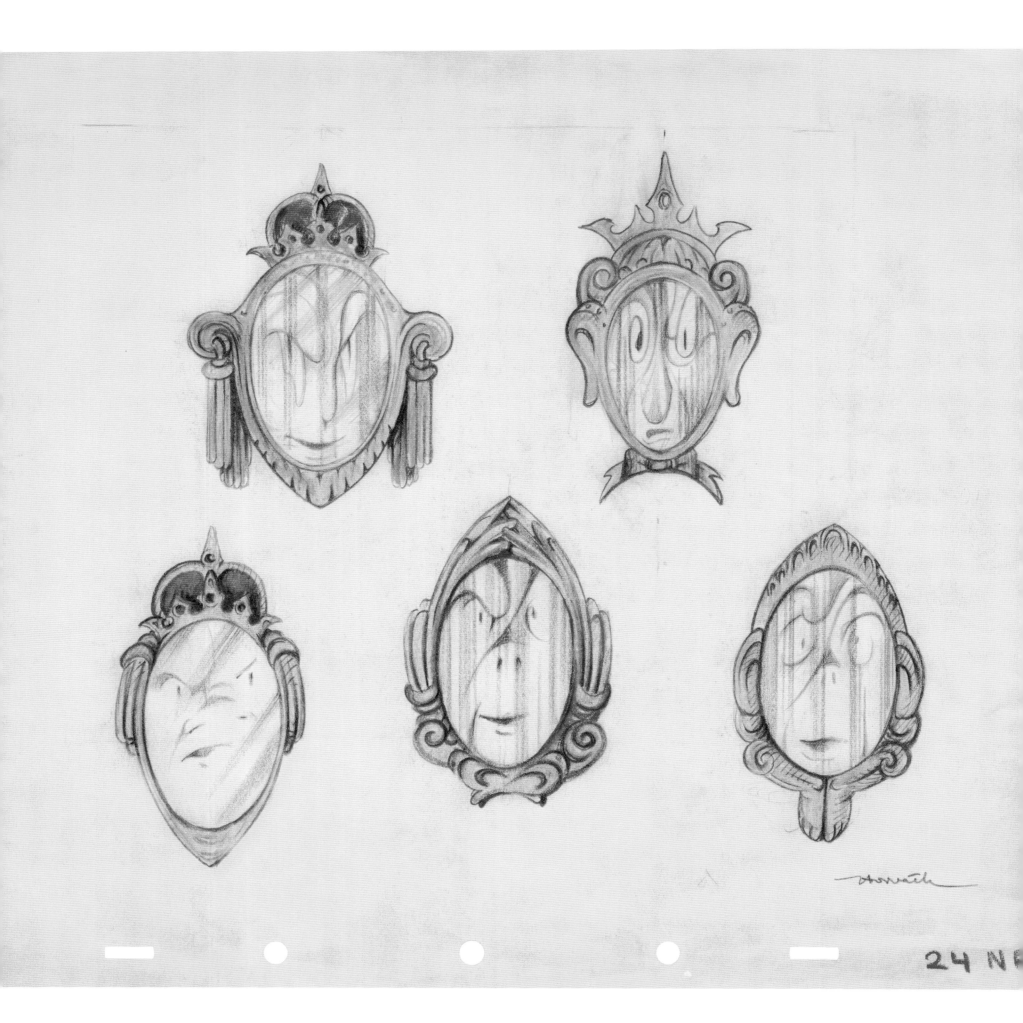

24 NE

THE MIRROR

In the Grimms' "Snow White," when the Queen wanted to learn who was currently the fairest one of all, she consulted a magic wall mirror. Early stage and film versions of the story consistently gave the Queen a hand mirror instead, usually hanging on a cord from her belt. In the Disney film the mirror returns to the wall, and the slave in the mirror not only answers the Queen's questions but becomes a full-fledged character. This was the first adaptation to give the mirror such a distinctive identity, and the Disney story team tried several approaches to the character.

The 1934 "Manuscript" outline proposes an outrageous episode involving the mirror: the Queen learns that Snow White has survived and angrily smashes the mirror—whereupon the mirror, like Frankenstein's monster, "stalks after her about the room, corners the frightened Queen and smashes itself upon her. The Queen, back turned, would not see the mirror step from the wall and move slowly, ominously toward her. But the audience would be breathless with suspense." Walt's own "Skeleton Continuity" of December 1934 dispenses with the walking mirror, but does depict the Queen—like the Queens in the various stage adaptations—smashing the mirror in her rage. The mirror itself reminds her of the bad luck that follows on breaking a mirror and "predicts that within a week the two of them will meet in hell." It laughs at her, she is further enraged and smashes it into many pieces, and "The mirror's laughs multiply and drive the Queen into a frenzy."

As the story continued to evolve, the mirror became more and more restrained. Walt gradually abandoned the idea of letting the Queen smash the mirror (although some members of the staff, in particular Ham Luske and Bill Cottrell, held out for such a scene). Even then, the slave in the mirror did remain a relatively volatile character for some time. Various outlines depicted him arguing with the Queen or laughing derisively at her when she learned that the Huntsman had brought her the heart of a pig. As envisioned at this time, the slave in the mirror would have related to the Queen more or less as Witch Hex had done in the Ames play: grudgingly cooperating with her, but disdainful of her ways and unafraid of her power. "I like the idea of intensifying the light on him when he gets angry," said Walt at one conference.

By the spring of 1937, even this measure of emotion in the mirror's character had been phased out, and he was evolving into the otherworldly, impassive, oracular presence we see in the finished film. Now Walt described the character in different terms: "He is a motionless type, almost a frozen face—a voice from out of space." Responding to lines of dialogue that had been suggested for the mirror, Walt said: "Make him more poetic, not have him come out with a plain statement. The Mirror should be more like an oracle . . . When the Mirror becomes ordinary in its conversation, it throws me all out."

A young Woolie Reitherman was given the unenviable job of animating this frozen face. Casting of the mirror's dark, sepulchral voice took place late in production, and various actors were considered: John Carradine, Irving Pichel, and even John Barrymore. In the end, the dialogue was recorded by Moroni Olsen, a former stage actor with a sonorous voice, who had made his movie debut in 1935 as Porthos in the RKO production of *The Three Musketeers*. "Are you going to try to get a trick way of recording his voice?" asked Larry Morey at one meeting. "Yes, just like he looks," Walt answered, "suspended in nothing." Disney technicians tried various tricks to achieve this vocal effect. One, described in the sound department's records, was to have Olsen speak into a long, hollow tube lying on a marble slab. A microphone, placed on the slab at the far end of the tube, recorded his voice. After the film's release, an article in *Photoplay* claimed that this was the method used in the film. But another, illustrated article in *Popular Science* reported an alternate method: Olsen inserted his head into a "hood" constructed from a square, box-like frame with drumheads stretched taut over five of the six sides, and spoke from inside it. Thanks to one or perhaps both of these devices, Olsen's disembodied voice did suggest an otherworldly being "suspended in nothing."

The final concept of the slave in the mirror: remote, impassive, inscrutable.

Opposite: Ferdinand Horvath's sketches of some alternate ideas for the mirror's personality.

An early exploratory character sketch for the Huntsman.

THE HUNTSMAN

Another of the Queen's minions, the Huntsman, is a relatively nondescript character in the Grimms' version of "Snow White." Assigned by the Queen to take Snow White to the woods and kill her, he impassively carries out his duties up to the point of the actual killing, then takes pity on the little princess and lets her run away. After killing a wild boar to fake the evidence of Snow White's death, he disappears from the tale. As we've seen, the various stage and film versions had built an increasingly complex and detailed character on this simple framework. By the time of the 1916 Paramount film, Berthold the huntsman had become a major character in the story, he and his children occupying an extended subplot that gave them more screen time than the Prince. (Indeed, in this version, it's Berthold and the Prince together who discover Snow White's body at the end of the story and then confront the Queen over her misdeeds.)

The Disney story team considered this approach, along with others, in creating their version of the Huntsman. At one point in 1936, an intriguing idea was suggested: the Huntsman might be shown as a sadistic killer who actually took pleasure in the idea of dispatching Snow White. "We won't let the Huntsman weaken anytime before the time he drops the knife," Walt suggested at one conference. "He doesn't say a word when the Queen talks to him. Get shots of Huntsman with a menacing face. When the Queen says 'Kill her,' the Huntsman's face brightens up as though he wants to do it." For a time there was also a halfhearted attempt to give the Huntsman a name, and at some point the name "Humbert" was suggested. (Apparently "Berthold," the name used in the previous stage and film versions, was never considered.) Walt continued to mention the possibility of "Humbert" from time to time—but, as Larry Morey pointed out, "No one seems to like that name," and it never gained wide acceptance.

In the end all these ideas were rejected, and the Huntsman reverted to a minor role. In the finished film he's anonymous, and he does mount a feeble but sympathetic plea on Snow White's behalf until the Queen angrily silences him. Technically, the Huntsman is yet a fourth "human" character like Snow White, the Prince, and the Queen, but—perhaps because of his stocky build and his coarse features—he seems to have posed less of an animation challenge than the others. He was animated by Errol Gray, one of the assistants in the Ham Luske unit.

His voice, like some of the others, was difficult to cast; character actors Reginald Barlow and Cy Kendall both recorded dialogue for the character, but both were found unsatisfactory. Finally, Paul Stuart Buchanan, hired in 1936 as studio casting director and dialogue coach, played the role of the Huntsman himself.[44]

[44] For the scene of the Huntsman calling after Snow White as she runs into the forest, Buchanan's dialogue was recorded outdoors between the wings of the inkers' building, his voice echoing off the walls.

This color callout displays the toy-like appearance of the *Snow White* deer, very different from the more realistic animals later created for *Bambi*.

ANIMALS

As Karen Merritt has pointed out, one of the major departures of the Disney *Snow White* was its generous use of a large crowd of animals and birds in the forest sequences. Some animals and birds had been mentioned in the Grimms' story; the Ames play had introduced the Brown Bird (played by a stuffed bird suspended on a wire); the 1916 Paramount film had retained the bird and added a few other creatures—but because of the inherent problems of getting animals to take direction, and the fact that the principal characters in the story were human anyway, little had been made of the animals in most versions.

The medium of animation, on the other hand, was tailor-made for a large animal population. "Animals will not talk," read an early treatment. "They are intelligent, clever, but will do nothing that is not plausible for animals and birds to do." Plausible, that is, with a certain level of cartoon license; these animals are not from the world of Mickey Mouse, but they are an integral part of Snow White's animated world and, in this film, become her devoted companions. In this film, in fact, they play an important role in the story. "We have taken the characters [from the Grimms' story] and haven't added any," Walt commented in 1936. "The only thing we have built in the story are the animals who are friends of Snow White's. This wasn't in the original fairy tale."

Animation of the animals and birds in *Snow White*, like that of the human characters, was assigned to specific artists who specialized in these characters. The principal "animal men" were Jim Algar (who would, coincidentally, write and direct many of Disney's later True-Life Adventure nature films), Bernard Garbutt, Milt Kahl, Eric Larson, and Louie Schmitt. These artists, with a corps of assistants, comprised a subunit within Ham Luske's larger unit, simply because the animals and birds interacted so closely with Snow White herself. Luske supervised their work and occasionally worked with them on their scenes, although most of his attention was reserved for the more pressing technical problems of animating the human characters.

In later years one of the "animal men," Eric Larson, would look back on the *Snow White* animals, in particular the deer, with disdain. "You could hardly call them deer," he told Michael Barrier. "They were sacks of wheat." He compared them unfavorably with the anatomically realistic deer that were later animated for *Bambi:* "When we got to *Bambi*, the idea was to be honest with them." But artists are notoriously poor judges of their own work, and it's worth pointing out that the visual style of *Snow White* was utterly unlike the style later created for *Bambi*. The more realistic deer of *Bambi* would have been as startlingly out of place in the storybook world of *Snow White* as the toy-like deer of *Snow White* would have been in *Bambi*. When Bernard Garbutt—one of the artists who would later animate the realistic deer in *Bambi*—submitted some of his first *Snow White* scenes for review, Walt admonished him: "Don't have the deer too real, but get them graceful and cute."

5

PRODUCTION

Production of *Snow White* presented a multitude of challenges that had never occurred before in animation. The various departments of the studio were obliged to find resourceful solutions. When the first color scenes of Snow White reached the screen, one of those challenges was immediately evident: the girl appeared to have a pale complexion. The ink and paint department was pressed for an innovation: how could they add a subtle, convincing touch of color to her cheeks?

For years afterward, a popular legend held that the painters, practiced in the art of applying their own makeup, had solved the problem by literally adorning each Snow White cel with a touch of rouge. In reality, of course, a messy substance like rouge, applied to those thousands of cels, would have been wildly impractical. The airbrush, already in use for other color effects in Disney films, likewise proved too clumsy for this purpose. In the end, the actual answer to the problem was a transparent red dye. Snow White's cels were inked and painted in the usual way—ink lines on the front surface, colors on the back—after which the red dye was carefully applied to the front surface. As it was absorbed into the celluloid, the red tint blended with Snow White's existing flesh tone to produce a lovely, natural glow.[45]

The effects artists seized on this technique, documenting it in a studio manual: "Certain transparent tones may be added over light opaque colors on the painted cel to give blended effects." The same treatment was applied to the Queen, enhancing *her* cold beauty with a healthy glow, and soon led to more extensive experiments in shading and modeling color. "Blended" color effects were added to the ink and paint department's arsenal of procedures, along with colored ink lines, airbrush, dry brush, and other specialized techniques. Similar innovations were being hatched in other areas of the studio, including, as we'll see, the camera department.

As the studio's activities expanded, it became clear that the staff would have to expand with them. In order to maintain the studio's quota of Mickey Mouse and Silly Symphony shorts *and* keep up with Walt's increasingly ambitious plans for *Snow White*, many more artists would be needed—story sketch artists, concept artists, layout artists, background painters, and above all animators. Beginning in 1935 and continuing into 1937, the studio launched a concentrated campaign to attract new artists, placing ads in major newspapers and magazines. Responses poured in by the thousands; not only had the Disney name become a magnet for artistic ambition, but artists in those impoverished Depression years were hard-pressed to find any employment at all.

Not just any artists would do, of course; the studio's increasingly high artistic standard was an obstacle that weeded out the majority of applicants. For some years Walt had maintained a training program for his artists, under the supervision of Don Graham, a former instructor at the Chouinard School of Art. Now Graham's duties were enlarged. Along with George Drake, the overseer of the inbetween department, Graham was charged with administering a series of tests to the new

Thanks to "blended" color effects, Snow White's cheeks had a subtle, convincing glow. Frame from an original 1937 release print.

[45] In an interview with Didier Ghez, decades later, ink and paint veteran Ruthie Tompson identified one particular artist who specialized in adding the blush to the girl's cheeks: an inker named Helen Ogger.

This ad, appearing in *The New York Times* in April 1936, invited prospective artists to apply to the training school.

[46] The 1934 addition was the new building, intended to accommodate feature production, that Art Babbitt had mentioned in his letter to Bill Tytla the previous November. Soon after the release of *Snow White,* when the Disney studio moved to its new quarters in Burbank, the 1934 and 1937 animation wings were physically moved from the Hyperion lot to the new property and joined into a single edifice, which then became the Shorts building.

[47] There were other hints of the growing relationship, including at least one that directly targeted *Snow White.* In the RKO feature *In Person,* produced in the summer of 1935 and released in November of that year, Ginger Rogers and George Brent interrupt a scene to engage in a short, inane snatch of dialogue about "dwarfs" and "Snow White." The passage is so awkwardly written that it seems an afterthought, gratuitously wedged into the script.

applicants, selecting the most promising candidates, and conducting an "art school" that would initiate them into the highly specialized skills of animation. "Some time ago," said *Daily Variety,* "Disney advertised for art students, got 1,700 replies. Of this number, 50 showed promise, but only one made good as animator." This was not much of an exaggeration. Few of the new recruits were put directly into the front lines on *Snow White,* of course, but the process did net some valuable new artists for the studio—among them John Lounsbery, who would assist Norm Ferguson on *Snow White* and who would himself become one of the top Disney animators within a few years.

Clair Weeks, one of the students from Chouinard, recalled the audition process: "We were all put into quick-sketch drawing classes, eight-hour days drawing from the model, from the live model. Two-minute poses, three-minute poses and all that kind of thing, and this went on for two weeks. On our time; we weren't paid for it, we weren't compensated for this at all. And I had to take leave from my drawing classes at Chouinard. And then these drawings were all collected at the end of the day. And at the end of the first week there was a cut and they decided, 'Well, we can't use you, you don't seem to have what we're looking for,' and so forth. So if you survived the first week, then you were invited to come back for the second week, and the second week was the final week. And then you were notified on Friday whether you had made it or not. So I survived the first week and I survived the second week, and on Friday I was told I had made it." Weeks's superior drawing ability won him a place in the Ham Luske unit, animating Snow White and the Prince.

As these new artists swelled the Disney ranks, office space at the Hyperion studio became increasingly cramped. New structures appeared on the lot; an apartment house and other buildings on adjacent lots were taken over. As early as the spring of 1934, as plans for the feature began to take shape, construction started on a new addition to the animation building. This new wing, completed in October 1934, was itself soon filled to overflowing, and yet another wing was added, this one completed in March 1937 and commonly known as "the feature building." [46]

In the spring of 1936, the studio intensified its efforts to find new talent on the East Coast. Ads were placed in major Eastern newspapers, and late in March, Graham, Drake, and business manager Carter Ludlow arrived in New York to screen applicants and conduct a miniature version of the studio "art school." After three months, they returned to the studio with several more new finds: Paul Busch, another addition to Luske's stable of Snow White animators; Les Novros, who moved into the Grim Natwick unit; John Elliotte and Nick de Tolly, who would assist two of the dwarf animators; and a few others.

Space for the New York class sessions was provided in the RKO building in Rockefeller Center. In 1936 the Disney cartoons were still distributed by United Artists, but in March of that year Walt and Roy signed a new distribution contract with RKO Radio Pictures, to become effective in 1937. This marriage was preceded by a long courtship: since 1932 the Disney soundtracks had been recorded with the RCA sound system (RCA being one of the parent companies of RKO), and since the spring of 1933 all of Disney's Technicolor cartoons had enjoyed New York openings at Radio City Music Hall, RKO's flagship theater and probably the most prestigious motion picture theater in the world. In 1935, after Walt had generally abandoned the use of copyrighted music in his cartoons, virtually the entire score of the Silly Symphony *Cock o' the Walk* was built around a single composition: Vincent Youmans's "The Carioca," from the RKO feature *Flying Down to Rio.*

None of these connections was especially remarkable in itself, but collectively they suggested the growing bond between Disney and RKO.[47] Coincidentally or not, the Disneys were simultaneously building a bond with Hal Horne, who had been a publicity director for United Artists in the early 1930s. Both Walt and Roy liked the energetic, resourceful Horne, and Walt consulted with him about word-of-mouth publicity for *Snow White* long before the feature was finished. "We used to meet at lunch," Walt told Pete Martin, "and he'd say, 'Well, here's your policy: keep 'em wondering, just so they keep talking.'" As Horne's relationship with the Disney studio continued to develop, he became the publisher of *Mickey Mouse Magazine* and resigned from United Artists in 1935. When this move led him into

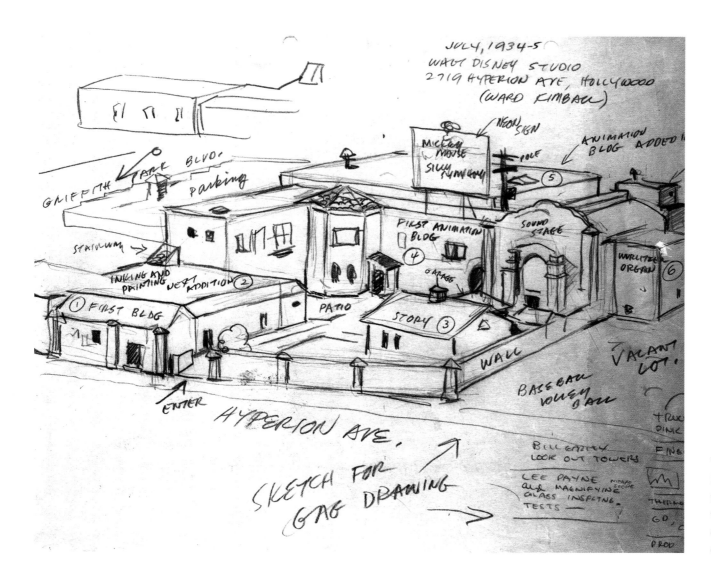

Within the sketch (handwritten labels):

JULY, 1934–5
WALT DISNEY STUDIO
2719 HYPERION AVE, HOLLYWOOD
(WARD KIMBALL)

NEON SIGN
ANIMATION BLDG ADDED
MICKEY MOUSE SILLY SYMPHONY
POLE
5
GRIFFITH PARK BLVD.
parking
FIRST ANIMATION BLDG
SOUND STAGE
WURLITZER ORGAN
6
STAIRWAY →
4
INKING AND PAINTING
NEXT ADDITION
2
GARAGE
1 FIRST BLDG
PATIO
STORY
3
WALL
VACANT LOT.
ENTER
HYPERION AVE.
BASEBALL VOLLEY BALL
SKETCH FOR GAG DRAWING

BILL GARITY LOOK OUT TOWERS
LEE PAYNE AND MAGNIFYING GLASS INSPECTING TESTS

Ward Kimball's sketch of the Hyperion lot, as he remembered it in 1934–35, reflects the constant expansion that took place during those years.

financial difficulty, Walt and Roy endeavored to help him in any way they could. In the summer of 1936, Walt purchased Horne's "gag file," a legendary collection of thousands of jokes and written gags (and the likely source of the excruciating puns that regularly appeared in *Mickey Mouse Magazine*). At the same time Dorothy Ann Blank, formerly of Horne's staff, was hired by the Disney studio and became a member of the story department. As we'll see, she made a substantial contribution to *Snow White* and went on to work on other Disney features. In the meantime, in August 1936, Horne made yet another career move of his own—to become an associate producer at RKO.

By spring 1936, then, when the Disney training program settled into RKO's New York building, the studio had already left United Artists to begin a long-term relationship with RKO. *Snow White* had been an important bargaining chip in these negotiations.

MUSIC

As the visual aspect of *Snow White* was taking shape, the musical side of the picture was also under construction. Music had played an important role in Disney cartoons since *Steamboat Willie*, and now, as the studio embarked on its most ambitious undertaking yet, it was clear that the music must be something out of the ordinary.

The single most important individual behind the music of *Snow White* was composer Frank Churchill, who had come to the Disney studio in 1930 after a varied career playing piano in honky-tonks and dance bands, on movie sets, and on the radio. Churchill's talent was the musical equivalent of Fred Moore's drawing ability: he was self-taught, instinctive, endlessly prolific, and had a knack for drawing catchy melodies out of thin air, seemingly without effort. "To have Frank play anything at all on the piano, in person, was a delightful thing," said Wilfred Jackson to historian Ross Care. "He seemed to have an endless variety of numbers, both classical and popular, in his repertoire, and when he really got wound up and going good,

Opposite: The song cover for Frank Churchill's early triumph, "Who's Afraid of the Big Bad Wolf?"

[48] In 1941, testifying in an (unsuccessful) plagiarism suit against the studio, Churchill would recall that he composed the melody "on or about" November 1934 and that the copyright on the song as an unpublished work was obtained 25 January 1935.

[49] Churchill may even have composed "With a Smile and a Song" independently of his work on *Snow White.* The earliest known pencil sketch is dated June 1935—a date that corresponds to the lull in *Snow White* story development, and to Walt's absence from the studio during his European trip. Special thanks to Leslie Smith of the studio's music department for this information.

[50] Churchill's composition of Dopey's theme seems to date to mid-1936. Walt, at a story meeting on the washing sequence, commented: "Frank had an idea to get goofy music for Dopey, but it should be tied in with the song."

seemed able to come up with an equally endless number of his own tunes . . . Frank could give a director so many satisfactory tunes to choose from, and could make each one of them sound so good as he romped through it on the piano, that it was often quite difficult to decide which one *not* to use with the action." Churchill had scored a sensational success by writing the song "Who's Afraid of the Big Bad Wolf?" for *Three Little Pigs* in 1933. When *Pigs* became an international hit, widely celebrated as a buoyant response to the Depression, "Who's Afraid?" had enjoyed a separate success of its own. The Disney studio's first hit song, it had single-handedly introduced the studio into the world of popular music.

From the beginning of work on *Snow White,* Churchill was designated to write the songs. The "Manuscript" outline of 1934, for all its unusable ideas, had suggested several possible song titles, and one of them was "Some Day My Prince Will Come." This title was immediately seized on by Walt Disney; it appears twice in the outline, and in Walt's copy of the document, preserved today in the Walt Disney Archives, the title is circled by hand both times. By December 1934, Churchill had obliged by composing a lovely melody that would go on to become perhaps the film's most popular song.[48] This was a significant development for the studio; earlier Churchill songs such as "Who's Afraid?" or "You're Nothin' But a Nothin'" (from *The Flying Mouse*), as popular as they might be, were unquestionably "novelty" numbers. "Some Day My Prince Will Come," by contrast, was a true romantic ballad that would become a standard part of the American musical repertoire.

The finished film includes this and eight other songs, all composed by Churchill with lyrics by Larry Morey. The songs for *Snow White* are a paradox: on one level they achieve the timeless quality that Walt desired for his story; on another, deeper level they ground the film in the 1930s—the golden age of American popular music. They embrace a variety of moods: further romantic songs for Snow White and the Prince, novelty numbers for the dwarfs. Walt had definite ideas about how to present these songs in the context of the film. "Really, we should set a new pattern," he said at one

conference, ". . . a new way to use music; weave it into the story so somebody doesn't just bust into song." And the *Snow White* songs *are* woven into the story, integrated with action and dialogue so that they seem to flow from the narrative, never tacked on as isolated production numbers. Even so, after release of the film several of them—not only "Some Day My Prince Will Come," but up-tempo numbers like "Heigh Ho" and "Whistle While You Work"—were taken out of context and became hit songs in their own right. "With a Smile and a Song," sung by Snow White to cheer herself up in the woods, unmistakably suggests (and was probably used as) one of the morale-boosting songs, like "On the Sunny Side of the Street," that had appeared throughout the decade to lift the spirits of a Depression-weary public.[49]

Along with the vocal numbers, Churchill was responsible for a large part of the film's incidental score. The art of musical scoring for sound films was being defined during the 1930s, largely by the work of composer Max Steiner. Steiner's groundbreaking scores for films as diverse as *King Kong, The Little Minister,* and *The Informer* had immeasurably heightened the effect of those films and had established a standard for the rest of the industry. Disney cartoon scoring, in the hands of Churchill and others, had likewise developed along its own lines. Now, however, with production of a feature-length film, the studio moved into that more wide-ranging, sophisticated musical realm that Steiner had pioneered. Churchill, with his easy musical facility, was equal to the task. In general he leaned away from Steiner's extensive use of *leitmotifs*—individual themes for each character, underscoring that character's scenes in the film—preferring, instead, to compose new cues for each mood or development in the story. For example, when Grumpy expresses his disgust with the other dwarfs for obediently washing their hands, Churchill doesn't give us a generic theme for Grumpy, but instead supplies two individual cues, "Defiance" and "Sissy Stuff." Two characters, the Queen and Dopey, did get their own instrumental themes, the former tense and foreboding, the latter light and rollicking.[50] Elsewhere the score sparkles with Churchill's endless supply of delightful, engaging melodies.

Privately, however, there was a dark side to

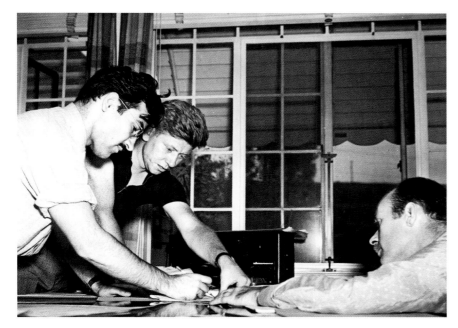

Churchill's sunny disposition. Happy-go-lucky on the surface, he was, like many artists, subject to morose turns of mind and a nervous condition, not helped by his heavy drinking. Early in 1937 he suffered a collapse and was absent from the studio for several weeks; even after returning, he continued to undergo a nervous strain and ultimately left the studio in mid-August, the *Snow White* score still unfinished. (He would return the following year, on a limited basis, and would contribute his touch to some of the studio's later films, before ending his own life in 1942.)

The task of completing the score fell to two other Disney composers: Paul J. Smith and, in particular, Leigh Harline. A prodigious musical talent in his own right, Harline was the temperamental opposite of Churchill: studious, serious, and with an extensive background of musical training. "I now have to write additional thematic material to complete the picture and, of course, must try to maintain the general atmosphere of what already has been composed," he told an interviewer. "So, fitting my ideas into those of the previous composer and escaping any hint of 'patchwork' is not easy." Some of his compositions *were* patchwork; for example, in the garden sequence, Harline contributes the short musical bridge between Churchill's songs "I'm Wishing" and "One Song." Conversely, in the long passage depicting the Witch's arrival at the dwarfs' cottage, her pressure on Snow White to eat the apple, and the dwarfs' futile race back to the cottage to save

their princess, *all* the music (except the interpolated strains of "Heigh-Ho") is Harline's work. Smith's contributions include a "Turtle Theme" for the slowest-moving of Snow White's animal friends, and the lovely "Prayer at Evening" as the inhabitants of the cottage settle down to sleep.

The first tentative recording of a section of the score took place late in August 1937, shortly after Churchill's departure. Harline used a 28-piece orchestra to record the music for two sequences: Snow White sending the dwarfs outside to wash their hands, followed by the washing sequence itself. On hearing this first attempt—as, so many times before, on seeing an artist's first pencil animation—Walt was dissatisfied with the result. Clearly, with the music under the same scrutiny as the story and the visuals, gathering a full orchestra for each new session was going to be prohibitively expensive. For subsequent sessions Harline recorded passages of music with small ensembles, or sometimes with an organ played by a single performer. Once the music was approved in this form, a full orchestra (36 to 40 pieces, Harline stated in the interview) was assembled for the final recording. Max Terr, vocal music director at Paramount Pictures, was engaged to conduct the chorus for the film's main title and final scenes.

CAMERA

Like all the studio's shorts at the time, *Snow White* was photographed in three-color Technicolor, based on

Technicolor's "three-strip" process. As the name suggests, the Technicolor camera housed three separate strips of film that moved through the camera simultaneously, filming three separate negatives that recorded the scene in three primary color values: yellow, cyan, and magenta. When these three separate negatives were combined in registration to make a single print, they produced a warm, brilliant range of colors that no other process, before or since, has been able to duplicate. The downside was the difficulty of using the Technicolor camera itself, a huge, bulky, cumbersome piece of equipment. The Disney studio had been producing cartoons in Technicolor since 1932, and for the first five years had used a standard three-strip camera, modified for stop-motion photography.

Shortly before starting color photography of *Snow White,* however, studio technicians had devised a *successive-exposure* camera that photographed all three records on a single strip of film, shooting successive frames through a color wheel. "First frame was shot through a blue filter," explained camera operator Bob Broughton, "second frame was shot through a red filter, and the third frame was shot through a green filter. And the opposites of that are yellow, cyan and magenta." The new, smaller camera greatly simplified the camera department's job. "It was a small camera, whereas the three-strip camera was a massive thing. Plus the thread-up of three strips of film, you know. The camera that we used . . . was just the old original Bell and Howell black-and-white camera, but with this added three-to-one drive so you'd shoot one frame, and the camera would automatically turn over three." The resulting negative was "skip-printed" to produce Technicolor prints in the usual way.

Today, probably the best known photographic aspect of *Snow White* is the invention of the multiplane camera crane, a towering structure with the camera perched at the top, shooting down through widely separated planes of animation art. While a normal camera table used a platen that held animation cels and background paintings pressed tightly together, the multiplane was built to position the cels and the individual foreground, middle ground, and background elements—all painted on separate sheets of glass—at wide distances from each other. First tested on the 1937 Silly Symphony *The Old Mill,* the multiplane allowed the Disney cameras to create the illusion of moving through a three-dimensional world.

In the opening scenes of *Snow White,* for example, the camera pulls through the edge of a forest to reveal a castle in the distance. As the foreground trees move past the camera, just as they would in a live-action dolly shot—the castle remaining at photographic infinity in the distance—it's clear that we're not simply looking at a flat painting. The cost of this magical illusion was a vastly more complicated and expensive photographic process, with individual technicians assigned to adjust the changes on each component level, as well as a separate operator for the camera at the top of the crane. (This, in fact, was one of the advantages of the new, smaller successive-exposure camera. The multiplane scenes in *The Old Mill* had been photographed with a standard three-strip camera, requiring a special hoist to lift that massive instrument into place at the top of the crane!)

The multiplane was still a relatively new device at the time of *Snow White,* and the camera department was still experimenting and learning its properties during production. The primary use of the multiplane was for forward or backward camera moves or "trucks"; lateral pans were limited by the six-foot length of the glass planes. Layout artists who wanted to create a pan shot on the multiplane were warned to limit their lateral movement to six feet, or else use two glasses and mask the seam with a tree or some other foreground object. At one meeting Dave Hand announced another discovery: "I would like to bring up something Tom [Codrick] has found on moving a multiplane: it is best to keep round objects rather than square ones—round tables, etc. The minute you put a square table in and start moving it on a multiplane you lose perspective. On round objects you are not conscious of things turning."

The photography of *Snow White* was complicated in other ways. Since 1935 the Disney studio had made use of *double-exposed shadows,* the most satisfactory way of rendering shadows in an animated cartoon. Earlier methods of depicting shadows in the studio's films had fallen short in various ways: solid black shadows had been blatant and distracting; efforts at a translucent

"shadow paint" had tended to streak. DX shadows, as they were called, were a perfect solution: the character's shadow would be painted in solid black on a separate cel, and the entire composite scene would be photographed at partial exposure. Then the film would be wound back in the camera and the scene rephotographed, on the same strip of film, completing the exposure *without* the shadow. The result was a convincingly transparent shadow.

This discovery soon led to others; the same principle could be used to create other illusions, such as the transparent clouds of dust as Snow White and the animals dusted the dwarfs' cottage. In Bashful's blushing scenes, his animation, featuring his normal skin color, was supplemented by a separate cel coloring his face a deep red. As the cameraman cross-faded between the two colors, an intense blush faded evenly into Bashful's face. Thanks to these and other effects, a great majority of *Snow White*'s scenes were photographed in multiple exposures. "We had many triple exposures in *Snow White*," said camera department head C.W. Batchelder. "We

have as high as seven exposures."

Closely related to the depiction of shadows was another Disney invention that is rarely recalled today: the Shadowgraph. This device, which was used to simulate convincing shadows against irregularly shaped backgrounds, involved an elaborate procedure. Beneath an ordinary flat camera table, on a tiny "stage" the same size as the animation field, the Shadowgraph artist modeled a three-dimensional "set" representing the background of a given scene. Then the characters in the scene, animated in register with the background, were inked and painted on cels in the normal manner and placed on the camera table. Through an opening in the table, the camera photographed the three-dimensional set, while a light, placed to simulate the light source in the scene, cast the characters' shadows from the cel onto the irregular surface of the set. The frames of the resulting film were then blown up and, like the rotoscope drawings of live-action performers, used as a guide for the artists to re-create the shapes of realistic shadows. This was a complicated, time-consuming procedure,

The Disney camera department in the 1930s. At right is a standard camera table; at the left is the multiplane.

Lillian Gish, as Lucy, whirls in terror in the closet scene in *Broken Blossoms* (1919).

"but with longer scenes," Bob Martsch noted, "there is an appreciable saving of animation cost." The Shadowgraph was not destined for a long life at the Disney studio, but it was patented and used in several scenes in *Snow White*.

SNOW WHITE AND THE MOVIES

In addition to all the other cultural influences embedded within it, *Snow White* affirms its place in film history by reflecting other important films that had gone before. We've already noted the influence of contemporary films such as *She* and *Bonnie Scotland* on the development of individual *Snow White* characters, but it's not hard to see other major films and filmmakers reflected elsewhere in this film.

From the American silent-film era, perhaps the most obvious influence here is the father of film technique, D.W. Griffith himself. Griffith's influence on *Snow White* is most evident in the climactic scenes of the dwarfs racing to save Snow White, their furious action suspensefully intercut with scenes of Snow White, at their cottage, slowly giving in to the temptation to eat the apple. Nearly three decades earlier, as Griffith experimented with the first principles of film editing in his historic Biograph films, he had created similar rides-to-the-rescue—and, like some of his rescues, the attempt in *Snow White* is unsuccessful: the dwarfs arrive too late to save their princess. Griffith is echoed in other scenes too; the pigeon that bears Snow White's kiss to the Prince in the garden suggests a similar love scene between Lillian Gish and Henry B. Walthall in *The Birth of a Nation* (1915). And Snow White, lost in the forest and imagining a host of dangers around her, whirls around and around in terror—recalling a strikingly similar action by Lillian Gish in the famous closet scene in *Broken Blossoms* (1919).

Certainly Walt and several of his artists were inveterate movie fans, and in story conferences were often inspired by specific films. Walt, discussing the Queen's magic mirror at one conference, suggested: "This mirror is draped with curtains, like *Dracula*." At another meeting he compared the same setting to one in Douglas Fairbanks's 1922 production of *Robin Hood*. Tarzan, appearing during the 1930s in a successful series of films at MGM, had his influence on *Snow White*: one early suggestion for the dwarfs' race through the woods had called for some of them to "swing on vines— 'Tarzan' to the rescue," and on another occasion Walt had suggested that the Witch might have a secret door in the rocks, inspired by *Tarzan and His Mate*: "the waterfall hid the entrance to the elephants' burial ground." Discussions of Snow White running into the woods, the Huntsman's voice calling after her, were marked by comparisons to Paramount's mental-health drama *Private Worlds* (1935), in which Joan Bennett had imagined a voice calling her name. As we examine *Snow White* in detail, we'll find other cinematic inspirations ranging from *Das Cabinet des Dr. Caligari* to "Our Gang." The artistic world in which Walt and his artists operated was not a limited one; they drew on the entire panoply of world cinema and the other arts. In the process, they created a film that would soon occupy its own place in that pantheon.

Nearly two decades later, Snow White reacts in the same way to her terrors in the forest.

Top: A cleanup animation drawing by Ham Luske and Jack Campbell.

Bottom: This cel setup is not a key setup from the film, but was assembled by Courvoisier Galleries, after the film's release, for sale to the collectors' market (see page 249).

Each day the Queen consulted her Magic Mirror, and each day the Mirror spoke the words she loved to hear, "Oh, Queen, thou art fairest in the Land."

ONCE UPON A TIME . . . *A storybook titled "Snow White and the Seven Dwarfs" opens, and in its pages we see an introduction to Snow White's story: her forced labor at the hands of her cruel and vain stepmother, the Queen, and the Queen's daily ritual of consulting her magic mirror to learn who is the fairest one of all. As long as the mirror answers that the Queen herself is fairest, Snow White is safe from her stepmother's jealousy. But as we watch, the Queen approaches the mirror and receives an unwelcome answer: there is another, more fair than she. Pressed to reveal the fair one's identity, the mirror replies enigmatically, but the Queen knows her rival can only be Snow White.*

Sequence 1A: Main title and storybook

Sequence 1B: First Queen and mirror sequence

6 THE FILM

The most common problem faced by any filmmaker adapting a story from another source is exposition: conveying the necessary story information to an audience, but trying not to bore them with the dull mechanics of the plot. In his career Walt Disney found a variety of creative responses to that challenge, but his usual instinct was to streamline wherever possible, and even eliminate cumbersome plot elements if he could. His opening passage in *Snow White* is even more economical than the Grimms'; we hear nothing of the birth of Snow White, the death of her mother, or her father's remarriage. The core conflict of the story is between the Queen and Snow White, and the film wastes no time in cutting straight to that basic situation.

The introductory text is condensed into two pages in a storybook, ornately lettered and punctuated with brightly colored illuminations. These pages were the work of Gordon Legg, a Disney artist who specialized in lettering and who had recently begun to paint the art title cards for the studio's short cartoons. Legg recalled in later years that Walt had closely supervised his work on these introductory titles: "Walt said, 'Make sure it's very legible.' You go into this Gothic style—not American Gothic, but the encryption that was current at the time of the Grimm fairy tales, or before that, you know—when you went into that, why, it was pretty hard to read, I guess. It's a German Gothic type of stuff. And Walt wanted to make sure it was legible so that people could read it."

The pages were bound into a large prop storybook that was shown opening on camera, and Gordon Legg, having designed the pages, now assisted in photographing them. Because they were live action, these shots were made not at the Disney studio, but at the Technicolor building in Hollywood.[51] "So we went to Technicolor," Legg recalled, "and they had a camera on a lathe bed or something like that. So we went there and we made several takes, and picked the best one. I turned the pages, but no hand was supposed to appear. So we would pull in close to the page before we'd turn to the next page, and by then my hand would be off-screen, of course."

As we read about the Queen's daily ritual with her mirror, the film draws us in, and we witness that ritual for ourselves. A pair of multiplane scenes, underscored by Leigh Harline's ominous, descending "Magic Mirror" theme, carry us closer to the castle and cross-dissolve into the first fully animated scenes of the film: the Queen at her mirror. This, the film seems to be saying to a late-1930s audience, is a rich, ornate world, a far cry from the world of Mickey Mouse or even the Silly Symphonies—charming and whimsical at times, but also, in these scenes, dark and foreboding.

The personality of the slave in the mirror was developed in story conferences and gradually became an oracular character, given to poetic speech. "The Mirror could say . . . something flowery," Walt suggested at one meeting. "Let him always talk that way . . . He answers indirectly." That detached, flowing speech, delivered in Moroni Olsen's hollow tones, adds greatly to the sense

Opposite: Gordon Legg, who lettered the elaborate storybook pages in the film, probably also created this preliminary sketch.

[51] At this time, early in the glory days of three-strip Technicolor, the Technicolor company maintained its high standard of quality by exercising a tight proprietary control over the process. No matter what studio was producing a color film, the cameras and other equipment remained Technicolor's property and were operated and maintained by its personnel. The Disney studio began producing Technicolor cartoons in 1932 but was not allowed to keep production cameras on its own premises until several years later. And of course the Disney Technicolor cameras were modified for stop-motion photography, while the storybook shots in *Snow White* were shot at the standard sound speed of 24 fps.

Two very different design concepts for the mirror sequence. The finished scene, shown on the facing page, adopted elements from both of them.

of mystery in this opening sequence. Note that the mirror's line, "Lips red as the rose," is softened from the Grimm original: "red as blood." Note, too, how this dialogue economically distills the ideas discussed in the story conferences. At another meeting Walt had mused analytically on the Queen's motives for preventing Snow White from leaving with the Prince: "Then Snow White would be out of her control. As long as she is at the castle she can keep her down where she won't be seen . . . The mirror tells [the Queen] . . . that these rags and things cannot hide her, but that word has reached the prince of another land . . . the Queen hasn't been able to disguise her by hiding her." None of this is overtly stated in the finished film. The only vestige of these thoughts is a single line in the mirror's dialogue: "Rags cannot hide her gentle grace."

The job of animating the slave in the mirror as he mouthed these words fell to Woolie Reitherman, a junior member of the animation staff who would go on to become one of the studio's "Nine Old Men." Reitherman struggled with this demanding assignment. "That was tough, because it was held," he later told a television interviewer. Not only was the character's disembodied head to remain rigidly still, its expressions were to be restrained, and the design of the face was to remain symmetrical at all times. "I did that thing over three, four, five times. I finally devised a way of splitting the head in half by folding the paper. I'd draw one half

[52] John Canemaker, drawing on other interviews, reports that Reitherman animated the mirror nine times before Walt was satisfied.

of the expression, and then I would fold the paper over and draw the other half right on the same line, and the same thing. So it didn't jiggle all over the place. And that finally worked; it got me out of a hole."[52] Sweatbox notes reveal that Reitherman was also coached by Ham Luske, who suggested creating a set of "anchor points" and moving them very slightly to control the raising and lowering of the character's eyebrows and eyelids. In the finished scene, of course, the face was overlaid with a distortion glass that obscured the symmetry Reitherman had struggled to perfect.

The other character animator on this sequence was Art Babbitt, who invested the Queen with a cold beauty and a menacingly regal air. This, as we've seen, was likewise a demanding animation assignment. Bill Justice, who would go on to a long career at the studio, was serving his apprenticeship as an inbetweener in 1937. "They just brought scenes over to the annex from the main building, and we would do whatever work on whatever scene they gave us," Justice said. "My first scenes were the wicked Queen, two or three scenes of the wicked Queen talking in the mirror." He laughed wryly as he recalled the assignment. "[The dwarfs] were more fun, you know, they were cuter and they have a lot more animation to them. The Queen was just, the lips were so—moved so close together, you'd use about a 6H pencil and keep it needle-sharp so you could squeeze the line in between."

Along with the character animation, this sequence was liberally augmented with effects animation ranging from the obvious to the subtle: the wind and flashes of lightning in the mirror as the Queen summoned her slave, John McManus's smoke effects when the slave appeared, the Queen's Shadowgraph shadow on the pillar behind her. Still more effects were planned for the sequence—including a series of overlaid colors from a color filter, rising from the bottom of the screen as the Queen gazed into the mirror—but later eliminated.

One of the most pleasing and subtle effects is in the layout of the final scene as it cross-dissolves into the next sequence: the Queen in one sequence, and Snow White in the next, momentarily occupy the same position on the screen. The effect is that of the cold, forbidding Queen inhabiting the same space as—and gradually replaced by—the innocent, lovely Snow White.

A cel setup representing the first character animation that appears in the film: the Queen's approach to her mirror.

Another cel setup, showing
Snow White at the wishing
well.

SNOW WHITE MEETS THE PRINCE *Snow White, dressed in rags, scrubs the steps in the castle garden and dreams of romance. Standing by the well, she tells the pigeons surrounding her that this is a magic wishing well. "Make a wish into the well, that's all you have to do; and if you hear it echoing, your wish will soon come true." As she sings the song "I'm Wishing," her voice is heard echoing from the well—and her wish does come true: the Prince, riding past on horseback, is attracted by her lovely voice and enters the garden. He declares his love in the song "One Song." Snow White, flustered and shy, runs inside the castle and listens from an upper room. Venturing onto the balcony, she sends a pigeon fluttering down into the garden to convey her kiss to the Prince. But the Prince's song is also heard by the Queen, who listens in mounting fury from her chamber window.*

Sequence 2A: Snow White and the Prince in the garden

This delightful sequence, which serves to set the stage and introduce Snow White to the audience, was one of the *last* sequences in the picture to be written, developed, and produced. This was no accident; Walt recognized very early that this would be one of the most difficult parts of the story for his artists to tackle. No slapstick action or gags, no cartoony characters, none of the properties that most audiences would expect from an animated cartoon—no, the business of this sequence was to establish an absorbing, enchanting fairy-tale world on the screen, drawing in the audience with its charm and sincerity, and without the aid of comic relief or easy shortcuts. Small wonder that Walt waited until late in production, allowing his artists to gain experience on other parts of the story, before attempting this one.

From the beginning of production, a wide variety of approaches had been considered for the opening of the story, some broadly comic, others more restrained. Most of the treatments had endeavored to explain the Prince's presence at the castle, that he was on a quest to find his loved one. One idea that was entertained briefly called for Snow White to construct an imaginary scarecrow Prince by mounting a bucket atop a fencepost, painting a face on it, and addressing the effigy as "Prince Buckethead." The real Prince, entering the garden unseen, was to observe her game and enter into it. The meeting of the two lovers would begin with Snow White, in surprise and embarrassment, hearing the Prince's voice apparently issuing from Prince Buckethead.[53]

Opposite: Snow White's reflection in the well, augmented in the film by a distortion glass (for the movement of the water's surface) and ripples animated in clear lacquer on specially manufactured cels.

[53] Although the "Prince Buckethead" idea was dropped from the film story, we'll see that it did appear later in the *Snow White* Sunday-comic adaptation and some of the other 1937–38 promotional materials. And, as we'll also see, the Disney story department returned to it two decades later.

By the spring of 1937, a more straightforward approach had been adopted. For this and other key sequences involving Snow White herself, Walt entrusted much of the story development to Larry Morey. Like Albert Hurter and Ham Luske, Morey played a special role in the making of *Snow White*. Today, history remembers him for his song lyrics—for many of the Silly Symphonies, for all the songs in *Snow White*, and for other songs in later Disney films—but as early as 1935 the multitalented Morey had combined his musical activities with story development at the Disney studio. In this position he could respond to Walt's request to "weave [the music] into the story"—creating an animation equivalent of Rodgers and Hart's sophisticated scores for *Love Me Tonight* and *Hallelujah, I'm a Bum,* which had seamlessly interwoven dialogue, rhymed dialogue, and song. This opening sequence was ripe for such a treatment. In the spring of 1937, Morey's was an important voice in the story conferences for sequence 2A.

Here again, the great challenge was exposition: the writers were faced with the burden of explaining a complicated situation, but in an entertaining way. Should the Prince be seen singing about his quest for the fair maiden? Should he approach the Queen to ask for Snow White's hand? Should the Queen disguise her treachery by pretending to send Snow White away to school, as she had done in the Ames play and the Paramount film? And if not, what other excuse could she give that would get the Prince out of the way long enough to dispose of Snow White? Step by step, in one conference after another, all these extraneous ideas were methodically pruned away as Walt strove for an ever greater simplicity of presentation. The sequence we see in the film today, unfolding on the screen with such seemingly effortless purity and clarity, was actually hammered out through painstaking labor.

At a story meeting on 5 April 1937, the team made the definite decision to develop the lovers' meeting from "the romantic angle." At this point the wishing well was not in the story; Snow White was to be seen scrubbing cobblestones, musing aloud that she wouldn't always have to work so hard, and leading into a short rendition of "Some Day My Prince Will Come"—with variant

Snow White performs her "Cinderella" work in the garden.

[54] It's possible that this idea was itself suggested by one of Walt's comments in the 5 April conference: as Snow White scrubs the cobblestones, "you'd see her reflection in the scrub bucket."

[55] Walt later expanded on this idea in *Cinderella:* as Cinderella scrubs the floor, singing "Sing, Sweet Nightingale," her reflections in the soap bubbles join in the song and become an overdubbed chorus. Unfortunately, the cutting records for *Snow White* sequence 2A, which might have explained how the echo effect was achieved, seem not to have survived. Our best clue is a fan-magazine article, based on interviews with Walt and the staff, which offers a simple explanation: "the echoes were recorded, played through a speaker into an empty room and then re-recorded."

lyrics, more general than the original ones, since she hadn't yet met the Prince. (It was at this conference that Walt made his comment that Snow White "should be doing some Cinderella type of work.")

Between this meeting and the next one, on 4 May, the sequence was transformed by the addition of the wishing well. This inspired device made the film's opening much more cinematic: instead of talking about her troubles, Snow White could stand beside the well, sing of her romantic longings, and see her reflection in the water below.[54] This invention inspired another one: instead of singing one more chorus of "Some Day My Prince Will Come"—clearly a clumsy fit for this revised concept of the sequence—Snow White would sing a new song, custom-tailored to the story by Morey and Frank Churchill. This was "I'm Wishing," one of the last songs written for the picture. Earlier cartoons had featured shadows or reflections that moved independently of their objects; "I'm Wishing" adapts that cartoon conceit in a new and sweetly whimsical direction. Snow White sings into the well, her own voice answers in the form of an echo, and then the "echo" assumes an independent life, singing counterpoint and then harmony with Snow White.[55]

"I'm Wishing" was also tailored to the vocal strengths of Adriana Caselotti (as Morey commented at one conference: "The girl does a good cadenza"). The melody is vintage Churchill, charming in its simplicity. But that simplicity is deceptive; Churchill incorporates a cunning musical design to link this song with Snow White's other song of romantic longing, "Some Day My Prince Will Come," which will not be heard until much later in the film. The verse of "Some Day" (written in November 1934) leads up to the chorus with an ascending five-note musical phrase to the words "He was so romantic . . ." Here, in the verse of "I'm Wishing" (written in April 1937), Churchill uses the same five-note phrase twice in a row—to the lines "Want to know a secret? Promise not to tell?"—then resolves the phrase in the next line: "We are standing by a wishing well." By this simple means he creates a subliminal connection between the two songs, and gives Snow White's character a subtle musical motif.

Another problem was the relationship between Snow White and the Prince. Morey and Churchill had devised an elaborate verse for the Prince's song, "One Song," which would have combined spoken dialogue with sung passages. The Prince would boldly declare

his love and press Snow White to declare hers; Snow White would deny her own obvious feelings for him while begging him to leave the castle before he was discovered; the Prince would defy all danger and obstacles: "I'll never leave as long as you/Keep standing there denying that it's true." The bantering, flirtatious nature of this exchange would have been well suited to some live-action performers, but the Disney story crew struggled to make it work for their animated lovers.

Part of the problem was that a definite personality had yet to be established for the Prince; the story crew was still striving to create a character that could be animated convincingly. Asked about the Prince's personality at the 4 May meeting, Walt replied: "I think we have

to figure out the business there and can't get down to his character until we do. Leave him as a romantic figure for now." This was a remarkable statement, considering that the personalities of the dwarfs and Snow White herself had been actively under construction for more than two years and the film's premiere was now a scant seven months away. But Walt was still trying to remain open to all possibilities, and he probably would have accepted this more mature concept of the Snow White– Prince romance if it could have been developed convincingly. It was he who suggested, in May 1937, that the Prince might impulsively kiss Snow White on his first meeting with her at the well. For her part, Snow White was to display a coquettish spirit when she ran

This story sketch captures the bold, bantering nature of the Prince's relationship with Snow White in an early version of the sequence.

Snow White primps in the mirror in another early story sketch. The mirror was not retained in the finished film.

Opposite: This story sketch explores possible camera fields as the Prince serenades Snow White.

inside the castle: outwardly she would pretend to be offended at the Prince's forwardness, but once inside the room she would instantly begin to primp at the mirror.

Underscoring this concept of the sequence is the selection of animators chosen to bring Snow White to life. In her earliest scenes, the scenes that give the audience their first glimpse of the character, Snow White is animated by Jack Campbell—originally an assistant to Grim Natwick, then a long-time stalwart of Ham Luske's animation unit and, by the time this sequence was produced, second in importance only to Luske himself. The Snow White we see scrubbing the steps and singing into the wishing well is Luske's version of the character, the wide-eyed little girl, vulnerable and shy. But from the moment she meets the Prince and runs inside, Snow White is animated by Grim Natwick and his unit, and her character shifts subtly. It's the Natwick Snow White, slightly older and more worldly-wise, who peeks from behind the curtain and advances onto the balcony. If the musical-comedy concept of the sequence had been retained, this Snow White would have been more believable as she feigned a haughty distance from the Prince, all the while falling willingly into

the arms of romance.

All through the spring and into summer 1937, the extended verse of "One Song" remained in the picture, and with it the kiss and the flirtatious tone of the romance. This version of the song was even recorded on the sound stage, and the story crew began to work with the recordings. Then, early in June, Walt suddenly suggested cutting out the verse. This was the turning point; the rest of the crew agreed that the verse should be cut, with a simpler and shorter transition between "I'm Wishing" and "One Song," and immediately the character of the sequence began to change. A less contemporary, more innocent, fairy-tale quality began to take over. Walt, who had earlier suggested the kiss by the well, now suggested taking it out. As the nature of the romance changed and he instinctively sensed the rightness of this direction, he began to curb Snow White's coquetry: "She is not getting too familiar." When Dave Hand suggested that Snow White, after drawing the curtains at the end of the sequence, might peek out one last time at the fadeout, Walt rejected the idea: "A little saucy."

The finished sequence, the distilled essence of this grueling process of analysis, bears out the wisdom of the process. Uncluttered by all the dialogue that had once been suggested for it, the film tells its story simply and directly through images and music. Walt is gambling on the loveliness of the imagery to carry the story, and it's a wise gamble; we're instantly drawn into this fantasy world. Snow White, scrubbing the bottom step, looks up at the rest of the staircase and sighs, expressing her weariness more eloquently than a surfeit of spoken dialogue could do. The Prince simply appears during her wishing song; no appeal to the Queen for her hand, no subterfuge about sending Snow White away to school. And, in fact, no explanation is ever given for the Prince's disappearance after this sequence—but we never miss it; wordy explanations are unnecessary because the film makes its appeal directly to our hearts. This is the simplicity of legend, of myth. As Walt had suggested, the Prince does remain simply "a romantic figure," an icon of romance. Snow White, hiding inside the inner room, does briefly adjust her hair, but there's no primping in the mirror—because there's no mirror. Here she's just a young girl, living out her fantasy of romance. And when she draws the curtains at the fadeout, with one final adoring smile at her Prince, the scene is reassigned from Natwick to Campbell.

Along with this simplicity, the sequence represents another gamble: it tells its romantic story absolutely straight, with no comic relief. To create this kind of enchanting atmosphere, populated by convincing human characters, was one of the most difficult challenges imaginable for an animation studio. Rarely had it been attempted before, even in Disney films. In films of later years, such an outpouring of warmth and sentiment might often have been undercut by a wise-cracking supporting character, distancing the audience from the sentiment with a nudge and a wink. There will be plenty of comedy later in *Snow White,* and of course there is gentle laughter in this sequence when the blushing pigeon delivers Snow White's kiss to the Prince—but this is mild comedy that works with the scene, not against it. In this opening, Walt and his artists offer us an unabashed romantic story that is not afraid to wear its heart on its sleeve. And, adult or child, we gladly submit to it.

THE HUNTSMAN'S MISSION *The Queen has heard and seen enough. Summoning her Huntsman, she tells him to take Snow White to the forest, find some secluded spot, and kill her. The Huntsman's protests are futile in the face of the Queen's menacing, unspoken threats. To ensure his compliance, she gives him a carved box and orders him to bring back Snow White's heart in it.*

Sequence 2B: Queen orders Snow White's death

For all its charm and romance, at the heart of the traditional "Snow White" story is a terrifying premise: a woman so jealous of a younger girl's beauty that she actually seeks to kill her. Some of the early stage adaptations had endeavored to soften this element of the story for the benefit of children in the audience. In particular, the Ames play and the resulting Paramount film had inserted a comic twist, hoping to distract the audience from the blunt horror of the Queen's murderous intentions.

At the beginning of Disney story development, there was some uncertainty as to how the Queen's instructions to the Huntsman should be handled. The August 1934 "Manuscript" outline—which, as we've already seen, had little in common with the finished film—suggested a jaw-dropping approach to this sequence. Here the Queen and the Huntsman were to perform a Gilbert and Sullivan–style musical number, the Huntsman bartering the lives of his children for the life of Snow White! How such a sequence might have played is difficult to imagine, but the writer (probably Dick Creedon) made it clear that his intention was to present the Huntsman in a "semi-comic" light.

In the end, the Disney film rejects any such evasions or sugar-coating and returns to the stark essence of the Grimms' plot. Here there's nothing humorous or comforting about it: the Queen literally wants to *kill* Snow White. This storytelling integrity alone would be remarkable enough; to attempt such a scene in the medium of the mid-1930s animated cartoon is doubly extraordinary. This sequence occupies less than a minute of screen time, but it takes the art of animation into strange new territory. Here two human characters engage in a scene of real dramatic intensity, played with deadly seriousness—and, again, no comic relief, no easy shortcuts.

And, to be sure, production of the brief sequence was grueling. Once again the chief burden was on Art Babbitt as he animated the Queen. Sitting on her peacock throne,[56] the Queen indulges in no wild, active histrionics—the kind of performance that most animators enjoyed—but instead underplays her scenes, projecting a cold, subtle cruelty. Even with the help of live action, sweatbox notes reveal that Babbitt labored over the Queen's scenes throughout the summer and autumn of 1937, reshaping the eyes here, lowering a hand there, as Walt and Ham Luske continued to scrutinize her performance. So critical were the details that negative tests, the usual means of testing pencil animation, were inadequate; Babbitt's animation was studied in positive tests and, in at least one case, fully inked and painted before Walt, Luske, and other key personnel could confirm that every detail was correct. The finished sequence is a tribute to their persistence and Babbitt's skill, particularly the last closeup, as the Queen looks directly into the camera and fixes it with a gaze of chilling intensity. Animation of the Huntsman was assigned to Errol Gray, one of the junior animators in Luske's unit.

Like sequence 1B, this sequence was also richly augmented by effects work that we sometimes take for granted today. The shadows that envelop much of the sequence were achieved by masks that were animated separately and then double-exposed over the inked and painted cels. Only the Queen's eyes and highlights on her clothing were left clear in painting these masks, so that her eyes seem to burn with a concentrated light even when she is in shadow.[57] This work was entrusted to effects-animation wizard Cy Young, who also contributed the details of the carved box that closes the sequence—the box that is meant to hold Snow White's heart.

[56] As late as October 1936, the Queen's panther was supposed to be present in this sequence, showing "the similarity of eyes between the Queen and the panther." By the time animation started, the panther had been cut from the film.

[57] The first scene in this sequence also made use of washoff relief cels, a device which—as we'll see in a later section—had been conceived during production of sequence 3D.

A Joe Grant character sketch of the beautiful but evil Queen.

A cel setup showing the
sequence in the finished
film, as the Queen gives
the Huntsman his awful
assignment.

SNOW WHITE FLEES INTO THE FOREST *On the following morning, the Hunts-man takes Snow White to the woods to carry out his mission. Snow White, unaware of her danger, happily picks flowers and helps a little lost bird. Moved by her innocence, the Huntsman cannot bring himself to kill her. Instead, he warns her of the Queen's intentions and urges her to run into the woods and far away. The terrified Snow White plunges deeper and deeper into the woods, imag-ining danger at every turn. Entangling vines hinder her way; branches catch at her clothing and seem to be clutching hands; logs in the water appear as ravenous alligators. Snow White reaches a clearing and, with a final terrified scream, col-lapses on the ground in utter despair.*

Sequence 3A: Snow White and Huntsman; Snow White into woods; montage

This sequence presented the studio with *two* formi-dable challenges: another dramatic situation, with two more or less believable human characters, that must present a real and palpable sense of danger; and the expressionistic montage of terrors as Snow White fled into the forest, which must *suggest* a host of perils without quite making them explicit. On a technical level—with the possible exception of the dream vision in sequence 8B, which was cut from the picture—this was perhaps the most challenging sequence in *Snow White.*

The attempted murder of Snow White had been covered by the Grimms in a few lines. The subsequent Görner, Merington, and Ames plays had fleshed it out slightly more, but they were written for children. The Disney film, in its treatment of this action, shared the burden of the preceding Queen-Huntsman sequence: it must bring out the inherent drama of the situation much more forcefully—which meant taking the art of anima-tion in an extremely unfamiliar direction. The August 1934 "Manuscript" outline suggested a remarkable version of this sequence, featuring an almost tomboyish Snow White who, on her initial ride into the forest with the Huntsman, "sings a gay hunting song" and "puts her horse over walls and water jumps." When she real-izes that the Huntsman intends to kill her, she shows no fear but instead, "rising proudly, tells him to strike."[58] Walt's own "Skeleton Continuity," dictated in December 1934, offered a version much more consis-tent with the finished film but was, indeed, only a skeletal outline.

[58] This particular idea, whether contributed by Creedon or someone else, was not wholly original; in the Merington and Ames plays, Snow White, learning that the Huntsman's children were in jeopardy, had bravely volunteered to sacrifice her life in order to save theirs.

In recent years, story development of the Snow White–Huntsman sequence has become a favorite example for authors who want to demonstrate the meticulous care taken by Walt and his writers. In truth, virtually *every* sequence in the film endured the same extensive process of analysis and development—and, in truth, the development of this one was perhaps even more exhaustive than most of these accounts suggest. Walt wanted to underscore Snow White's goodness and innocence by showing her kindness to a baby bird, but he and the story crew debated a range of details: should the bird actually be sick or have a broken wing, or should it simply be lost? Perhaps its foot should be caught in a twig. Perhaps it should be pursued by a larger bird of prey, paralleling Snow White's own situation. Perhaps they should do without the bird altogether! And how should the Huntsman's stealthy approach behind Snow White's back and his change of heart be depicted? If the bird stayed in the picture, should it see the approaching Huntsman, chatter, and fly away, causing Snow White to turn around? Should Snow White remain unaware of her danger, keeping her back to the Huntsman ("which gives you a swell position for the knife in the back," Walt noted) until he weakened and dropped the knife, and she heard it clatter on the ground?

The biggest problem in this sequence was depicting the Huntsman's change of heart. The Huntsman was to be a believable human character, and just to animate him in convincing movements would be challenging enough, let alone to portray complex, shifting emotions in his pantomime. "Even [for] actors in pictures," Walt pointed out, "changing attitudes is a very difficult thing to do." Part of the problem was that the Huntsman's personality had not yet been fully established: should he be a sympathetic character as in earlier versions of the story, forced against his will to attempt the murder of this innocent girl, or should he be the sadistic killer suggested in some conferences? "If you build up the Huntsman as a tough guy who is drooling at the mouth when the Queen tells him to cut Snow White's heart out," Bill Cottrell observed, "it may be pretty hard to put over why he weakens." This may have been the major consideration in bringing the Huntsman back to a more sympathetic characterization.

Gustaf Tenggren created this striking thumbnail concept painting, in which Snow White imagines that the half-submerged logs are ravenous alligators.

When production started on this part of the sequence early in 1937, some of these questions were still unsettled. Much of the action was animated in experimental tests, viewed by Walt and by groups of studio employees, and then modified according to their reactions. One of the first ideas had been to insert closeups of the Huntsman's feet stealthily approaching Snow White—conveying his menace, but avoiding the problem of animating his facial expressions. When the rough reel was screened for a studio group in mid-March 1937, the shots of the feet were almost universally criticized. They "seemed a little clownish," Grim Natwick complained: "You're expecting something ominous and all you see is a pair of feet." The feet came out of the sequence soon afterward. As late as May, when one of the layout artists noted that the Huntsman should be seen in the opening scenes carrying the box given to him by the Queen—which otherwise would never be seen between sequences 2B and 7A—Dave Hand could tell him: "That sequence . . . is all being done over, the Huntsman's part of it. So we could very easily have a box if we needed it." The box was duly inserted in the sequence—then, still later, removed again on Walt's orders.

The finished film does retain the episode of the lost baby bird, staged as briefly and economically as possible. (The bird and his parents will reappear later in the film. Note that the parents' call, heard offscreen here, will be repeated in the next sequence and will lead into a song.[59]) Snow White's attempted murder is cannily staged so that we *think* we see the Huntsman's change of heart, but the actual turning point takes place offscreen. We see the grim determination in his face as he approaches Snow White, we see his urgency immediately afterward as he implores her to run away into the forest, but the moment of change itself is conveyed by dialogue and by a closeup of his upraised hand shaking, opening, and letting the knife fall.

Snow White's terrified flight into the forest was a different kind of challenge, and occasioned even more extended debates in story conferences. Here, in the already fantastic world of animation, the artists must convey the dangers surrounding Snow White, but make it clear that they were all in her imagination and not in the "real" world. This was an extremely fine distinction. The result was the film's—and, to date, the studio's—deepest foray into the world of expressionism. Today

[59] Note also that Grim Natwick animated the lovely opening long shots of Snow White in this sequence, her hair and cape blowing gently in the breeze. For some reason he was also given her closeups with the bird—perhaps because Ham Luske and his crew were carrying a heavy workload of their own in this sequence, including animation of the Huntsman.

Two story sketches for the Huntsman sequence.

the rise of expressionism in cinema is generally traced to the German horror film *Das Cabinet des Dr. Caligari* (1920), which had boldly translated the work of the Expressionist painters into cinematic terms. The impact of *Caligari* had quickly spread to other German films, then to American films as well, as many of the German directors and cameramen emigrated to Hollywood. By the late 1920s, the dark visual magic of these stylists had permeated much of Hollywood cinema. Even as late as 1935, so American a director as John Ford was employing a strongly expressionist style in *The Informer*. Considering this prevailing influence—and considering the strong Old World influence of some of the Disney artists, not to mention the Germanic roots of the "Snow White" story itself—it's hardly surprising that expressionist techniques were used to project Snow White's terror in the forest onto her surroundings.

Too, some of the devices in this sequence could be traced to earlier Disney shorts. In *Alice in the Jungle* (1925) and in *The Castaway* (1931), first Julius the cat and then Mickey Mouse had discovered that what they thought were harmless fallen logs were actually hungry alligators. *Snow White* reversed the illusion: here the terrors *were* logs and other harmless objects, but the fright in Snow White's mind must be vividly projected to the audience—yet still understood as imaginary. "When she hits the branches in back, she disturbs them," Walt said at one conference, "and that is what

makes them start to move, and she imagines that they are hands. We have to watch that they don't come to life, but just have them do like bramble bushes do that could catch on her dress."

The climactic montage was discussed, dissected, and analyzed in minute detail. Some artists felt that the escalating series of terrors should be separated by quick dissolves; others argued for rapid cuts. Walt left both possibilities open: "They are all short, fast blends. You can overlap, too, and get some double exposure stuff . . . Work it out that way and it can easily be reshot in straight cuts."

Like the other part of the sequence, this section went into production while still in an experimental stage, the better to test multiple ideas and see which ones were most effective on the screen. "The montage I want to shoot in black and white," said Walt, "rehearse it and then shoot it in color, or even shoot it in color as a test. I plan on shooting that twice, not inking and painting but shooting it twice. I don't know how you can do it otherwise. There are a lot of dissolves in there." Studio records would later identify sequence 3A (along with 3B, 3C, and 3D) as jointly directed by Ham Luske and Perce Pearce, but in reality the crew remained very loosely organized, with no real leader other than Walt. "Some of the sequences don't have a director," Mike Holoboff noted at one meeting, "like with Larry [Morey]. He is more or less responsible, but he turns

the stuff over to Ham Luske." Hal Adelquist agreed: "Originally Larry prepared the story on it. Sequences 3A and 3B, the montage sequence, and so on—Larry originally handled the story on this stuff, but due to working on other sequences it has been more or less up to Ham and myself as assistant director." The continuity remained in a constant state of flux. Some scenes, including Snow White's second fall into the water, were planned and animated but then dropped from the final cut.

Some of the changes had the effect of making the sequence much more strongly expressionist. In story conferences, Walt had leaned toward conveying Snow White's fears through subtle suggestion: "I think it all has to be dark so you can't see the detail too much . . . The shapes in the darkness would look like things and not be too definite like trees with mouths. Lots of mystery. Never see too clearly that it's a tree with a big mouth." But when the experimental scenes started

showing up in sweatbox in the spring of 1937, it was clear that some of them were *too* subtle. Now new scenes were added, superimposing onto the trees the horrific faces haunting Snow White's imagination. When she falls into the hole above the pool, the hole itself becomes a gaping mouth, the "jaws" dripping with cobwebs and surmounted by large yellow eyes. By the time she reaches the clearing, the eyes are everywhere around her, pressing angrily in upon her as, in a paroxysm of terror, she collapses to the ground.

An expressionist idea not used in the film: in Snow White's frightened imagination, harmless vines appear as deadly snakes.

More expressionism: Gustaf
Tenggren's clutching branches
(above) were used in the film;
Ferdinand Horvath's nightmare
image of a giant wolf (opposite)
was not. Tenggren's painting
is not actually production art,
but one of his illustrations
for the *Good Housekeeping*
serialization of the story
(see pages 228-229).

SNOW WHITE MEETS THE FOREST ANIMALS *The woods are not full of monsters after all. Snow White discovers that the creatures watching her are really harmless, friendly birds, deer, rabbits, and other small animals. Reassured, she dries her tears, introduces herself to the animals, and sings "With a Smile and a Song." She asks the animals if they know a place where she can stay, and they assure her that they do. Her spirits lifted, Snow White is led through the woods by the animals toward an unknown destination.*

Opposite: In this display setup, against a decidedly inauthentic background, Snow White sings to the animals.

[60] In addition to the animals themselves, the transition from sequence 3A to 3B—the idea of terrifying visions that are revealed to be harmless, benign creatures or objects—was a familiar device by 1937. The Silly Symphony *Babes in the Woods* (1932) had used this device in a way very similar to that of *Snow White*, and this was not the only point of contact between the two films.

[61] Special care may have been exercised with this song because, in the summer of 1936, it was planned as Snow White's first song in the film. As we've seen, "I'm Wishing" was added to the score nearly a year later. In the finished film, "With a Smile and a Song" is preceded by "I'm Wishing" and by Snow White humming "One Song" in the woods.

Now the mood of the film shifts dramatically, suffused with a reassuring wave of hope. Some filmmakers revel in the dark, terrifying, villainous sides of their stories but make only halfhearted gestures on behalf of happiness and virtue. No such lazy measures for Walt Disney: he's shown us the terror of Snow White's flight into the forest, but this sequence evens the balance. When Snow White discovers that her fears were imaginary, the film is flooded with an almost palpable sense of joy—due in part to Frank Churchill's "With a Smile and a Song," which surely reminded 1938 audiences of earlier morale-building songs of the Depression. This song, in addition to its pleasing melody, helps to advance the plot: the timid animals of the forest are, at first, more frightened of Snow White than she is of them. It's her singing of the song that draws them to her, and by the end of the first chorus they gather around her adoringly—devoted companions who will remain faithful throughout the rest of the story.

With the introduction of these animals and birds, Walt makes one of his most radical departures from "Snow White" tradition. But this change is not carelessly made; it's perfectly in keeping with the spirit of the story and simply one of the ways that the medium of animation is uniquely suited to enhance the plot. For *Snow White*'s first audiences, this sequence may have had an extra significance that we miss today. From its opening scenes, the feature had been something boldly, strikingly different—unlike anything the audience had seen before, and peopled by characters unlike any others in animation. Apart from the pigeons in sequence 2A and the baby bird in 3A, the woodland animals here were the film's first characters of the kind moviegoers *expected* from a Disney film in the late 1930s: cute,

appealing animals that could exist only as cartoons. Now, eleven minutes into the film, we're entering something like familiar territory.[60] Walt Disney hasn't abandoned his well-loved cartoon world; it can still exist within the larger universe of the feature.

As with the preceding sequences, the action that seems to flow so simply and spontaneously on the screen was the result of long, arduous work. And, again, much of that work was in pruning away extraneous dialogue and business. Originally Snow White was to ask the animals, "Maybe you know of someone who needs a housekeeper?" At one conference the story crew bogged down in a discussion of who would be living in the woods—perhaps a woodcutter—and of whether Snow White was planning to work for a man or a woman. It was Ted Sears who uncluttered the dialogue: "The way you have straightened this out, the only clumsy thing is the long explanation of the place she is looking for. It is not necessary to say anything more than her only worry is where she would sleep at night and do they know of any place and they say yes."

The lead-in to Snow White's song was another problem. Because of Walt's aversion to having characters suddenly "bust into song," an effort had been made to integrate Snow White's dialogue with the beginning of the song. This time it was Ham Luske who felt the transition was still too abrupt. "It has what I was afraid of," he complained. "It sounds as if it were written . . . [as if she] had been told to sing a song at this spot." Walt, usually the most critical member of the group, found himself in the odd position of trying to placate Luske: "I wonder, if the music and business is effective enough, if the audience would mind . . . I like the pickup. What is the objection to it, Ham?" Luske persisted: "I try to say to myself: does the audience care?"[61] He felt Snow White should ease into the song more gradually.

On the other hand, Bill Cottrell felt this approach entailed too much dialogue. "We are just getting one scene after another with dialogue in it," he pointed out. "I had the impression it was a lot of talk." Finally the team arrived at a continuity that balanced all these concerns: Snow White, recovering from her fright and beginning to cheer up, trades vocal cadenzas with a baby bird—the same bird she had encountered in the

Longue — 426-1½
Bottom of feet — 7738-3

685-1|✓
606-½

906-3

965-4

olive green -1

7738 - 3

(normal)

A color callout for the slowest-moving member of Snow White's animal retinue.

Huntsman sequence. This provides a musical bridge into the first chorus of "With a Smile and a Song." Her dialogue about finding a place to sleep, trimmed to its bare essentials, is delivered in rhyme and functions as the "verse" of the song. Then comes the second chorus, played instrumentally on the soundtrack as the animals and birds lead Snow White through the forest.

As the sequence that introduces the animals, sequence 3B is also the film's earliest opportunity for the "animal men" to show what they can do. Eric Larson animated the birds, and his early work was so appealing that the scenes featuring proud parent birds and precocious baby bird were expanded: baby sings to Snow White and shows off his vocal range; parents beam with pride until Junior embarrasses them by hitting a sour note. Bernard Garbutt animated key scenes of the deer, a specialty that he would develop in coming years. One of the fawn's actions during Snow White's song, animated by Milt Kahl, would later be singled out by critic Otis Ferguson in his review of the film: "shy but sniffing forward, then as she starts to pat it, the head going down, ears back, the body shrinking and tense, ready to bound clear; then reassurance, body and head coming up and forward to push against the hand—half a dozen motions shrewdly carried over from the common cat."

One animal character who makes his bow in this

sequence is the turtle. "I introduced the turtle character into the picture," Grim Natwick recalled in later years. "I'd grown up on the Wisconsin River, and we used to catch turtles by the hundreds when we were kids. And in effect I was thinking of different animals and what they could do, and then I thought, hell, a turtle'd be kind of cute in here." Natwick made his suggestion at a story conference in January 1936. The story men seized on the character's possibilities, and turtle gags began to appear on the *Snow White* storyboards. Here, Walt suggested, as Snow White sings, "the turtle's head could just come out of the weeds and listen, then back into shell." It's a modest introduction to a character who will become familiar later in the film.

As for Snow White herself, a single scene in this sequence—Snow White rising from a sitting position to her knees, then standing up, a technical challenge in animating the human form—was animated by Natwick. The rest of her scenes were the work of Ham Luske's unit. But many artists worked in Luske's unit at one time or another, and an unlikely name joins the ranks in sequence 3B. This sequence, alone in all the picture, offers an artistic mystery: did Ward Kimball—an animator known for wild, cartoony, slapstick action—animate some of the delicate, charming scenes of Snow White in the forest? Late in life he claimed more than once that he did, and production papers from this sequence seem to support his claim: his name doesn't appear on the draft but does appear on some of the exposure sheets—suggesting that he was not originally assigned to those scenes, but worked on them after the

drafts were typed. Six scenes, some of them closeups, are candidates for Kimball's work. In view of all the Kimball animation that was eventually cut from *other* sequences in the picture, this is worth mentioning. The scenes in question don't differ greatly from most of the other Luske-dominated scenes in the feature[62] and, in any case, are a far cry from Kimball's usual forte. But then, *many* artists stretched beyond their usual limits in the making of *Snow White*.

One effect in this sequence was supplied by an unusual device. A stream runs through Snow White's forest, and in two scenes the water in this stream has a distinctive appearance—dark, tranquil, gently flowing. Both the scenes in question were shot on the multiplane. The "water" in these scenes was a sheet of highly polished tin, mounted at an angle to the contact planes, positioned to reflect Snow White and the animals as they moved above, with "flow" lines scored in it, and drawn through the scene frame by frame. Walt was impressed with this striking effect and sought other ways to use it in the picture. During story work on sequence 2A, in which Snow White meets the Prince in the garden, he suggested that tin might be used either for Snow White's distorting mirror or for the water in the wishing well.[63] But the mirror was eliminated from sequence 2A altogether, and in the end the reflections in the wishing well were photographed through a standard distortion glass, augmented by specially animated ripples.

The fawn's action, as suggested in these story sketches, remained in the scene as animated by Milt Kahl.

Overleaf: A preliminary concept painting of the Dwarfs' cottage by Sam Armstrong.

[62] It's true that some individual drawings in the closeups vary slightly from the Luske standard— but *so* slightly that the difference is imperceptible onscreen, and may be nothing more than an inker having a bad day. In one of these closeups (scene 12B, Snow White saying "I'm so ashamed of the fuss I've made"), the girl's teeth have an odd appearance in some individual frames, but this again seems to be simply an anomaly in painting the cels.

[63] Walt made these comments early in June 1937. He was clearly inspired by seeing the first stream scene in sequence 3B, which was photographed around the same time in June 1937, one of the earliest multiplane scenes to be shot for *Snow White*.

THE DWARFS' COTTAGE *The animals lead Snow White to another clearing, where she is delighted to discover a small house, "just like a doll's house." Finding that no one is home, she hesitantly ventures inside. There she finds seven small chairs and decides that the house must be inhabited by seven children—and, from the cluttered state of the house, that they must be very untidy children. She decides to surprise them by cleaning up the house, in the hope that she will be allowed to stay. Enlisting the help of the animals and birds, Snow White sets to work sweeping and dusting the house and washing the dishes and clothes, to the tune of "Whistle While You Work."*

Sequence 3C: Snow White discovers Dwarfs' house

Sequence 3D: Snow White and animals clean house

[64] The first 1934 story outlines had followed the sequence of earlier versions of the story: Snow White would discover the house, meet the dwarfs, and then clean house the following day. During story conferences in 1935, it was decided to streamline the film's continuity by combining the discovery and housecleaning sequences in one long passage.

[65] This gag may be hard to visualize, but a similar idea surfaces in a later Disney film, *Johnny Fedora and Alice Blue Bonnet*, released as part of the package feature *Make Mine Music* in 1946. The stars of this love story are a couple of hats— hardly promising subjects for an animated film—but the Disney artists use the natural shapes of the hats, especially Johnny Fedora's, to suggest a remarkable range of "facial" expressions.

Of the many talented animators who worked on *Snow White*, we've already seen that certain artists were singled out as leaders. In particular, Ham Luske set the standard for animation of Snow White, while Fred Moore and Bill Tytla similarly established the dwarfs. In the early months of 1936, after months of story and character development, production officially started on the feature. Each of these three key artists was given a sequence and started work on it—experimentally, but with the understanding that the finished results were intended for production. Ham Luske's section of the picture was Snow White's discovery and cleaning of the dwarfs' cottage, a passage that combined two separate sequences.[64] By February 1936, Snow White's first scenes were being animated.

Not that those February 1936 scenes are the same ones we see in the finished picture. On the contrary, "Ham's sequence," as it became known at the studio, established the pattern for the rest of *Snow White*: experimental animation was filmed, studied, subjected to endless review in sweatbox, revised again and again. In November 1936 the work done to date was screened for a large studio group and critiqued in minute detail by Walt and by many of the artists, including Luske. The group examined not only the technical details of drawings and movement, but also the effect that those details, such as the relationship of eyes and eyebrows, might have on Snow White's personality. ("I cannot make this girl frown," Luske confessed. "Every time we do, her eyebrows just travel.") Walt pointed out that some techniques were producing a better effect on the screen than others, and that Luske and his team should

play to their strengths: "If we could get a line on just the type of stuff that we are more sure of getting over, we could . . . get some 'don'ts' and 'do's' and keep them in mind when writing dialogue and building business." In all, sequences 3C and 3D were subjected to a process of refinement that went on for nearly two years, up to completion of the feature.

Delighted to discover a house deep in the woods, Snow White crosses the little bridge to the dwarfs' doorstep, accompanied by yet another sparkling Frank Churchill musical theme. Frank Thomas and Ollie Johnston later wrote of their admiration for the "bubbling quality and friendly spirit" of this musical passage and added: "we asked Ed Plumb [another Disney musician] what gave the music that extra something. Ed squinted his eyes, 'Y'know, I've memorized every note in that orchestration and I still can't figure out what does it.'" The interior scene of Snow White, framed in the window as she looks in from outside (paralleled by a similar scene in the silent Paramount *Snow White* of 1916), was added late in the summer of 1936, a good six months after work started on the sequence.

We've already seen that the untidy dwarfs in the Ames play and the Paramount film were a departure from the traditional Grimm dwarfs, who had kept their home spotless. The Disney version enlarges on this idea and plays it for comedy: here the dwarfs aren't just untidy, they're slobs. Snow White is greeted by the spectacle of a pick embedded in the table (with a dirty sock hanging from the handle), stacks of dirty dishes, a cooking pot with a shoe inside, and dust and cobwebs everywhere. Clearly, if she wants to work as a housekeeper, the occupants of this house can use one. One gag planned for sequence 3C was later eliminated: the various articles of dirty clothing, strewn around the house, were to be wrinkled in ways that suggested "faces." Snow White was to pick up a pair of pants, wrinkled so as to suggest a glum expression, and shake them out so that they seemed to break into a smile. This gag was animated and remained in the picture as late as the spring of 1937 before being cut.[65]

The discovery of all this disarray leads directly into the housecleaning sequence, set to the tune of Churchill's cheerfully catchy "Whistle While You

Work," one of the first songs written for the film.[66] This is one of the most joyous and memorable sequences in *Snow White*, seemingly overflowing with inventive gags. And, indeed, it did overflow; Disney staffers had been invited to submit housecleaning gags, and had responded with such an outpouring of imaginative ideas that only a portion of them could be used. (Later, during story conferences on sequence 11B—the Bed-Building sequence, ultimately cut from the film—Walt directed one of the writers to "Get the gag folder on the house cleaning sequence" because, in the surplus of unused gags, there was still plenty of good material left over.)

If this section of the film was an introductory assignment for Luske and his fellow Snow White artists, it served the same purpose for the animal animators who were also part of Luske's unit. Animals and birds dominate the screen during much of this action. "I didn't realize," said Eric Larson to a television interviewer, "that when I got onto *Snow White* I'd be having maybe ten, twenty animals on one page, trying to move them around in a composition that would be interesting." He

and the other "animal men" quickly learned that their work would be subjected to much closer scrutiny than in the earlier shorts. Sweatbox notes reveal the subtle nuances of detail that were expected of them. "I don't like the bunny stopping and looking at Deer while he is dusting under chair," Walt wrote to Louie Schmitt. "He should come out and look at the Deer with the cock of his head and a blink. The little bunny holds his looking too much straight out instead of looking at the Deer—he looks in the wrong direction." As the birds arrange flowers in the vase, Walt suggested to Larson: "Personality touch: Last bird comes in with flower and goes a little higher and pauses momentarily before dropping it right straight down into the center of the bouquet. Will give feeling of finishing it off. Flies up and out." The scene of the two squirrels, reprimanded for sweeping dust under the rug, who sweep it into a mousehole instead and incur the wrath of the mouse, was labored over for months by Leonard Sebring before being reassigned to Milt Kahl.

One side benefit of the sweatbox notes is that they

The wood-grain background here is part of the Courvoisier setup; the actual scene in the film employs a neutral light background.

[66] The Disney music department retains a lead sheet for "Whistle While You Work," with lyrics varying from those heard in the film, signed by Churchill and dated 21 December 1934. Walt's "Skeleton Continuity," typed five days later, mentions the song by name as the "little work song" that Snow White teaches to the birds.

The "pants gag" (see page 126) as pictured in story sketches.

[67] This gag was poorly received at the 17 March 1937 studio screening of rough reels, the same session where some artists objected to shots of the Huntsman's feet in sequence 3A. As in that instance, the group reaction may have contributed to the decision to trim the scene. Similarly, the "pants gag" in sequence 3C was roundly criticized by the group and seems to have disappeared within a few weeks afterward.

[68] A similar scene had been animated by Ken Anderson for the studio's Oscar-winning 1935 Silly Symphony, *Three Orphan Kittens*, depicting the title characters scampering through a room as the walls and furniture seemed to pan behind them. Although the finished scene in *Kittens* looks impressive, Anderson later claimed to see a "jitter" in it. In that connection it's worth noting that, while Anderson's animated furniture had been solidly inked on cels, the floorboards in *Snow White* are rendered in soft focus, perhaps to prevent any such problems.

reveal more gags that were planned, animated, and then dropped from the final cut of the film. The chipmunk who falls into the sock was originally supposed to have a longer fall: as the toe of the sock unraveled, the chipmunk would slip through and tumble to the floor.[67] The birds arranging flowers in the vase were supposed to be supervised by a "boss bird," but after several attempts to animate that character failed to please Walt, the "boss bird" was removed from the scene. Later, when the dwarfs' dirty clothes were washed outside in the stream, they were to be hung up to dry by means of "pinch bugs" that would act as living clothespins; this too was eliminated.

On a technical level, two especially notable scenes are the panning shots of animals carrying dirty dishes across the room in one direction, then dirty clothes in the other. These scenes are staged near floor level and depict the floorboards (and, in the second scene, a pickaxe) panning past the camera in perspective. Such an effect might have been easily staged with the Fleischers' lateral camera setup, but at the Disney studio the floorboards are *animated* along with the characters, and the effect is remarkable.[68] The first of these pan shots, with the turtle carrying a precarious stack of bowls and teacups on his back, was the scene of another eliminated gag. Here the turtle was to collide with an obstacle, causing the tower of cups to sway and then come cascading down toward the floor. The turtle hastily ducked inside his shell, but the birds came flying to the rescue with a tablecloth stretched between them, deftly catching most of the falling china. As the turtle looked out of his shell in relief, the last cup alighted unbroken on his head, a spoon landing harmlessly

inside it. Like some of the other missing gags, this complete scene was animated and then cut. It may have been reduced simply to reduce the overall footage of the sequence; the scene, originally running nearly 32 feet (roughly 20 seconds of screen time), is just under 4 in the finished film.

A curious fact of the sweatbox notes for this sequence is that almost all are devoted to the animals and birds. The character most difficult to animate, Snow White, is rarely mentioned at all. The reason for this seems to be Ham Luske's central role, second only to Walt's, in the review process. It was Luske himself—Walt's fellow architect of Snow White's performance—who was also its severest critic. His improvements and refinements, striving for an ever higher standard in the girl's animation, seem to have been made silently; only occasionally did Walt find it necessary to offer additional comments of his own.

Another precedent in Snow White's animation was established in this section: Grim Natwick was given a semi-autonomous unit of his own but was assigned only the full or long shots of Snow White—and not all of those—while, for the time being, close shots of the girl's face remained the province of Luske and his team. One of Natwick's scenes, Snow White standing on the porch at the end of the sequence as the camera pulls away, occasioned another technological innovation. "In my youth," said Natwick, "when I first left home and began doing drawing professionally, I did a lot of song covers, and I got acquainted with the engravers who engraved these. And I found that they could reduce my large drawings, which might be eighteen or twenty inches large, down to an inch and a half or something and still

Within the sketch:
INTERIOR · DOWNSTAIRS · SHOWING FRONT DOOR

© 1936 W.D.P.

INTERIOR · BEDROOM

INTERIOR DOWNSTAIRS SHOWING PUMP AND SINK

PUMP DETAIL

PRODUCTION FI- "SNOWWHITE" 1151-139

retain a perfect picture." This experience was recalled to mind when Natwick tried to animate the final, distant image of Snow White at the end of the scene. "Marc Davis [his assistant] re-drew that, finally, with a 6H pencil, and still, when we projected it, it had a jitter because it was too small. So I remembered this old engraving thing and suggested to Walt that these things could be drawn larger and reduced, photographically, onto celluloid, which they did." The solution was the introduction of *washoff relief cels*. The figure of Snow White was drawn in a comfortably large size and photographed; then a reduction print was made on a cel coated with a special photographic emulsion. When the emulsion was washed away, only the exposed part of the image remained. The cel was then painted in the usual way and became part of the scene, with Snow White

perfectly rendered in miniature. "Because you could take a 6H pencil and draw as carefully as you want to," said Natwick, "and there's a point beyond which you cannot do good work."[69]

Preliminary sketches of the cottage interior show the artists' careful attention to detail.

Overleaf: A cel setup from the housecleaning sequence.

[69] A similar account of the introduction of washoff cels was given by Bill Garity in *Popular Mechanics* after the film's release. Paul Sprunk, one of the studio's camera-effects specialists, apparently played a part in this innovation; the exposure sheet for the scene includes a note: "drawings on second cel [level] are to be reduced as per Paul Sprunk's contraption."

INTRODUCING THE DWARFS AT THE MINE *Meanwhile, far away, the occupants of the house—not children, but seven dwarfs—are working at their daily occupation, digging precious jewels in a mine. As they work, they sing a song about their labors. A clock strikes five, announcing the end of their workday. Gathering their tools and taking up the chorus of a marching song, the dwarfs prepare for their daily walk home.*

Sequence 4A: Dwarfs at mine

Now, and only now, nearly three reels into the picture, we're ready to meet the Seven Dwarfs. At an early story conference Walt suggested introducing the characters in a sequence at the mine, by way of a roll call. He soon abandoned this idea in favor of a subtler approach, and in the finished film the introduction of the dwarfs seems casual, almost offhand.

In discussions of the famous sequences planned for *Snow White* and then discarded, it's often forgotten that this sequence, 4A, was very nearly one of them. For a good nine months during production, sequence 4A was cut from the picture; the mine was eliminated altogether, and the dwarfs were simply introduced marching home from work at the end of the day. Only very late in production, in the late summer of 1937, was the mine sequence reinstated. Why was it cut in the first place?

The problem, as usual, was an overabundance of story material, far more than could be contained even in a feature-length picture. The idea of the dwarfs as miners, established in most versions of "Snow White" from the Grimm Brothers on, inspired the Disney story department to concoct an elaborate mine sequence, rich with mining gags, personality gags, and ingenious details of the mining equipment the dwarfs had built themselves. Frank Churchill supplied a song, "Dig Dig Dig," to introduce the sequence and propel it at a jaunty tempo. Walt suggested that these dwarfs, like those in the Ames play, might be so accustomed to the fabulous wealth in their mine that it meant nothing to them: "Funny if they had all these diamonds and found a doorknob mixed in there. All of them look at it with interest, keep it and throw the jewels away." Other gags were designed to advance character; Sneezy, for example, might sing a line of the song and end it with a violent sneeze, bringing down a rock on his head. The

dwarfs' homemade equipment might include an ore crusher, its pistons and gears working to the rhythm of the music.

As conceived at this time, much of this sequence revolved around the dwarfs as hardworking miners. *Santa's Workshop* (1932) and *Father Noah's Ark* (1933)—two earlier Silly Symphonies setting industry to music (gnomes making toys, animals helping to build the ark)—were invoked at some of these meetings. As an extension of this theme, the idea of the dwarfs as ingenious craftsmen was inspirational to Walt. His suggestions included an elaborate homemade clock that would make use of a live owl to announce the end of the workday: "The old owl is perched up there. When it hits 5, something comes out and gooses the owl and he goes WHOOOO! like a whistle." This in turn led to a variety of gag suggestions built around the clock. Another artist suggested a gem polisher, powered by a squirrel running in a circular cage. When the squirrel's energy started to flag, Dopey would place two large diamonds in his own eyes, the facets producing the bizarre appearance of a score of eyeballs. Frightened by this fantastic spectacle, the squirrel would run for his life.

This proliferation of ideas, wonderful as it was, came into direct conflict with another of Walt's roles: that of ruthless story editor. In meeting after meeting, he and the story crew wrestled with these opposing drives—constantly hatching creative new gags that no one could bear to part with, while simultaneously striving to pare the film's continuity down to its essentials. Because this sequence would be followed immediately by another featuring the dwarfs, an arbitrary limit of roughly 230 feet (about 2½ minutes) was established, and the writers did their best to cram the maximum number of gags into that footage. Perce Pearce felt they were straining for an impossible quantity of material. "Make little miners of them, and put across a few good gags. Have a clock in the mine and Doc's forge in the corner, but mainly plant the idea that there are seven of them and that they work in a mine," he advised. "You can't break them down to individuals in this footage . . . I feel you are not putting individuals across and you are losing both ways."

Finally, at a meeting on 2 November 1936, the

Opposite: This Courvoisier cel setup cobbles together several cels from the mine sequence into a single image.

Early plans for the mine sequence called for an elaborate array of homemade machinery.

matter came to a head. Once again Walt and the writers struggled to reduce the sequence to its essentials, even as new gags were being suggested. Something had to give, and finally Walt made the difficult decision: cut sequence 4A from the picture altogether. "Cut all mine stuff and 'dig dig dig' song, and fade out on her cleaning the house to them marching home singing HI-HO." Better to do without the mine sequence entirely than to present a rushed, strained version of it. Immediately the other members of the crew chimed in with suggestions to make this new continuity work. "What does it matter where they work or what they do," Walt added a few minutes later, as if trying to convince himself. "It really has nothing to do with your story."

Whether or not he was happy with this decision, the mine sequence remained out of the picture all through

the winter, spring, and summer of 1937, while intensive production work continued on the rest of *Snow White*. Some of the gags and music were tentatively moved to other parts of the picture, but the introduction of the dwarfs in their workplace was out. Then, late in the summer—in August or early September 1937, judging by production papers—the mine sequence was quietly restored. By the second week in September, new animation was appearing in sweatbox.

As viewers of *Snow White,* we know, of course, that sequence 4A *is* part of the finished film, but the version we see onscreen is drastically reduced from the one discussed in 1936. Gone are the crusher, the forge, and other elaborate details of settings and gags that had been suggested for the sequence—and, not being privy to those earlier conferences, the audience never misses

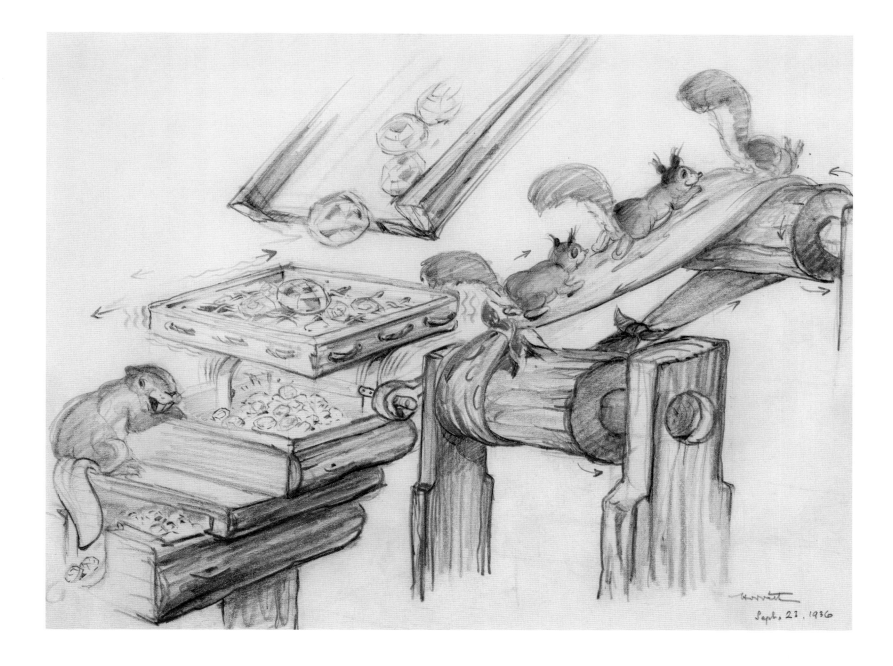

them. Dopey still puts the diamonds in his eyes, but the squirrel cage is nowhere to be seen; Dopey is simply indulging in the sheer joy of silliness. Walt's point about the dwarfs' careless disregard for their wealth is expressed in the simplest possible way: we see the gems being sorted and the less-than-perfect specimens swept into a dustpan and tossed away like so much garbage. The clock, which had inspired so many gag suggestions, is no longer a complicated device but simply a charming little clock with two carved figures—representations of the dwarfs themselves—which emerge from tiny doors and strike the hour on a tiny anvil. (This and the film's other "cuckoo" clock, the one in the dwarfs' cottage, were both animated by effects animator Andy Engman. In a modest way, they suggest the delightfully intricate Old World carved clocks that would be featured much more prominently in the studio's next feature, *Pinocchio*.)

Most pertinently, as Perce Pearce had suggested, no concerted attempt is made to establish *all* the dwarfs' personalities in this first sequence. Doc and Dopey (thanks to Fred Moore's animation) make a strong first impression, but the other dwarfs are simply sketched in. Happy looks happy, Grumpy looks grumpy, Sleepy seems more than a little drowsy as he lazily drives the mine car. Beyond that, the dwarfs remain simply seven intriguing little characters who work in a mine. We'll get to know them better soon enough.

This Ferdinand Horvath sketch features more homemade mining equipment, driven by squirrel power.

THE DWARFS MARCH HOME *The dwarfs emerge from their mine into the surrounding hill country, still singing their marching song. As the setting sun casts their long shadows across the hills, they march across a fallen log that spans a chasm, then set off through the woods toward home.*

Sequence 4B: Dwarfs march home from the mine

Early in story development, a generic "Dwarf Song" had been suggested for the film, an all-purpose song "to be sung by the dwarfs when they are working in the mines, the forest or around the house." This idea was soon elaborated as "their marching song," which they were to sing while marching home through the woods: "'We're seven men of the woods,' and so forth." By the spring of 1936, Frank Churchill had produced the song "Heigh-Ho." It's heard several times in the course of the film, but most memorably when the dwarfs sing and whistle it during their walk home from the mine, picks slung over their shoulders, the evening shadows lengthening around them.

During production, this sequence assumed an added importance. When sequence 4A was temporarily dropped from *Snow White* late in 1936—and for the better part of a year, until it was reinstated—this following sequence, the dwarfs' homeward journey from the mine, became more prominent. This was now to be the dwarfs' first appearance in the picture. As such, it became a concentrated exercise in character animation: how best to introduce each individual dwarf to the audience, based solely on his walk? A long meeting of the dwarf animators, in November 1936, focused on sequence 4B as a laboratory of character development. For more than two hours, the animators—some of whom had been animating the dwarfs for a good nine months—debated the different walks that might instantly distinguish each character from the others.

George Stallings, the writer who had been working on the sequence, stressed that the characters' movement should convey their personalities *without* exaggeration. "They do this every day," he pointed out. "They go home each and every day this same way . . . Don't let them put on a show . . . Don't let them look at the camera. Don't let them get out of character." He suggested some basic characteristics: Doc's walk would be a strut, Happy would have more of a rolling

movement, Sleepy would drag his feet. Dopey's main concern was to get in step with the others. Soon the animators were chiming in with more suggestions. The dwarfs would carry their picks slung loosely over their shoulders, not uniformly; and Sleepy would be too lazy to hold the pick in his hand but would simply hook his wrist over the handle. Bashful would enter into the singing "as though he were putting his soul into the music." Grumpy, by contrast, might refuse to sing at all.[70] Walt, not present at the meeting, had already given Stallings his thoughts about Dopey: "Walt has mentioned two or three times that Dopey thinks this is all a game . . . He is never serious about anything. Even in this walking home business, his whole attitude is that he has got to go along with them and he is making a play thing out of it."

Before the next meeting, some of the story crew met on the sound stage and filmed live-action footage for this sequence, committing to film their ideas for the various walks. Stallings played the role of Happy; Perce Pearce walked for Bashful. The irrepressible Pinto Colvig played four different dwarfs: Grumpy and Sleepy—both of whose voices he supplied on the soundtrack—as well as Doc and Sneezy. The animators studied this footage together and compared their impressions of the various mannerisms suggested for the dwarfs.

The focus of most of this work was one key scene in the sequence: a semi-closeup running 28 feet (just under 20 seconds). In this panning closeup, all seven dwarfs would march across the screen, the camera lingering on each dwarf just long enough to capture the essence of his personality. Bill Tytla, one of the leading dwarf animators—and the one who had taken the initiative in filming live-action reference footage—was assigned this scene, which would serve as a model for the other animators. Some modest business was devised here: Sleepy, dangling his pick over his shoulder, inadvertently got it caught in the seat of his pants and pulled himself up on his toes, drowsily oblivious to the fact that he was walking on tiptoe. Tytla's group scene, gradually refined and much discussed and studied by the other animators throughout most of 1937, was approved for inking late in September.

[70] In the finished version of the sequence, Grumpy does sing and whistle along with the others, although he doesn't look very happy about it.

Two early story sketches for the mine and marching sequences.

This evocative reverse-angle
story sketch was followed very
closely in the finished film.

Then a surprising thing happened: sequence 4A, depicting the dwarfs in the mine, was replaced in the picture after all, and suddenly the combined weight of the two dwarf sequences was too much. Sequence 4B was no longer the audience's introduction to the dwarfs, and after mulling it over for several weeks, Walt decided—in consideration of the feature's overall running time—to condense the dwarfs' homeward march. Tytla's panning closeup, which had served for the better part of a year as a benchmark for the other animators, was one of the scenes cut from the film.

The other cut scene was the one intended to follow immediately afterward: the dwarfs, continuing on their way, march underneath the exposed root of a giant tree.[71] Essentially, the combined effect of the cuts was to remove one chorus of "Heigh-Ho" from the film. The finished version of the sequence cuts directly from the fallen log to the reverse angle, the dwarfs marching away from the camera as Dopey tries vainly to get in step with the others.

The removal of these two scenes meant that the final version of sequence 4B was animated in its entirety by one man. Both Woolie Reitherman and Bill Roberts were considered for this assignment, but in the end it was given to Jimmie "Shamus" Culhane. The three scenes remaining in the sequence, each one a group shot of all the marching dwarfs, totaled a combined running time of just over 70 feet. This, along with the beginning of the song in sequence 4A, was the sum total of Culhane's animation assignment in *Snow White*[72]—but as he remembered it, that was plenty. In each of these scenes he was required to maintain all the distinctive walks devised for each individual dwarf *and* to march them in perspective and over uneven terrain. "It took me almost six months of backbreaking work to finish the sequence," he recalled in his 1986 autobiography.[73] As his scenes reached sweatbox, they were scrutinized by Walt and sequence director Ben Sharpsteen, and returned to Culhane again and again for minute changes in the dwarfs' walking action.

One day, several months' worth of this meticulous work nearly went up in flames. Culhane's chain-smoking assistant, Nick de Tolly, accidentally set a sheet of paper on fire, and the fire quickly spread. "My whole goddamn sequence was on fire in seconds!" Culhane wrote. "Before I could help, Nick had grabbed a towel and smothered the flames. The miracle was that none of the drawings was damaged, although in some cases the fire had burned to within a quarter of an inch of the figures." A disastrous loss had been narrowly averted.

The changes made in these sequences during production illustrate differing approaches to story construction. If sequence 4A had remained out of the picture, the dwarfs would have been introduced in classic Hollywood fashion: first their shadows on the face of the cliff, then a distant glimpse of the characters, then a closer approach that would gradually reveal their characteristic movements. Instead, in the finished version, we get to know the dwarfs in a more oblique manner: seemingly random vignettes of action at the mine, followed by a group portrait of all the dwarfs as they march home. In this version the shadows on the cliff are simply a picturesque touch. More picturesque yet is Culhane's scene of the dwarfs marching across the log against a sunset sky, perhaps the film's single most iconic image of the dwarfs. In the meantime, as we'll see in Part III, Bill Tytla's benchmark scene *would* eventually reach the screen after all—but in an unexpected and heavily altered way.

[71] Apparently, all the dwarfs except Dopey had to stoop in order to pass underneath the root. Layout artist McLaren Stewart was instructed to "change the root on the tree so that the dwarfs are in the clear as they squat," while the animator was to "prepare a new rough on Dopey's action, cutting down his size as he goes beneath the root and enlarge the hand that feels above his head."

[72] His later scene of the dwarfs in sequence 14B, marching back to the mine, was actually one of his scenes from this sequence, reversed to show them marching in the opposite direction.

[73] The conclusion of this sentence, "but it went through the sweatbox without my having to change a drawing," is belied by the sweatbox notes—which, like most of the *Snow White* sweatbox notes, call for *dozens* of changes.

SNOW WHITE DISCOVERS THE BEDROOM *The ground floor of the house has been thoroughly cleaned, and now Snow White decides to investigate upstairs. There she finds a bedroom, with names like Doc, Happy, and Sneezy carved on the footboards of the small beds. "What funny names for children!" The sight of Sleepy's name reminds Snow White that "I'm a little sleepy myself," and she lies down across several of the beds and quickly falls asleep. The animals and birds find resting places too, but just as they're beginning to nod off, the distant sounds of the singing dwarfs alert them that the house's inhabitants are approaching. Snow White slumbers on, but the animals race downstairs and out the door, and hide in the bushes.*

Sequence 4C: Snow White discovers bedroom

Having paused to introduce the dwarfs, the film returns to Snow White just in time to bring the two threads of the story together. In addition, this sequence serves subtly to continue the "introduction" of the dwarfs: we've *seen* them in the mine and marching home, and here for the first time we learn their names.

The scenes of Snow White climbing the stairs and entering the bedroom are enhanced by a new special effect. In the just-completed Silly Symphony *The Old Mill,* the fireflies that appeared in an early scene had glowed with a light that seemed real—because it *was* real. First the fireflies had been animated and photographed in the usual way. Then, on the multiplane crane, a second exposure had been added with miniature lights attached underneath the cel level, following the trajectories of the animated fireflies. On the screen, the fireflies seemed to shimmer with a luminous halation. Now the same technique was applied to the candle in Snow White's hand. The flame of the candle was doubled by a small light attached underneath the cel, and the camera department experimented to determine the best exposure levels for each part of the scene. As a result, on the screen, the flame of the candle was surrounded by a tiny glow. Combined with the dark, atmospheric background paintings and the double-exposed shadows cast by Snow White and the animals, the effect was magical.

In this sequence the turtle, still trying to keep up with the other animals, gets some additional comedy business. Unable to trip lightly up the stairs after Snow White like the rest of the animals, he fastens his jaws on the next step and *pulls* himself up, one step at a time. Assistant director Hal Adelquist dubbed in a repeated "crunch" sound effect for this exercise, which someone, probably Walt, asked to have taken out again: "It is not necessary to have sound effect crunch for turtle going up the stairs; music can carry this effect with an accent on each bite." Whether by oversight or because the decision was reversed, this sound effect never was removed from the film and is still in the soundtrack as we hear it today.

The turtle's laborious ascent of the stairs, in addition to offering comic relief, serves a storytelling function. When pencil animation of this sequence was shown to a general studio group in March 1937, writer Dick Creedon objected to the sudden reawakening of the animals in the bedroom. "I always have the feeling that we go too quickly from the sleeping mood to the waking up," he explained, "that it moves . . . too abruptly . . . The whole feeling is going to sleep quickly and waking right up." Dave Hand replied uneasily that the change in lighting (when the candle is snuffed out) and the music would help to bridge the transition. Later on, however, a new scene of the turtle was inserted during this passage. Now, thanks to his dogged persistence, the turtle is nearing the top of the stairs, and his moment of near-victory is underscored by a muted fanfare. We cut back to the bedroom in time to hear the dwarfs' voices, and the animals suddenly open their eyes. The cutaway to the turtle has masked any feeling of abrupt change.

By this time, of course, we've forgotten all about the turtle, and he reaches the landing just in time to be bowled over by the other animals stampeding from the bedroom. He falls, and his considerably faster trip back down the stairs was animated by Milt Kahl, who later told John Canemaker that he had collaborated with Frank Churchill on the timing of the action: "He worked out a musical pattern for it. He helped me decide. You know, I said, the guy ought to pick up speed [going] down [the] stairs. And we've got a thing at the foot of the stairs where he slides across and hits the wall, so we can make it as long as we have to, to get the proper length into the timing."

This turtle action is followed immediately by another gem of animal animation. Bernard Garbutt was

still a junior member of the staff in 1937, but offered a subtle glimpse of his brilliance in this sequence. His animation of the deer family as they race out the front door, if we slow it down and examine it more closely, belies the insinuations of inexpert deer animation in *Snow White*. The buck is the first to reach the partially open door, and wheels and turns awkwardly in his attempt to charge through the narrow opening. Just as he's about to pass through the doorway, the doe catches up with him and, in her blind panic, strikes the door with her shoulder, knocking it farther open. Cut to the exterior of the house, where all the animals race out and leap over a low railing—all except the fawn, whose legs are too short to clear the railing. He hesitates, then turns

to go around as the camera pans past him. These actions, easily overlooked in the pell-mell crowd action of the animals' escape, suggest the virtuosity Garbutt would bring to the deer in *Bambi* just a few years later.

A story sketch of the turtle's ascent of the stairs, suggesting a moving camera field to follow his progress.

Discovery of the Dwarfs' beds, with their names carved on the footboards.

Opposite: Snow White, in the form of rotoscope tracings of Marjorie Belcher, starts up the steps to investigate upstairs.

SOMETHING'S IN THE HOUSE! *As the dwarfs approach their home, they are suddenly met by a terrifying sight: lights in the windows and smoke issuing from the chimney. Someone or something is inside the house! Cautiously, they enter the house and find it in an alarming state—clean, dusted, the floor swept, dishes washed and put away, a kettle of soup cooking in the fireplace. Clearly, something is terribly wrong. The dwarfs soon realize that their uninvited visitor must be upstairs, and elect Dopey to go up and investigate. Dopey, petrified with fear, enters the bedroom and sees what appears to be a ghost—actually Snow White, stretching and yawning beneath the sheet. The terrified Dopey bolts from the room, tears downstairs and out of the house, and conveys to the other dwarfs that something unspeakably awful is asleep in their bedroom. Summoning up their courage, the dwarfs reenter the house, prepared to do battle with this fearsome creature.*

Sequence 4D: Spooks

This sequence illustrates the divergence between the Disney *Snow White* and traditional versions of the story. The action it describes—the dwarfs' return to their house and their discovery of Snow White, asleep in their beds—is a comparative non-event in earlier versions. The Brothers Grimm toss it off in a few paragraphs: the dwarfs return home and find, like the Three Bears, that someone has been sampling their food; discover Snow White asleep; and are so charmed by her beauty that they allow her to sleep undisturbed the rest of the night, leaving introductions until the morning. The Winthrop Ames stage version elaborates *very* slightly on this premise ("Brothers, there must be Robbers in the house!" "Or Pirates!" "Or Burglars!") but, again, resolves the matter quickly. The 1916 Paramount film, which young Walt saw in Kansas City, is even more straightforward.

The Disney version, on the other hand, spins this slight incident into a major episode in the story. Here again, the change is determined by Walt's priorities: his purpose is not simply to retell the traditional story, but to use it as a vehicle for his medium, the art of character animation. From that standpoint, this sequence is a pivotal moment in the introduction of the dwarfs. We've glimpsed them in action at the mine, seen them marching home from work, and heard their names. Now, for the first time in the film, we are to hear them speak, watch them interact with each other, and observe their varied reactions to a common crisis: someone or something is inside their home!

Walt Disney, a born showman, was not about to waste such an opportunity. The threat of the unknown intruder inside their home would bring out each dwarf's distinctive response, and their frightened investigation of the house was a natural situation for slapstick sight gags. At a series of story conferences, Walt encouraged his writers and artists to expand this moment into a full-fledged sequence, contributing more than a few of the ideas himself. Here again, more story material was generated for the sequence than could possibly have been used. One interesting angle in the earliest conferences suggested a streak of cowardice in Doc, the nominal leader. An October 1934 treatment, couched in rhyming dialogue, had suggested these lines for Doc as the dwarfs approached the house: "Some scoundrel lurks within, I fear./Forward, boys. I'll guard the rear." (The other dwarfs promptly pushed him to the head of the line.) This was soon replaced by a simpler gag: Doc announced "Follow me!" while, in fact, pushing the other dwarfs ahead of him into the house. In the end these ideas were discarded from the film; but three years later, when the film was released, the latter gag did appear in the *Snow White* Sunday comic continuity and in at least one of the storybooks.

Several elaborate gags were suggested for the turtle, last seen falling down the stairs when the other animals bolted from the house. One gag called for the dwarfs, frightened by the sound of the birds, to dive into various hiding places, Doc in his haste dropping the candle he had been carrying. The candle was to land on the turtle's head. By now thoroughly frightened himself, the turtle was to make his way through the house, the candle on his head illuminating each of the dwarfs in turn as he passed them. When the turtle passed too near Doc's hiding place, Doc's tender anatomy was to be burned by the flame of his own candle. As an alternative to this, Walt suggested that the turtle might hide under a pair of pants, confounding Dopey when he saw the pants apparently moving by themselves. Still another variation called for two frogs to hide in a pair of shoes, so that

Opposite: Studio artists, asked to submit gags for the Spooks sequence, responded with a flood of suggestions. A few of them are pictured on this and the following pages.

AS RETURNING DWARFS DISCOVER HOUSE IS
OCCUPIED. DWARFS — FAN OUT TO ONE
SIDE OF DOC AND EXPOSE SLEEPY, WHO
HAS BEEN WALKING IN HIS SLEEP AT THE
END OF THE LINE. — SLEEPY SUDDENLY
WAKES UP. —EYES POP OPEN

[74] These gags were discussed at a story conference in May 1936. They were not used in the film, but—in what seems an impossible coincidence—two of the more distinctive ones did find their way into another film, produced by another studio, exactly concurrently with *Snow White*. Warner Bros.' *Sh! The Octopus*, starring Hugh Herbert and Allen Jenkins, is a very odd little comedy released in December 1937. The two comics, cast as police detectives, are lured to a spooky lighthouse where they do battle with a mysterious arch criminal known as The Octopus. Among the uncanny sights Herbert and Jenkins witness at the lighthouse are a turtle carrying a candle on its back, and two frogs that hop into a pair of shoes, so that the shoes appear to be walking by themselves! Adding to the suspiciously coincidental nature of these devices, examination of the Warner Bros. production file reveals that the turtle and frog gags were late additions to the script of *Sh! The Octopus* and were, in August 1937, essentially the last scenes shot for the picture. Special thanks to Sandra Joy Lee Aguilar and Taylor Nygaard of the Warner Bros. Archives (USC), and extra-special thanks to Scott MacQueen for bringing this very strange film to my attention in the first place.

[75] Art Babbitt challenged this line of dialogue because it seemed unrelated to any sort of superstition: "If you used something like 'I walked under a ladder today,' people would understand it, but I think 'M'corns hurt' pertains to weather." As a precaution Grumpy's dialogue was retaken in two variations, with both "felt it in my bones" and "felt it in my corns," but in the end his original dialogue remained in the picture.

Dopey would think the shoes were *walking* by themselves.[74]

In the finished sequence, all these ideas are discarded in favor of gags stemming from the dwarfs' own characteristics or personalities. The dwarfs, still singing "Heigh-Ho" as they near home, are frozen in their tracks by the signs of life in the cottage. Their individual reactions are animated by Bill Tytla, Fred Moore, and others. Grumpy pessimistically announces that there must be trouble ahead; his corns have been hurting all day.[75] Doc, attempting to lead the group, becomes flustered and garbles his words. Inside the house, the sight of a vase of goldenrod on the table appeals to Bashful's sentimental nature, and he impulsively thrusts the flowers in Sneezy's face—bringing on the first of Sneezy's colossal, gale-inducing sneezes. All the dwarfs react to the changes wrought in their home in droll lines

of dialogue that bear the stamp of Ted Sears: Bashful laments that "Our cobwebs are missing"; Happy observes that the dishes "ain't stole, they're hid in the cupboard."

This passage leads to Dopey's unwilling trip up the stairs, candle in hand, to apprehend the monster. Beginning with the dwarfs' solemn conference at the foot of the stairs and continuing through Dopey's sighting of what he thinks is the monster, this episode is notable as Art Babbitt's one extended piece of dwarf animation in the picture. Babbitt was currently best known at the studio for his animation of another loose-limbed, simple-minded creature: Goofy. Here he offers a memorable vignette of character animation in Dopey's jittery, terrified sneak up the stairs and into the dark bedroom, the candle (enhanced by more double-exposed flame effects) shaking violently in his hand. In

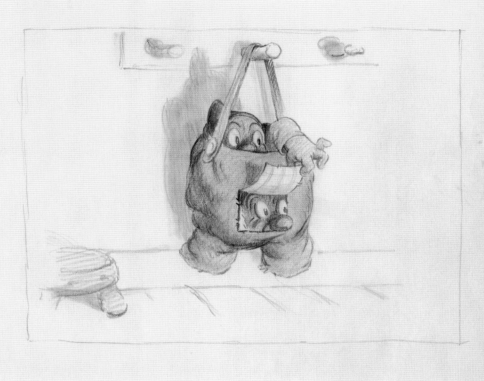

Dopey's state of suspense, that nondescript form stretching and yawning beneath the sheet is more than enough to send him flying in panic out the door and down the stairs.

Dopey's "Joe E. Brown yell" in the bedroom is the one remaining vestige of the earlier plan to make him a talking character. At one meeting, in fact, "There was much discussion as to whether Dopey should make some sound [outside the house] trying to describe what he saw, but the general comment was that it may be repulsive for him to try to talk, although we will make some takes of him trying to talk. It is okay for him to yell." Further yells were suggested for him as he ran outside, as well as other sounds including a horse's whinny, but by late April 1937 all these further vocal sounds had been abandoned.

The remainder of the sequence—the dwarfs' tumble down the stairs and headlong flight out the door; their assault on what they think is the monster and discovery that it's really only Dopey, entangled in a mass of pots and pans; Dopey's attempt to describe the awful creature he saw upstairs; and the group's grim determination to march back inside—was animated in its entirety by Fred Spencer. This passage, too, is notable as the film's first concentrated serving of slapstick comedy. If

1938 audiences were relieved to see Snow White meeting familiar Disney-style animals in the forest, they may have been further reassured by this sequence. It's true that we're in an enchanting fairy-tale world, but—as we see the dwarfs, armed with clubs, wildly clobbering what they think is their intruder—it's clear that traditional slapstick cartoon action still has a place in that world. As Perce Pearce had commented, "At times there is great violence done [Dopey], just like the Duck . . . whether he gets socked on the head or whatever it is, it never hurts him."

Above and opposite: Frightened by the birds' mischievous screeches, the Dwarfs scramble into unlikely hiding places. The gag on the opposite page, Happy hiding under the broom, was retained in the film; the others were not.

SNOW WHITE MEETS THE DWARFS *Picks and clubs at the ready, the dwarfs reenter the bedroom to kill the monster hiding in their beds. As they raise their weapons to attack, Doc yanks aside the blankets—to reveal the lovely, slumbering form of Snow White. The dwarfs are bewildered, but before they can gather their wits, Snow White awakens and an awkward introduction takes place. Having read the dwarfs' names on their beds, Snow White makes a game of guessing which dwarf is which. She immediately melts the hearts of all the dwarfs—except Grumpy, who declares that "all females is pizen" and belligerently demands that she leave at once. Snow White pleads to be allowed to stay and promises to keep house and cook for the dwarfs. Her promise of gooseberry pie seals the bargain: Grumpy is outvoted as the other six dwarfs eagerly welcome Snow White into their home. Suddenly she remembers the soup kettle boiling on the fire, and rushes downstairs to attend to it.*

Sequence 5A: Bedroom

During the early months of 1936, while Ham Luske and his unit were embarking on their first experimental animation of Snow White, the dwarfs were also being animated for the first time. Walt, having decided that Fred Moore and Bill Tytla would be the two principal animators of the dwarfs, assigned each of them a key sequence in the picture. Moore's assignment was sequence 5A, the Bedroom sequence.

Technically, of course, the Bedroom sequence is not our *introduction* to the dwarfs; they've already been on the screen for the better part of two reels. But if the audience is not meeting the dwarfs for the first time, Snow White is, and the initial meeting of the story's principal characters is a turning point in the plot. Walt's comments indicate how thoroughly he had analyzed this sequence and its place in the story: "What we have to keep in mind is that this is one of the longest straight dialogue sequences we have in the picture of the dwarfs. The rest of them have more action. We . . . get the whole thing solved as to whether she stays or not. This helps to establish [the dwarfs]. Grumpy, as a woman-hater, has never been established before."

The meeting of Snow White and the dwarfs had, indeed, been recognized from the very beginning as one of the most crucial sequences in the picture. As early as October 1934, when most of the feature's story existed only as a vague outline, writers were preparing specific treatments for this section. One thing was certain from the start: unlike the Grimm dwarfs or the Ames dwarfs, the Disney dwarfs would not unanimously welcome Snow White into their home. Grumpy, the lone holdout, would defiantly resist her intrusion. As story development continued, studio personnel were invited to contribute their own ideas. Ward Kimball received a bonus for suggesting one of the most fondly remembered gags in the sequence: as the dwarfs cautiously rise from their hiding place behind the beds to face Snow White, their knobby noses pop over the footboard, one by one, with a "ping" effect. Dialogue was recorded in February and March 1936, and by April Moore was at work on the animation. For the rest of the year, sequence 5A was known around the studio as "Fred's sequence."

As we watch the Bedroom sequence, then, we're seeing more than an entertaining episode in the story. In effect, this is a template: Moore is establishing a guide for the rest of the animators who will work on the dwarfs. From the moment the dwarfs first behold Snow White, the encounter brings out the essence of each one's personality: Doc's excited befuddlement, Bashful's ecstasy of embarrassment as he ties his beard in knots, Sleepy's dim comprehension of events around him, Dopey's mindless eagerness to participate in a world he'll never understand. To Snow White's "How do you do?" a scowling Grumpy responds with perhaps his best line in the feature: "How do ya do *what*?"[76] All are suffused with Moore's special quality, an endearing warmth that binds us to the characters.

Moore is, in fact, defining the dwarfs' personalities not only for the other animators' benefit, but also for himself. In periodic sweatbox sessions that continued for more than a year, well into the summer of 1937, Walt and Moore continued to review and refine the sequence together—changing an eye-blink here, retiming a line of dialogue there—transforming the raw diamond of Moore's animation into a polished jewel. The general effect of all the revisions was to deepen and strengthen the personalities of the dwarfs. For a scene of Grumpy furiously describing the Queen's magical powers ("She can even make herself invisible!"), Walt and Dave Hand asked Moore to reanimate Grumpy so as to make his paranoia even more intense, "almost as

[76] This dialogue exchange had been suggested as early as October 1934, but the punch line had originally been given to Sleepy instead of Grumpy.

though he had the Witch in his hands and was going to explode." It was during work on this sequence that the artists noticed a problem with Roy Atwell's dialogue for Doc. Atwell had been cast partly because of his specialty of mixed-up words, but on timing his dialogue recordings for the frame-by-frame needs of animation, the crew noticed that the mixups sounded deliberate. "It sounds like he was doing it on purpose instead of not helping it," Ken Anderson complained. Walt agreed: "It doesn't sound funny enough to me." In all likelihood, Atwell himself had never analyzed his performances with such intense scrutiny. He was called back to the studio, and the dialogue retaken.

As planned, Moore's animation in this sequence served as both a highlight of the finished picture and a training ground for the other animators. In June 1937, when Moore was asked to lead a "dwarf meeting" to teach the inbetweeners the fine points of animating the characters, all his examples were drawn from this sequence. As late as August 1937, when Les Clark was required to animate Sneezy sneezing in another part of the picture, Walt referred him to the model sneeze Moore had animated in the Bedroom sequence.

By the spring of 1937, the dwarfs were well enough established in "Fred's sequence" that other animators could begin to make their contributions. Now Ham Luske and his unit, having a full year's experience in animating Snow White, went to work on her scenes. Her warmth and innocence were a refreshing foil to the dumbfounded dwarfs' reactions: she projected, first, terror at the discovery of seven pairs of eyes watching her, then a little girl's delight at the prospect of making new friends. Here again, Luske prefaced his work by filming live action with Marjorie Belcher, devising creative business that would help to express the girl's naturalness: Snow White's teasing imitation of Grumpy's body stance, or her careless gesture as she shrugs off the Queen's threat: "But she doesn't know where I am."

Another animator emerged from Moore's shadow and came into his own on this sequence: Frank Thomas. The precocious Thomas had been working as Moore's assistant, and in fact had worked with Moore on some of his earliest scenes in the Bedroom sequence. Now Thomas graduated to the position of full animator, his place as Moore's assistant taken by Ollie Johnston.[77] Like his mentor, Thomas was made a dwarf animator and was likewise assigned to the Bedroom sequence. Moore was at work on all the dwarf animation beginning with the characters' first glimpse of Snow White; now Thomas was given the scenes of the dwarfs *before* that first glimpse, sneaking into the room with picks and clubs to kill what they thought was a monster. For their stealthy entrance, Thomas used an intriguing effect: he animated the group of dwarfs as a single mass, then

The gag suggested by Ward Kimball: one by one, the Dwarfs' noses pop over the footboard.

Overleaf: A cel setup depicting Snow White's awakening.

[77] In later years, of course, both Thomas and Johnston would become members of the fabled "Nine Old Men" at the Disney studio. Through hindsight, this gives the Bedroom sequence an added resonance today: two generations of master Disney animators have left their mark on it.

broke the mass down into individual figures. As the trembling dwarfs advance slowly on tiptoe, as they draw back in fear at the sound of Snow White's voice, they move, think, and react as one.

Some action that had been planned for the sequence was eliminated. At Grumpy's suggestion that the Queen "might be in this room right now," Dopey was to have more extended "looking" business, including looking under his own skirt, before peering under Happy's beard as he does in the finished film. At one meeting Walt commented that there had been discussion of a song about gooseberry pie. In the end all these extraneous ideas were cut, the better to concentrate on the main business of the sequence: the first meeting of the principal characters in the story.

By far the most notable of these cuts was an extended passage that has come to be known as "the Bedroom Fight." As the sequence was originally planned, Grumpy was (literally) not about to give up without a fight. Instead:

Overjoyed at Snow White's promise of a gooseberry pie, six of the dwarfs cheer as they welcome Snow White into their midst—but Grumpy remains adamant. Rebelling against Doc's authority, he insists that Snow White must leave. The argument between Grumpy and Doc becomes a shouting match, which escalates into a shoving match, and soon the two are brawling with each other as the others try to pull them apart. To stop the fisticuffs, Snow White volunteers to leave, but reminds the dwarfs of the dangers she will face in the woods at night. Grumpy is unmoved by her predicament, but in the end he is won over by a more selfish consideration: the gooseberry pie. Reluctantly he concedes that Snow White can stay—until the dwarfs get their pie. Snow White's effusive thanks are cut short when she remembers the soup kettle on the fire downstairs. With a shriek she runs out of the room, leaving the startled dwarfs to wonder what's the matter.

This is one of the famous discarded sections of *Snow White*, fully produced but then eliminated from the final cut. The fight between Grumpy and Doc had been planned from the start as part of the sequence, and Walt had definite ideas about how it should be staged. As always, he urged the story crew to take advantage of the unique opportunities before them—in this case Grumpy's prominent nose, which was just asking to be yanked and twisted. "We want to make use of the noses," he said at one meeting, "you can clunk anyone on the head." He had a practical suggestion for the sound effect: "Get the tweak of the nose to sound something like a nail being pulled out of a piece of wood. They have some kind of a contraption in the sound efx department of a round thing in wood." Other planned business included a sort of inside joke: as Doc squared off for his fight with Grumpy he assumed two fighting poses, one reminiscent of John L. Sullivan, the other a hopping action, one foot extended, brandishing one fist while swinging the other at his side. This was recognized by the animators, as it would have been by many audiences, as Donald Duck's traditional fighting stance, introduced by animator Dick Lundy in *Orphans' Benefit* (1934).

The story crew worked over the fight as carefully as they did the rest of the Bedroom sequence; the music and dialogue were written and recorded; Fred Moore labored for months over the animation; the cels were inked and painted. As late as September 1937, it was still considered part of the sequence. So why was it cut? None of the surviving evidence answers that question directly, but there are some clues. At a staff screening of rough *Snow White* reels in March 1937, this part of the sequence was received uneasily by some viewers. Grim Natwick criticized the dwarfs' fighting action: "I expected to see them roll over and over in a lot of fast stuff. It seems too planned, they never really get to fighting . . . All I'm conscious of is that they grab each other's nose." More striking, however, was the general reaction to Snow White, who had been animated in this section by Natwick himself. As depicted in this sequence, Snow White interrupted the dwarfs' fight by petulantly snapping, "Don't let me break up your happy home, I'll go," then proceeded to whine: "I'm not afraid of the dark woods at night—and the goblins." This self-consciously manipulative ploy was jarringly at odds with the character who had seemed a happy little girl a few moments before. At the March screening, Charles Philippi tried to articulate his objections: "Her line 'I don't want to break up your happy home' is

SW: "NO – NO! SHE'LL NEVER FIND ME HERE!" ⑰

SW: "YOU MEAN, YOU WANT ME — ?"
GRUMPY: "WE DIDN'T SAY SO!"

out of line too much . . . I didn't feel it was Snow White all during that." Perce Pearce had already noted at least one similar objection: "Mary made this comment on Snow White's manner of walking out on the dwarfs; she said it impressed her that Snow White had a snippy attitude. If that is so, we have failed to get our point across." Had this dialogue remained in the picture, it would have been the film's most glaringly obvious contrast between the little-girl and young-woman sides of Snow White's character.

The fight remained in the sequence for the time being, but during the summer months Walt began chipping away at it, eliminating short sections of footage. One casualty of this editorial process was what had been planned as the closing scene in the sequence. When Snow White remembered her bubbling soup kettle, then shrieked and bolted from the room, the startled dwarfs were to dive for cover. As planned, the sequence would end as they cautiously emerged from their hiding places, Grumpy declaring: "I knew it—she's crazy!" This last scene was animated by Moore and was in the picture as late as June 1937, but it was gone by the time the sequence reached the ink and paint department.

And then, sometime during the autumn, the entire Bedroom Fight—comprising more than a third of the overall sequence 5A footage—was dropped from the picture. The finished sequence cuts directly from Snow White's promise of gooseberry pie and the dwarfs' group cheer "Hooray! She stays!" to the soup kettle in

the fireplace and Snow White's flight down the stairs to retrieve it. To the viewer who knows the missing material, the raw edges of the cut are fairly obvious; in the finished picture we can even see Grumpy's anticipation to the line of dialogue—"Wait a minute, ya crazy fools!"—that he never gets to say. But in the decades since 1938, countless viewers, *not* knowing of the missing scenes, have followed the visual logic of the remaining scenes—the cheering dwarfs, the bubbling soup kettle, Snow White's dash down the stairs—without difficulty. And if we lose an entertaining episode in the story, we gain a streamlined continuity and a Snow White who remains a more consistent character, without the odd lapse that had been suggested for her here.[78]

Early story sketches for the bedroom sequence, picturing Snow White as a blonde.

[78] In 1987, on the occasion of the film's 50th anniversary, the Disney studio's Dave Pacheco rephotographed the Bedroom Fight from the cleanup pencil drawings (since few of the inked and painted cels had been retained). The resulting reconstruction was later included on the *Snow White* laserdisc and DVD releases. By the time of this reconstruction, some of Fred Moore's scenes, intended as closeups, had been reframed as medium shots instead. One of these was scene 38BB, originally planned as a closeup of Grumpy during his argument with Doc. Since the preceding and following scenes were also medium shots, this had the effect of causing Doc to vanish from the scene and suddenly pop back in again.

LET ME SEE YOUR HANDS! *The dwarfs, venturing out of the bedroom, sniff the tempting aroma of soup and come stampeding down the stairs, ready to dig into a delicious meal. Snow White announces that they'll just have time to wash, a word that stops them in their tracks. Wash? Seeing that the dwarfs are unfamiliar with this concept, Snow White asks to see their hands, which are, indeed, badly in need of washing. She commands the dwarfs to march outside and wash their hands, and six of them willingly obey—but Grumpy, his worst suspicions of this female intruder confirmed, defiantly refuses to cooperate.*

Sequence 5B: Snow White tells Dwarfs to wash

In this sequence another vein of comedy springs from the newly established characters of the dwarfs. Ordered to wash their hands for supper, they're not so much defiant (always with the exception of Grumpy) as mystified. Exchanging baffled looks, they try to fathom the reason for this strange request: "Why wash?" "What fer? We ain't goin' nowhere!" "'Tain't New Year's!" It's an appealing and well-written situation, tailor-made for another vivid morsel of character animation, and this time Frank Thomas, having proved himself on the previous sequence, was handed the plum assignment. With the exception of some fast action scenes by Fred Spencer and some solo Grumpy scenes by Bill Tytla, all the dwarf animation in this short sequence was Thomas's work.

It's clear that he enjoyed the challenge. *Snow White* stands poised at a critical juncture in Disney history: the great artists who had established the principles of Disney animation—Moore, Tytla, Ham Luske, Norm Ferguson, and a few others—dominate the film, and it's a rich banquet of some of their best work. But another group waits impatiently in the wings, the group that will soon displace those pioneers—the group that will become known in later years as the "Nine Old Men"— and *Snow White* is liberally seasoned with their scenes too. Thomas was one of the strongest presences in that second group, and sequence 5B was his first extended opportunity to show what he could do. He seems eager to seize the opportunity. His dwarfs are almost indistinguishable from those of Fred Moore, and display much of the same charm and appeal—especially in their beaming smiles when they think they've pleased Snow White, and their sudden crestfallen countenances when

they understand otherwise. At the same time, Thomas seems eager to add his own unique, quirky touches, such as Doc's nervous half-smile as he proffers his hands for Snow White's inspection. And, of course, some of the psychological nuances of these scenes had been determined in story conferences, as in Walt's observation that "Doc would sort of slip into the word RECENTLY—then beam with surprise after saying it."

(As if to underscore the fact that Thomas had trained under Moore and not Tytla, he gets one closeup of Tytla's signature character, Grumpy. This is scene 6A, Grumpy disgustedly saying "Heh! I knew they was a catch to it!" It's a good scene, but Grumpy's half-hearted gesture of throwing down his spoon is a far cry from the seething rage he exhibits in Tytla's own scenes a couple of minutes later.)

As for Snow White, her role in this sequence calls for her more mature side. Here she's the little mother, alternately instructing, cajoling, and gently scolding her charges. It's not surprising, therefore, that her scenes were assigned to Grim Natwick. But Ham Luske continued to supervise and review Natwick's scenes, and in at least one case he reworked Natwick's drawings. The result is the one instance in the picture in which both Natwick's and Luske's conceptions of Snow White were combined in a single scene. When the young-woman Snow White leans over behind Grumpy, teasing him with "What's the matter? Cat got your tongue?" Grumpy whirls and furiously sticks out his tongue at her—and as she draws back in surprise, she's suddenly the wide-eyed little girl again. Then, as Grumpy turns on his heel and stomps away, she reverts to her young-woman persona. It's a quicksilver moment, and one that most viewers miss, their attention riveted on Tytla's bold animation of Grumpy.

As six of the dwarfs exit the house to carry out Snow White's request, Dopey, at the rear of the line, performs his little hitch step to get in step with the others. This, as we've seen, was claimed as a key scene in establishing Dopey's hitch step, although the action had already been introduced elsewhere. In any case, the hitching action does appear to good effect in this scene. Certainly Walt enjoyed it here, and even asked Thomas to embellish it: "Everything is okay up to the time Dopey takes a

hitch—have Dopey at this point take a double hitch, then near the end of the scene have him take another double hitch, keeping his head facing in front of him during this whole scene." Thomas complied, and this is the action that appears in the finished film.

Grumpy's anger in this Frank Thomas scene is compounded soon afterward in Bill Tytla's animation.

Overleaf: The Dwarfs caught off guard by Snow White's strange request.

THE DWARFS WASH FOR SUPPER *Outside the house, the dwarfs, except Grumpy, obediently gather around the tub to wash their hands for dinner. To guide his companions through this unfamiliar ritual, Doc leads them in song. Grumpy, watching the others in disgust, can scarcely contain his scorn. "I'd like to see anybody make* me *wash, if I didn't wanta!" he declares. This challenge cannot go unanswered; the other six dwarfs surround Grumpy, seize him, and plunge him bodily into the tub, clothes and all. Struggling mightily, the furious Grumpy is vigorously dunked, lathered, and scrubbed by the others. Dopey, while fetching an extra bar of soap, swallows it and begins to hiccup, filling the air with soap bubbles. When Snow White calls that dinner is ready, six of the dwarfs drop everything and race for the door, leaving Grumpy in the tub, still spluttering with rage.*

Sequence 6A: Dwarfs at tub washing

This was the third of the three key sequences with which, in the spring of 1936, the first experimental animation of *Snow White* began. As the Bedroom sequence was assigned to Fred Moore, so the Washing sequence was entrusted to the other leading dwarf animator, Bill Tytla. As sequence 5A was "Fred's sequence," so 6A became "Bill's sequence." And because the story of sequence 5A was not quite finalized, Tytla went to work on 6A before Moore's assignment was ready. In the Washing sequence, then, the dwarfs came to life on the screen for the first time.

The idea behind the Washing sequence derives not from the Brothers Grimm, but from Winthrop Ames. Ames's 1912 stage production of *Snow White* had introduced one scene of the dwarfs' washing ritual, and another in which they forcibly washed the dirtiest of their number. Both of these scenes were retained in the 1916 Paramount film, which young Walt saw in Kansas City, and the earliest Disney *Snow White* story notes indicate that he intended to return to the washing idea in his own film.[79] By November 1935 he had assigned Earl Hurd to develop this part of the story, but here, by rooting the washing action in the personalities of the dwarfs, Walt completely transformed the nature of the scene. At a story conference in 1935, he succinctly stated the difference: "dwarfs are driven by Grumpy's sarcasm to douse him in the tub." The washing action in Ames's play had been merely a quaint, whimsical bit of

business, lasting only a few minutes. Here it was to be grounded in the personalities of the individual dwarfs: their initial mystification, as if they'd never seen soap and water before; their willingness to take a chance on this odd custom if it would make Snow White happy; Grumpy's defiant refusal to wash for her or anyone else; the determination of the others to punish his rebellion. As a result, the washing action became a key sequence and a hilariously memorable part of the picture.

The Ames dwarfs had dunked Quee in their water barrel to the accompaniment of rhyming dialogue: "Here's the pump to *douse* him with!/Here are suds to *souse* him with!" and so on. For the Disney film, Larry Morey and Frank Churchill composed a song for Doc to sing as he led the other dwarfs through the alien procedure of washing themselves. The song's chorus ended in a loud blubbering sound that the dwarfs made as they rubbed their faces with water, and the story team tried to find a way to refer to this noise or describe it in written transcripts. At a story meeting in December 1935, Walt spoke of Doc "joining the others in the 'blub-lub-ubub'." By the spring of 1936, the onomatopoeic term "bluddle-uddle" had been coined. Throughout the rest of production, this expression was used in the studio as a technical term: "2' 4 frames blank film between end of Doc's bluddle uddle [and] start of quartette," remarked a sound technician's recording notes, and Walt instructed an effects animator to "Have bubbles come up from Dopey's bluddle-uddle." Morey's and Churchill's song was officially titled "Bluddle-Uddle-Um-Dum (The Dwarfs' Washing Song)."

Just as Fred Moore was defining the dwarfs by his work on the Bedroom sequence, so Bill Tytla worked to define them as they gathered around the washing tub in this sequence. As he explained to an action analysis class: "The [dwarfs'] hands are on the side of the tub. The only thing you can rely on is their reaction, not their mannerisms—only how they would react to a sentence—how fast they would do it. This is merely in the timing. Each one has his own way of reacting at a different time. This handling gave the scene a soft kind of feeling and not a mechanical one as if a company of infantry were present and on the order, 'Eyes right' all eyes went right." The subtly droll humor of the

[79] The "Manuscript" of August 1934 had suggested that "Awful" would be tossed into the well by the other dwarfs. At a story conference two months later, Walt led a discussion of a washing scene, including such details as "action of catching soap" and "one blindly reaching for a towel."

preceding sequence continues in this one, as each dwarf, utterly bewildered at the prospect of washing, reacts in his own way. "Will our whiskers shrink?" drawls Sleepy (in a curiously unintelligible reading of the line by Pinto Colvig), while a blushing Bashful coyly inquires: "Do you have to wash where it doesn't show?" Blustering, officious Doc demonstrates his style of leadership: as he talks the five obedient dwarfs through the ritual of washing, reassuring them that "'tain't no disgrace," he nearly succeeds in never getting wet himself. Water approaches Doc only twice in the course of the song, once when Happy abruptly shakes his head and sends forth a spray of water from his beard—to Doc's extreme irritation.

But the real star of the sequence, and Tytla's overriding triumph as a character animator, is unquestionably Grumpy. Anticipating the challenges and the opportunities of animating Grumpy in this sequence, Tytla took the initiative late in 1935 by filming live-action reference footage. Pinto Colvig, the voice of Grumpy, performed Grumpy's action in the opening of the sequence—furiously stomping out of the house and hoisting himself onto a barrel, from which he delivers his diatribes—under Tytla's and Walt's co-direction. When Tytla studied this footage and then incorporated Colvig's mannerisms into his animation, the results were startling. "There are very definite attitudes and positions in what he does," Tytla later explained. "Basically there is a lot of good stuff in Pinto's actions, but we have to go further by accenting it stronger. In order to accent, you don't have to [copy] what he did." By exaggerating and expanding on the basis of live action, Tytla

Animation pioneer Earl Hurd was working in the Disney story department by the mid-1930s. He suggested this dialogue exchange for the Washing sequence.

A rough layout sketch picturing Grumpy's path of action as he leaves the house. The finished scene depicts the same action from a different angle.

had vividly captured the essence of Grumpy's character. The effectiveness of his results led to much more extensive live-action filming by the other dwarf animators.

But Tytla was just getting started. As Michael Barrier has written: "Tytla had completely mastered the physical demands of his 'role' . . . but rather than stop there, he had used that mastery to make Grumpy not just physically but emotionally three-dimensional." Seething with resentment, belligerently challenging everyone and everything in his path, Grumpy emerged in this sequence as a vividly forceful personality, setting the tone for all the other animators' handling of the character. Some of the subtlety of Tytla's animation can perhaps be appreciated only by slowing down the film; as Grumpy mocks the other dwarfs' bluddle-uddles and their efforts to prettify themselves, there is embedded in his actions a deep vein of comedy that defies a casual viewing. In the end, of course, as the furiously struggling Grumpy is thrust under water by the other dwarfs, he emits a strangled, livid bluddle-uddle of his own—right on the beat.

Like the Bedroom sequence, the Washing sequence was subject to periodic reworking during 1936 as the design of the dwarfs changed. Walt was understandably concerned about maintaining a consistent appearance of the characters throughout the picture. After his first sweatbox viewing of rough animation from the two sequences, he wrote to Moore and Tytla: "Your characters of Grumpy should match—it is very important that they do. You two should get together and figure on making the same Grumpy." Grumpy's design had always featured a large nose, but as production went on Walt began to feel that perhaps Tytla was making Grumpy's nose *too* prominent. Scene after scene, otherwise approved as to the action and personality of the character, was recalled so that Tytla could reduce the size of Grumpy's nose.

Because the story for the Bedroom sequence was not quite ready for Fred Moore's animation in March 1936, he was initially put to work alongside Tytla on the Washing sequence. Moore was assigned the scenes of *his* signature character, Dopey, vainly trying to get his hands on the slippery soap and then accidentally

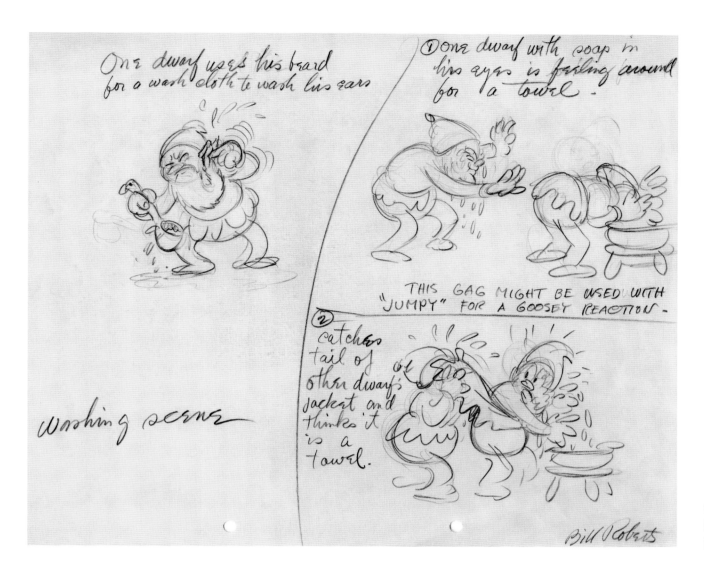

More washing gags, suggested by animator/director Bill Roberts.

swallowing it.[80] When Moore redesigned Dopey later in 1936, phasing out some of his mutant-imp quality in favor of a more babyish look, the scenes were reanimated—but, oddly, not by Moore. This was one of the Dopey passages reassigned to Fred Spencer. It's not immediately clear why (unless it was simply to relieve some of Moore's workload); in fact, Spencer's Dopey scenes retain some elements that had appeared in Moore's original animation. In March 1936, one of Dopey's facial features had been a wide, reckless grin. As Moore refined the character, his mouth became smaller, with chubby cheeks and a protruding lower lip. Tytla, in reworking his own Dopey scenes, followed Moore's lead and reduced Dopey's mouth—but in Spencer's animation in the finished film, Dopey retains something of that same wide-mouthed grin.

As in other sequences, Walt continued to improvise new business for the characters. In one continuity, Dopey, after washing his face, was to grope blindly for a towel and dry his face on Bashful's shirttail instead. Watching rough animation in sweatbox in June 1936, Walt suddenly suggested: "It would be funny to have one guy shake his head to get water out of his ears and have a sound of water moving around [inside his head] . . . He should hit head first and then shake and hear splash and gurgle sound." No sooner said than done. Dopey was clearly the ideal dwarf for a gag like this, and before the end of the sweatbox session, new head-sloshing action was being planned for Dopey. This meant Dopey must be replaced in the other scene: now it was Sneezy who pulled Bashful's shirttail out to serve as a towel, while Sleepy, approaching from the other direction, made similar use of Bashful's beard. Pulled in two directions at once by the other dwarfs, Bashful was suspended between them. "Have Bashful open his eyes like 'what the hell'," Walt told Tytla. "While he is suspended in the air, let his legs dangle a little bit . . ." Conversely, Walt also eliminated some gags that had originally been planned for the sequence. The story crew had suggested that, after Grumpy had been deposited in the tub, Sneezy might sneeze, causing a mighty splash that drenched *all* the dwarfs. With all the other gags in the sequence this seemed unnecessary, and Walt vetoed the idea.

[80] Some of Moore's original cleanup drawings from this sequence, as drawn in spring 1936, are reproduced in Thomas and Johnston, *Disney Animation*, p. 127.

In addition to establishing a precedent for the character animators, the Washing sequence became an important test case for the effects animators. The effects animation department had been formed to animate water, fire, smoke, ripples, and other non-character movement in the studio's cartoons; many character animators regarded such work as drudgery, while other artists came to specialize in it. The Washing sequence, of course, featured plenty of water, and the effects animators met periodically with Tytla's assistant, Bill Shull, to ensure that their water effects were perfectly coordinated with his character movement. The effects department's notes show vividly the meticulous care taken with *Snow White:* when Doc accidentally sprinkled a few drops of water near his own face, the effects department was directed "to clean up the water and drops in the scene so they will not look like the stock, cartoon, tear-shaped drops, but will be handled more realistically, as in *The Old Mill.*" Walt, viewing rough animation of Grumpy surfacing in the tub, instructed effects animator Cornett Wood: "Don't have so many suds on Grumpy's face when you cut to this scene—amount of suds should tie in with the amount of suds on Grumpy's face in previous scene. Little bubbles could be coming up from the mass on Grumpy's face and a little movement of suds running down." Further: "Have a bigger splash when Grumpy is doused in the tub, and instead of the water running down the side of the tub, have it drop off the edge."

Another case of attention to detail surfaced at a layout meeting in December 1936. Layout artist Tom Codrick, setting up the interior scene in which Snow White called the dwarfs to supper, found himself confounded by the geography of the house. If Snow White, standing by the fireplace, called in the direction the dwarfs had gone—that is, in the direction that was geographically correct—the screen continuity looked wrong. "If she called in the direction facing the dwarfs," Codrick explained, "it would give the impression that she was calling into the room instead of towards the back door. The argument was whether it was bad to have her call in the [screen] direction of the dwarfs, which would be wrong as to direction of setup, or whether correct with the setup, and have her facing in

the same direction as the dwarfs face in the next scene." A long debate ensued from this seemingly minor problem. In the end, the decision was made to "cheat" the background in favor of a continuity logic that *looks* correct on the screen.

This was one of the sequences in which Sleepy's fly was briefly allowed to steal the show. Here Riley Thomson animated a single closeup of the fly, perched on a bar of soap, busily scrubbing himself and performing a tiny bluddle-uddle of his own. Apart from this scene, Fred Spencer's scenes of Dopey with the soap, and Grim Natwick's single scene of Snow White calling the dwarfs to supper—and the important water and soap action contributed by the effects crew—the entire Washing sequence was animated by Bill Tytla. Like the Bedroom sequence, it stands as an extended tour de force by a master animator.

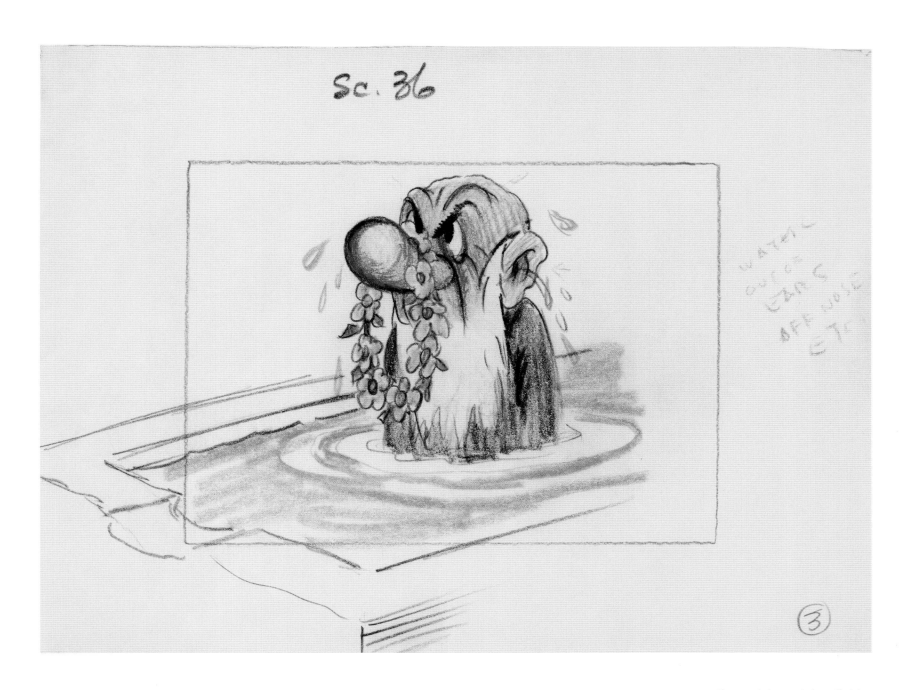

Grumpy's ignominious finish
in the tub.

THE SOUP SEQUENCE *Cut from the film: The dwarfs come stampeding in the door, crowd around the table, and begin slurping the soup Snow White has prepared for them. Even Grumpy, still fuming over his forced washing, enters the room and surreptitiously tastes the soup, then joins in the feeding frenzy. Snow White, alarmed at the dwarfs' crude manners, tries to teach them proper dining etiquette, a lesson that is only partly successful. The dwarfs continue to slurp noisily, and Dopey, in his enthusiasm, accidentally swallows his spoon. The other dwarfs' attempts to extract the spoon are unsuccessful until, finally, a well-aimed kick from Happy ejects both the spoon and the soap that Dopey has swallowed. Launched from Dopey's mouth, the two foreign objects sail across the room and hit the opposite wall, the handle of the spoon spearing the soap in place.*

Cut from the film

Sequence 6B: Soup

Of all the sequences planned for *Snow White* and then eliminated from the final cut, the "Soup Sequence" is easily the most famous (partly because of its television showing in 1956; see page 278). It has become a classic example of Walt's overarching vision: his willingness to sacrifice a single section, entertaining as it was, for the good of the film's overall continuity.

The sequence had been planned as part of the film almost from the beginning. Walt's "Skeleton Continuity," dictated in December 1934, had described the "Soup Symphony," complete with Dopey swallowing his spoon and "Funny business of the gang trying to get the spoon out of Dopey's throat." By February 1936, experimental soup-slurping sound effects were being recorded. Later publicity stories, at the time of the film's release, would claim that the sound-effects men had had to "drink countless thick malted milks . . . perfect sound effects were obtained by recording the process of noisily drinking a thick malt through a straw. None of the sound effects crew has any taste left for a malted milk." In reality their efforts were far more extensive than that and included such experiments as recording a vibraharp and a marimba, then slowing the tracks down and playing them backward.

Like other sequences, the Soup sequence appealed to Walt as a vehicle for rich personality animation of the dwarfs. In story conferences he made it clear that he particularly enjoyed the idea of the dwarfs missing the point of Snow White's etiquette lesson. She used a little

Opposite: The Dwarfs, trying conscientiously to follow Snow White's instructions, manage to miss the point anyway.

rhyme to help them remember the proper way to hold their spoons: "Spoon in the hand/Bending the wrist/Into the bowl/And out with a twist." The dwarfs repeated her words, imitated her actions, demonstrated perfect form in holding their eating utensils—and then continued to slurp their soup as loudly as before. Walt's comments at some of the story meetings indicate that he meant the label "Soup Symphony" literally: the dwarfs' eating noises were to assume a musical form (hence the use of "disguised" musical instruments for the slurping effects). "Make the sounds rhythmic . . . Work also for different registers in soup sounds . . . Pick up first with a vamp, then a melody . . . Like a waltz rhythm with prominent bass . . . Must be funny, but pleasant to listen to . . . Anything that will create an unconscious feeling that they are doing a musical symphony." This concept never quite materialized; when Frank Churchill and Larry Morey unveiled the song "Music in Your Soup" in December 1936, it was a more conventional number like their washing song. The slurping effects were still heard in rhythm, but were used mainly to underscore the visual gags: Doc using his bread as a sponge to squirt soup into his mouth, Sneezy using two spoons at once like paddle wheels.

Now that the dwarfs' personalities were firmly established, there was some debate over which dwarf would deliver the kick to Dopey's backside. Doc and Grumpy were two strong candidates, but Walt resisted the idea of using Grumpy: "The kick that they give Dopey isn't a kick that hurts." Ultimately the job was given to Happy. Similarly, it had first been assumed that Doc, the leader, would sing "Music in Your Soup"—but Roy Atwell, the voice of Doc, was not an accomplished singer. (The "Washing Song" had deliberately been designed so he could *talk* the lyrics.) When the suggestion was made that the soup song, too, might be given to Happy, Walt agreed: "Yes, Harlan sings better." This in turn led to further debate. At another story meeting three weeks later (at which Walt was not present), Bill Tytla and his assistant Bill Shull mounted a long and passionate argument for giving the soup song back to Doc. Perce Pearce vigorously defended Happy's right to the song: "If you see [Doc] as a leader all the time you get too much of one character . . . It is entirely in

A story sketch depicting a rare starring moment for Happy, leading the singing of "Music in Your Soup."

character for Happy to be leading the song." Finally Fred Moore spoke up: "Perce, tell the other reason why Happy is leading the singing: that Walt wanted Happy there." There was no countering *that* argument, and Happy remained the singer of choice.

Another objection on the grounds of personality was raised by Wilfred Jackson. Why, he asked, was Grumpy sneaking into the room and furtively tasting the soup? Jackson argued that it would be more in character for Grumpy to stomp angrily into the room, especially after his forced washing outside. Pearce was nonplussed: "I was trying to think back on this, and it has never been questioned . . . You bring this point up, and it is definitely a question there." Walt later explained that Grumpy's appetite got the better of his temper in these scenes: "I think the way Grumpy peeks around the door

and sneaks over to the table with a grouchy look on him, that right away you would recognize the Grumpy character—it would be a laugh."

Ward Kimball, just emerging from the ranks of junior animators into what would become a stellar Disney career, was assigned most of the dwarf animation in this sequence. In latter-day Disney lore, the Soup sequence has been inextricably linked with Kimball's name as if he had animated it singlehanded. In truth, it may be worth pointing out that of the eight animators who worked on the sequence, Kimball was one of the *last* assigned to it. As late as mid-February 1937, Walt was considering dividing the Dopey animation in this sequence (including the key scene in which Dopey swallows the spoon) between Bill Roberts and Art Babbitt. In the end, Roberts did animate the closing

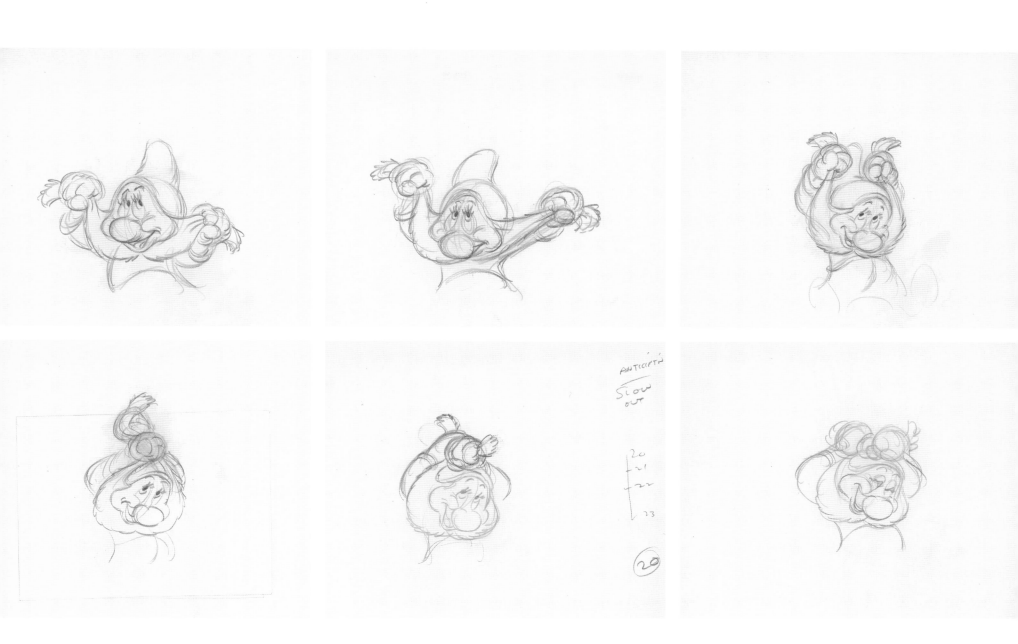

episode of the dwarfs manhandling Dopey, while Tytla was given all the Grumpy closeups. Other snippets of dwarf animation were assigned to Fred Spencer, Marvin Woodward, Dick Lundy, and Les Clark, and Grim Natwick was given all of Snow White's scenes.

But the majority of the dwarf animation—Happy singing, dwarfs eating, Dopey swallowing his spoon—was Kimball's work, and it was a traumatic blow to him when the sequence was cut from the film. In later years he never tired of telling the story: "Everybody thought it was a great sequence, Walt thought it was good—it was even cleaned up, I think, and in the picture. But the picture was running very long, almost two hours . . . And when Walt sat and looked at the picture every day, and saw it over and over, and really had to cut something out, he decided that the soup sequence had to go . . . He felt the soup sequence, as funny as it was, with all the different characteristic ways the dwarfs would slurp up their soup, stalled the story, and he wanted to

get on with it. And I agreed with him, really, at the time, even though there were tears in my eyes for all that work I had done."

The cutting of the Soup sequence from *Snow White* remains an object lesson in story construction. If we lose an isolated gem of character animation, we gain a more pleasing overall contour of the story. Along with Kimball's animation, the casualties of this cut are Happy's starring moments—his chance to stand out from the rest of the dwarfs—and a striking transitional device to what would have been the next sequence, the Queen at her mirror. As planned, the Soup sequence would have ended with the comic scene of the spoon handle spearing the soap against the wall, then dissolved into a similar scene with a more sinister import: a closeup of the clasp on the Queen's box—with a dagger symbolically thrust through the heart of Snow White.

In Ward Kimball's animation drawings, Bashful, ever fastidious, ties his whiskers above his head to keep them out of his soup.

Believing that the Huntsman has disposed of Snow White, the Queen returns in triumph to her magic mirror—only to learn the truth: the Huntsman has deceived her. She holds in her hands the heart of a pig, and Snow White, her hated rival, still lives. The furious Queen determines to find Snow White and kill the girl herself this time. Descending the steps to her dungeon laboratory, she concocts a potion that will effect her disguise. As her pet raven watches in terror, the coldly beautiful Queen undergoes a violent transformation, emerging as a horrific witch. Then, delighted with the disguise, she consults her library for a suitable poison to destroy Snow White.

Sequence 7A: Queen leaves mirror, prepares disguise

In this dramatic sequence, the Disney *Snow White* reconciles two variant strains of tradition. In the Grimms' tale, the Queen, armed with magical powers, had disguised herself (several times) as a peddler in order to make her attempts on Snow White's life. The Ames play and the Paramount film had introduced a new character, a witch, who supplied the magic behind the Queen's misdeeds. Here the Disney film returns to the Grimms' original concept: the Queen works alone and magically disguises herself—but her disguise *is* that of a witch; and the Witch and her transformation are far more terrifying than anything Ames had envisioned.

Even as part of the mammoth undertaking that *Snow White* represented, the writing and production of this sequence were unusually difficult. The time devoted to story development rivaled that of sequence 2A, Snow White and the Prince in the garden. As late as autumn 1936 the idea of the furious Queen smashing the mirror was still under consideration, and one possible version would have shown her transformed into a hag *because* she had broken the mirror, not by her own choice.[81] Walt himself entertained this idea for a time, but by February 1937 he had abandoned it because it weakened the character of the Queen. If she was to be shown killing Snow White, then exulting, "Now I'll be fairest in the land," the transformation must be under *her* control, not the mirror's.[82] Instead Walt became fascinated with the idea of the Queen in her secret laboratory, crafting her revenge. "I'd like to see her come down those steps into this place and slam the door," he said at one meeting. "You could have the raven asleep. It knocks him off his perch, and maybe knocks a couple of bottles down.

She's madder than hell. She's been tricked . . . It gives you a chance for this queen—she's not the hag here, but the Queen—to be more active, to make her actions more forceful. She slams books and everything around."

The dark, Gothic atmosphere of the laboratory was a departure for the Disney studio, and some of the visual ideas for this sequence were pretested in a remarkable Mickey Mouse short. *The Worm Turns*, released early in 1937, concerns a "Courage Builder" formula that Mickey concocts in his home lab and its effects when he tries it out on several animals, including his dog Pluto. Mickey's laboratory, shown at the beginning of the short, is remarkably similar to the Queen's laboratory: gloomy atmosphere, ominous shadows, suspicious liquids bubbling in retorts. Mixing his ingredients, Mickey consults a musty book of "Ancient Formulae," propped up on a human skull, the pages looking like aged parchment. When the formula is complete, the brooding Old World atmosphere instantly vanishes, and we're back in a contemporary American suburban neighborhood. This sequence was used to test not only the *look* of the Queen's lair, but also the sound effects of her bubbling potions—and Walt was dissatisfied with the results. "Get them all working together," he said of the *Snow White* sequence, "the sobs and everything, like a lot of people chattering. I believe the stuff cooking could look very interesting. It didn't work out in this thing [*The Worm Turns*] because I don't think it was featured right where the stuff coughed and sputtered."

Even after the basic direction of the sequence was determined, Walt and his writers fussed over the dialogue with meticulous, painstaking care. Over a period of months every word of dialogue was polished and weighed for maximum clarity, economy, and poetry. At one meeting in March 1937, a debate over the Queen's choice of ingredients led Bill Cottrell to consult *Macbeth* to see what ingredients Shakespeare's witches had used. The following month, rather late in the process, the line "A special sort of death for one so fair" was suggested for the Witch, and Walt took to it immediately, relishing the sound of the words. At the same time, the concept and layout artists were devising the details of an appropriately fantastic setting for the Queen's dark deeds. Hugh Hennesy, the principal layout artist for this

[81] A variation on this idea was that the mirror, like Dorian Gray's portrait, concealed the Queen's true nature. "Would he tantalize her with thoughts of what she would look like?" asked Walt at one meeting. "Finally pulling off his mask."

[82] Walt made this point in answer to an objection from Bill Cottrell at a meeting in February 1937. A month later Ham Luske was still grumbling: "You have lost your biggest punch when you don't break the Mirror."

sequence, pointed out in May 1937 that some of the background paintings suggested a subterranean setting—and yet the Queen was seen standing at a window, and in a later sequence exited downward to reach her boat, which meant that the laboratory must still be above water level.

The finished sequence reflects this extra care on the screen. It begins by establishing atmosphere: two beautiful multiplane shots, painted by Sam Armstrong, depict the castle at night. The camera draws nearer, and we see that the entire castle is dark save for one lighted window, revealing the obsessive, driven soul inside. (As a distant shot of the tower dissolves into a closer view, the position of the window in one scene overlaps with the same window in the next—a technical device that was praised when Orson Welles borrowed it in *Citizen Kane* a few years later.)[83]

Inside the Queen approaches her mirror with a sense of self-satisfaction: "Who *now* is the fairest one of all?" Her triumph is short-lived; the mirror—not emotionally, as some outlines had suggested, but cold and impassive as ever—reveals that Snow White is still alive, that she is in the cottage of the Seven Dwarfs, and that the Queen's box contains only the heart of a pig. Like the Queen's

earlier exchange with the mirror, this is a far cry from the genial banter of Winthrop Ames's play, softened for juvenile audiences. This encounter is, rather, in deadly earnest and draws far more heavily on the rich visual tradition of classic 1930s horror films. But it's nothing compared to what is coming next.

A new hand is evident in the Queen's animation in this sequence. Bob Stokes, a highly talented but today somewhat forgotten animator, joins Art Babbitt in animating the Queen—and, in fact, dominates the Queen's scenes in this sequence. Stokes was a former Chouinard instructor, and his singular drawing ability had quickly won him a place in the studio's animation hierarchy. Here he contributed all of the Queen's animation in the upper chamber, then alternated with Babbitt in the laboratory scenes, *and* worked over some of Babbitt's drawings even in those scenes. In Stokes's passage the Queen faces the camera head-on—the most difficult kind of animation for a character of this kind—and plays an extended scene with arrogant confidence, seeming slightly more mature than Babbitt's Queen at the same angle.

The most difficult part of this sequence, both in planning and in execution, was the Queen's transformation into a witch, described by Walt on several occasions as "a

A Bob Stokes cleanup drawing of the Queen, showing his close attention to detail.

Overleaf: In this cel setup, the Queen enters her secret laboratory.

[83] These two scenes, AA1 and AA1X, were added after the Soup sequence was cut. We've noted the transitional device that had been planned: the bar of soap, speared against the wall of the dwarfs' cottage, would cross-dissolve into a tight closeup of the Queen's box, with its ominous dagger-heart clasp. That closeup still appears in the film, but without the need to link it to a preceding image, we are afforded these darkly beautiful establishing shots instead.

A strikingly atmospheric story sketch of the castle at night.

Opposite: Even after the staging of the sequence was determined, shadows on the wall remained an important visual element.

Jekyll and Hyde." Even after the rest of the sequence had been established, writers and concept artists continued to struggle with this essential story point, trying to determine the most powerful and dramatic way to present it on the screen. By March 1937 they had concocted some imaginative scenes as the Queen mixed her various ingredients, but they depicted the transition itself simply by means of shadows on the wall, accompanied by stirring music. When this concept was presented to Walt, he rejected it: "I felt terrifically disappointed in your transition here." He and the writers wrestled with the problem in succeeding months, trying to make the transformation more compelling but still essentially working with shadows. Among other ideas, it was suggested that the Queen's shadow on the wall might become the shadow of a giant bat, then metamorphose into the Witch's shadow before revealing her face—a striking motif that might have suggested the Queen's kinship with Dracula.

Finally, late in the summer of 1937—months after animation had already started on other parts of the sequence—an answer was found. The inspiration came from the movies; not *Dracula,* but the film that Walt had indirectly been citing all along: *Dr. Jekyll and Mr. Hyde.* In the classic 1931 film version of that story, director Rouben Mamoulian had underscored Fredric March's transformation scene with a remarkable effect: from a vantage point in the center of a room, he had spun the camera rapidly in a circle. The result was a subjective shot from Jekyll's point of view, showing the room literally spinning around him as flashback scenes were superimposed over it. Now a similar device was used for

the Queen. The moment she drinks her dread potion, the room begins to revolve around her, leading into a montage: rapidly dissolving images of the bubbling liquid, lightning flashes, wind, a violent whirlpool. By this means, some details of the transformation—the Queen's hair turning white, her hands becoming bony claws—can be sandwiched into the mounting frenzy of images, while still saving a shocking closeup of the Witch's face for the final climactic moment.[84]

Even after this solution was found, Walt maintained a close and critical eye on the sequence as it progressed: "I wanted to get away from the conventional montage stuff that everybody's been doing in pictures." As with the earlier expressionist montage of Snow White in the forest, he insisted on shooting scenes experimentally and changing them as needed: "you can't tell until you try something." Work on the montage proceeded slowly, scene by scene, it was assembled by trial and error. In the finished film, it unfolds rapidly, smoothly, and with vivid effect; in a film that would sometimes be criticized for its frightening effect on children, the transformation scene would remain an unforgettable highlight. The sequence ends with the Queen, now transformed into the Witch, gleefully selecting a "special sort of death" for Snow White: the poisoned apple—the Sleeping Death! Contemplating this prospect with maniacal glee, she stares directly into the camera and the scene starts to fade. Even this fadeout is marked by a special effect: a double exposure that maintains the full brightness of the Witch's eyes while the rest of the scene darkens. Those burning, malevolent eyes are the last thing we see.

[84] Besides *Dr. Jekyll and Mr. Hyde,* it's tempting to see other contemporary horror films reflected in this sequence. We've already observed the similarity of the Queen's costume to that of Helen Gahagan in *She* (1935), but it's also worth noting the climax of that film, punctuated with horrific closeups of Gahagan as, standing in the Flame of Life, she ages hundreds of years in a few minutes. Too, the long shot of the Queen crossing the dungeon to enter her laboratory, her robes swirling behind her, recalls a strikingly similar shot of Frances Drake in the opening scenes of Universal's *The Invisible Ray* (1936).

THE PARTY *Supper over, Snow White and the dwarfs enjoy a party with plenty of carefree dancing and singing. The dwarfs play homemade musical instruments, including an unusual pipe organ, and take turns singing verses of a "Silly Song" of their own composition. As the dancing becomes livelier, Dopey stands on Sneezy's shoulders and dons a long coat to become a "tall" dancing partner for Snow White. The dance builds to a climax but is interrupted by an impending sneeze from Sneezy. All the partygoers seek hiding places as they hear the sneeze starting to build. When it comes, the volcanic sneeze blasts Dopey out of the coat and into the air, and leaves him sitting high on one of the rafters, while Snow White and the rest of the dwarfs (except Grumpy) collapse in helpless laughter.*

Sequence 8A: Entertainment

From the beginning, Walt had planned to picture a musical interlude at the dwarfs' cottage. One of the earliest surviving *Snow White* documents includes his handwritten note: "Snow White dances with & for dwarfs." There was no precedent for this idea in the Grimms' story, and the musical episodes in the Ames play (some of them represented in the 1916 Paramount film) had included nothing of the kind Walt had in mind: a rousing musical party in which Snow White and the dwarfs would sing, dance, and forget their troubles. Such a sequence, he knew, would be a refreshing highlight of the film and (apart from the difficulty of animating Snow White) would be made to order for his medium.

By November 1935 his ideas had taken firmer shape; while much of the story still existed only in a nebulous form, Walt was making definite plans for what was now known as the "entertainment sequence." In a memo to his production team, he announced the two animators he expected to carry the sequence: Dick Lundy would animate the dwarfs, and Les Clark (one of the two principal animators of Persephone in *The Goddess of Spring*) would be responsible for Snow White. In the end both Lundy and Clark would contribute heavily to the sequence, but both their roles and the sequence itself would change considerably in the course of production.

At this early stage, Walt entrusted story development of the entertainment sequence to Pinto Colvig. In the finished version of *Snow White* we can hear Colvig in the voices of Grumpy and Sleepy, and "see" him, in a

sense, by way of his performances in the live-action film shot for the dwarfs. But Colvig left his mark on *Snow White* in other ways too, and, as originally planned, he was to have had a determining influence on the "entertainment sequence." At this time his cheerful, corny, irrepressible sense of humor seems to have appealed to Walt, who felt that Colvig could develop the dwarfs' musical party along lines that would be consistent with their personalities. By November 1935 Walt had appointed a story crew for the sequence: Colvig, fellow story man Erdman Penner, and Walt Pfeiffer, a boyhood friend of Walt Disney's who was currently employed at the studio. Besides story material, Walt also pressed for Colvig to help write the lyrics of the dwarfs' song: "Ted [Sears] and Pinto can help on this. They're good on these comic things." At one point, plans for the entertainment sequence even included a fanciful musical instrument of Colvig's invention called the "Pintophone": a bizarre hybrid of ocarina and bagpipes, played with both hands and feet. Gags were devised for the Pintophone and the musicians improvised a sound for it, made up of a peculiar combination of woodwinds, but in the end it was not used in the film.

Although the entertainment sequence was one of the earliest conceived for the picture, it was one of the last to be finished. One reason was the music: the song that the dwarfs perform in the film was only the latest in a long list of songs that were proposed for this sequence. Before the "Silly Song" was composed in the summer of 1937, no fewer than *four* earlier candidates were written, developed, and ultimately discarded. The "Songs" memo of mid-1934 had tentatively suggested a song called "Funny Little Bunnies" in which one dwarf would sing a series of verses poking fun at the others.[85] This idea didn't last long, but it represented an attempt to introduce the individual dwarfs in an entertaining way. In any case, the short-lived "Funny Little Bunnies" idea seems to have paved the way for the first song seriously considered for the sequence:

Eenie, Meenie, Miney, Mo. This song was planned for the film during late 1934; references to it (with a wide range of spellings) turn up in story conference transcripts from October to December of that year. We have no evidence that a melody was actually com-

[85] *Funny Little Bunnies* had been the title of an Easter-themed Silly Symphony released earlier in 1934.

An early sketch of Snow White's and the Dwarfs' musical party.

posed for this number, but there was general agreement on the *idea* of the song, and the story team proceeded to develop that idea. The premise of "Funny Little Bunnies," one dwarf poking fun at all the others, was to be expanded in "Eenie, Meenie, Miney, Mo." This time "each dwarf sings a jingle, caricaturing another dwarf"—a device that presumably would have allowed even more opportunity to develop the characters. At the general sound-stage meeting in November 1934, all the studio personnel were invited to submit lyrics for the song, much in the manner of the story outlines which were routinely circulated throughout the studio to solicit gag ideas for the shorts. Responses from the artists included this proposed verse from layout artist Charlie Philippi: "Now there's 'Grumpy' Gus, he's an ornery cuss/He's the joy killer of the hour/He fills his mug from the vinegar jug/To keep him good and sour."

Walt endorsed the song in his "Skeleton Continuity" of December 1934: "Dwarfs sing their special little song, called 'Eenie, Meenie, Miney, Mo,' in which every one gets up and sings a verse with the whole gang joining in the chorus. All the dwarfs get up and do some kind of stunt, dancing and acrobatics and various gag things that we can work in here for entertainment. The atmosphere is very happy and gay . . . Even Grumpy has changed and is beginning to enjoy things." This description does bear a strong resemblance to the finished version of the sequence. But story work on the entertainment sequence, and the rest of the film, was sidelined during much of 1935, and "Eenie, Meenie, Miney, Mo" languished. By December 1935 it had been replaced by a new number:

The Lady in the Moon. This intriguing song idea told a story about a group of animals: tentatively an owl,

86 The professional musicians
were clarinetist Glen Johnson,
oboist Joe Barrett, and fifer Joe
Petkere. Among the participating
studio artists were animators
Frank Thomas and Ward Kimball
and writer Ed Penner, all of
whom would perform in later
years in the well-known Disney-
artists–Dixieland combo, The
Firehouse Five Plus Two. At
this 23 December 1935 session,
none of these artists played his
later instrument of choice (piano,
trombone, and tuba, respectively).
Thomas and Kimball simply blew
on bottles to simulate a jug-band
effect, while Penner doubled on
ocarina and tin whistle.

87 In this connection, note the
dwarfs in the 1932 Silly Symphony
Babes in the Woods, who are seen
playing a jug-band arrangement of
"Little Brown Jug."

a frog, a mockingbird, a cricket, and a fish. "Now when the moon came up at night, they'd all burst into tune/ For each one thought himself in love with the Lady in the Moon." Several of the dwarfs were to be cast as the animals in the story (Sleepy as the fish) and act out their parts as the narrative progressed. In the story, jealousy quickly broke out among the competing animals, who proceeded to fight with each other every night—until they discovered that "the lady in the moon" was actually "the man in the moon," whereupon they all lost interest in their former idol and decided to be friends again. "Walt liked this song for its animation possibilities," noted the transcript of one story meeting. The dwarfs were to enter enthusiastically into playing their roles, and an early idea to costume them with simple props (such as a feather duster representing the mockingbird's tail) was vetoed in favor of using as few props as possible ("'A big hoot owl': show two fingers at the side of the head"). Walt suggested that after the song's introduction, about friends who got into trouble, Grumpy might pointedly add: "because of a woman."

Unlike its predecessor, "The Lady in the Moon" was fully composed with a melody and a more or less definite set of lyrics, and a rough recording was made late in December 1935. A few professional musicians were hired for this session, but most of those present were musically inclined studio artists, giving the dwarfs' performance a ragged, improvised sound.[86] At this writing the composer of "The Lady in the Moon" is unknown, but Frank Churchill was conspicuously absent from the recording session, and the musicians were conducted by Paul Smith.

Besides "The Lady in the Moon," at the 13 December 1935 story meeting it was agreed that the sequence should have an additional song, possibly improvised by the dwarfs as a jug band. This separate song would be an introductory number at the beginning of the sequence, and some of the artists suggested traditional rounds such as "Three Blind Mice" or "Little Brown Jug."[87] Walt preferred a simple original song, and asked Pinto Colvig to supply one. By the time of the "Lady in the Moon" recording session ten days later, Colvig had produced his response:

Music Everywhere (or Everything's Music). The idea behind this song was that musical (or at least percussive) sounds could be produced with ordinary household objects, a principle the dwarfs would illustrate as they tapped out rhythmic sounds on brooms and chairs. Of course Colvig built in some slapstick humor as the dwarfs ribbed each other: "If a tune's about a big rose/Just [HONK] like this on Grumpy's nose." The 23 December recording session, besides "The Lady in the Moon," produced several takes of "Music Everywhere," sung by Colvig and sound-effects specialist Jim Macdonald.

Both "Lady in the Moon" and "Music Everywhere" found favor with Walt, at least temporarily, and the production team continued to develop them. Another recording session on 29 January 1936 produced several more takes of each (including one take of "Lady in the Moon" featuring Otis Harlan's vocal, and another performed on the Pintophone). By that time, however, yet

another song had been introduced that would supersede them both:

You're Never Too Old to Be Young. Larry Morey and Frank Churchill unveiled this song at a story conference on 6 January 1936. Sung by Morey and accompanied on piano by Churchill, "You're Never Too Old to Be Young" made an instant hit with the story crew. As its title suggests, the song celebrated the dwarfs' youthful spirit, which belied their long white beards. A bouncy song filled with infectious good humor, it proved to be a flexible workhorse: at this early meeting Morey and Churchill offered the story crew a choice of two endings to the chorus, and other members of the team quickly began to improvise new verses.

Of all the unused songs written for the entertainment sequence, "You're Never Too Old" is easily the best known among Disney enthusiasts today because of the surviving demo recording. This demo, never intended for public consumption in the 1930s, was widely disseminated for a later generation: included as a bonus track on the *Snow White* soundtrack CD in 1993, reprised on the *Snow White* DVD released in 2001. Internal evidence suggests that the demo was recorded shortly after the song's introduction at the 6 January meeting; the chorus is the version selected by Dave Hand at that meeting from the available options, and the verses are the same as those sung by Morey in that debut performance, with none of the alternate lyrics that would be suggested in later months. The early version of "You're Never Too Old" represented in the recording may well have evolved into something

entirely different in the course of production. Perhaps because of that flexibility, it proved a durable candidate for the entertainment sequence. "The Lady in the Moon" had been discarded after a few months; "You're Never Too Old to Be Young" remained the song of choice for nearly a year and a half.

One unusual feature of this song was its yodeling chorus. "Anybody could do the yodel," said Walt on first hearing the song—but the next story meeting was attended by a half-dozen professional yodelers, among them Reynard Fraunfelder and Freeman High. As the music track was built up in succeeding months, more yodels were included in the mix, performed partly by the professional singers but also by Jim Macdonald, of the studio staff. Macdonald was employed as a sound-effects expert, but he could sing and had already sung on the "Music Everywhere" demo. He was later quoted by Frank Thomas and Ollie Johnston: "I had never yodeled in my whole life, but when Walt said, 'Yodel!' you yodeled."

During those succeeding months, under the supervision of Walt and sequence director Wilfred Jackson,[88] sequence and song evolved together as the verses were adapted to individual dwarfs. Morey's original verses had suggested comic turns on the minor ailments of old age: baldness, creaky joints, and so forth. New verses detailing other infirmities were quickly suggested, and soon the crew had more verses than they could possibly use. Walt pressed for using the best of these verses in an improvisational spirit, as if each dwarf was making up his verse as he went along: "It's like each guy sits there

Photostats from live-action reference footage for the Entertainment sequence. Marjorie Belcher, in costume as Snow White, dances with sequence director Perce Pearce.

[88] Wilfred Jackson had been appointed director of this sequence by early January 1936. One of the studio's top directors, "Jaxon" had a musical background and had employed it to good advantage on a number of shorts during the 1930s, including two particularly brilliant examples released in 1935: *The Band Concert* and *Music Land*.

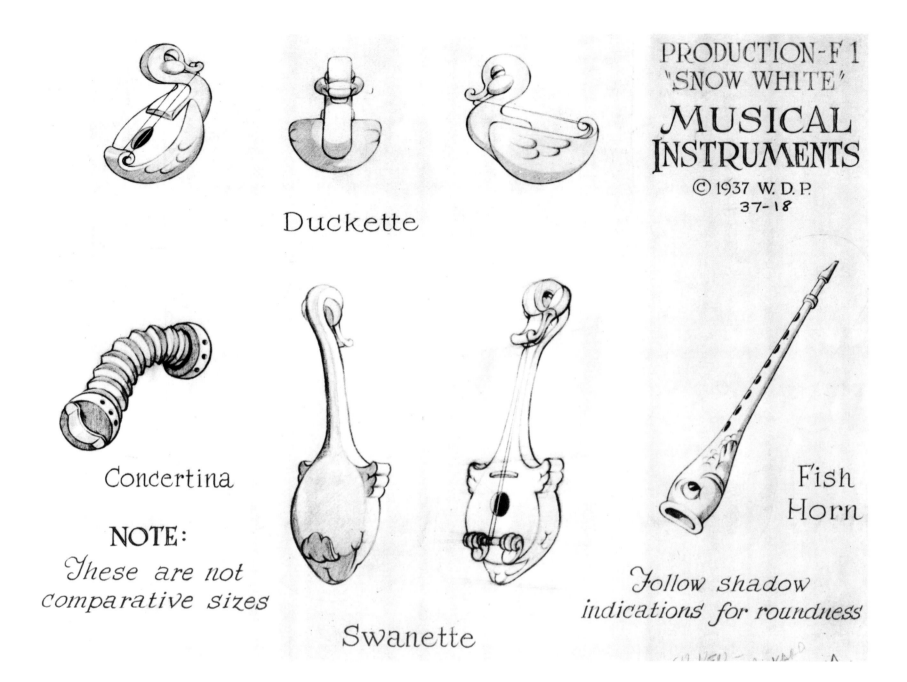

Duckette

Concertina

NOTE:
These are not
comparative sizes

Swanette

PRODUCTION-F1
"SNOW WHITE"
MUSICAL
INSTRUMENTS
© 1937 W. D. P.
37-18

Fish
Horn

Follow shadow
indications for roundness

The Dwarfs' musical instruments were designed with as much care as the animated characters.

[89] At one meeting Walt suggested a gag in which Sneezy, playing the Pintophone, would sneeze and blow the instrument to pieces.

thinking and when his turn comes he will get up and sing." The verse we hear in the demo, beginning "When you know your legs are going to give out soon," was given to Doc, and other verses were fine-tuned for other specific dwarfs. One verse about indigestion, a particular favorite of Walt's, was temporarily given to Bashful—who was pictured blushing and giggling at the line "Eat some pickled parsnip pie"—before finally being assigned to Grumpy.

Along with the mock-improvisational nature of the song, Walt focused on the dwarfs' musical instruments. The dwarfs, living in a quaint cottage filled with their own hand-carved furniture and improvised utensils, would not play ordinary musical instruments. Instead Walt urged the creation of fanciful homemade

instruments that looked and sounded like no others: "Their instruments have got to be unique and unusual . . . If you get a regular jazz organization you've not taken advantage of the opportunity." Over and over he stressed this idea: "I don't want a flute to sound like a flute; I want it to sound like something else—whatever we have got drawn." "If you use clarinets, trick them so that they don't sound legitimate." The Pintophone was one of the odd instruments devised for the sequence, and was to be played by Sneezy.[89] Other instruments, likewise not used in the film, included the Gourdaphone—a string instrument made of a row of gourds with faces painted on them—and the Squirrel Horn, a horn carved in the shape of a squirrel. Other inventions did appear in the finished film, including the

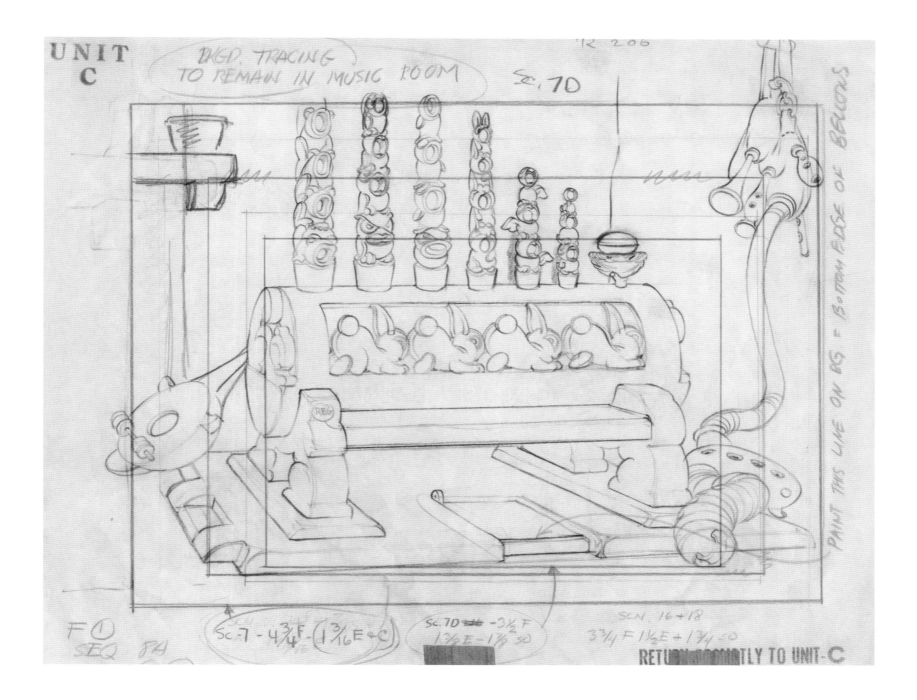

Swanette, a sort of string bass carved to resemble a swan; a smaller counterpart called the Duckette, which was played somewhat like a mandolin; and the Fish Horn. In the finished version of the sequence, Doc alternated between the swanette and the duckette, while Sleepy, who had been cast as a fish in the aborted "Lady in the Moon" number, played the fish horn.

By far the most notable of these imaginary instruments was the organ. As early as 1934, a pipe organ had been envisioned in the dwarfs' cottage. As Walt continued to develop his ideas, he gave special attention to the organ. This fanciful instrument was so meticulously developed during the years of *Snow White*'s production that it very nearly qualified as another character in the story. Like everything else in the dwarfs' homemade

environment, the organ pipes would display their ingenious creativity: "The smaller pipes would be carved as birds, the larger ones squirrels, owls, and bullfrogs, all carved like totem poles." Walt demonstrated how an owl pipe might work: a carved wing, placed over the owl's mouth, would be mechanically opened by the key to emit a "hooting" bass sound. All these pipes were to be brightly painted. Another refinement was suggested by Albert Hurter: the organ's air supply was powered by a bellows underneath the organist's seat. While Grumpy sat playing the keys, he energetically pumped the bellows with his fanny. Soon still more embellishments were added to the organ, including some that were not used in the film: "We cut to a C.U. of Grumpy who pushes a button and a drawer flies out with minia-

This rough layout sketch includes, at the right, a rare glimpse of the Pintophone.

ture keyboard—he plays a little trill in the drawer."

Along with the organ's appearance, its *sound* came in for special attention. As with the other instruments, Walt was adamant that the sound should bear little or no resemblance to the sound of an actual pipe organ. The idea of the dwarfs forming a jug band, to perform "The Lady in the Moon" and/or "Everything's Music," had been abandoned when those songs were discarded—but the *sound* of the jug band was adopted, along with other sounds, to represent the homemade organ pipes. "I think you ought to figure out the organ with bassoons for the bass and on down," said Walt at one meeting, "but tied in so you have a complete scale. If we use jugs we have to get them to tie in with everything." Stuart Buchanan was incredulous: "You're not going to use an organ at all?" "We might use an organ," Walt responded. "It's got all these pipes that get the sounds of tin whistles and ocarinas, etc. He can run the whole scale. When he is in the bass it's the bassoon and he gets down here and he's playing tin pipes . . . Grumpy can run the whole scale changing instruments as he goes up. Nobody has ever heard it, but they are instruments that tie together." In the end, the musicians and the sound-effect specialists worked together for months to build a track representing the overall sound of the music. Much of the melody was carried by a concertina, the one "legitimate" instrument that Walt allowed to appear in the sequence. The organ's sound was a combination of bottles, jugs, flutes, ocarinas, and a clarinet played without the mouthpiece;[90] and still other miscellaneous sounds were layered on top of that. "Use a few legitimate instruments the way they are played," said Walt, "with

enough illegitimate instruments thrown in to throw it off, to make people wonder how you got the sounds."

Other aspects of the sequence were developed with similar care. One problem facing the story crew was finding a way to end the sequence; with all that infectious energy, the number needed some kind of climactic topper. Late in March 1937, veteran story men Webb Smith and Earl Hurd found the solution. More than once, in the course of story development, it had been suggested that one dwarf might stand on the shoulders of another to dance with Snow White. Now Smith and Hurd expanded on that idea: Dopey would stand on Sneezy's shoulders and then don a long coat so that the two, together, would appear to be one very tall "dwarf."[91] This odd stand-in, nicknamed "Dozey" by the artists, would enjoy a dance with Snow White until the music and the sequence were interrupted by a violent climactic sneeze from Sneezy. This idea proved to be the perfect topper, ending the sequence on a note of laughter.[92]

Of course many other gag ideas were proposed for this part of the film, far more than could actually be used. Among the gags that did *not* appear in the finished picture:

- As Dopey sits playing the drums, he tosses drumsticks into the air, where the birds in the rafters catch them. Dopey is mystified when the sticks fail to come back down, then confounded when *all* the sticks descend on him at once. (Several variations on this idea were suggested, and a remnant does remain in the film.)

- Sleepy, harassed by the fly, follows it around the room and swings at it, but hits one of the other

[90] This may have been Pinto Colvig's famous trick clarinet; it was Colvig who enumerated this recipe of sounds at the 31 March 1937 story conference. After *Snow White*'s release, the clarinet-without-mouthpiece was mentioned frequently in publicity.

[91] Like so much of *Snow White*, this idea may have been inspired by other contemporary films. In the Our Gang comedy short *Teacher's Beau*, released in April 1935, Spanky stands on Alfalfa's shoulders and dons a long coat, in an effort to impersonate a "tough guy" and so scare away their schoolteacher's fiancé.

[92] This complete sequence of gags was jointly presented by Smith and Hurd at the 31 March 1937 meeting. Later, however, in a letter to his son, Hurd specifically claimed credit for the climactic sneezing gag.

The same gag, in later sketches by Fred Moore.

Overleaf: A cel setup representing the finished scene.

dwarfs (possibly Grumpy) instead. A fight breaks out between the two dwarfs and continues while the other dwarfs carry on playing their song.

• As Dopey watches Sneezy's gyrating Adam's apple, the Adam's apple disappears from view, and Dopey yanks Sneezy's shirt collar out to see what happened to it. (This latter action was actually animated by Fred Moore but then eliminated from the final cut, leaving only the basic action at the beginning of the scene.)

• Some of the organ pipes, jarred by some collision, fall out of place, and Grumpy quickly jams them back into their holes so that he can continue to play. In his haste he accidentally replaces one of the larger pipes with Dopey, who then tries to function as an organ pipe by working his hands over his mouth. When Grumpy notices the change in the organ's sound and sees the reason for it, he glares at Dopey, who instantly vacates his spot.

• Dopey climbs onto Sneezy's shoulders to form the composite figure "Dozey," who walks jauntily

forward—straight into a ceiling beam, where Dopey conks his head. (This scene, too, was animated by Fred Moore but then eliminated from the final cut.)

By early 1937, the team was having second thoughts about the song "You're Never Too Old to Be Young." "It's kind of cold trying to get anything from it the way it is," Walt commented in February. "It begins to sound cut and dried." His concern was that the musical pattern had been established in such precise detail that it restricted the development of new ideas and action for the sequence.[93] Others felt that the verses were too long and unwieldy for the dwarfs to sing; Ted Sears even suggested cutting out the verses altogether and letting the chorus, yodeling, and visual gags carry the sequence. "You're Never Too Old" survived this growing discontent for several months, but by early summer the decision had been made to write yet another new song in its place—six months before the film's production deadline.

Once again the job was initially entrusted to Pinto Colvig. Early in June 1937, Colvig submitted a sheet of lyrics to a song that he called "Gee, Ain't This a Silly

[93] Pinto Colvig, Ed Penner, and Walt Pfeiffer, the story team assigned to the entertainment sequence, had in the meantime also been given charge of a Mickey Mouse short released in April 1937 as *Mickey's Amateurs*. The short had featured an appearance by Goofy performing as a one-man band. After the music was recorded, Walt pointed out, "you got that and afterwards we couldn't make it over because too many things were animated to it." He was concerned lest *Snow White* be similarly hampered.

Song?" This time the lyrics had no "theme" at all; they were simply silly and spontaneous lines, sung just for fun. The song was immediately taken in hand by the story crew, who proceeded to refine it as they had refined its predecessor. The new number retained the yodeling chorus from "You're Never Too Old" (newly recorded by a different group of yodelers), but otherwise was custom-tailored to the sequence—incorporating the visual gags and ideas that had already been devised, but allowing more latitude to develop and polish them. Once again the dwarfs would take turns contributing individual verses, but this time the verses would be shorter and catchier. The end result of all this development was the number we hear in the finished film, known alternately as "The Silly Song" and "The Dwarfs' Yodel Song." Like the other songs in *Snow White*, it was credited to Larry Morey and Frank Churchill.[94]

In August 1937, this long-awaited, carefully worked-out sequence finally went to the animators. True to Walt's 1935 plans, Dick Lundy and Les Clark were among the animation crew—but the animation hierarchy had changed dramatically in the intervening two years. Now both Lundy and Clark were among a large group of dwarf animators, while Snow White's action was in the hands of other specialists. Lundy contributed some Grumpy animation in this sequence, notably Grumpy's forceful, belligerent performance at the organ. Fred Moore invested most of "Dozey's" action with his characteristic charm; Fred Spencer animated much of Dopey, including his wild drum solo; and Marvin Woodward lent his special touch to Bashful, including his exquisitely embarrassing verse in the "Silly Song."

Even at this late date, the entertainment sequence was still subject to change if Walt or anyone else had a better idea. As late as September 1937, it was planned that Dopey would prompt Snow White to kick the cymbal, then would "go right on out of the scene doing a hot rhythm dance, hitting the cymbal, getting a bobble in his head and looking back at S.W. while he is dancing out." By mid-October this action had been replaced by

the coolie-hat gag we see in the film. The "Silly Song," which has two verses in the finished picture, was supposed to have three. In between Happy's and Bashful's verses, Sneezy was to step forward and sing: "The minute after I was born, I didn't have a nightie/So I tied my whiskers 'round my legs and I used 'em for a didee"—the last word interrupted by another prodigious sneeze. This verse was recorded by Billy Gilbert and animated by Les Clark, and was in the picture as late as 29 October 1937, yet did not make the final cut.[95]

Even Grumpy's pipe organ, which had been the focus of so much careful development, continued to be fussed over as the sequence moved through production. When Walt saw Dick Lundy's first scenes of Grumpy at the console, he immediately called for the console to be made smaller, "more like the original layout sketches," so Grumpy wouldn't look so small in proportion to it, nor have to reach so far for the keys. The sequence was gradually refined, but Walt was still dissatisfied with the organ pipes. After the Pomona preview in December 1937, four background paintings were recalled so that the pipes could be repainted—*eleven days* before the opening at the Carthay Circle.

In its finished version on the screen, this sequence seems to unfold in a single unbroken thread, its spontaneous sense of delight never betraying the years of labor behind it. Audiences are swept along with the sheer joyful momentum of the sequence, accepting the dwarfs' quaint homemade musical instruments and their quirky sounds without question. As Walt intended, the months of reworking story and song have the effect of distilling the essence of the team's best ideas in a few wonderful moments on the screen.

One casualty of all that reworking is Happy's role in the sequence. At the time of "You're Never Too Old to Be Young," Walt had pictured Happy taking a leading part in the song and perhaps even conducting the other dwarfs as they played: "Doc takes quite an important part in the picture. Happy hasn't done much, so he shines here and in the Soup sequence." Now the Soup sequence had been cut from the film altogether, and, in the switch from "You're Never Too Old" to the "Silly

[94] Although Colvig participated in the early development of the "Silly Song," his position at the studio was becoming tenuous by this time, and it seems unlikely that any of his material remained in the final version of the song. Colvig's original lyric sheet, bearing his name and dated 10 June 1937, contains eleven verses, none of which was used in the film. A second sheet, five days later, is unsigned but does include some notes in Colvig's handwriting. Only one of the typed verses on this second sheet, the verse sung by Bashful, is heard in the film.

[95] Sneezy did sing this verse when the "Silly Song" was performed on the *Mickey Mouse Theater of the Air* radio broadcast on 9 January 1938 (with slightly altered lyrics) and on the *Lux Radio Theatre* on 26 December 1938 (with the lyrics as written for the film).

A beautifully rendered layout sketch of the organ.

Song," Happy's leading role had been lost. He does perform his verse, but in the finished version of *Snow White,* Happy remains a minor character.

On another level, however, the entertainment sequence accomplishes something seemingly impossible. We've already noted that Snow White and the dwarfs, in terms of design, look and move like members of entirely different species. It's a tribute to the Disney animators that they can believably depict both Snow White and the dwarfs inhabiting the same space, even without any direct contact between them. One unidentified artist had even warned: "Snow White does not come in actual contact with the dwarfs. If she did, she would become a giantess." In this sequence, however, she does more than make contact—she joins hands with the dwarfs and dances with them—and the effect is not only believable, but completely natural. In one near-miraculous scene, Snow White, animated by Jack Campbell, starts near the camera and dances in turn with Doc, Bashful, Sneezy, and Doc again, moving in perspective toward the background and then back toward the camera. The dwarfs, animated by Dick Lundy, join hands with her and likewise move in perspective through the dance with her. It's an especially challenging scene, pulled off with grace and style, and so naturally that we never think to question it. It's anything but realistic, and yet Snow White and the dwarfs exist in a reality of their own that defies disbelief.

As do all the elements of this charming sequence. In less than five minutes it's all over, and Dopey is sliding down from his perch to the laughter of the other dwarfs.

A BEDTIME STORY *Now everyone at the party is thoroughly winded, and the dwarfs ask Snow White to tell them a story. The story is her own, of a princess who fell in love—but it's an unfinished story, and Snow White sings of her longing for romance in "Some Day My Prince Will Come." The dwarfs listen, enraptured. By now it's time for bed, and the dwarfs (most of them) insist that Snow White must sleep upstairs in their beds while they remain downstairs. Snow White accepts their hospitality. As she says her bedtime prayer for the seven little men who have been so kind to her, the seven little men are downstairs finding unlikely places to sleep—a cupboard, the sink, the soup pot. To the gentle cacophony of their snores, peace settles over the little cottage.*

Sequence 8B: Story Telling
Sequence 8C: Going to Bed

In contrast to the wild action of the preceding sequence, the film now moves to a quietly romantic interlude. "Some Day My Prince Will Come," arguably the most beautiful and best-known song in the film, is introduced in this sequence. It had been one of the first songs composed for *Snow White*, and early plans had called for numerous reprises throughout the story. In the finished film it's sung only twice, in this sequence and at the finale. Snow White's performance of the song, and the determination of sleeping arrangements that follows immediately afterward, occupy a scant six minutes of screen time in the finished film—but they represent two full sequences, because originally much more story material was planned for each one.

Sequence 8B, the Story Telling sequence, was in fact envisioned during 1936 as something far more spectacular than we see today. Walt's earliest outlines of the feature, in late 1934, had depicted the Story Telling sequence in a simple and straightforward way: Snow White would tell the dwarfs of her love for the Prince and perhaps "teach them a dance of the court." As story development proceeded, this sequence became more elaborate: now Snow White's rendition of "Some Day My Prince Will Come" would be illustrated by dream images picturing that future reunion with her Prince. In a vision, wandering in a starry sky, she would see the Prince approaching from the distance, riding a winged horse and escorted by tiny humanized stars. Joyfully reunited with Snow White, the Prince would sweep her up beside him, and the two would ride away through the clouds.

By January 1936, plans for the sequence had become even more elaborate. Now the winged horse had been replaced by a swan-shaped boat with a heart-shaped sail, piloted by the Prince through the "sea" of a night sky. The writers and artists, encouraged by Walt to let their imaginations soar, created an ever more spectacular dream landscape for this sequence: massive clouds assumed the shapes of trees, hills, and a "shoreline" to which the Prince's boat sailed. Snow White entered this dream world by wandering through a field twinkling with star "dew." The little humanized stars were back too, guiding the Prince's boat and casting a romantic light on the proceedings by illuminating the clouds from behind and below. As the Prince's boat reached "land," Snow White and the Prince would run to meet each other, dancing on the clouds. The tiny stars would form a double line leading to the ship, beaming their rays to form an archway of light, beneath which Snow White and the Prince would run up a "gangplank" of clouds to the boat. Then the happy couple would depart, sailing over the Milky Way as clouds parted in the distance to reveal their destination: the Prince's castle, illuminated from behind by a sunburst. "I felt this sequence would be for the women," Walt admitted at one conference. "After all, 80% of our audience are women. If we got something they loved it would help, because there is a lot of slapstick stuff that women don't like so well."

As the dream sequence continued to expand, the song "Some Day My Prince Will Come" alone seemed inadequate to underscore it. To avoid endless repetition, Walt proposed a break in the pattern, a spoken verse in which Snow White would begin to describe her dream as it unfolded on the screen. It was at this point that Kathleen Millay joined the story team. The younger sister of Edna St. Vincent Millay and an accomplished poet in her own right, Kathleen Millay was hired in late November 1936 and worked at the Disney studio for a couple of months. During that time she worked on character development of the Queen and acted as a dialogue consultant, but it's clear that her primary function on *Snow White* was to devise a verse for Snow White to speak during the dream sequence.

Oddly, Millay's verse seems not to have been preserved in studio files. Walt read from it during one of the

An unusual piece of concept art by Ken Anderson: Snow White surrounded by a ring of stars—with several overlays suggesting different color combinations.

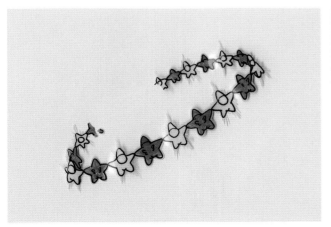

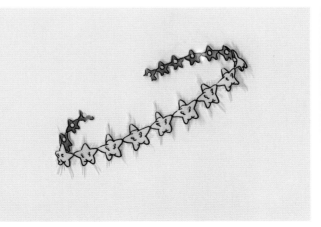

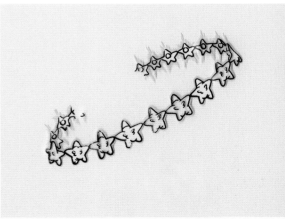

Plans for the dream sequence
included fantastic
cloudscapes like this one, with
stars standing in for a field of
"flowers."

story meetings, and the transcript of his comments gives us a glimpse: "I thought somehow I wandered in the sky—up a high cliff—neither feet nor wings to climb nor fly, but strangely drifting—lighter than air . . . Till at length I stood at night alone on such a lovely cloud—all pink it was at nighttime—all pink and gold beneath the rainbow of the moon—Then soft from out the distance of the sky a white ship like a swan . . . came to me." These words were to follow the singing of "Some Day My Prince Will Come," and would be illustrated onscreen by the beginning of the dream sequence. As the picture escalated into ever more fantastic imagery, an instrumental reprise of the song would begin, and as the lovers sailed away the orchestra would be joined by a choir—represented on the screen either as the chorus of stars, or as the voices of the wind.

As recorded by Adriana Caselotti in spring 1937 (after Millay's departure from the studio), the verse had been considerably altered:

I see myself all in the loveliest gown
Woven of moonlight and fairy wings.
Thru drifting clouds I wander in the sky—
Clouds that turn to trees and flowers;
Through fields of shimmering stars I go—
Stars like golden daisies all around me.
You cannot think how beautiful it is!

Only a dream can find such loveliness.
Then, from out the distance of the night
Thru the soft light of the radiant moon,
The friendly stars come sailing down the sky
Bringing the Prince of my dreams to me.

Discussions of the dream sequence continued through the early months of 1937, but they were increasingly tinged with a kind of uneasiness. Fine points of the story were debated, spectacular effects were planned, but little was said about character animation—which would be an important and very difficult part of the sequence. Wilfred Jackson was the nominal director of sequence 8B, but because Snow White and the Prince were featured so heavily, much of the responsibility for this section rested on Ham Luske. In January 1937 Walt asked Luske point-blank: "Ham, how do you feel about the whole sequence? We have never attempted anything like it before, you know." Luske responded: "The way you talked it, I think I like it." But while production proceeded briskly on other parts of the film, the dream sequence languished in uncertainty. At a layout meeting in late February, Dave Hand made a casual but telling remark: "There is Jaxon's dream sequence that I didn't mention. It is actually in production but not so much now." By midsummer the dream sequence had been quietly dropped from the picture.

At one time the Prince was pictured piloting a swan-shaped boat through the sky. This sketch shows the relative scale of the boat to the Prince, Snow White, and the humanized stars.

How would *Snow White* have been affected if the dream sequence had remained in the picture? Through hindsight—now that the finished film as we know it has been absorbed into our culture for so many generations—it's easy to write off the dream sequence as an ill-conceived notion, a mistake that was wisely discarded. We should keep in mind, however, that Walt and his story artists, the same team responsible for the genius of the rest of *Snow White,* labored over this sequence for more than a year, and that it seems to have been dropped mainly because of technical considerations. One thing is certain: if the dream sequence had remained in place, *Snow White* would have been vastly different from the film we know today. Far more than any of the other cut sequences, Snow White's dream would have radically altered the contour of the story—shifting from a delightful fantasy world, created by the studio for the film as a whole, to an altogether different, heightened dimension of fantasy. As it is, one element of the dream sequence does remain in the finished film: the Prince's dream castle, illuminated by a sunburst, appears at film's end. And the imagery of cloudscapes and humanized stars didn't go to waste either: some of these visual ideas were incorporated in the elaborate Silly Symphony *Wynken, Blynken & Nod,* released in mid-1938.

No such elaborate plans were made for sequence 8C, "Going to Bed," but one prominent piece of business was planned and then dropped: the "woodpile gag."

This was planned as a transition from one sequence to the next. As Snow White finished describing her dream, the camera would return to the room to show the dwarfs listening to her, happily lost in romantic reverie. One by one they would sigh dreamily—then would be interrupted by a loud snore: Sleepy, curled up on the woodpile, had slept through the whole sequence. One of the dwarfs would dislodge a log and the entire woodpile would collapse, logs and Sleepy clattering noisily to the floor. Rudely awakened, Sleepy would rouse himself and say: "Tell us a story"—the same line he had spoken at the beginning of the song.

Like every other major gag in the film, the woodpile gag was dissected and analyzed. Would Sleepy's dialogue register with the audience? Should the woodpile collapse by itself? If one of the dwarfs triggered the collapse deliberately, which dwarf would it be? Dopey was one popular choice, but Walt pointed out that this was an opportunity to show a neglected side of Happy's personality: "I see that we have yet to build up Happy as the one little guy pulling tricks on the others . . . Just showing that Happy is the practical joker." Dave Hand, for one, was surprised to hear this: "I am glad to know that about him. I never heard of that angle in his character." By the time Les Clark animated the scene, Dopey had been chosen as the practical joker, but in the end the gag was dropped altogether.

In the finished film, the combined sequences 8B and 8C opt for warmth, gentle humor, and quiet understatement.

DWARF SLEEPS WITH BEARD TIED
HOLDING HIM UP.(HIS PANTS ALSO.)

The Dwarfs' search for places to sleep inspired these and other gag suggestions.

[96] Natwick made these remarks with reference to Snow White's bedroom scenes in sequence 5A, but all the evidence suggests that, nearly half a century after the event, his memory was playing tricks on him. In the bedroom sequence, all the Snow White closeups were the work of the Ham Luske team; but Natwick and his unit were explicitly assigned to sequence 8B, production papers confirm Les Novros as the key cleanup artist, the finished animation bears Natwick's unmistakable stamp, and Snow White's chin and nose are inked with the light gray line he describes.

[97] This staging was a rare instance of Walt being outvoted. During development of this sequence Ken Anderson had suggested the long pan along the line of dwarfs, but Walt had pushed for individual cuts instead. Several artists campaigned for reinstating the pan, and in March 1937 Walt agreed to it. In the finished version of the sequence, only Grumpy and Sleepy are isolated in separate scenes.

[98] Wilfred Jackson commented: "When Walt told me about the sequence he mentioned a cuckoo clock in this instance, with a frog coming out instead of a bird, and it seemed like a good hunch for me to use it." Here again, more detail was suggested for the clock than we see in the film.

The dwarfs ask Snow White for a story, and her rendition of "Some Day My Prince Will Come" is simple and unadorned, letting the beauty of the song speak for itself. In this sequence Snow White is no longer the little girl, but the young woman longing for romance, and her animation is in Grim Natwick's hands for the duration of the song. "She was sitting in a chair singing a song," Natwick recalled in later years, "and there isn't much a singer can do sitting in a chair." Live-action reference and rotoscope drawings had been provided, but Natwick claimed that he used only the first and last drawings and improvised all of Snow White's action in between: a turn of the head here, a clasp of the hands there. To compound the difficulty of these scenes, Snow White is shown from a nearly direct front view. "When you take a nose and lips and two eyes left in an open space—we always tried, where we moved from one side to another, to do it very quickly so that we wouldn't get a jitter on the drawings as they went by." Natwick relied heavily on the skill of his assistants and gave Les Novros particular credit for these cleanups and inbetweens. "Les Novros did a beautiful job," he recalled, "he really worked on it, and I never bothered him at all, I just let him! . . . However, they were very smart; she was not inked in black lines the way most of the characters were. And particularly this front view, they inked her chin with a light gray line that more or less vanished. However, the contour, the front view was satisfying."[96]

To help Natwick further with this animation challenge, Snow White's singing scenes are broken up by cutaways to the dwarfs and animals. One 26-foot scene by Les Clark pans slowly across the faces of five of the dwarfs, listening adoringly to Snow White's song. Grumpy sulks in the corner; Sleepy, beginning to nod off, is awakened not by a slapstick gag but by a piercing high note from Snow White.[97] At song's end the dwarfs sigh, not individually but in unison.

And the romantic mood is broken by a laugh, but it's a gentle laugh prompted by another "cuckoo" clock. This clock, suggested by Walt,[98] is another of the dwarfs' ingenious creations: while a carved squirrel rings a tiny chime in the shape of an acorn, a carved frog emerges from a door and "croaks" the hour with a funny sound effect. Like the clock at the mine, this one was animated by effects animator Andy Engman. Snow White, suddenly realizing the lateness of the hour, tries to send the dwarfs upstairs to bed but is persuaded to accept their bedroom, while the dwarfs themselves remain downstairs.

There follows a gag that is enjoyable in itself: even before Snow White enters the upstairs bedroom, Dopey spies the one large, soft pillow in the downstairs area and surreptitiously tries to claim it for himself. The instant the bedroom door closes, *all* the dwarfs descend in a mob on that one pillow, tugging and yanking at it until it's ripped to pieces, the air filled with floating feathers. Dopey, left with a single feather, fluffs it up as a "pillow" and settles down contentedly with it. Viewers, enjoying this gag, seldom realize that it's inserted—like the turtle's second appearance on the stairs in sequence 4C—partly to cover up an awkward continuity problem. The problem: to get Snow White from a position *behind* the dwarfs, who were already starting up the stairs, to a position *ahead* of the dwarfs, looking down at them from the top of the stairs. The pillow gag was the answer: an exchange of dialogue closeups, and Dopey's stealthy maneuver to claim the pillow for himself, provide a convenient series of cutaways. The first time we cut back to the group, Snow White is standing parallel to the dwarfs; the second time she has started up the stairs; the

A charming story sketch depicting Snow White's prayer. In the film this action is shown from the rear.

third time she's at the top of the staircase—having gracefully bypassed a staging problem *and* paved the way for a pleasant moment of slapstick.

Snow White's prayer in the upstairs bedroom is worthy of note. In the studio's first outlines of the story, as in some of the earlier stage versions, a *lot* of praying had occurred in *Snow White:* the heroine prayed in the forest when abandoned by the Huntsman, said grace at the beginning of the Soup sequence, and prayed over the dwarfs at bedtime; and the dwarfs themselves knelt in prayer after Snow White had succumbed to the poisoned apple. One by one these scenes were eliminated, but the prayer in the bedroom remained,[99] although, like every other scene in the film, it was pared down to essentials as the continuity of the film was tightened. Walt, in his role of ruthless story editor, approved all these cuts, but long after the film's release he commented at another story meeting: "I feel in *Snow White* we should have had . . . something a little slower. I know they kept cutting that prayer of Snow White's,

and I would like to have been slower with that, but there was that pressure everywhere—'You've got to keep moving.'"

The sequence concludes with a chorus of snores as the dwarfs settle down to sleep in their cramped makeshift quarters. Grumpy grumbles as he tries to get comfortable in the soup pot; Dopey whimpers and stirs like a dog in his sleep; Sleepy's fly, also like a dog, turns in circles before bedding down for the night on Sleepy's nose. All of this action is underscored by two lovely musical themes: "Pleasant Dreams" by Frank Churchill and "Prayer at Evening" by Paul J. Smith. In the film, much of this latter music is drowned out by snores; both themes—like much of the other *Snow White* music—are worth seeking out on the soundtrack CD.

[99] And this scene was not unprecedented in Disney films. See *Mickey's Nightmare* (1932), in which Mickey Mouse is seen saying *his* bedtime prayers.

THE WITCH AT THE CAULDRON *Deep in her secret laboratory, the Queen-turned-witch brews a special poison for Snow White. When the mixture reaches its full potency, the Witch dips an apple into the cauldron, allowing the deadly liquid to soak through. Now her plan cannot fail: Snow White will eat the apple, fall victim to the Sleeping Death, and be buried alive—a prospect that fills the Queen with cruel delight. As a misty dawn begins to break over the countryside, the Witch emerges from her lair and sets out on her deadly mission to the dwarfs' house.*

Sequence 9A: Witch at cauldron, prepares apple

This sequence is essentially a continuation of sequence 7A. We've seen the Queen transform herself into a witch and the beginnings of her plan to kill Snow White; now, after an extended "cutaway" to the scenes of happiness at the dwarfs' house, we return to see her carrying out that plan.

The difference is that this time the continuity is relatively straightforward: the Witch simply prepares the poisoned apple, exults over her wicked scheme, and departs. Story development for this sequence was far simpler than that for the earlier passage, and, in fact, sequence 9A was in animation months before the story had been finally determined for sequence 7A.

Briefly in the transformation sequence, and far more prominently in this one, a major animator is introduced. It's generally agreed that, even among the extraordinary array of talent that populated the Disney studio in the 1930s, four legendary animators stood out: Norm Ferguson, Ham Luske, Fred Moore, and Bill Tytla. We've seen how the animation of *Snow White* is dominated by the work of Luske, Moore, and Tytla, but until now Ferguson has been conspicuous by his absence. Belatedly, with the introduction of the Witch, he makes his appearance. For several years Ferguson had been one of the leading pioneers of personality animation at the Disney studio. One of his early triumphs had been the Big Bad Wolf in *Three Little Pigs*, a character whose dimwitted psychology had been illuminated by Ferguson's expressive animation. It's a long way from the clumsy skullduggery of the Wolf to the crafty schemes of the Witch in *Snow White*, but Ferguson's hand is evident in both characters. Both Wolf and Witch take a special delight in their respective villainies, and that delight is unmistakable on the screen, especially in their eyes. Clearly, disguising herself as a witch is a liberating experience for this Queen: the cold, austere behavior of her earlier persona is now replaced by a flamboyant performance style, reveling in the sheer joy of evildoing for its own sake.

Along with the Witch, Ferguson was charged with animating her pet raven. Working at the head of a small unit, Ferguson was directly or indirectly responsible for *all* the character animation in the poisoned-apple sequence. One of his assistants was a young John Lounsbery, who worked with him on the scene of the Witch descending through the trap door, laughing: "Buried alive!" The exposure sheet indicates only that the two men worked together on this scene, but in later years, as one of the "Nine Old Men," Lounsbery would recall that Ferguson actually handed the scene over to him to animate by himself.

A half-dozen scenes from the beginning of this sequence, after being fully animated, inked, and painted, were cut from the version of *Snow White* that we see today. The eliminated passage, running just over thirty seconds, introduced the Witch in a long shot and then moved toward her as she added the final ingredient to her deadly mixture, uttering the incantation: "Boil, cauldron, boil/Boil, cauldron, boil/Death within your depths I see/For one who dares to rival me/Brew the magical recipe/Boil, cauldron, boil!" This isolated fragment of film was preserved at the studio and is widely available to *Snow White* enthusiasts today.[100] It's been suggested that these scenes were part of the film when it premiered at the Carthay Circle in December 1937 but were cut before general release because they would be too frightening for small children—an odd assertion, since there's nothing excessively frightening about them. The shapes of skulls do appear briefly in the steam billowing from the cauldron, but this is far less harrowing than some scenes that *were* retained in the film. In any case, the evidence indicates that this passage was cut before the premiere. In November 1937—two months after the sequence had been photographed in Technicolor, and one month before the Carthay Circle

Opposite: A Joe Grant pastel depicting the Witch with the apple.

[100] Disney Home Video included this "lost" section as a bonus chapter in both the 1994 laserdisc and the 2001 DVD releases of *Snow White*.

QUEEN FLOATS INTO FOREST

Two pieces of concept art depicting the Witch's journey to the Dwarfs' cottage. On this page, Ferdinand Horvath pictures an eerie, nightmarish forest. On the opposite page, Sam Armstrong paints an atmospheric misty dawn more akin to that in the film. Armstrong also contributed a mist effect when the sequence was produced.

opening—sequence director Bill Cottrell issued a retake order for the closer shot of the Witch, surrounded by clouds of steam, dipping the apple in the cauldron. THIS IS NOW THE FIRST SCENE IN SEQ. 9-A, he wrote. ADD FADE-IN AT HEAD END. This is, indeed, where the sequence now begins. Without any further evidence, we can only assume that the opening scenes were cut for the same reason the Soup sequence and other passages were cut: simply to tighten the continuity and move the film along at a brisker pace.

If any part of this sequence did run the risk of censorship, it was a brief episode immediately after the Witch's exit through the trap door. Making her way along the dungeon passage, she comes to a cell in which a skeleton lies on the floor, its arms stretched between the bars toward a pitcher—presumably once filled with water—that lies *just* beyond its reach. "Thirsty?" cackles the Witch. "Have a drink!" She kicks the pitcher, scattering the skeleton's bones as a spider scuttles out of the overturned pitcher. A vestige of the Prince-in-the-dungeon idea, this grim little vignette is a vivid illustration of the Witch's cruelty; if the transformation scene is the single most frightening moment in the film, this one is a close second. Some observers, particularly writer Al

Perkins, found it *too* strong. As late as January 1938, after the film had already opened, Perkins was still campaigning to have the skeleton scene taken out. He wrote to Walt that some viewers had objected to it: "My reason for disliking that shot from the first was because I thought it was too gruesome and would scare the kids. The people I talked with, however, objected on a much more serious ground: that the scene is the only thing in the picture that is in bad taste . . . I think the picture as a whole would gain rather than lose if that shot could be deleted and we could take the old girl right down to the boat."

We know that Walt approved the scene because of his comments in story conferences—and from the most compelling evidence of all: the scene did remain in the film. At the same time, Walt, practical as ever, recognized that there might be objections from other quarters, including the Production Code Administration (PCA). Before the sequence was photographed, Walt asked Cottrell to shoot a second version *without* the skeleton scene: "Arrange a dissolve for safety's sake to be shot on her . . . in the same negative—dropping this trap door and dissolving to her walking down into the boat, so we've got that shot and can match it in . . . in

case we run into objections on the horrible nature of the skeleton and skull. Same thing with the music. Call for a connection with the music to be recorded at the same time so it all can be spliced in." In the end this precaution proved unnecessary; the PCA approved the entire film without any cuts.

As in sequence 7A, the work of the character animators in this sequence was enriched by strong support from the effects animators. As the Witch leaves the castle—stepping into the boat, which rocks gently, sending slight ripples through the dark water; casting dim reflections on the wall behind her; gliding silently through the enveloping mist on her way to the forest— the effects department surrounds her with a breathless, foreboding atmosphere.

THE WITCH AND THE BRIDE

Like the earlier sequence 7A, this one reflects a subtle link with the American horror-film tradition, and once again Scott MacQueen has pointed it out. As the Witch bends over her bubbling cauldron, the musical theme underscoring her (Leigh Harline's "Theme Sinister") is propelled by a slow, throbbing, insistent rhythm that helps to build suspense. It unmistakably suggests a similar device used by Franz Waxman in his score for the 1935 horror classic *Bride of Frankenstein*, during the scene in which the Bride is brought to life.

There is, in fact, an additional and more obscure link between the two films. Among the other early ideas proposed for *Snow White*, it had been suggested in the August 1934 "Manuscript" that the Queen might keep a collection of "dozens of little people ranging in height from six inches to one inch"—her former enemies, reduced to miniature size. These tiny humans would move and speak like little automata, and "the Queen plays with them like a cat with a tiny mouse, or like a child with soldiers." Walt's handwritten notes on this document suggest that he considered this idea either for *Snow White* or for a short subject. But after the April 1935 release of *Bride of Frankenstein*, with its scene of Dr. Pretorius (Ernest Thesiger) and his homunculi—pictured very much as described in the "Manuscript"—the Disney studio did not pursue this idea.

THE DWARFS LEAVE FOR THE MINE *Morning, and after a refreshing night's sleep, the dwarfs leave the house for a day's work at the mine. Snow White sees them off at the door. One by one, the dwarfs warn her to be careful and beware of the Queen's trickery. Snow White assures them she'll be all right and gives each dwarf a good-bye kiss on the top of his head. This is a wonderful and unexpected treat for most of the dwarfs, especially Dopey, who comes back for seconds and thirds. Grumpy pretends to resist, but clearly wants Snow White to kiss him too. When she does, his heart melts and he openly shows his love for the little princess—just for a moment. Quickly catching himself, he reverts to his truculent self and stalks away defiantly. But his distraction is all too obvious; he jams his nose into a tree trunk and then walks off a bank and falls in the stream.*

Sequence 10A: Dwarfs leave for mine

Once again, an episode that was only a cursory incident in the Ames play—Snow White kissing the dwarfs good-bye as they leave for work, the dwarfs trying to wheedle extra kisses out of her—becomes the springboard for an inspired set-piece of character animation. And, once again, *story* development is determined by *character* development: confronted with the prospect of a kiss from the beautiful princess, how would each dwarf react?

The answer is this series of "variations on a theme." One by one the dwarfs emerge from the doorway, and each one responds to Snow White's kisses in a way dictated by his personality. Doc, the leader, is naturally the first dwarf to walk out the door, and Snow White's spontaneous gesture of lifting his cap and planting a kiss on the top of his head is unexpected. It catches him off guard, in the midst of his warning to beware of the Queen; suddenly his officious manner vanishes and he's happily surprised, and more than a little flustered. Bashful, next in line, can scarcely believe his eyes. He hastily removes his own cap and, avoiding eye contact, mumbles a warning of his own; and when he receives his kiss, he blushes a bright crimson and twists the cap beyond recognition. Sneezy, on the verge of another sneeze, is so moved by Snow White's kiss that his sneeze is dispelled—temporarily. Dopey, for his part, may be a prepubescent character, but Snow White's kiss brings out the Harpo Marx in his personality. None of this top-of-the-head business for him; he turns his face to Snow

White's and puckers up for a big smooch. And even though this bold approach still earns him only a chaste top-of-the-head kiss like all the others, Dopey is delirious with joy and—now identifying the doorway with kisses—tears around to the side of the house, dives through the window, and races back to the doorway for a second helping, then a third.[101]

These delightful scenes were assigned to Fred Moore (Doc, Sneezy, and Dopey) and Frank Thomas (Bashful). Years later, it was revealed that the animators themselves were surprised at the touching effectiveness of these scenes. "It was not until we had the believable characters in *Snow White*," wrote Thomas and Ollie Johnston (who assisted Moore on this sequence), "that anyone realized how provocative the act of touching could be. No one could have guessed how much the audience would be moved by mere drawings of the girl kissing the dwarfs."

The key character in this sequence, of course, is Grumpy, and once again his animation is in the hands of Bill Tytla. In the Snow White–Grumpy subplot, this sequence marks a significant milestone. Thanks to the subtleties of Tytla's character animation, *we* already know Grumpy is secretly smitten with Snow White, but here, for the first time, he briefly lets down his guard. At a story meeting, Walt described Grumpy's mixed signals: "Grumpy still has sort of a sourpuss expression; [but] when the dwarfs aren't looking, he takes off his hat and shines his head as though he would like to be kissed. He then assumes his grumpy attitude and walks by Snow White . . . He pretends to let her kiss him on the head so that it will make *her* feel better." (At one point in production, in response to Snow White's "Why, Grumpy, you do care!" Grumpy was to snap: "I *don't* care, but I just don't wanta git the place messed up!" This was one of the lines eliminated from the final cut.) In the film Grumpy's embarrassment is increased: Snow White, waving good-bye to the other dwarfs, doesn't notice him at first, and poor Grumpy is forced to march in place, coughing and harrumphing until she finally does notice him—so that he can pretend he doesn't want to be kissed.

In sequence 6A the interior of the dwarfs' house had posed a staging problem for the layout artists; in this

101 As early as a preliminary story conference in October 1934, the suggestion had been made: "Snow White, in the early morning light, is sending dwarfs off to work, kissing them—one gets on the end of the line again for a second kiss." The transcript doesn't tell us who made this suggestion, but it may have come from someone who had seen the Fleischer cartoon *There's Something About a Soldier*, released a couple of months earlier in 1934. In the Fleischer short, Betty Boop recruits soldiers for the army by offering a kiss to each new recruit, and one goofy little character sneaks back into line several times for multiple kisses.

SMACK!

HAPPY GETS FIRST KISS THAT DOPEY HAS BEEN EXPECTING—

HAPPY SNEAKS AROUND TO BACK OF LINE

sequence they had a similar problem with the exterior. In addition to the issue of "lighting"—painting the shadows to represent an early-morning scene, rather than the afternoon light in which Snow White had first discovered the cottage—the artists were faced with the problem of staging the characters' action in the relatively small, cramped area of the doorstep. "It confines you so much," artist Tom Codrick complained, "trying to keep her standing up there in the doorway with the dwarfs. I feel you might get into trouble, particularly with Dopey sliding in." But when he had tried to vary the setup, letting Snow White walk farther away from the door, "the objection was that it looked as though *she* were going to leave *them* and they were seeing her off." Codrick and a group of his fellow layout artists debated this problem for the better part of an evening meeting in March 1937. Charles Philippi suggested the solution adopted in the film: the sequence begins with Snow White walking out onto the doorstep, then cuts to close-ups featuring Snow White and the dwarfs. By now the audience understands the situation, and the next time Snow White appears in a full shot, she's standing a few steps farther from the door. As in the washing sequence, the layout continuity was "cheated" in order to preserve the *sense* of the action.

Meanwhile, Tytla's animation of Grumpy's undignified exit was turning out so well that Walt decided to add more footage. Snow White's kiss has a profound effect on Grumpy. As he walks away, we can feel his heart melting; his step slows and, dropping his tough-guy act for a moment, he gazes back at Snow White with

a sweetly shy expression. But just as quickly he recovers his cantankerous spirit, and pays for that moment of weakness by running a gauntlet of slapstick accidents. Embarrassments multiply: the distracted Grumpy walks straight into a tree trunk, pulls his nose loose, then falls in the stream; sitting in the water, he jams his cap on his head and drenches himself with another capful of water; he tries to stand up and conks his head on the bottom of the bridge; and finally he tries desperately to maintain his aplomb as he sloshes across to the opposite bank and retreats. In order to accommodate this extended litany of humiliation, several other scenes were cut. One of them was Snow White's good-bye to Happy; viewers seldom notice that, in the finished film, Snow White kisses only six of the dwarfs good-bye.[102] In return the sequence gains a satisfying resolution— Grumpy stalking imperiously away with as much dignity as he can muster, squishing at every step, water running freely from his pants.

The writers experimented with the multiple-kisses gag. In these story sketches, it's assigned to Happy.

[102] Technically, only five. Sleepy's kiss takes place offscreen while the camera is watching Dopey at the side of the house.

A DEADLY JOURNEY *The Queen, in her witch disguise and carrying her basket of apples, makes her way through the forest toward the dwarfs' house. Two vultures sitting on a branch see her coming. Instinctively realizing the nature of her mission, they leave their perch to follow her. As the Witch hobbles away down the path, the vultures flap silently through the forest behind her.*

Sequence 10B: Queen on way to Dwarfs' house

This short sequence (only three scenes) serves a mainly expository function: it charts the Witch's progress through the woods toward the dwarfs' cottage. Tony Rivera, one of the Snow White animators in Ham Luske's unit, also worked with Ferguson on the Witch's scenes in this and other sequences. It's worth noting the subtleties of the Witch's animation here as she crosses the log, one arm weighed down with the basket of apples, the other upraised, maintaining a precarious balance as she mutters feverishly to herself.

This sequence also serves to introduce the two vultures, ominous harbingers of death. The villain in the 1932 Silly Symphony *Flowers and Trees*, a grouchy old tree, had been attended by two vultures that symbolized his foul nature. Following this, a similar pair of vultures had been planned for *Snow White* from the beginning of story development in 1934. One outline had proposed introducing them early in the picture, as Snow White fled from the Huntsman into the woods,[103] and for more than a year Walt pictured them as comedy characters. In the finished film they are introduced at this later juncture in the story, and their appearances are anything but comical. Observing the Witch's progress, they turn to each other with chilling, evil grins and silently follow her on her way, a dark portent of what is to come.

After considering both Ferguson and Luske, Walt assigned animation of the vultures to Ward Kimball. With both the Soup and Lodge Meeting (see page 202) sequences cut from the film—a sort of wholesale purging of Kimball animation from *Snow White*—the vultures would remain his most memorable contribution to the finished picture. Their menacing presence is enhanced by slow, deliberate movements, carefully supervised by Walt and by sequence director Ben Sharpsteen. When the birds left their perch to follow

the Witch, Kimball was instructed to vary the pace of their movements: "In the take-off, look for a chance to speed the exposures in one spot so as to once again take away from too great an evenness [of movement]." As the birds flew through the forest, their shadows on the ground, drawn by effects animator Cy Young, came in for their own share of scrutiny: "Extend the neck and head considerably so as to positively identify them as vultures, as they now give the appearance of sea gulls."

As for the Witch, her path through the woods was marked by dead foliage and withered trees—subtly suggesting that, like Dracula, she left a trail of decay in her wake. "Do not show cast shadows from the foliage at the point where the Witch goes behind the tree in making her exit," layout artist McLaren Stewart was told. "Show that the trees are dead along the path she takes." This idea was underscored by the understated death's-head motif in the backgrounds.

As we see the film today, this sequence functions as a brief prelude to the Witch's confrontation with Snow White. As originally planned, however, the two sequences were to be separated by an upbeat passage featuring the dwarfs.

Opposite: A Joe Grant character sketch of one of the vultures.

Overleaf: A pan cel setup showing the Witch's progress through the woods. Note the subtle death's-head motifs "hidden" in the scenery.

[103] Walt's "Skeleton Outline" includes this: "The Huntsman is very sad. He looks up and sees two buzzards leaving their roost in an old dead tree, following Snow White as she goes into the dark woods."

BUILDING A BED FOR SNOW WHITE *Cut from the film: Arriving at the mine, the dwarfs hold a meeting to discuss making a special gift for Snow White. After some discussion, they agree to build a bed for her. Work at the mine is suspended for the day as the dwarfs tackle the various tasks of building the bed: Doc supervises, Grumpy and Sleepy cut wood, Bashful carves angels on the frame, Happy sews a quilt, Dopey gathers soft materials for the quilt and mattress. When we last see them, the bed is still unfinished but nearing completion.*

Cut from the film
Sequence 11A: Lodge Meeting
Sequence 11B: Bed-Building

Opposite: A story sketch of the Lodge Meeting sequence, showing the Dwarfs' meeting space, customized with homemade conveniences.

Like the Soup sequence, the other dwarf-centered episode cut wholesale from the film, the dwarfs' construction of a bed as a gift for Snow White had been planned as part of the story from the beginning. It was described in the earliest story conferences in 1934, and it wasn't cut from the film until the summer of 1937—and then only reluctantly.

The bed episode was divided into two sequences, the first depicting the dwarfs' meeting in the woods. At a story meeting in October 1934, it was agreed that "one [dwarf] gets up on a stump and conducts meeting like a lodge or convention gathering." One month later another outline suggested: "The meeting at which they decide on the bed will be a burlesque of a typical American lodge meeting." From that time on, sequence 11A was known as the "Lodge Meeting" sequence.

This sequence opened with the dwarfs seated around a large stump, just outside the mine entrance, that served as their conference table. This was another opportunity to explore the dwarfs' personalities through character animation: Doc, the officious leader, pompously presided over the meeting and tried to maintain order; Grumpy scowled and criticized; Dopey, oblivious to whatever was going on, indulged in silly pranks. One gag involved Dopey noisily cracking and eating nuts, disrupting the business of the meeting —much to the displeasure of Doc, who was standing next to him. As Doc pounded his gavel, Dopey slipped a nut underneath so that Doc cracked it for him. Doc retaliated by thumping Dopey on the head with the gavel; Dopey, anticipating another blow, quickly placed a nut on top of his head so that Doc cracked that one too. This gag

remained in the sequence for several months as more and more variations were suggested; finally it became much too elaborate and was cut from the picture altogether.

Gradually, all such extraneous gags were eliminated so as to focus on the main plot point: the dwarfs' attempts to think of an appropriate gift for Snow White. The "finished" sequence opens with the dwarfs grouped around the stump, straining to think of an idea. As inspiration strikes, one after another springs to his feet with a suggestion, only to be voted down by the others. Happy proposes a crown studded with precious jewels; Bashful a golden harp decorated with angels; Doc's idea is a royal coach "with six white hearses—er, horses"; Sneezy's suggestion is lost in another prodigious sneeze. Grumpy sourly exclaims: "Aw, give her somethin' useful, like a mop!" None of these ideas is suitable, and it's Sleepy, naturally enough, who suggests a bed. To a group who have just spent a painfully uncomfortable night sleeping on benches and in cupboards after giving up *their* beds, this is an inspired notion. The dwarfs seize on it and eagerly volunteer for various details of the bed's construction; Sleepy makes himself available to try it out when it's finished.

This leads directly into sequence 11B, the Bed Building sequence. If the Lodge Meeting sequence had been long on personality animation, this one was stuffed to overflowing with gags. The bed was to be a four-poster, built from ready-made posts: four trees growing in symmetrical positions in the woods. "The best way to come back to the bed might be to leave them working on four trees," said Walt. "Come back and here's the bed as though it's finished, but truck [the camera] back and the trees are still growing." After building a complete framework from the four trees, the dwarfs' last step would be to chop off the top branches and cut the trees loose from their stumps. Much footage was devoted to Dopey's efforts to supply raw material for the quilt and the mattress. The quilt was to be made largely from the dwarfs' own shirttails, snipped off surreptitiously by Dopey with a large pair of scissors. The mattress was to be stuffed with anything soft that came to hand. Birds

"LOOK OUT BELOW!" "HERE SHE COMES!" "HURRAY!" "C...

voluntarily sacrificed their feathers for Snow White's mattress, rabbits their soft tails. Dopey was to supply some of the mattress stuffing, too: the ends of the other dwarfs' beards, snipped with that same wicked pair of scissors, and—unfortunately for Sneezy—large clumps of dandelions. The bed still half-finished, the sequence was to end with another mighty sneeze from Sneezy, causing the mattress to swell up like a balloon and then gradually subside.

Much of the story development for these sequences took place in December 1936 and the early months of 1937, immediately after the decision to cut sequence 4A, the introduction of the dwarfs at the mine, from the picture. As a result, some of the ideas that Walt and the story crew had been loath to sacrifice in the Mine sequence were temporarily diverted into the Bed Building sequence instead. Frank Churchill's song "Dig Dig Dig," shorn of its mining lyrics, was borrowed as an

The bed approaches completion.

Opposite: The Dwarfs in action, carving their ready-made bedposts.

instrumental theme for this section.[104] Doc was seen spelling out Snow White's name with jewels inset in the bed's headboard, providing a perfect excuse to reprise his diamond-sorting business from the mine sequence—complete with Dopey's gag, inserting diamonds in his eyes to frighten the squirrel.

Walt was also anxious to establish the atmosphere of the dwarfs' mine, since, according to the current plan, this would be the audience's only look at the mine. "We show the mine entrance," he suggested, "the tracks and the mine car." He was particularly taken with an Albert Hurter sketch that had shown a tree trunk with drawers carved in it. Expanding on that idea, Walt stressed that the mine and the cottage, the dwarfs' two customary habitats, should be filled with their handmade, custom-carved implements and decorations. "I see these guys living here for years and years," he said, "and they have

had time to do all of this carving. They are real artists." When Fred Spencer questioned the idea of the drawers, Walt defended it: "They have carved these trees; they keep their tools there . . . [There is] a hole on the trunk of the tree and they have a bell hung in it. The place is full of atmosphere like that."

The continuity established, scenes were assigned to the animators. Pencil animation commenced, numerous scenes being completed in May and early June of 1937. Then, late in June, the Lodge Meeting and Bed-Building sequences were dropped from the picture. Like the Soup sequence, they were entertaining in themselves but simply slowed down the story. Ward Kimball, who had animated so much of the Soup sequence, had also been assigned most of the dwarf animation in sequence 11A, and had completed much of it—only to see both sequences cut from the picture.

[104] This was the plan in January 1937; later Paul Smith composed new themes for both sequences. A demo recording of some of Smith's music for sequence 11B, recorded in April 1937, survives today.

The birds, with help from Dopey, supply dandelions for the stuffing of Snow White's mattress.

"That was kind of a tragic period in my animation life," he recalled wryly in later years.

Much of the animation for sequence 11B had also been completed before this section was scrapped. Five decades later, surviving pencil animation was combined with story sketches to "reconstruct" the Lodge Meeting and Bed-Building sequences as bonus chapters for the *Snow White* laserdisc and, later, the DVD.[105] Today's *Snow White* enthusiast can view these passages as a fascinating sidebar to the story of the film.

As with the Soup sequence, it's easy to see through hindsight that the cutting of these sequences benefits the overall flow of *Snow White*. If anything, Walt's reasoning is easier to understand in this instance: at this point in the film we've seen the Queen/Witch brewing the poisoned apple, we've seen her on her way to kill Snow White, and suspense is beginning to build—suspense that would surely be diluted by the dwarfs' extended bed-building comedy. The tradeoff, here and in the Soup sequence, is that we lose nuances of character development in the dwarfs. Bashful's observation in the Bedroom sequence, that Snow White looked "just like a angel," had originally been the beginning of a full-fledged obsession. Here, when the dwarfs determined to build a bed, Bashful was to volunteer excitedly to carve angels on the frame, asking Doc: "Big angels or little angels?" Doc, preoccupied with something else, would answer: "Both." Bashful would next be seen

chiseling the images of angels on the wooden bed frame, using a squirrel or rabbit as a model, leaves affixed to its back to suggest wings. Similarly, Dopey's unused scenes in sequence 11B, stalking one dwarf after another and pilfering their shirttails, suggest a mischievous side of his personality that we rarely see in the finished film. And Sleepy's knack for suggesting ingenious ideas, then sleepily forgetting what he had said, was to be illustrated here too. When he suggested building a bed, the other dwarfs were to seize on the idea: "A bed! That's it! A bed!" Whereupon Sleepy would rouse himself and ask drowsily: "A bed?" Dave Hand commented at one meeting: "That's why I wonder if it might not be well to include Sleepy in this section. We have cut him out of everything."

More Dopey mischief: stealing shirttails for a patchwork quilt.

[105] This reconstruction, like that of the Bedroom Fight in sequence 5A, was carried out in 1987 by the Disney studio's Dave Pacheco on the occasion of the film's fiftieth anniversary. Unlike the Soup sequence or the Bedroom Fight, sequences 11A and 11B were abandoned before animation had been completed, and the surviving fragments have a raw, unfinished quality that gives them an added measure of interest today. For example, Kimball's scene of Doc saying "Covered with fancy filigree" is only partially animated, without inbetweens. For the version preserved on the laserdisc and DVD, the rediscovered demo soundtracks were used where possible, the remaining audio newly recorded or improvised from miscellaneous music tracks. Although "Dig Dig Dig" had been planned in 1937 as musical underscoring for the bed-building action, the laser/DVD version substituted some instrumental tracks from the "Silly Song" instead.

THE WITCH AT THE DWARFS' COTTAGE *Snow White happily busies herself in the dwarfs' kitchen, baking pies—with a special one for Grumpy—as the animals and birds help her. She is shocked when the leering face of the Witch suddenly appears at the window, but the Witch pretends to be an apple peddler. The birds, instinctively uneasy at the Witch's presence, become alarmed when she attempts to press an apple on Snow White. Swooping down on the Witch, they attempt to drive her away, but Snow White takes pity on what she thinks is a harmless old lady and kindly takes the Witch inside the house. The animals and birds, now frantic, race away toward the mine to warn the dwarfs of danger.*

Sequence 13A: Snow White making pies, witch enters house

Now the film shifts into a new key as two major threads of the story are brought together. With the elimination of the Lodge Meeting and Bed-Building sequences, we dissolve directly from sequence 10B—the Witch on her way to the cottage—to Snow White happily singing as she bakes pies for the dwarfs. It's a brief respite, a last look at Snow White's innocent world before the Witch arrives to destroy it.

The respite was originally meant to be longer; as with almost every part of *Snow White,* more story material was planned for this sequence and then cut. At one point in story development, Walt became intrigued with the idea of showing several pies in progress, including some freshly baked ones inside the oven: "have that oven with her putting in maybe Doc's pie, you know, and here the pies are all made—you see them bubbling as she opens the door and puts in a fresh one . . . out of the holes the birds make you see the juice bubbling . . . There's something in seeing a finished pie and then seeing her make one. The interest comes then in the way it was done." The finished film dispenses with this idea, and we merely see Snow White rolling out the dough for a single pie. The birds who assist her, hopping onto the crust and crimping the edges with their feet, came in for some debate in story conferences. Notwithstanding the difference between real birds and cartoon birds, some writers were simply uncomfortable with the idea of birds wiping their feet on the surface of a pie. "I wouldn't like that in a picture," said Dorothy Ann Blank. "If I were seeing it and had had nothing to do with it, I would not like it."[106] But the general consensus was that the birds were harmless, and they remained in the picture.

Bob Stokes, the talented pinch-hitter who had animated most of the Queen in sequence 7A, was called upon for all the Snow White animation in this and the following sequences, as the girl is gradually persuaded to bite into the poisoned apple. These scenes are an anomaly in the picture, the only Snow White scenes *not* animated by Ham Luske, Grim Natwick, or one of their assistants. Strictly speaking, the Stokes version of Snow White doesn't quite resemble either the Luske or the Natwick model. She might be described as the Luske Snow White on an off day, retaining much of her wide-eyed little girl expression, but with features that suggest a slightly more mature woman. Stokes, working with a measure of relative autonomy, also adds some idiosyncratic touches of his own to the character. Snow White's "takes," for example—especially the second one, as she looks up and gasps at the sight of the Witch in the window—are more pronounced than anything comparable in other parts of the film.

As for the Witch, her animation remained in the capable hands of Norm Ferguson and his corps of assistants. Walt's sweatbox notes reveal that he enjoyed the Witch's theatrical performance style as much as Ferguson did. When Snow White comes to the Witch's aid after the birds' attack, and the Witch smiles wickedly to herself, Walt told Ferguson: "The smile should be more Lionel Barrymore, more subtle." Immediately afterward, however, the Witch redoubles her bid for Snow White's sympathy. "You are to get a more 'dying calf' expression at this point," Walt said, "that is, with the lids partly down and the eyes up."

The Witch's appearance is also augmented by another subtle color effect: in these scenes her nose has a slight reddish tint, suggesting that she's suffering from a cold. When she sniffs the air, she's commenting on the aroma of the pies, but thanks to that nasal discoloration her sniffs also insinuate something vaguely unhealthy.

The animals and birds, now barred from the house, are unable to do anything further to prevent the Witch from carrying out her plan. (This staging was discussed at length in story conferences: since the birds fly freely in and out the window at the beginning of the sequence, and can only watch helplessly through the closed

[106] Two weeks later, at another meeting, Bill Tytla objected to a proposed gag for the Soup sequence that would have shown a fly, the one that continually plagued Sleepy, sipping the dwarfs' soup. When Ham Luske pointed out the bird putting its feet on Snow White's pie, Tytla replied: "That wouldn't disturb me. We always think of birds being much finer than flies."

window after Snow White takes the Witch inside, it follows that Snow White must have closed the window at some point. The final decision was to "cheat" this action, *implying* that Snow White had closed the window, off camera, before going out the door to help the Witch.) With no other recourse, the animals leave the house and go racing through the woods to summon help from the dwarfs.

An early story sketch, suggesting Snow White's extended pie-baking activities.

Overleaf: A cel setup depicting the animals' frantic race through the forest to alert the Dwarfs.

THE RACE TO SAVE SNOW WHITE *The dwarfs are just beginning their workday at the mine when the animals stampede into the clearing. Frantically pushing, pulling, and tugging at the dwarfs' beards and clothing, the animals and birds try to make them understand that something awful is about to happen. The dwarfs finally realize that Snow White must be in danger, and race back to the cottage on deerback to save their beloved princess. Meanwhile, the Witch continues to coax Snow White to try a bite of the apple. The dwarfs, riding furiously, are too late; Snow White bites into the apple and falls to the floor unconscious. The Witch exits the cottage, exulting in her triumph, just as the dwarfs approach. Through a gathering storm they chase her up the side of a mountain. The Witch, in desperation, tries to roll a huge boulder down the mountain to crush her pursuers, but lightning strikes the crag on which she is standing, and she plunges to her doom. As the dwarfs peer over the edge of the precipice, the two vultures circle silently down through the mist after her.*

This is the climactic passage of the story—a climax that occurs nowhere in the Grimms' version, or in most other versions for that matter. The traditional story of Snow White offers danger, apparent loss, sorrow, and redemption, but never suspense. And although other producers had committed the story to film, it's Walt Disney who fully realizes the possibilities of his medium—remaining faithful to the *essence* of the story, but at the same time rendering it fully cinematic. His method is the uniquely cinematic tool of cross-cutting. This was a principle D.W. Griffith had pioneered a quarter-century earlier in his Biograph films: if one character is in danger and another character is rushing to the rescue, the filmmaker can work the audience into a state of unbearable suspense by skillfully cutting back and forth between them.

But if Walt's finished chase sequence suggests Griffith, his techniques are, necessarily, vastly different. Griffith, in constructing his chase scenes, had the luxury of shooting his raw material in advance, then experimenting in the cutting room to determine by trial and error the most effective editing pattern. Because of the carefully pre-planned nature of animation, no such option was available for *Snow White*. Here the cross-cutting was meticulously planned in advance, and what

appears on the screen as a wild, freewheeling race to the rescue was calculated and formally broken down into seven separate sequences before the animation even began.

The key to this section, of course, is in the birds and animals who have observed Snow White's danger and who rush to warn the dwarfs. This is part of the genius of *Snow White*: the Disney animals and birds, which are unique to the medium of animation and have already helped to give this version of *Snow White* its warm, distinctive quality, now also function as the engine to drive the film's climactic action. We've seen how the 1916 Paramount film depicted a bird and a rabbit creeping down into the mine to whisper the news to the dwarfs. This was an admirable attempt to go beyond tradition with an effect not possible on the stage, but even so, the Paramount filmmakers were hampered by the limitations of the real world. The *idea* of their scene is charming, but the effect remains clumsy and weak. The Disney animals suffer no such limitations; roused by Snow White's danger, they become an army galloping to the rescue and propel the film into an extended, exciting climax of action.

At the time this section of the film was planned, the Bed-Building sequence was still a part of the story. The first part of sequence 14B was essentially a continuation of the bed-building action (and in fact the original working title of the sequence was "Dwarfs finish bed, animals warn them"); the effect was that the camera, after lingering on Snow White and the Witch for an extended time, would return to the dwarfs and show the final stages of their work on the bed. As they started to carry the bed back to their home, the animals would come racing into the scene.

Accordingly, during 1936 and much of 1937, more bed-building gags were planned for the first part of this sequence. Now that the bed was more or less complete, the dwarfs would be seen cutting off the top branches of the four "corner post" trees and chopping them loose from their bases. Walt suggested that one dwarf would be seen cutting off the top branches of a tree while still sitting in them, and would ride them down to the ground with a loud crash. This hapless dwarf probably would have been Sleepy, although Dopey was also nominated

at one meeting. Doc would be seen polishing the gold letters "SNOW WHITE" inlaid in the headboard; Sleepy, true to his word, would settle down for a test nap.

When the Bed-Building sequence was removed from the film in the summer of 1937, the corresponding action in this sequence was necessarily eliminated too. These cuts had the combined effect not only of uncluttering the story line, but of compressing time in the action onscreen. Now the army of animals and birds would arrive at the mine just minutes after the dwarfs themselves arrived. One of Jimmie Culhane's scenes from sequence 4B, showing the dwarfs marching home from the mine, was reversed and reused to show them returning to it. As they picked up their tools and started to work, some layouts and animation, already completed with the bed-building action in mind, were ingeniously adapted to the new continuity. "After a new layout has been given you, replacing the bed with the mine car," Eric Larson was told in one sweatbox note, "get a new test and change the actions of Happy so as to show him dragged across the scene during about the last 2 feet."

Of course the main benefit of the cuts was to streamline the *emotional* continuity of the film at this point in the narrative. We've already seen Snow White threatened by the Witch's ominous presence and felt the excitement of the animals who sensed her danger. Now, instead of detouring into extended comedy business with the dwarfs, the film maintains its emotional pitch as the animals come bursting into the clearing, frantic with the urgency of their mission.

The frenzied animals and birds surround the dwarfs, pushing and pulling them back in the direction of their home. In one early version of the story, Grumpy had been seen as the dwarf who finally understood what the animals were trying to tell them; in the finished film, it's Sleepy who wakes up long enough to suggest that Snow White may be in danger. This was to be another instance of Sleepy eliciting a reaction from the other dwarfs and then reawakening in surprise, forgetting that he had made the statement in the first place.[107] But here again the film maintains its taut pace, not pausing for such niceties. Snow White is in danger! Doc, the nominal leader of the group, is completely flustered and helpless in the face of a real crisis, but Grumpy instantly takes command and leads the charge to save Snow White. Leaping (or stumbling, or being helped) onto the backs

Grumpy, instantly taking command, leads the charge.

[107] In fact, Sleepy's closeup here, animated by Les Clark, is borrowed from another such moment in the discarded Lodge Meeting sequence (11A). Scene 12 in the earlier sequence—"Why don't you make her a bed?"—is now adapted as scene 2 in sequence 14E: "Maybe the old Queen's got Snow White."

of the deer, the dwarfs ride furiously back through the woods to save their princess.

As the chase builds in excitement, all the action is similarly streamlined. At one time Walt had pressed for scenes of the animals and birds registering happiness when the dwarfs finally understood them, and at another meeting it was suggested that Dopey might fall off his deer while crossing a stream, be whisked down a waterfall, and intercept the deer again just as he reached the bottom.[108] The finished film dispenses with all such business; nothing is allowed to clutter the action. The only remaining gags are absorbed into the relentless tempo of the chase: Happy loses his grip on his deer and is hauled back into place by helpful birds; Dopey, desperately hanging onto the tail of another deer, is yanked along behind it, his feet occasionally touching the ground in wild, elongated strides. The turtle, still plodding doggedly in the direction of the mine, is bowled over by the animals stampeding back in the opposite direction.

Beginning with sequence 14E, when the chase begins, the film cuts back and forth six times between the house and the dwarfs (counting a single cutaway to the dwarfs in the midst of sequence 14H, "Snow White dies"). All the action sequences were directed by Ben Sharpsteen and animated by the second-string dwarf artists and the animal specialists. The animation of Bernard Garbutt, in particular, shines in these sequences. One of his scenes in 14B, showing the deer and other animals charging through the woods to warn the dwarfs, reappears a few minutes later—reversed, to show the deer running back in the other direction, and with dwarfs mounted on their backs.

The scenes at the house are essentially extensions of sequence 13A, still directed by Bill Cottrell. Now the staging becomes more sophisticated, subtly enhancing the Witch's menace as she advances toward the camera. These scenes introduce another of the film's distinctive innovations. In earlier versions of the story, Snow White had simply eaten the apple unquestioningly, but here Walt urged "a reason for Snow White to take the apple instead of just being hungry." Now a new fantasy element was added to the story: the Witch tells Snow White that this is no ordinary apple, but a magic wishing apple. Walt defended this idea: "I believe any fairy tale can have wishing things . . . I believe in fairy tales you want those things." As in the earlier sequence, most of Snow White's animation is in the hands of Bob Stokes, and once again she adheres loosely to the Ham Luske little-girl model, all wide-eyed innocence as she repeats credulously: "A wishing apple?" Her death scene takes place offscreen, the camera remaining on the Witch as she whispers in keen anticipation: "Her breath will still . . . her blood congeal . . ."

She hasn't long to enjoy her triumph; as she emerges from the cottage, the army of dwarfs and animals is fast approaching. The ensuing chase takes place in a driving rainstorm. During the previous sequences, the sky has been gradually darkening; now we see the first flashes of lightning and the first raindrops, beginning softly, then becoming heavier. The effects animators labored long and hard over this sequence, but Walt felt the rain

[108] The exposure sheets suggest that vestiges of this gag survived long enough to be animated.

important to the picture: "You know a chase in the rain is twice as effective to me. You feel they are going to slip and it's cold and wet . . . I can see some marvelous setups with the chase with the wind blowing and the rain beating down. It complicates our animation, but it sure makes things nasty." As the Witch flees through the pelting raindrops, she becomes tangled in the same vines that had encumbered Snow White on her own terrified flight into the forest. As she starts up the rocky slope, the rocks are dark and slippery, rivulets of water running down as the rain intensifies.

During early development of this sequence, it had been suggested that Doc and Grumpy might remain behind at the cottage with Snow White while the rest of the dwarfs pursued the Witch. By this time, however, the film has built up a driving momentum and is not about to abandon it. The dwarfs spot the Witch escaping and, without much more than breaking stride, all seven gallop furiously after her (and it's still Grumpy who leads the charge). Similarly, the climactic action at the top of the rocky crag was built up only gradually during story development. In some early outlines, the Witch simply slipped off the ledge and fell to her doom; even her attempt to roll the boulder down on the pursuing dwarfs appeared only intermittently in early treatments. No such ambivalence in the finished version: the combined effect of the dark sky, the wind and heavy rain, the portentous presence of the vultures, the racing music, the Witch's desperation, and the precariously teetering boulder creates a nightmarish vision. As the Witch anticipates her grisly victory, a powerful bolt of lightning, animated by Josh Meador, shatters her rocky perch and she falls, her screams lost in the wind.

This is the climactic moment of the sequence; although the rain continues to fall, the surging excitement of a few seconds earlier now gives way to an ominous stillness. Walt had intended to end this section with a scene of the vultures circling down into the chasm, but on seeing an early version of the scene he was disappointed in the result. "I was thinking this thing isn't working out," he said at a September 1937 sweatbox session. "I pictured them going down and down, but it's not going to register. The rumble of the stuff falling we can carry in that scene, cut up to the vultures and they leave and start to circle down. Just get them started down and cut to the cliff and the dwarfs come and look over, then fade out." But two months later the scene was rephotographed, saved by a soft-focus mist effect. The finished sequence ends as Walt intended: the dwarfs gather and peer over the cliff; the vultures leave their perch and are soon shrouded in mist, circling down and down into the silence to claim their prey.

THE DWARFS MOURN SNOW WHITE *The dwarfs are too late to save Snow White, and as she lies dead, they gather to mourn her. Outside the house the animals and birds are watching too, and as the rain softly falls, nature itself seems to be weeping for the little princess. Unable to bear the thought of burying her in the cold ground, the dwarfs build a glass coffin for Snow White and keep watch over her in the forest. The Prince, still searching for his lost love, hears the story of the beautiful maiden who sleeps in the glass coffin.*

Sequence 15A: Snow White dead
Sequence 15B: Titles

This sequence is the moment of truth. The bold intention declared in the film's opening, of telling a new kind of story in animated cartoons, has been leading up to this challenge: to depict a deeply emotional scene on the screen. The audience, long conditioned to expect comedy in cartoons, must be so deeply immersed in the story by this point that they feel the sadness of the scene—no laughs, no shortcuts, no easy way out. Winthrop Ames had removed a similar scene from his play in 1912 because it had proved too distressing for his young audience.[109] But Ames was writing for children. The Disney studio had a different problem; if they faltered before this sequence, it was because of the immense challenge of convincingly conveying such deep emotions in animation.

In the earliest stages of story development, the writers had suggested that the dwarfs would return from chasing the Witch and find Snow White dead, and that Doc would lead them in prayer. As late as November 1936, the story was still planned along these lines. But as Walt and his story crew continued to refine the sequence, the action became simpler. Step by step, overt action and dialogue were eliminated. The most effective way to communicate the mood would be to show the dwarfs speechless with grief, tears in their eyes, and even that would be an enormous challenge in animation. At a conference in May 1937, Walt and the writers debated the risks of this sequence. Ken Anderson suggested doing away with closeups and simply showing the dwarfs in full shot from the rear. "Is there more value in showing closeups of these fellows crying?" he asked. "They might look funny crying." "I don't think so," Walt replied, "I think you'll really feel for them." A few minutes later, perhaps trying to convince himself,

he reiterated: "I think we can handle the stuff so it won't be laughable. You know the characters so well by this time."

But Walt was well aware of the pitfalls in this sequence, and later in the same conference he reluctantly suggested that it might be cut altogether. "You know what happened to Snow White, you have seen what happened to the Queen—would it be good to fade out on the vultures and fade in on our titles, not showing the house shot?"[110] The group, including Walt, voted overwhelmingly to keep the mourning dwarfs in the picture, but to postpone production and finish sequence 16A first.

Finally, in August 1937, the dwarf animation was assigned to Frank Thomas. During production Thomas had distinguished himself with his dwarf animation; this sequence would be the acid test of his abilities. Years later, writing with his longtime friend Ollie Johnston, Thomas recalled the difficulties of animating this passage: "It just felt like they should all move as little as possible . . . They'd have strong body attitudes that could be held for the most part, and maybe a sagging move on the head here and there, just enough to keep it alive. Even a sniff seemed too much action for the mood." Thomas continued to strip away overt actions, reducing them to an absolute minimum. One scene of Dopey staring straight ahead, then breaking down in sobs and burying his face in Doc's shoulder, did elicit an unwanted laugh from early viewers; the scene was promptly shortened, and in the finished film begins with Dopey already turning to Doc's shoulder.[111] As Thomas noted: "There was an unexpected bonus from this cut, because now Grumpy was the only dwarf with a major body move." Grumpy, who has so stubbornly resisted Snow White's charms, now seems the dwarf most profoundly moved by her death; he stares in disbelief and then turns and hides his face from the camera, choked and sobbing. The slow movement in these scenes made extraordinary demands on the inbetweener, and "so," Thomas told John Canemaker, in addition to his regular assistant Art Elliott, "you have to pick an inbetweener that you can either whip or lead or inspire." He identified Bob McCrea as the artist who filled this role.

As Thomas's animation began to appear in sweatbox, it was examined with possibly even greater intensity than

[109] Technically, the scene Ames removed in 1912 was that of the dwarfs and the glass coffin in the forest, which actually corresponds to sequence 16A in the Disney film. But his object was to spare his audience a scene of intense sadness; and in the Disney film, the dwarfs are far more visibly grief-stricken in the present sequence than in the later scenes in the forest.

[110] The context of the conversation suggests that Walt was motivated not only by the story material, but also by his desire to reduce the overall running time of the feature.

[111] It's not clear when the preliminary screening of the Dopey animation took place; the exposure sheet for the scene, dated October 1937, shows no evidence of the change in footage. But some of Thomas's cleanup drawings from what was originally the first part of the scene are reproduced on page 476 of *Disney Animation*.

The Dwarfs inside the house, and the animals outside, mourn Snow White in these story sketches. The camera move suggested in the sketch at left was replaced by a shifting-focus effect in the finished film.

usual. "Ham [Luske] thought perhaps there were parts of the face moving which wouldn't move," read one sweat-box note, "said the eyes could stay where they were and the eyebrows take the extreme drop; he thought the head tilts should stay as they are. Fred [Moore] suggested that instead of hitting the extreme at the bottom, you hit it halfway or a third of the way down, then inbetween from there down. Modify the action, anyway. Also slow down the tears. The welling up of the tears in the eyes should be slower." The effects artists, animating the tears as they ran down the dwarfs' faces, came in for the same scrutiny: "Get more roundness in the tears; bring out the highlight and don't let the tears be so blue. Don't get so much contrast between the water in the eye and the eyeball as was shown in the color test."

As the dwarfs watch over Snow White inside the house, the animals and birds, animated by Milt Kahl, are keeping their own vigil outside in the rain. (Considering the tarnished reputation of the Silly Symphony *The Goddess of Spring*, it's worth noting that Walt commended the mourning animals in that short as a model for their counterparts here.) All of this is underscored by Frank Churchill's "Chorale for Snow White," played on a reedy organ.

The scenes of the grief-stricken dwarfs and animals give way to a transitional sequence that bridges the change of seasons, and Snow White's interment in the glass coffin, in a series of intertitles. Like everything else in the film, these titles were carefully analyzed by Walt. Dorothy Ann Blank was assigned to write them, and Walt continually pressed for brevity, urging Blank to

express the story points with a minimum of words. Otto Englander suggested the title background we see in the film, a classically simple composition of blank sky punctuated by a single tree branch, which would convey the changing seasons by falling leaves, blowing snow, and budding blossoms. At the May 1937 story conference, where Walt had considered dropping the scenes of the mourning dwarfs, he was—in his effort to simplify this part of the picture—similarly prepared to sacrifice the titles. "Suppose you left out the titles and . . . faded in on the snow falling. From that dissolve into a spring effect and then dissolve into the coffin and pick up without any titles."

But again it was clear that Walt and the rest of the team preferred to retain the titles; they would simply have to be as understated as possible. The day after the meeting Dorothy Blank submitted her text—then continued to revise it for several days as Walt insisted on fewer and fewer words. Blank's four titles were conflated to three, and Walt personally rewrote the third one before the final lettering began, reducing it to its essence. The result is an elegantly simple passage, with the economy and grace of the best silent-film titles, bridging the transition into the forest scenes:

. . . so beautiful, even in death, that the dwarfs could not find it in their hearts to bury her . . .

. . . they fashioned a coffin of glass and gold, and kept eternal vigil at her side . . .

. . . the Prince, who had searched far and wide, heard of the maiden who slept in the glass coffin.

In a quiet forest glade the Prince finds his Snow White, attended by the grieving dwarfs and animals. Sadly he sings to her a song of love, the song he had sung so long ago in the garden. He kisses her and then kneels beside the glass coffin. But the kiss of true love is the antidote to the apple's poison. Suddenly Snow White blinks, opens her eyes, and awakens as if from a deep sleep. She is alive! As the dwarfs and animals dance wildly with joy, the Prince lifts Snow White from the glass coffin and carries her to his horse. She bids the dwarfs goodbye and departs with the Prince toward his castle, shining in the sky beyond the horizon. And the storybook closes, assuring us that they lived happily ever after.

Sequence 16A: Snow White in coffin, back to life, away with Prince

Not having spared us the deep sorrow of Snow White's apparent death, the film now allows us the full measure of joy at her revival. Although the Grimms' tale and most other versions of "Snow White" had brought the princess back to life by dislodging the morsel of poisoned apple stuck in her throat, Walt and his team seem never to have considered resolving the story in this mildly unpleasant way. Instead, beginning with their earliest outlines, they borrowed a device from another fairy-tale heroine, Briar Rose (Sleeping Beauty): the poison casts her into a deep sleep, from which she is awakened only by the kiss of true love. The Disney film tells us of this possible outcome long before it occurs, when the Witch discovers it in her book of spells, but then distracts us with all the action that follows afterward.

Along with the opening sequence of Snow White and the Prince in the garden, this happy reunion of the lovers at film's end was one of the last parts of the picture to be developed and produced. In the finished film, it flows directly out of the montage of titles and even seems to be part of the montage itself: during the last of the titles we hear the Prince singing "One Song"—not passionately, as he had sung it on that long-ago day in the garden, but tenderly and plaintively. His voice continues to underscore the picture as we see the dwarfs, coming with flowers to pay tribute to their departed princess. Then we *see* the Prince singing, and suddenly we're not in the abstract world of the montage any longer; the Prince has finally found Snow White and is singing of his everlasting devotion. He advances toward

[112] Very early in story development, it had been suggested that the dwarfs' first instinct would be to protect their beloved Snow White from this stranger: "They refuse to let him approach the coffin, but when he breaks into a song of lamentation for his dead love, they fall back." Such ideas were dropped as the story was simplified and uncluttered.

the glass coffin, and the dwarfs, who have never seen him before, instinctively step aside so that he can approach his lost love.[112]

During story conferences, Ham Luske proposed extending the montage effect still further with a series of cross-dissolves as Snow White came to life and the Prince carried her away. Luske's concern was motivated by the sheer mechanics of the sequence: such dissolves would bridge gaps in the action, so that the potentially awkward scene of the Prince lifting Snow White out of the coffin could be omitted altogether. Walt argued for retaining it: "Lifting her up seems important to me. If he has her in his arms you can cut to the rest. You can't jump from her in the coffin to him carrying her . . . You could even have him put her up on the horse. He's a real he-man." Luske and some of the other artists had been picturing the glass coffin at ground level. To depict the Prince lifting Snow White from ground level and rising to a standing position, moving with convincing weight *and* without clumsiness, might have been an impossible demand on any animator. But Walt was envisioning something different: "I think the coffin should be like Napoleon's tomb, sitting on a sort of base that raises it up—something that can be carved." In the film, the glass coffin is indeed set on an elevated base, and the Prince lifts Snow White both times—out of the coffin, onto the horse—convincingly and gracefully.

It's fitting that this last sequence in the picture unites the talents of both the major Snow White animators: Grim Natwick animates both the Prince and Snow White until she sits up in the coffin, after which both characters are taken over by Luske's unit. The dwarfs are animated principally by Frank Thomas, as a complement to the scenes of the mourning dwarfs. It's a natural transition: here he takes them from the utter despair of their scenes by the coffin, through their astonishment as Snow White begins to stir—with interpolated scenes by Dick Lundy and Fred Spencer as the dwarfs go wild with joy—to their last bittersweet farewells as she kisses them good-bye. (At this point the montage idea does return, with a series of cross-dissolves as Snow White kisses the dwarfs good-bye and departs with the Prince. What we get is a generalized *sense* of

Snow White's leave-taking, and in fact we see her kiss only six of the dwarfs. Sleepy, whose good-bye kiss in sequence 10A had taken place offscreen, is similarly passed over here.)

As Snow White and the Prince set off into the distance, their final scenes of happiness are enriched by other familiar effects. Their distant figures, walking toward the horizon, are reduced by means of washoff relief cels, like our earlier view of Snow White sweeping the dwarfs' doorstep. One scene, fully animated but cut at the last minute, depicted the lovers passing a flowing stream with the special reflective water effect that we first saw during Snow White's walk through the forest.

And the film's final animated image is a lavish multi-plane shot of the Prince's castle appearing majestically against the sun, a remnant of the discarded dream sequence. Accompanied by a choir singing a final exultant chorus of "Some Day My Prince Will Come," Snow White is allowed her dream vision at last—and now it's a dream come true.

A composite cel setup, depicting Snow White attended in the forest by dwarfs and animals.

Overleaf: A story sketch depicting the final "sunburst" multiplane shot of the castle.

7

FINISH THE PICTURE!

Early in the summer of 1937, Dave Hand called an emergency meeting of the dwarf animators. The emergency was a remarkable one: after three years of meticulous work by the entire Disney staff, reaching unprecedented and ever higher standards in every area of animated filmmaking, the dwarf animators had become *too* meticulous. Dwarf scenes that had been okayed in rough animation were not being sent to the inbetween department, simply because animators like Fred Moore, Bill Tytla, and Frank Thomas didn't trust any of the artists outside their respective units to make the inbetween or cleanup drawings. So devoted to *Snow White* had they become, so proprietary about "their" characters and "their" scenes, that the scenes were being hoarded in their units while they and their assistants did the supplementary work themselves. The result was a bottleneck in the operation, an increasingly serious impediment to finishing production of *Snow White* on time.

Hand was sympathetic to their dedication and, being a former animator himself, understood that concentrated attention *was* required to maintain fine details of the dwarfs' appearances and personalities in closeup dialogue scenes. But for fast action scenes, he insisted, the inbetween department could and should be trusted to take up the slack. "In some cases where the figures are moving around, all you fellows who have been in the business any length of time at all know how a drawing will flash through and never be seen again, and how foolish it is to dress it up too much," he pleaded. He cited a scene in the "Spooks" sequence, "a scene where the seven dwarfs scramble around into a bunch and come around into a whole position with their picks raised . . . That scene has been returned into sweatbox with every drawing very carefully cleaned up. It is foolish. That fast action takes place for three feet. There are seven dwarfs and that makes [the equivalent of] twenty-one feet of a single character." He proposed to combat the problem by appointing animators from the studio's shorts units to go from one dwarf unit to another as "shock troops," sitting in and helping to move the unfinished scenes through production. Upon completion of the current crop of shorts, *all* the studio's inbetweeners would be put to work on the feature. Fred Moore's response was instant and wary: "Do they know anything about the dwarfs?"

That such a conversation was even necessary is a testament to the dedication of the artists who worked on *Snow White*. But Hand's concern was a valid one. *Snow White* had now been announced as a Christmas 1937 attraction, and Walt and his team had mounted a desperate drive to finish production in time to release the picture on the first of December. Assessing the amount of animation still to be completed, Hand had calculated that 70 feet of finished animation must move through the studio *every day* in order to meet that goal. A new sense of urgency was taking hold throughout the studio, an urgency that would drive the artists to heroic lengths throughout the long, hot summer and autumn of 1937. All of the company's resources were riding on this terrific gamble, and the entire staff pitched in with an extraordinary unity of purpose. Background painter Maurice Noble was moved into an office close to the

An inker carefully traces a
Snow White cel in 1937.

hub of the L-shaped production building. "And the
room was on an angle with Walt's room," he recalled, "a
right angle, so he could look into my window and I
could look into his window. And of course I worked
very hard!"

Particularly hard-pressed during this frenzied time
were the ink and paint department and the camera
department. These were the final links in the chain of
production, and with every delay at earlier stages, the
pressure on these departments was increased. The
inkers and painters were given unexpected relief in
October: the addition of new help. The Harman-Ising
cartoon studio, which had been releasing its cartoons
through MGM, suddenly lost its distribution contract.

Desperately trying to keep their studio afloat, Hugh
Harman and Rudy Ising turned to Walt, their friend
and former employer, for help; this was the situation
that led Walt to subcontract production of the Silly
Symphony *Merbabies* to them. The first step in this
cooperative enterprise, however, was the loan of
Harman and Ising's entire ink and paint staff to the
Disney studio to help finish *Snow White*. The new
inkers and painters reported for work on Monday, the
4th of October; by this time the department was
working round-the-clock shifts, as were some of the
studio's other departments. The lights on Hyperion
Avenue burned brightly far into the night.

Late in the summer, a screening of the complete

A longer view of the Hyperion ink and paint department.

Opposite: A.P. Giannini (left) and A.H. Giannini (right).

[113] Sadly, Ames did not live to see the Disney *Snow White*. He died in November 1937, a scant seven weeks before the opening.

[114] Another early booster was W.G. Van Schmus, managing director of New York's prestigious Radio City Music Hall, who was an admirer of Walt's pictures and regularly featured the latest Disney short on the Music Hall's program. Throughout production of *Snow White*, Walt recalled, Van Schmus maintained an unflagging faith in the film and promised to book it into his theater. When "Mr. Van" died in 1942 he was succeeded by his assistant, Gus Eyssell, who had crossed paths with Walt during his early days in Kansas City, but who was notably cooler toward the exhibition of Disney features at the Music Hall.

rough cut was held on the sound stage for the entire staff. Artists who were focused on isolated details of the film had an opportunity to see them in the overall context of the picture as it took shape. The screening had a powerful impact on one important attendee: Walt's daughter Diane, who was three and a half years old at the time. Years later she retained a vivid memory of the occasion: "When the Queen gulped down her potion and began to turn into the Witch I became terrified. I remember screaming in terror, over and over again—and suddenly I found myself outside the sound stage, just outside that big door, with a strange man looking down at me . . . not unkindly, actually." Walt laughed as he told reporters about his daughter's reaction to *Snow White*. "She hated it," he told one journalist in 1938. "She got up and left, protesting." (Two years later, having finished *Pinocchio*, he told another reporter that Diane had watched the considerably more frightening scenes in that film without incident: "Now, he says, he doesn't think she would be scared at all by the Witch.")

During the summer of 1937, the studio had finalized its acquisition of rights to Winthrop Ames's theatrical version of *Snow White*. This may seem surprising at

such a late date; the Disney film story was firmly set by this time, and the writers had used little, if anything, from Ames's script. But the acquisition was strictly a protective measure on the part of the Disneys' attorney, Gunther Lessing. Lessing had already contacted Ames personally in 1936 to purchase the rights to his play. Ames had commented at the time that "Mr. Disney's attorneys say he means to use none of this material in the film. In that case he need safely pay me nothing . . . Besides I have so much admiration for the charm and art of Mr. Disney's work, that I should give him every benefit of any reasonable doubt."[113] At Lessing's insistence, the studio had paid Ames for a license anyway, but Lessing was still concerned that Paramount's contract for the motion-picture rights in 1916 had created a vague situation that left the Disney studio in a dubious position. "We were alarmed," he wrote to Walt, "over the fact that many members of our organization had seen the Ames version play on the stage and had had other access thereto." Now, in June 1937, the studio purchased the animated-cartoon rights from Paramount and settled the matter.

The studio's single biggest concern at this point, of course, was money. Theoretically this was Roy's concern, not Walt's, but *Snow White* had already cost far more than anyone had expected and was continuing to run up heavy expenses, and Walt was now being forced to consider the financial aspect of his picture. Roy had approached the Bank of America on three separate occasions since 1935 for large loans to complete the film, and when yet another infusion of cash was needed in the fall of 1937, Roy prevailed on Walt to show his work-in-progress to the bank's Joe Rosenberg. Walt was apprehensive. In later years he explained to Pete Martin that Rosenberg, still new to the film business, had prepared for the *Snow White* screening by asking around for advice on this Disney matter and had received discouraging replies from some Hollywood insiders. (One notable exception was producer Walter Wanger, a friend of Walt's who had believed in the *Snow White* venture from the start.[114]) On 11 September, the day of the screening, Walt wryly recalled, "Roy didn't show up . . . just the two of us sat in this big projection room." As the still-uncompleted film unreeled, Walt sat next to Rosenberg, nervously explaining away the gaps and rough edges that appeared onscreen. After the finish he walked Rosenberg to his car, waiting in an agony of suspense for the banker's verdict. "He talked about everything but the picture . . . He started talking about the weather and he was [saying] he had to get somewhere." Finally Rosenberg reached his car and got in. "He says, 'That thing is going to make a hatful of money,' and he drove off . . . That's all he said, 'This thing is going to make a hatful of money.'" The loan was promptly approved.

THE BANK OF AMERICA AND THE GIANNINI BROTHERS

During production of *Snow White*, Walt and Roy Disney were drawn increasingly into the orbit of another remarkable pair of brothers, the Gianninis. The rise of Amadeo Peter "A.P." Giannini and his banking empire is one of the great American success stories. From modest beginnings in San Francisco in 1904, he rose quickly through a combination of toughness, intuitive skill, and innovative thinking. By the early 1930s, through his efforts, the Bank of America had become one of the largest banks in the world. Giannini's rapid rise and success were remarkable, but equally noteworthy was his continuing concern for the middle class. His initial expansion had been based on small loans to California fruit growers and other clients that most banks regarded as poor credit risks. Throughout his career he continued to champion these "small borrowers," and thus played an important role in bringing banking services within the reach of ordinary Americans.

His younger brother, Attilio Henry "A.H." Giannini, had a more direct bearing on Walt's and Roy's fortunes. A.H. began his career in medicine but changed professions in 1909 to join his brother's banking empire. Almost immediately he challenged another banking convention by making loans to the motion-picture industry. His involvement with the movies increased during the 1910s and 1920s, and by 1928, "Doc" Giannini was such a fixture in the film business that the AMPA awarded him its Sam Harris cup "for the best suggestion or deed in promoting a spirit of goodwill and cooperation between the public and the film industry." Walt could hardly have been unaware of this highly publicized ceremony; it was held at New York's Biltmore Hotel on 20 November 1928—two days after the opening of *Steamboat Willie* at the Colony Theater.

Shortly after this, the younger Giannini returned to his home base in Los Angeles, where he became even more involved in financing film production, at the Disney studio and others. He established a friendly rapport with Walt and Roy, becoming yet another important "Doc" in Walt's life. It was Giannini's friendship with the Disneys that initially paved the way for financing of *Snow White*, and when he resigned from the Bank in 1936 to become president of United Artists, his successor, Joe Rosenberg, continued to approve the extended loan. "The Doc's been more than a banker to the movies," Walt told a journalist. "Everybody in Hollywood's cried on his shoulder."

8

THE OPENING

As *Snow White* moved inexorably toward completion inside the Disney studio, a wave of anticipation was building on the outside. At this time *Snow White* was still envisioned as a Christmas 1937 attraction, and the combined publicity forces of the Disney and RKO studios had been working to whet the appetites of the moviegoing public for the treat in store for them. Tantalizing reports had appeared sporadically in the press throughout production, and as early as September 1936 Walt made a guest appearance on Cecil B. DeMille's *Lux Radio Theatre* to promote his forthcoming feature.[115]

Early in 1937, RKO Radio, fresh from its triumphant acquisition of the Disney distribution contract, began a campaign of Disney publicity and joined in the promotion of *Snow White*. At RKO's request, a unique promotional tool was created: a short film that would show the inside of the Disney studio and offer an advance glimpse of *Snow White*—to be shown not to theatrical audiences, but to RKO exhibitors. In the summer of 1937, Walt assigned the project to Al Perkins and the head of his technical staff, Bill Garity. Perkins had come to the Disney studio from the staff of the *March of Time* newsreel and was a natural choice to write and direct such a promotional short. Garity, a fast and efficient worker, shot most of the scenes during two days in July 1937. "Al Perkins . . . wanted me to come over and take the part of an animator," said Jack Kinney. "I sat at a desk and they shot me; it was done for a promotional job. And all I did was come in and sit down and do flipping the papers and whatnot."[116]

This promotional reel, known as *A Trip Through Walt Disney Studios*,[117] survives today as a precious historical record of the Disney studio in 1937. A slightly nervous Walt, photographed in his office, makes an impromptu address to the RKO exhibitors, hoping that the short "might help you in the selling of the product." Kinney, sitting at his desk, labors intently at a drawing before crumpling it up in disgust and throwing it in the wastebasket. Other studio stalwarts are similarly glimpsed: Webb Smith pounds at a typewriter, Dave Hand confers with Frank Churchill, Norm Ferguson grimaces in a mirror as he sketches Pluto, Les Clark peers into a Moviola. Fred Moore's legendary drawing ability is captured in closeup as, sketching quickly and confidently, he executes two consecutive animation drawings of Mickey Mouse. Along with its *Snow White* connection, this picture inadvertently offers us a time capsule of Disney shorts in production in mid-1937: *Lonesome Ghosts*, *Donald's Ostrich*, and *Little Hiawatha* are all seen in various stages of production. In one scene Leigh Harline conducts a studio orchestra in a passage of the *Donald's Ostrich* score, and registers great annoyance when a voice from the control room interrupts him in mid-take.

It's always been claimed that, until the opening, *Snow White* had been ridiculed in Hollywood establishment circles as a quixotic venture, labeled "Disney's Folly" by industry cynics.[118] Such ridicule is not evident in the trade press of the time, which tended toward positive, supportive coverage of all filmmakers, and certainly of Walt's pictures. Leon Schlesinger, producer of Looney Tunes and Merrie Melodies for Warner Bros., did sound a note of dissent in June 1937. "Brevity is the secret of the success of the short subject," Schlesinger

[115] This appearance by Walt, on the *Lux* broadcast of 28 September 1936, was made at the invitation of DeMille and his sponsors and was encouraged by Roy Disney as a way to help support the "Mickey Mouse birthday week" promotion then being staged by United Artists. Walt obligingly discussed Mickey's early years and spoke to the audience in Mickey's voice, but the conversation quickly turned to *Snow White*.

[116] By the summer of 1937 Kinney was working in the story department, but he had started at the studio as an animator.

[117] This was the generic title assigned to the film, although no actual title card appears on the screen.

[118] These claims appeared in print as early as December 1937, just after the film's sensational opening.

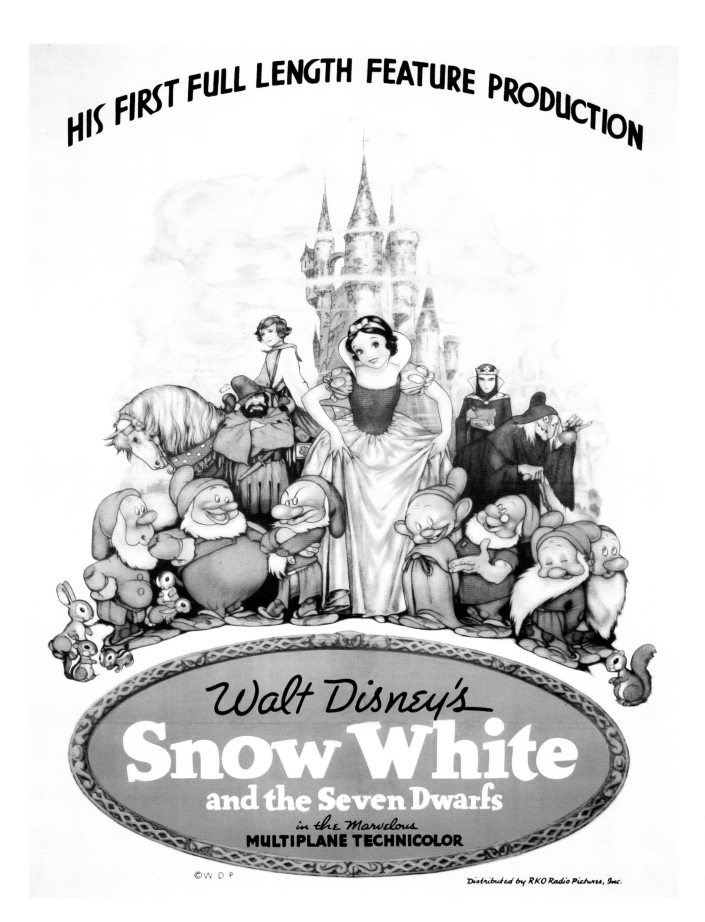

This classic poster art by Gustaf Tenggren afforded many moviegoers their first glimpse of the film's characters.

opined. "Give the theater patron just a little bit less than he wants and he goes away satisfied and waiting for more. Cartoon makers have been in business for 20 years on that policy, and I have my doubts as to the success of a cartoon which will run at least an hour in length." But even this polite skepticism was qualified: "For the present, at least, I do not intend to follow Disney's lead. If the public accepts *Snow White*, however, and cries for more, I'm frank to say I will be forced to follow."

Whatever the climate within Hollywood, the general public looked forward to *Snow White* with eager anticipation as December approached. The age of the great American department store was in full swing in 1937, and as early as October, huge, ornate *Snow White* displays began to appear in department-store windows across the nation. A different kind of publicity appeared in magazines. Since 1934, *Good Housekeeping* magazine had featured a monthly Disney page in color, each page showcasing a current or forthcoming Disney short. A standard format had been established for the *Good Housekeeping* pages, with art by Disney artist Tom Wood and a text, usually written in rhyme, that presented a condensed or simplified version of the film's story. For the November and December 1937 issues of the magazine, these simple pages were replaced by a far more elaborate presentation of *Snow White*. Wanting illustrations that captured the spirit of the film, Walt asked Phil Dike in July 1937 to recommend a member of

the background staff who might illustrate the *Good Housekeeping* adaptation. Dike agreed with part of Walt's idea—"I have talked with Tom [Wood] and he realizes the need for a professional illustration job"—but, in the summer of 1937, he was hard-pressed to spare any background artists from their duties on the film: "What help we could give from the background department would not be skilled in the character painting nor the reproduction angle. We cannot afford to pull our best men off backgrounds because of the pressure of work."

Instead, Dike suggested Gustaf Tenggren. In the end Tenggren did illustrate the *Good Housekeeping* feature, and he was an inspired choice. The opening of the story was illustrated with his classic poster art in its original sketch form (that is, before the image was reversed and the birds were removed from the upper part of the scene). In this and the rest of Tenggren's illustrations, the characters were somewhat at odds with their appearance in the film—including his telltale rendering of the dwarfs' hands—but the lush fairy-tale *atmosphere* of the film was beautifully captured in his images.

For the magazine text, Walt abandoned the simple rhyming couplets of the earlier *Good Housekeeping* pages in favor of a quasi-storybook retelling of the story. This was assigned to another veteran of the film, Dorothy Ann Blank. Considered as promotion for the film, Blank's version of the story is quite remarkable; remnants of different developmental stages of *Snow*

Left and opposite: The "Prince Buckethead" idea, long since dropped from the film, resurfaced in the Sunday-comic continuity.

White are cobbled together in a single text. The opening, detailing the naming of Snow White and the death of her mother—episodes that had never been planned for the film—is lifted straight from the Brothers Grimm, down to the phrase "when snowflakes were falling like feathers from the sky." Elsewhere Blank follows the Disney scenario, but not always closely, sometimes manufacturing elaborate passages of dialogue and inner psychology. Vestiges of the Bedroom Fight, the Soup sequence, and the Bed-Building sequence all appear in the story. The language, mostly couched in timeless storybook vernacular, suddenly lapses into contemporary slang: as the animals help Snow White clean the cottage, they "sneezed like sixty while they dusted," and when Snow White's account of the Prince is interrupted by the eager dwarfs' questions, she cracks, "Who's telling this story?" Two of the film's songs, "I'm Wishing" and "Heigh-Ho" (the latter rendered as "Hi-ho"), figure in the *Good Housekeeping* adaptation, but the film's other songs are never mentioned. On the other hand, when the Prince first meets Snow White in the garden, he sings a song that is heard nowhere in the film or in the published music, but seems to be related to "Snow White, the Fairest of All," a song that had been proposed in 1934 during the earliest story conferences.

The Silly Symphony newspaper comic page, a feature of Sunday comic supplements since 1932, was similarly adapted to *Snow White*. Beginning on 12 December 1937 and continuing for another nineteen weeks, until late April 1938, readers of the Sunday funnies were treated to the story of *Snow White*. For this continuity the strip's regular artists were replaced by writer Merrill de Maris and artist Hank Porter (assisted by Bob Grant), who took further liberties with the story, wandering from both the version in the film *and* the *Good Housekeeping* version. Story ideas that had long been discarded from the film reappeared in the comic continuity: here, once again, Snow White playfully constructed an effigy in the garden and dubbed it "Prince Buckethead," and here again the Queen captured the Prince and imprisoned him in her dungeon, the Prince heroically escaping just a little too late to save Snow White from the Witch. (Here, too, the Huntsman was named "Humbert," the name Walt had suggested for him in the film.)

The first installment of the story in *Good Housekeeping* had been preceded by the announcement that the film "will be released around the first of the year." Walt's original plan to release *Snow White* as a Christmas attraction had been gradually eroded by the pressures of reality. As he continued to tinker with the myriad details of the picture, he and RKO scaled down their plans for an early release and decided the film would open by Christmastime only in the nation's key cities. Then, because of the time required by Technicolor to manufacture release prints, even that goal proved impossible. Eventually the Hollywood premiere was set for 21 December 1937; *all* other openings of the film would have to wait until early 1938. "New York—especially the younger generation—is keenly disappointed in the fact that Walt Disney's *Snow White and the Seven Dwarfs* is not ready for Christmas release here," reported the *New York Post.* But the film's publicity and promotion, already planned for the Christmas season, proceeded on schedule and served to whet the public's appetite still further.

Meanwhile, RKO was still fiddling with its plan for national distribution. The RKO sales department had considered a large-scale roadshow presentation, but had abandoned that idea by August 1937, announcing that *Snow White* would be part of its regular release schedule.[119] Then the latter statement was retracted: *Snow White* would be given special treatment and released separately from the studio's own product. Still later it was announced that the film would be test–marketed in a half-dozen key cities before final distribution policies were set. Determined to exploit this exceptional motion picture, RKO announced that exhibitors would pay an advanced rental scale for *Snow White*—a move that caused resentment within the film industry and would actually hurt the picture's box-office returns in some American cities. In at least one case, that resentment spilled over into the popular press. "Don't make the children any promises of seeing Walt Disney's first feature length cartoon in color," wrote one journalist who evidently thought the high rentals had been imposed by the Disney studio itself. "Studio, after spending more than two years and $1,000,000, is demanding eyeballs for the films [sic]."

In November, production of the film's trailer was assigned to Al Perkins and Bill Garity, who had produced *A Trip Through Walt Disney Studios* earlier in the year. For the trailer, Garity made a special arrangement to shoot Technicolor scenes of Walt in his office. The scenes were photographed on the morning of Friday, 26 November 1937. Relaxed and more self-assured than in the earlier promotional reel, Walt addresses the camera directly, displaying small models of the dwarfs and describing their personalities. Dopey, as always, brings up the rear: "He's nice, but sort of silly," Walt smiles. It's a classic piece of footage, one that has thankfully

been preserved. Both the "A" trailer and one of the shorter "B" trailers have survived in truncated form, marred by crude jump cuts, but Walt's scenes in the longer trailer appear to be intact.

Early in December, while *Snow White* was still in the throes of frantic last-minute production, a sneak preview was held in Pomona. On Monday evening, 6 December, Walt and a group of studio employees arrived unannounced at the Fox Theater in Pomona, carrying a rough cut of the film. This might have been considered an acid test of *Snow White*'s appeal to an audience, for patrons of the Fox had come that evening to see William Wellman's sophisticated comedy *Nothing Sacred*. "But how they enjoyed it," reported a local critic. "To hear the spontaneous laughter and the unrestrained applause was indeed catching." RKO vice president Ned Depinet, in the audience that evening, was thrilled with their response to *Snow White*. CROWDED HOUSE GAVE PICTURE EXCELLENT RECEPTION AND SPONTANEOUS APPLAUSE, he wired the studio's New York office. AT CONCLUSION WE LISTENED TO COMMENTS OF DEPARTING PATRONS AND TALKED WITH SEVERAL. EVERYBODY RAVED BOTH YOUNG AND OLD AND I NOW HAVE A HIGHER OPINION OF THIS SHOW THAN BEFORE IF THAT IS POSSIBLE.

Encouraged by this enthusiastic response, Walt and his artists returned to the studio to plunge into the last-minute details of production: repainting the organ pipes in the entertainment sequence, retaking scenes with minor camera flaws, and performing countless other bits of fine-tuning. The premiere was now a scant two weeks away, set for the Carthay Circle Theater in the Wilshire district of Hollywood. The Carthay Circle, with a seating capacity just over 1,500, was not Hollywood's largest theater, but it was a prestigious showcase.[120] During the previous decade a number of Disney shorts had opened there, including *The Skeleton Dance*, the first Silly Symphony, in 1929. This time, however, there was a gratifying difference: Walt was no longer the scrappy underdog whose short subject would unexpectedly steal the show. This time his picture *was* the show. Outside the theater in Carthay Vista, a small strip of land fronting on San Vicente Boulevard, an elaborate display called "Dwarfland" was erected, with a miniature cottage, garden, diamond mine, and a small brook

[119] "It was figured by RKO," said the *Hollywood Reporter*, "that Disney's chief following is among kids, who couldn't afford the roadshow price."

[120] In addition, the Carthay Circle was itself featured onscreen in some movies as a symbol of Hollywood glamour. Coincidentally, one such movie, the Warner Bros. musical *Hollywood Hotel,* could be seen by American audiences as it opened around the country in late 1937 and early 1938, concurrently with the openings of *Snow White.* One of the key scenes in *Hollywood Hotel* was an opulent movie premiere, filmed on location at the Carthay Circle.

that turned a water wheel.

As the opening drew near, anticipation continued to build in Los Angeles. Robinson's department store offered a "Snow White" puppet show for visitors to the toy department. Tickets to the Carthay Circle opening, priced at all of $5.50, were offered to members of the motion-picture industry and were available directly from the Disney studio. Long before the big night arrived, the house was sold out. Breathless *Snow White* news items continued to appear in the press and were broadcast on the radio. The Disney studio scrambled to fix last minute-details in the film: retake orders were issued for two final troublesome scenes on Friday, the 17th of December—*four days* before the opening. On Sunday, 19 December, the popular ventriloquist Edgar Bergen and his dummies hosted Snow White and the dwarfs on their *Chase & Sanborn* radio program, where Charlie McCarthy engaged in his customary verbal sparring matches with Grumpy, Sneezy, and Doc. The following night, on the eve of the premiere, Walt made a return appearance on Cecil B. DeMille's *Lux Radio Theatre*, received DeMille's congratulations, and talked of the years of hard work he and his artists had put into *Snow White*. Their conversation was scripted, but Walt sounded sincere as he confessed to a case of stage fright. "You've got premiere fright," chortled DeMille, "which is much worse."

Tuesday, the 21st of December, dawned fair and mild. The showing of *Snow White* at the Carthay Circle

was scheduled for 8:45 p.m., but crowds began to arrive hours in advance to get a glimpse of the festivities. Special displays of Disney animation art had been set up for onlookers, and as the hour of the screening drew near, fans were treated to "personal appearances" by a costumed Mickey and Minnie Mouse and Donald Duck. From "Dwarfland," brightly illuminated against the night sky, emerged another group of special guests: the Seven Dwarfs themselves—seven little people hired for the occasion, costumed and wearing character masks designed by "soft sculpture" artist Ted Wiedhaus. A special radio broadcast had been arranged over the NBC Blue Network, with announcers Don Wilson and Buddy Twiss interviewing Hollywood celebrities as they arrived. An orchestra played songs from the picture, and Adriana Caselotti and Harry Stockwell were on hand to sing their numbers. Shirley Temple posed with the dwarfs; Marlene Dietrich, Douglas Fairbanks Jr., Helen Vinson, Claudette Colbert, Gail Patrick, Hedy Lamarr, Preston Foster, and even Chaplin were captured by newsreel cameras or spoke on the radio as they entered. But many other Hollywood notables were also in attendance: Joe E. Brown, Frank Capra, George Cukor, Sidney Franklin, Jesse Lasky, Mervyn LeRoy, Ernst Lubitsch, and Spencer Tracy, among others. Both "Doc" Giannini and Joe Rosenberg of the Bank of America were on hand. Rival animation studios were represented, too: Leon Schlesinger and Bob Clampett were both present, as was Rollin "Ham"

Left: Newsreel cameramen film the "Dwarfs" in the special Dwarfland display in front of the theater.

Right: The Carthay Circle heralds the world premiere of *Snow White and the Seven Dwarfs*.

Hamilton, the first animator Walt had hired in 1924,
shortly after his arrival in Hollywood. Hugh Harman
bought a block of eight tickets.

Along with all the "outside" celebrities, Walt and
Dave Hand were asked to speak to the radio audience
too. Scripts had been prepared for both of them, and
Hand stuck closely to his script. Walt, caught up in the
festive spirit of the evening, improvised his comments,
and was so happy and excited that he couldn't remember the dwarfs' names—an endearing moment that was
noted by several columnists.

Then, at last, came the showing of the picture itself.
The audience packed into the Carthay Circle included
several hundred Disney artists who had purchased
tickets so they could attend the premiere. For all of
them, this was the moment of truth. All their monumental effort for the previous four years was riding on
this evening. What would this glittering array of Hollywood royalty make of their picture?

From the moment the opening titles flashed on the
screen, it was clear that the audience was utterly capti-
vated with *Snow White*. "Laughter was induced at
will," wrote one correspondent, "and spontaneous
applause occurred at a half dozen points in the exhibition." The celebrity audience willingly gave its collec-
tive heart to Snow White, laughed at the dwarfs, shud-
dered at the Witch, thrilled to the dwarfs' ride to the
rescue. Sequence 15A, the dwarfs gathered at Snow

White's bier—the sequence that had caused so much
nervous apprehension at the studio—elicited real tears
from the sophisticated crowd. "Everybody in the audience is sniffing and I heard people blowing their noses,"
said Ward Kimball to historian Jim Korkis. "It's hard to
believe, but the people in the audience were really
blowing their noses . . . We knew it was a winner then."
At the end of the screening, one journalist reported,
"the Hollywood intelligentsia stood around the lobby of
the theater for more than an hour with dazed looks on
their faces, trying to find adjectives to carry on." *Motion
Picture Daily* summed up the evening: "Men, women
and children attending the premiere surrendered in
concert to the delicate charm of the opening sequence
and the Disney spell upon them was broken only by
their irrepressible applause at half a dozen points in the
narrative and the velvet crackle of recurrent laughter. It
is an inescapable conclusion that a picture capable of
making happy kiddies out of the bluebloods of Hollywood . . . will captivate the plain population as perhaps
no other motion picture ever has or will."

The next day the reviews were rapturous. "Walt
Disney has so perfectly captured the spirit of this
famous Grimm fairy tale and surrounded it with such
charm that we are newly impressed with his creative
ability," reported Louella Parsons. "The settings are
breathtaking in their beauty; the loveliest thing of the
kind ever brought to the screen, and the color is equally

HIS FIRST FULL LENGTH FEATURE PRODUCTION! *Walt DISNEY'S* **Snow White** *in the Marvelous* **MULTIPLANE TECHNICOLOR** and the Seven Dwarfs ©WDP

Christmas Eve in the dwarfs' cottage.

COUNTRY OF ORIGIN U.S.A.

exquisite." "It is a masterpiece of entertainment for people of every age," said the *Hollywood Reporter. Daily Variety* exulted: "*Snow White* is the genius of craftsmanship which can make an endless series of line drawings and color washes so eloquent in human expression and trouble and antic joy, so potent in evoking audience emotion, laughter, excitement, suspense, tears. Yes, indeed—tears!" Other reviewers chimed in, vying with each other for superlatives. The paying customers echoed their fervent enthusiasm, thronging to the Carthay Circle box office, and would continue to pack the theater to capacity in the coming weeks and months. *Snow White* was not only a success, but a vast, overwhelming success; more than that, a milestone that would leave a lasting mark on film history.

For Walt Disney, this was a turning point. During the previous decade, he had achieved worldwide recognition as the creator of a fascinating and delightful new form of entertainment—but always within a prescribed

niche. Thanks to his efforts, the cartoon short was no longer as disparaged as it had once been, but it was still a supplement, an adjunct, an outbuilding separate from the main arena. Now, suddenly, Walt had moved to the center of the arena and had made it his own, in a unique, original, and thoroughly beguiling way. If critics and audiences had been amused and charmed by his earlier shorts, they were utterly enthralled by *Snow White*—and they couldn't get enough of it. This was the doorway to further and seemingly unlimited conquests. In the years to come, Walt would experience a wildly varying series of ups and downs, triumphant successes balanced by setbacks and sometimes heartbreaking personal disappointments. But in December 1937 he was on top of the world. For four years he had stubbornly clung to his dream, and now it had come true—and the whole world happily surged forward to share in it.

No such scene as this was ever planned for the film, but the marketing forces, anticipating a Christmas opening, cannily produced this image for one of the film's promotional lobby cards.

PART THREE

After 1937

THE UPS AND DOWNS OF SUCCESS

As the year 1938 dawned, *Snow White and the Seven Dwarfs* was riding a wave of success—while still showing in only one theater. The star-studded premiere in December had been no more than the beginning; *Snow White* settled into the Carthay Circle for what was clearly going to be a record-breaking run. In Hollywood, at least, the film had succeeded as a Christmas attraction. Both Marjorie Belcher and the costumed dwarfs, who were still making nightly appearances in "Dwarfland," had joined Santa Claus in his sleigh for the parade along "Santa Claus Lane" on Christmas Eve, and capacity audiences continued to jam the theater. "Christmas Eve, one of the year's worst headache nights for showmen, only a few side seats were empty," reported one newspaper.

On New Year's Day 1938, Marjorie Belcher and the dwarfs made another public appearance, riding a "Snow White" float that became the hit of the Tournament of Roses Parade.[121] At the Carthay Circle, *Snow White* entered a second week that drew even greater attendance than the first, then another week, then another. Theater management began giving away a free color etching of Dopey, the popular favorite among the dwarfs, to each patron. Celebrities of filmland were still among *Snow White*'s biggest fans. Harpo Marx confirmed that he had come back to see it three times; Mary Pickford opined that "Walt Disney again proves himself a supreme artist"; Chaplin himself declared that Dopey was "one of the greatest comedians of all time."[122] The Los Angeles Public Library reported a dramatic new surge of interest in *Grimm's Fairy Tales* since the film's opening. In late April 1938, after more than four

months, *Snow White* came to the end of its historic run at the Carthay Circle—and even then the theater reported that the film was still drawing capacity crowds, but must be withdrawn to honor previous bookings.[123]

As gratifying as this reception was, *Snow White* had not been produced for only one theater. Technicolor was busily working to turn out more release prints, and early in January the film began to open in other cities across the United States. On 13 January 1938 the long-awaited New York opening took place at Radio City Music Hall, the prestigious showplace where Disney shorts had enjoyed distinguished New York openings since 1933. Just as in Los Angeles, *Snow White* was a tremendous hit. "Sheer fantasy, delightful, gay and altogether captivating, touched the screen yesterday," wrote Frank S. Nugent in the *New York Times*. "Let your fears be quieted at once: Mr. Disney and his amazing technical crew have outdone themselves. The picture more than matches expectations . . . If you miss it, you'll be missing the ten best pictures of 1938." The Music Hall's seating capacity was more than four times that of the Carthay Circle, and in place of the Carthay's two showings per day, the Music Hall offered five. Even so, after several weeks the box office still had patrons standing in line for three blocks, waiting to get in. A special telephone line was installed to help the theater's staff handle the calls for reserved seats, and they received calls at the reported rate of 150 per hour. The theater's previous record booking had been three weeks, but *Snow White* played for five—and, again, was withdrawn only because of the pressure of previous commitments. *Motion Picture Herald* reported in tones of awe

[121] Before the premiere, Walt had hoped to commission giant Snow White and dwarf balloons, like those in the annual Macy's parade in New York, to parade along Wilshire Boulevard on the day of the opening. Unfortunately time did not allow this.

[122] Later in 1938, the *Los Angeles Times* compared Dopey's pantomime to Chaplin's gag with the whistle in *City Lights*.

[123] The film's second Los Angeles run began in July at the Pantages Hollywood and RKO Hillstreet theaters, and again drew record crowds.

Marjorie Belcher plays Snow White again, riding a special float in the 1938 Tournament of Roses Parade. Her costume for the filming (see page 49) had been designed simply to "read" well on black-and-white film; this one is more glamorous.

that, once again, business actually increased from one week to the next; and that *Snow White* would earn back half its negative cost from its five weeks at this one theater. The Music Hall's engagement ended on 16 February; three days later *Snow White* opened at the RKO Palace and Brooklyn's RKO Albee for long runs, and the neighborhood houses followed early in March.

One unusual outcome of the Radio City engagement was a special recording of *Snow White* for the blind. Harry Braun, the Music Hall's sound director, collaborated with the American Foundation for the Blind to produce a special adaptation of *Snow White* for the

Foundation's "Talking Book" series of recordings. These discs were dubbed from the film's soundtrack, with interpolated narration that attempted to describe the action onscreen. The writer of the narration, William Barbour, listened to the soundtrack and discovered for himself some of Frank Churchill's musical virtuosity: "By hearing, rather than seeing the film, Mr. Barbour discovered that Dopey alone among the dwarfs has a theme song all his own which is heard when he is on the point of some amusing antic. When Dopey's theme comes into the sound track the narrator describes his antics."

There is another curious sidelight on the New York

Gustaf Tenggren's finished poster was reproduced for the cover of the Carthay Circle souvenir program.

[124] Roy's mention of "faulty registration" is a reference to the washing and reusing of cels. As a cel was used multiple times, the peg holes were apt to stretch out of shape, causing some play in the cel's position and, therefore, less precise registration of the cel to other cels and to the background. "Walt said," Roy added, "if I hadn't been so damn tight they could have bought fresh celluloid where the holes weren't big and that wouldn't have happened. So it was my fault for not buying the celluloid."

run: we have reason to believe that some of the Prince's scenes in sequence 16A, the closing moments of the picture, may have been rephotographed and replaced *after* the film opened at Radio City. In the rush to finish the picture by the December 1937 deadline, both Walt and Roy had been frustrated and dissatisfied with some details, including the action of the Prince as he approached Snow White. "As he walked down the path he was shimmying and shaking quite a bit, due to the faulty registration under the camera," Roy told an interviewer decades after the fact.[124] "I said, 'Gee, I hate to see it go out that way.' [Walt] said, 'Well, we can fix that. It will delay the picture going out for two or three weeks and will probably cost $250,000, $300,000 more.' I said, 'You've said enough. Let him shimmy!' So the Prince has been shimmying ever since."

But has he? A viewing of the film today reveals the Prince's action in scene 3, the approach to the bier, as more than acceptably smooth, and some press accounts in 1938 suggested that a substitution *had* been made:

"even after the film was running in New York, [Walt] was still working on new animation for the Prince. He sent it on, too, and made the theaters use it." Newspaper and magazine accounts are naturally suspect, but these accounts are clearly based on interviews with Walt or someone else at the studio. Normally a mystery like this would be settled by the presence or absence of a retake order for the scene in question. Retake orders were filed with the corresponding exposure sheets, and today are found in the files of the studio's Animation Research Library. A check of those files reveals no retake order for scene 3—but, at the same time, no exposure sheet and no animation drawings! This gap in the record does suggest an unusual circumstance of some kind, and prevents a conclusive answer either way. The mystery remains a mystery.

Meanwhile, on 13 January—simultaneous with its Radio City opening in New York—*Snow White* opened at the Sheridan Theater in Miami to "smash biz," according to *Film Daily*. As a special attraction, the same little people who had appeared in person as the Seven Dwarfs at the Carthay Circle in Hollywood were flown to Miami to make similar appearances at the Sheridan. Marjorie Belcher didn't make this trip; instead Betsy Walker of Chicago—"one of the noted Miami Beach bathing beauties this winter," as a local paper observed—filled in as Snow White. The costume Marjorie had worn in her personal appearances in Hollywood was flown to Miami for Miss Walker's use.

While in Florida, one of the dwarfs made headlines by taking time out to get married. Billy Curtis, the 3-foot-7-inch "Sneezy" of the troupe, took Lois de Fee, a 6-foot-4½-inch nightclub bouncer and former showgirl, as his wife on 18 January. After one day of wedded bliss, Curtis departed Miami with the other dwarfs, leaving his bride behind. (Lois later revealed that she had married him on a bet, and the marriage was annulled.) Under the supervision of RKO publicity man Harry Reiners, the dwarfs continued to make their way up the East Coast, appearing in major cities long before the local openings of Snow White, and concluding their tour at Radio City in New York. By the time they arrived in Washington, D.C. on 20 January, it was clear that their thin dwarf costumes, perfectly adequate for Hollywood and Miami weather, were no match for an East Coast winter. "You can say for me," one of them told a reporter through chattering teeth, "that I'm damn sorry you have no Florida climate around here!"[125]

While these promotional activities were taking place on the East Coast, Pinto Colvig, in Hollywood, was attempting to turn Snow White publicity to his own advantage. Colvig, whose careless work habits had rubbed Walt the wrong way once too often, had departed the studio in August 1937, after all his Grumpy and Sleepy dialogue had been recorded but before completion of the film. Now, riding Snow White's wave of success in January 1938, he placed ads in the trade papers congratulating "my former associates at the Disney Studios . . . the animators who so skilfully [sic] and faithfully interpreted my characterizations of the dwarfs, and the directors who so masterfully incorporated many of my story situations, gags, dialog and sound-effects." This characteristically brazen stunt probably did little to improve Colvig's standing with

Walt. Still less helpful was an item that appeared in Variety soon afterward, announcing that three of the vocal talents from Snow White, Adriana Caselotti, Roy Atwell, and "Walter Pinto," would soon appear in a vaudeville act based on their movie characters. "Miss Caselotti will warble and her partners will do comedy," the article claimed. Disney publicity chief Gregory Dickson lost no time in following up this story and reported to Walt that there was no real cause for alarm: "It appears that, as usual, the trade papers have distorted the story completely. The three above-named people came to them ([vaudeville promoters] Fanchon and Marco) requesting a booking in an attempt to cash in on their association with Snow White. However, nothing has been done about this so far and Mr. Schultz assured me that Fanchon and Marco would not do anything until they checked with Roy."

If his fellow performers were dissuaded, Colvig was not. By September 1938 he was back, opening at the Los Angeles Orpheum in a solo act that openly touted his Snow White connection. "It was his voice that issued from Grumpy in Snow White," one reviewer noted, "from the grasshopper in 'Looney Tunes' [sic] and many others. Now he comes along to the stage with a lot of jokes on himself and lets you see him as he makes those sounds."[126] And the irrepressible Colvig wasn't finished yet; his voice continued to be heard in other studios' films, even after he returned to the Disney studio in 1941 to resume Goofy's vocal duties.

By February 1938 Technicolor was beginning to catch up with the demand for release prints, and Snow White was opening in other cities around the United States. The openings were still erratic, not only because of the paucity of prints but because RKO was making separate arrangements for each booking, rather than including Snow White in its regular release schedule. The distributor had announced an advanced rental scale: exhibitors, who normally paid an average of 35 percent of their gross receipts in film rentals, would be charged 50 percent or more for Snow White in most markets. This move created a wave of resentment among some exhibitors, especially the independents. It was actively opposed in Philadelphia, where local theater owners had banded together in a tacit agreement

The Radio City program reproduced Tenggren's original art instead.

[125] At least two of the little people in the dwarf troupe—veteran performer Major Doyle, who played "Grumpy," and Curtis—went on to appear as Munchkins in MGM's The Wizard of Oz (1939).

[126] Colvig was not the last performer to capitalize on his connection with Snow White. Early in 1940, Marjorie Belcher—presumably with Walt's blessing—toured in a revue titled Seeing Stars, billed as Marjorie Bell. Although she was advertised as "Disney's Model for 'Snow White'," her act did not derive from anything in the film. Variety called her "a cutie who comes through with a fair toe dance in addition to the [ballroom dance] bit with [Alexander] D'Arcy." The tour headliners were the Three Stooges and, notably, Cliff Edwards, who was just on the threshold of a new wave of fame as the voice of Jiminy Cricket in Pinocchio—but was still best known at this time by his long-running showbiz tag "Ukulele Ike."

127 Even this eloquent tribute was scaled down from a still loftier assessment. Hal Horne wrote to Walt that Pegler, after attending the New York opening, "remarked that he was beside himself and said to his party that 'Walt Disney's *Snow White and the Seven Dwarfs* is the greatest thing since the Resurrection.' . . . You will notice that in his article he settles for the Armistice."

128 Along with screen credit, the artists were rewarded financially. The following spring, with *Snow White's* epic profits rolling in, the entire Disney staff received a bonus. *Variety* reported that "the average to be given each [employee] will roughly amount to 12-15 weeks salary." Another gesture, a staff picnic and "field day" at the Norconian Resort in June 1938, backfired when the proceedings got wildly out of hand. Fueled by alcohol and months of pent-up energy, the party degenerated into a drunken orgy that lasted all night and became notorious in studio lore. Dick Huemer, interviewed in later years by Joe Adamson, avoided the details but commented succinctly: "Oh boy! Walt never did that again!"

to refuse high rentals. RKO, in its turn, stood firm. "As a result," *Variety* noted, "cartoon is getting practically no bookings from the nabe [neighborhood] houses." But RKO had a hot property on its hands; *Snow White* continued to play to unprecedented business wherever it was shown. Many cities followed New York's example and extended the film's first run, moving it to secondary "moveover" theaters for weeks at a time before releasing it to the neighborhood houses.

Along with other forms of promotion, RKO promoted *Snow White* from theater screens. Besides the trailers, and coverage of the Carthay Circle premiere in *Pathé News* (a newsreel distributed by RKO), the studio also released a special behind-the-scenes short subject. This was nothing other than the earlier promotional reel for exhibitors, *A Trip Through Walt Disney Studios*, now revised and released to theaters under the title *How Walt Disney Cartoons Are Made*. Seen today, this second short does seem somewhat more polished than its predecessor. Al Perkins's background with *The March of Time* is evident in the film's narration: Walt and "his hard-boiled directors" work on a story, "hundreds of pretty girls" ink the cels, "more pretty girls" paint them. The second short differs from the first primarily in the quantity of new *Snow White* material which could not be included a few months earlier in 1937. Now, as artists sit in a sweatbox watching pencil animation, they're looking not at *Donald's Ostrich* but at the dwarfs; shots of musicians conducted by Leigh Harline are now synchronized to a performance of "Whistle While You Work." The short concludes with scenes from the premiere and (in black and white) from the trailer, includ-

ing Walt's direct-to-camera address about the dwarfs' personalities.

As *Snow White* continued to open around the country, the first wave of critical adulation became a torrent. "To say of *Snow White and the Seven Dwarfs* that it is among the genuine artistic achievements of this country takes no great daring," wrote Otis Ferguson. Rival producer Leon Schlesinger, who had expressed his doubts about animated features six months earlier, now graciously capitulated: "We're businessmen. Walt Disney's an artist. With us, the idea with shorts is to hit 'em and run. With us, Disney is more of a Rembrandt." "It is astonishing," enthused the *National Board of Review Magazine*, "how these pictures create a life in a world of their own, totally unreal in fact but absorbingly real to the entranced imagination." Critic Westbrook Pegler declared that *Snow White* was "the happiest thing that has happened in this world since the Armistice."127 Several critics took note of the screen credits, which were far more extensive than movie audiences were accustomed to seeing in live-action features in 1938. "Disney gives credit to his directors, animators, musicians in a way that is heartening to see," wrote Otis Ferguson, "and a list as long as your arm."128

Some of the tributes to *Snow White* came from unexpected sources. *Soap* magazine, a trade journal of the soap industry, praised the film for promoting the use of soap, particularly in the dwarfs' washing sequence: "We have been told that if the soap industry itself directed the production of this picture, and underwrote its cost, a job more to its liking could not have been done." As reviewers and audiences continued to take

More *Snow White*
merchandise. The Dopey
money clip at left was Walt's
own; the Dopey figure at right
was a popular tin toy.

the dwarfs to their hearts, *Hollywood* magazine conducted a contest to determine which dwarf was the most popular. Not surprisingly, Dopey was the clear winner, with Grumpy a distant second.

Amid all the praise, there were a few discordant grumbles over the animation of Snow White and the other human characters. Archer Winsten of the *New York Post*, while strongly recommending the film, found in Snow White herself "faint similarities" to Betty Boop: "I am completely at a loss to understand how any one [sic] can fail to sense the difference in the quality of draftsmanship between the animals and the dwarfs on the one hand and Snow White, Prince Charming, the Huntsman and the Wicked Queen. Now to place it on an artistic plane, one can say that the former come to life completely whereas the latter remain drawings, not very pleasing ones, that move." Winsten, of course, was not an artist himself, nor did he have the luxury of screening the film repeatedly and studying the animation in detail, as we can do today. A more surprising dissent came from the noted caricaturist Al Hirschfeld, who admired the dwarfs but disparaged Snow White as "an anatomic automaton" and "a ventriloquist's dummy," and called for a return to the world of the shorts: "I merely wish to point out that Mickey Mouse is great art and not a clever novelty, and Disney should not underestimate the genius of his original invention."

Thanks to Kay Kamen, Disney's energetic licensing wizard, a vast array of *Snow White* merchandise was available in stores long before the film opened in most cities. A glance through Kamen's 1938–39 catalog reveals the expected assortment of pull toys, sheet music, handkerchiefs, stuffed toys, children's wear, neckties, shoes and boots, banks, pencil sets, costumes and masks, rubber stamp sets, wrapping paper, brushes and toothbrushes, silverware, hats, bookends, lampshades, soap, wind-up toys, night lights, sweatshirts, drinking glasses, sand pails, games, stationery, furniture, rubber toys, umbrellas, salt and pepper shakers, candy, and dolls by Ideal, Knickerbocker, and Richard G. Krueger. But there were unusual items too: marionettes by Madame Alexander, jewelry by Cartier, a Snow White radio by Emerson, flower seeds by Germain Seed & Plant. The Miller Corset Company offered Snow White foundation garments, embroidered with tiny images of the princess, while American Toy Works marketed a Snow White target game that allowed the player to shoot rubber-tipped darts at the dwarfs, or a larger target with the Witch's face in the center!

One significant piece of merchandise was the soundtrack record album. Records of Disney music, including soundtrack recordings from the Silly Symphony and Mickey Mouse shorts, had been issued for years on various record labels. For *Snow White* the Victor label contracted for something more elaborate: a three-record set of double-sided 78 rpm records, featuring soundtrack recordings of all the film's songs, packaged in an album illustrated with full-color studio art. Like some of Victor's earlier Disney releases, the same records were issued in England on the British HMV label, the individual discs adorned with beautiful color labels. In addition to the soundtrack recordings, new

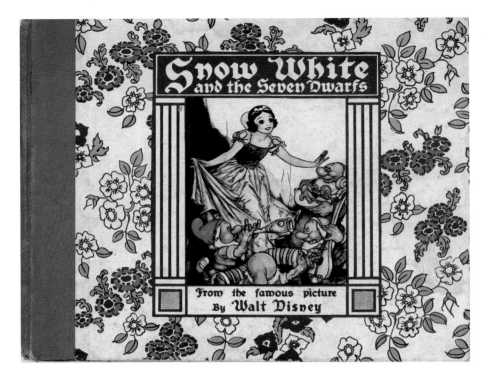

Two of the many licensed storybook editions of *Snow White,* both with covers adapted from Tenggren's art.

recordings of the *Snow White* songs were made by popular singers and orchestras, and all the film's songs—along with at least one related song *not* heard in the film—were issued in sheet-music form. Almost invariably, these printed versions included verses not sung in the film, as well as the familiar choruses.

Another important part of *Snow White* merchandising was the storybooks. By 1937 the Disney studio had a well-established relationship with the Whitman Publishing Company, which published Disney books under its own imprint and several others: Harper & Brothers, David McKay, and Grosset & Dunlap. These ranged from large, full-color storybooks to Whitman's own "Big Little Books," the tiny but thick editions that sold for 10 cents. A wide variety of *Snow White* books were published, coordinated with the planned Christmas 1937 opening of the film, and were eagerly snapped up by the buying public. All were heavily illustrated, some with scenes directly from the film. Of the most elaborate book, a large color Harper edition, *Publishers' Weekly* reported in February 1938 that "there were only 5,000 copies, issued on December 1st. These were sold out by December 20th; no others were made and the edition is now out of print." Other editions were similarly in demand; for the Grosset & Dunlap edition "Orders for more than 50,000 copies have piled up . . . truckloads of from 5,000 to 10,000 copies have come in [from the printer] every day, but the supply has as yet been insufficient to fill orders completely."

These storybooks make for a fascinating comparison today because, like the *Good Housekeeping* pages and the Sunday-comic continuity that preceded the film's release, they vary widely in their versions of the story. Several of them, prepared in 1937 before the film's continuity was firmly established, include discarded material such as the Soup sequence and the Bed-Building episode. On the other hand, the death of Snow White's mother, which was never planned for the film, appears in almost all the storybooks. Several of the books recycle the Prince's song, "Fairest in the Land," which had appeared in *Good Housekeeping* but is never heard in the film. The *Snow White* Big Little Book, like most other Big Little Books, is illustrated with art from the newspaper comics—but this one also draws illustrations from other sources, and its text includes ideas that appear nowhere in the comic continuity, including the Queen smashing the mirror and Dopey speaking dialogue! Most of the storybooks, written for very young children, soften or eliminate the more distressing aspects of the story—yet, after the Witch falls from the mountain, one edition includes the line: "When the dwarfs found her she was dead, maimed and disfigured."

One interesting variation, *Walt Disney's Famous Seven Dwarfs,* tells the story of the film with the accent entirely on the dwarfs. The first part of the story eliminated, this book begins with the dwarfs leaving the mine and marching home. Later, at the party, when they ask Snow White to tell them a story, she obliges with a

Some of the publications blurred the line between storybooks and toys, such as this book of paper dolls.

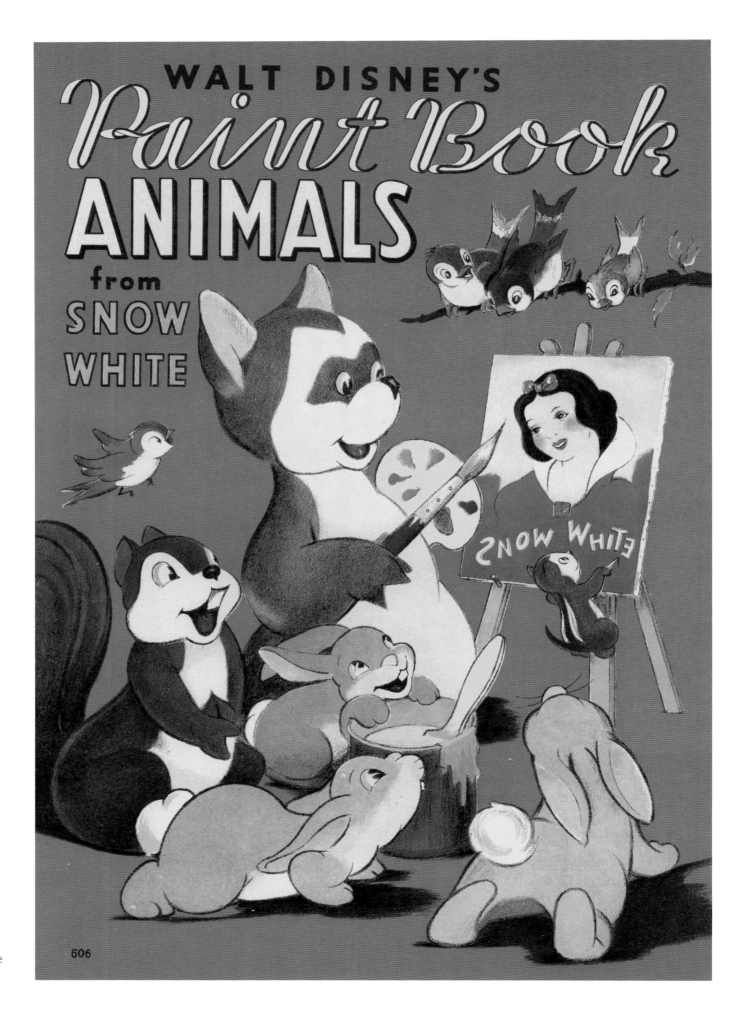

606

A paint book focusing on the
animal cast of the film.

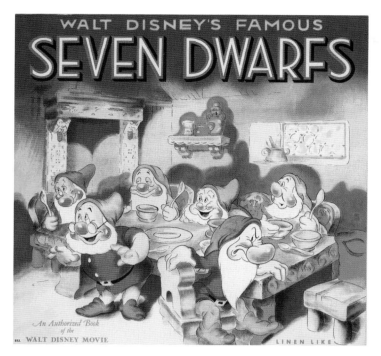

More offshoots: the story as told from the Dwarfs' point of view, and a book celebrating the characters' appearance on Edgar Bergen's popular radio program.

flashback that amounts to a quick summary of her own previous history. Whitman's "Story Of" series, beginning with *The Story of Snow White*, continued with "stories of" each of the dwarfs, *after* Snow White had left with the Prince. *The Story of Grumpy*, for example, includes two stories: one in which Grumpy accidentally reveals his true soft-hearted nature by rescuing a baby bird, and one in which the other dwarfs discover the date of his birthday and throw him a surprise party. Among the more unusual books were *Dopey's Christmas Tree*, a promotional coloring booklet issued to department stores for Christmas 1938, and *Edgar Bergen's Charlie McCarthy Meets Walt Disney's Snow White*, which reproduced much of the dialogue from the characters' radio meeting in December 1937.

And still more radio coverage was coming. Radio was a pervasive force in American life in the 1930s, a medium second only to the movies, and inevitably it reflected the phenomenal popularity of *Snow White*. We've already observed the broadcasts that preceded the premiere, but once the film began to score its historic success, the radio floodgates opened. The *Snow White* music and songs were widely performed by popular singers and orchestras, and two songs, "Whistle While You Work" and "Heigh-Ho," broke into the Top Ten on *Your Hit Parade* and remained there for months. Two of the dwarf voices, Roy Atwell and Billy Gilbert, appeared in character as guests on variety programs. Fibber McGee, Joe Penner, and other radio comedians weighed in too; Jack Benny and his troupe, noting that "none of us look like dwarfs," mounted a satiric skit called "Snow White and the Seven Gangsters."

Walt himself was uniquely positioned to promote the film on radio, by way of a new Disney-produced program, *The Mickey Mouse Theatre of the Air*, which had just debuted on the NBC Red Network in January 1938. The program's second episode, on 9 January, was designated as "Snow White Day" and served to introduce Mickey and his gang to Snow White, the dwarfs, and the Witch. Several of the film's songs were featured, and Walt appeared both as himself and as the voice of Mickey Mouse (a radio role he would surrender shortly afterward to Joe Twerp, the comic who had been considered as a voice for one of the dwarfs). One running gag involved a feud between Donald Duck and the show's announcer, John Hiestand, who vowed to keep Donald from entering the studio during the program. But Donald managed to slip in twice anyway: the first time hidden in the Witch's basket of apples (from one of which he took a bite, after wishing for Shirley Temple), the second time disguised as an eighth dwarf!

On two occasions before the opening of the film, Walt had appeared as a guest on the prestigious *Lux Radio Theatre* to promote his upcoming picture. At the end of the triumphant year of 1938, on the day after Christmas, *Snow White* was itself presented as the featured attraction on the Lux program. Walt returned as an "intermission" guest, interviewed by Cecil B. DeMille, and the cast featured four voices from the original film: Roy Atwell as Doc, Billy Gilbert as Sneezy, Moroni Olsen as the slave in the mirror, and Stuart Buchanan as the Huntsman. Unofficially, the tally of original voices was higher than that: Snow White was played by Thelma Hubbard—who, as we've seen, had

In addition to individual song sheets, fans could also buy this book featuring all the songs heard in the film—and one that wasn't.

FIFTEEN CENTS

December 27, 1937

TIME

The Weekly Newsmagazine

Color photograph for TIME by Robert Mack

Volume XXX

**HAPPY, GRUMPY, BASHFUL, SNEEZY,
SLEEPY, DOC, DOPEY, DISNEY**
The boss is no more a cartoonist than Whistler.
(See CINEMA)

Number 26

Circulation Office, 330 East 22nd Street, Chicago.   (Reg. U. S. Pat. Off.)   Editorial and Advertising Offices, 135 East 42nd Street, New York.

Walt featured on the cover of *Time* magazine, introducing the Dwarfs as he had done in the film's trailer.

The Courvoisier Galleries continued to market original Disney art well into the 1940s.

supplied some of the character's miscellaneous voice tracks for the film—and the vocal chorus included at least two singers, Harry Stanton and Freeman High, who had similarly filled in for the dwarfs in their singing scenes.

Like the storybooks, the Lux radio adaptation of *Snow White* varied from the film in interesting ways. Later radio plays, confined to half-hour time slots, would necessarily abridge the story; the Lux program ran for a full hour and so hewed much more closely to the film continuity—but that fidelity only made the differences more obvious. The birds that befriended Snow White in the forest sounded nothing like those in the film, and one of them had a whistle that imitated human speech patterns so that it was practically a talking bird, intelligible to Snow White (if not to the listener). Among other things, this meant that Snow White knew the dwarfs were "little men," not children, *before* she met them. Radio listeners heard a quantity of original dialogue from the script, from the finished film but also from the excised Bedroom Fight. Most of the songs were also heard (as was some of the incidental score), but the dwarfs performed the "Silly Song" without the chorus or yodels, singing only the verses—including Sneezy's verse (which had also been heard in the *Mickey Mouse Theatre* broadcast). Perhaps the most obvious

variation from the film was the treatment of Dopey. Here he was first heard as a wood-block sound effect, to represent his knees knocking in fright when the dwarfs saw their house inhabited. Later, during the introductions, Doc explained to Snow White that the other dwarfs had supplied Dopey with a bell around his neck, so that he could alert them in an emergency; after that the bell was used to represent Dopey for the rest of the broadcast.

A darker aspect of the *Snow White* phenomenon was that, once it was clear that the film was going to be fabulously successful and there were great sums of money to be made, the Disney studio became the target of several lawsuits. Walt had anticipated this; as early as September 1937, Art Babbitt had reported to him that "Fleischer intends to sue us as soon as our picture is released; it seems we are supposed to be infringing on his dimensional cartoon photography." In reality, of course, there were fundamental differences between the Disney multiplane camera (for which a patent application had already been filed) and Fleischer's "setback" system. Perhaps realizing this, the Fleischers refrained from litigation after all. The Stereoplane Process Pictures Company did file a patent-infringement suit against RKO and the Disney studio in 1938, but this came to nothing.

And other lawsuits were filed over *Snow White*. The

most famous and possibly most surprising of these came from Adriana Caselotti, who may still have been smarting from her thwarted personal-appearance tour, and Harry Stockwell. In October 1938 the voices of Snow White and the Prince filed suit over the Victor soundtrack recording of *Snow White*. The Disney studio and RCA, they contended, had made millions from their vocal recordings, over and above the grosses from the film itself, with no extra compensation to the vocalists. The studio countered that both artists had originally signed agreements giving Disney the right to use the recordings "in any manner whatsoever." The case was decided in favor of the studio in June 1940; an appeal in 1941 was denied.

Other lawsuits centered on alleged cases of musical plagiarism. Reynard Fraunfelder, of the yodeling Fraunfelder family, charged in October 1938 that the use of his yodels in the "Silly Song" constituted unauthorized use of his compositions.[129] Modest Altschuler, composer of a "Russian Soldier's Song," alleged that "Whistle While You Work" was an infringement on his composition. And Thornton Allen, a publisher of college songs, claimed that "Some Day My Prince Will Come" had been plagiarized from the Yale "Old Eli March"! ("Was the Prince a Yale man?" mused the *New York Times*.) Nothing came of any of these charges, and all were eventually dismissed or decided in the Disney studio's favor; they were simply part of the price of success. "There's a plague of these song cases," studio attorney Gunther Lessing told one journalist. "We've elected to fight every case and we've never lost one."

And *Snow White* endured the downside of success in other ways. In June 1938 Dr. Stuart Rice, addressing the American Association for the Advancement of Science, opined that society was seeking escape from "fear of universal warfare and the general breakdown of existing social institutions" by taking refuge in fantasy. He cited as examples the popularity of *Snow White* and of James Hilton's *Lost Horizon* (neglecting to mention that Hilton's novel had itself been produced as a film by this time). Dr. Rice's comments were widely reported and brought a kind of rebuttal from the *Christian Century*, which pointed out that much of *Snow White*'s audience was made up of small children "who are

certainly not much agitated about the imminence of Armageddon." Further, art could be seen as a "diversion" akin to imaginative thought, love, and religion: "These are all avenues of escape—not *from* reality, but *to* a larger reality." Another dubious recognition of Walt's success came in December 1937, shortly after the premiere, when the Screen Cartoonists' Guild filed a complaint with the National Labor Relations Board, demanding better wages and working conditions for animation artists. *Daily Variety* reported that the Guild represented workers at all the major animation studios, but was moved to file its complaint "after enthusiastic reception accorded first showings of Disney's *Snow White and the Seven Dwarfs*." The full irony of this distinction would become all too clear in the spring of 1941, with the onset of the infamous Disney strike.

But if success brought a new host of nuisances, the rewards were sweet. Walt Disney had been recognized for some of his earlier achievements, but now the recognitions moved into a new league. In the summer of 1938, he was awarded honorary degrees by three major universities—the University of Southern California, Yale (the "Old Eli March" notwithstanding), and Harvard—prompted at least in part by *Snow White*. Disney exhibits had appeared in art museums as early as 1933, but now the studio entered into a new contract with Courvoisier Galleries of San Francisco to market original *Snow White* art to museums and collectors. Soon galleries across the country began to mount special exhibits of original *Snow White* cels and backgrounds. Of these exhibits, a *Snow White* acquisition by the Metropolitan Museum of Art in New York—a cel setup showing the vultures landing on a branch in driving rain—aroused exceptional comment. Metropolitan curator Harry B. Wehle's description of Walt as "a great historical figure in the development of American art" was widely quoted.

At the end of 1938, as film critics began to review the year's cinematic output, there was a fresh wave of adulation. The National Board of Review named *Snow White* one of the ten best films of the year in mid-December, and a couple of weeks later the New York Film Critics similarly singled it out. (The New York awards ceremony was broadcast on the radio, and the press noted

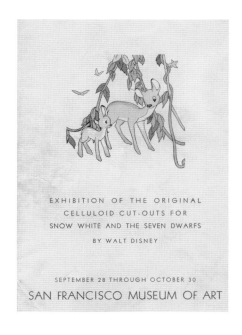

EXHIBITION OF THE ORIGINAL
CELLULOID CUT-OUTS FOR
SNOW WHITE AND THE SEVEN DWARFS
BY WALT DISNEY

SEPTEMBER 28 THROUGH OCTOBER 30
SAN FRANCISCO MUSEUM OF ART

An announcement of one of the many gallery exhibitions of *Snow White* production art.

[129] In fact, the final *Snow White* soundtrack contained neither Fraunfelder's compositions nor even his voice. When "You're Never Too Old to Be Young" was replaced by the "Silly Song" in the summer of 1937, the yodeling chorus had been completely rerecorded. Fraunfelder, Freeman High, Jim Macdonald, and most of the other original vocalists were replaced by a new group in this final recording.

The historic special award for the film from the Academy of Motion Picture Arts and Sciences.

Opposite: At the Academy Awards ceremony in February 1939, child star Shirley Temple presents the award to Walt.

[130] The *Film Daily* tribute may have been especially meaningful to Walt for another reason. Jack Alicoate, the paper's publisher, had encouraged and supported the fledgling Disney studio as early as the 1920s. During Walt's visits to New York in 1928, Alicoate had provided valuable counsel in the upheavals of Walt's contract dispute with Charles Mintz and, months later, the recording of the *Steamboat Willie* soundtrack. As Walt's and Roy's fortunes rose in the early 1930s, Alicoate had continued in his supportive role; *Film Daily* had led the other trade papers in coverage of Disney events, including Walt's first public announcement of an animated feature in July 1933. Years later Roy told an interviewer: "Up to the time Jack died, he was a good friend of ours."

[131] The feature was also announced as *Aladdin and His Wonderful Lamp*. Lantz, with impressive audacity, told the press that he was "going Disney one better" in the animation of human figures: "Lantz says that he will use the rotoscope for timing, and then will reanimate the figures to get a convincing element of unreality in them"—in other words, exactly what the Disney studio had already done in *Snow White*. If the *Aladdin* feature had been completed, it would have boasted the talents of another *Snow White* veteran: Frank Churchill. During Churchill's eight-month hiatus from the Disney studio, he was snapped up by Lantz and wrote musical scores for twelve of his cartoon shorts, besides working on the unfinished feature.

Walt's short acceptance speech: "All I can say is thanks a lot.") Both these distinctions were qualified; the NBR announced several alternate rankings of its choices, only one of which named *Snow White* at the head of the list, while the New York critics gave it a special award, isolated from the other contenders "because of its unique character." By contrast, the *Film Daily* poll of the nation's critics, announced later in January 1939, was unequivocal: *Snow White* was, simply, the best film of the year. Perhaps because of this clear-cut endorsement, Walt seemed to take a special pleasure in the *Film Daily* award. Buying multiple copies of the announcement issue, he distributed them to some of his key staff members with a memo: "I thought you might like to stow away the attached copy of *Film Daily* with all the other memoirs you may be saving for your grandchildren."[130]

And if some Hollywood cynics had once regarded *Snow White* with skepticism, the filmmaking community as a whole made spectacular amends at the Academy Awards ceremony in February 1939. There, to deafening applause, Walt was presented with a special award for *Snow White and the Seven Dwarfs*: one full-size Oscar and seven miniature ones. The award was presented by Hollywood's favorite child star, Shirley Temple. "No grownup could have been so unself-conscious as Shirley Temple when she presented the big and little statues to Walt Disney for *Snow White and the Seven Dwarfs*," wrote Hedda Hopper. "That was a combination which will be long remembered—our Little Princess and Snow White's creator. And Disney meant it when he said, 'I'm really flabbergasted.' He was!"

By this time *Snow White* was a trendsetter; cartoon producers who would scarcely have considered a feature-length film two years earlier were now inspired to make the attempt. Max and Dave Fleischer, at their new studio in Florida, were hard at work on *Gulliver's Travels*, featuring the talents of Grim Natwick, Jimmie Culhane, and other *Snow White* veterans. Walter Lantz, Universal's house animation producer, had undertaken a feature-length *Aladdin and His Magic Lamp*,[131] and at one point announced he would produce *four* animated features. Leon Schlesinger, at the instigation of Warner

Bros., had tackled *Rip Van Winkle* in feature length. MGM, emboldened by *Snow White*'s success to produce a live-action fantasy feature, *The Wizard of Oz*, likewise issued periodic announcements of its own animated features. But resident producer Hugh Harman, claiming that his feature-length ambitions had been repeatedly denied, finally left MGM in 1941 to form an independent studio and announced that *he* would produce a feature. Walt's dream of an animated feature had once seemed an impossible gamble; now, said the *Hollywood Reporter*, "The trail blazed by *Snow White* promises to become a heavily trafficked highway."

In the end, apart from *Gulliver's Travels* and one additional Fleischer feature, none of these projects was completed. Most of these producers had seriously underestimated the difficulty of producing an animated feature, let alone a successful one. But by this time, of course, Walt had an intimate firsthand knowledge of both the risks and the rewards, and *he* was firmly committed to a program of further feature-length pictures.

THE "SNOW WHITE COTTAGES"

One of the oddest pieces of the *Snow White* legacy was the story of the "Snow White cottages," a court of small, quaint cottage-style houses located between 2900 and 2912½ Griffith Park Boulevard in Hollywood. For decades, rumors persisted of a connection between these cottages and the Disney studio, and in particular with *Snow White*. Perhaps the most persistent of these urban legends was that Walt had ordered the cottages built as residences for his artists, in order to inspire them to create the charming fairy-tale atmosphere of *Snow White*. The stories seemed to gain credence from the location of the cottages directly behind the Disney studio lot (which fronted on Hyperion) and the fact that a number of Disney staffers did live in them over the years. Doubtless because of their proximity to the studio, Hal Adelquist, Claude and Evelyn Coats, Chuck Couch, Dick Lundy, Ham Luske, Fred Moore, Lee Morehouse, Herman Schultheis, and Erwin Verity all occupied houses in this court at one time or another, some of them during the making of *Snow White*.

As much as one would like to believe the stories, there was, in fact, no formal connection between these residences and the Disney studio. The Griffith Park cottages were built by developer Ben Sherwood in 1931–32, after the Disney studio lot was established but long before Walt began to contemplate his animated feature. Writer Steve Vaught, who specializes in Hollywood's historic architecture, describes Sherwood as "a prominent Los Angeles builder/designer who was responsible for a number of speculative ventures throughout the 1920s and 1930s. Although he worked in various styles, Sherwood favored the same sort of fanciful fairy-tale type of French Norman styling he utilized in the Griffith Park Cottages." Other examples were built and can still be seen throughout Los Angeles. Special thanks to Steve Vaught and Joe Campana for providing information on this subject.

10

SNOW WHITE IN OTHER LANDS

Clearly, a phenomenon like *Snow White* could not be confined to the United States. It must be exported to the rest of the world, and that meant that special alternate editions must be prepared for showing in other countries.

For English-speaking countries, of course, no changes were required, and *Snow White* could simply be exhibited there in its original domestic version. Accordingly, RKO planned an opening in England shortly after the American release. But there was an unexpected problem in England: the censors. After a viewing of *Snow White* early in February 1938, the British Board of Film Censors announced that the more frightening scenes were too intense for very young viewers. "The *Sunday Graphic*," wrote an American correspondent, "says that British children are apparently held to be more easily upset by fairy stories than their 'tougher' American counterparts." *Snow White* was given an "A" certificate, denying admission to children under 16 unless they were accompanied by adults. An outcry ensued in the public press as writers debated the pros and cons of the Board's decision. The *Times* of London criticized it, editorializing: "No, the plain truth is that all fairy stories are wildly unsuitable for children. But fortunately, in the days when they were written, adults had not yet begun to dabble in 'child psychology.' If they had, the books of Messrs. Andersen, Perrault, and Grimm would have been suppressed at once, and the world would have been the poorer." The Disneys could not have been comforted by RKO's response to the "A" certificate: it was rumored that the distributor would deal with the problem simply by cutting the offending scenes out of the film.

This was not Walt Disney's first brush with the censors, and it would not be his last. Fortunately, in this instance the controversy was quickly squelched. Within two weeks of the Board's announcement, representatives of individual British counties viewed the film and made their own recommendations, overriding the Board's decision. *Snow White* would now be shown with a "U" certificate, allowing universal admission, in London, Essex, and Middlesex counties. On 24 February the film was given its European premiere at London's New Gallery cinema, where it settled in for a run of no less than eight months. Other county councils quickly followed this lead, granting "U" certificates for their respective territories. In the meantime, as the *Hollywood Reporter* noted, the uncut film had been shown to Princess Elizabeth and Princess Margaret with no ill effects: "By virtue of the fact that the picture was shown in a Command Performance at Buckingham Palace for the Royal Children, it is expected this will influence other local authorities in reaching a similar decision." By late summer—while still playing to capacity crowds in London—*Snow White* had reached the seaside towns, still uncut and with all ages admitted. Australian audiences first saw it in May 1938; its first run in Sydney extended into late October.

In the meantime, the studio had started to work on alternate editions of the film for non–English-speaking countries. Foreign editions were not a new idea for the Disney studio in 1938; Disney cartoons had long been international favorites. During the silent era, preparation of the Alice Comedies for foreign markets had amounted to simply replacing the English titles with

France had its own assortment of *Snow White* storybooks.

translations into the appropriate languages. The coming of talking pictures hadn't posed a great problem at first; the Disney sound cartoons had still been primarily visual and had kept English dialogue to a minimum. Later Walt, like the live-action filmmakers, had begun "dubbing" his films into other languages for foreign release—a much easier process in animation than in live action, since cartoon soundtracks were recorded separately anyway. Title cards, too, were translated from English into the appropriate language, along with lettering that appeared within the film—signs, banners, labels—where such translations were feasible.

The worldwide release of *Snow White* would be a far more visible and significant event than that of any short subject. Consequently, the Disney studio lavished special attention on the foreign versions of its feature. As always, the studio drew on past experience but aimed for a higher standard. By the end of December 1937, Erwin Verity had prepared a list of the *Snow White* scenes that contained English lettering. A surprising number of them did: "20 karat" and "50 karat" labels on the bags of jewels at the dwarfs' mine, the dwarfs' names carved on the footboards of their beds, titles of books on the Witch's bookshelf.

Most of these scenes would be replaced by specially photographed inserts in each foreign edition of the film. Wherever possible, the original backgrounds were reused for these inserts, with appropriate changes. Scenes in sequence 4C, in which Snow White reads the dwarfs' names on the footboards of their beds, were rephotographed with new overlays that replaced the original names with the dwarfs' alternate foreign names. Other scenes in the same sequence were rephotographed at closer range, putting the names outside the frame area—and, curiously, still other background paintings remained unchanged, the original English names still plainly visible on the screen. The pages of the book in the film's opening sequence were translated and relettered in the appropriate languages. Instead of rephotographing the action of the book's turning pages, as in the domestic version, the camera department simply shot the book's pages as if they were title cards, cross-dissolving from one to the next. Only one scene in the feature actually had to be reanimated: the closeup, in the pie-baking sequence, in which a small bird used a strip of dough to spell out the name "Grumpy" on the surface of a pie.

Meanwhile, the studio had also turned its attention to recording the alternate foreign-language soundtracks. Work on the Spanish translation started as early as the summer of 1937, long before completion of the feature. Soundtrack recordings began in October, and the Spanish edition of the film was completed by late February 1938. The Carthay Circle theater unveiled *Blanca Nieves y los siete enanos* at a special preview on Sunday, 27 February, during the tenth week of *Snow White's* 19-week engagement, and continued to play the Spanish edition once every Sunday afternoon thereafter. Subsequently *Blanca Nieves* was released in Mexico and in Central and South America. A separate Portuguese edition, prepared for showing in Brazil, was recorded in Rio de Janeiro in May 1938, supervised not by the Disney staff but by the Brazilian office of RKO. Latin American audiences generally enjoyed *Snow White,* but the Spanish adaptation came in for some criticism. "The Spanish version has certain flaws quite apparent in title and dialogue translation, considering the various customs of speech in the Latin countries where it will undoubtedly be shown," wrote one correspondent, observing however that "Disney's creation has lost little of its effectiveness as presented in Spanish."

For *Snow White's* introduction to continental Europe, the studio pinned its hopes on the French edition. The French government, which normally insisted that the dubbing of French soundtracks for American films must be performed in France, waived this regulation for *Snow White,* and work went ahead at the Disney studio in Hollywood. Marcel Ventura, a multilingual radio producer and actor who had played small parts in some live-action features, was hired to cast the actors and direct the recording sessions; he also cast himself as the Prince. The French recording sessions began late in February 1938 and continued into March.

In the meantime, Roy Disney and Paul Buchanan left the studio in early March, traveling cross-country by train to confer with RKO's New York office on the sensational success of *Snow White.*[132] On Friday, 11 March, they sailed on the *Bremen* for Paris, intending to remain in Europe for several months. Their missions were to prepare the way for the opening of *Snow White* in Paris, to oversee that opening personally, and to launch an ambitious program to record further foreign-language editions of the film. While dialogue for the Spanish and French editions had been recorded in Hollywood, the studio had determined to record voices for the other editions in Europe, hiring European directors and casts and working in European studios.

Although Buchanan had urged a mid-April Paris opening, the French edition could not be completed and shipped in time. *Blanche Neige et les sept nains* opened at the Marignan cinema in Paris on 4 May—and, despite the delay, was a smash success. The opening "was quite a gala affair," Buchanan wrote to Dave Hand at the studio a week later. "It really was a great turnout, and the reviews were quite good." Although he and the distributors privately expressed disappointment at the singing voices, French audiences embraced the film as warmly as had their American and English counterparts. *Blanche Neige* extended its stay at the Marignan for four months, then immediately moved to a second run at the Imperial and continued to play Paris until December.

By the time of the Paris opening, Buchanan and Roy had been in Europe for nearly two months and had already started work on the Dutch and German soundtracks for *Snow White.* Using Paris as a home base, Buchanan had been traveling to some of the other European capitals to investigate the availability of actors and recording equipment and to arrange for the recording of the various editions of *Snow White.* A plan was taking shape: the Dutch and German vocal tracks would be recorded in Amsterdam, the Italian in Rome, the Swedish in Stockholm, the Polish in Warsaw, and possibly the Czech in Prague. "We have definitely decided against a Danish version," Buchanan announced—but by August that decision had been reversed, and the Danish version was in the works. All of these various vocal tracks were recorded in synchronization with the picture and with a music-and-effects track that had been sent from Hollywood. The resulting vocal tracks were cut and assembled in Europe, then shipped back to the Disney studio in California for rerecording. ("Rerecording" was the contemporary term for what today would be called "mixing": combining the voices with the instrumental music and sound-effect tracks to create a single composite soundtrack.)

Spanish poster art for a later reissue.

Opposite: This French poster loosely reflects Gustaf Tenggren's influence.

[132] The Paul S. Buchanan who traveled to Europe with Roy Disney in 1938 was the same man as the Stuart Buchanan who had recorded the Huntsman's dialogue in *Snow White* (and also supplied voices for some other Disney films). At the studio he was addressed interchangeably as both "Paul" and "Stuart," a fact that has caused some confusion for latter-day researchers, but his letters from Europe to the studio were invariably signed "Paul."

RITORNA SUGLI SCHERMI ITALIANI LA PIÙ DELIZIOSA FAVOLA DEL MONDO

Biancaneve e i Sette Nani

REALIZZATO DA **WALT DISNEY** *in TECHNICOLOR*

DISTRIBUZIONE R K O RADIO FILMS

Note that this Italian poster advertises a reissue after the end of World War II.

Opposite: The magnificent Great Art Trophy, which caused such controversy at the Venice International Film Festival in 1938.

The German edition of *Snow White* was completed in late summer 1938, but *showing* the film in Germany was a problematic issue—not only because of the war clouds gathering over Europe, but for a variety of reasons, many of them financial. In 1933 and again in 1934, United Artists' European offices had contracted for the release of two series of Disney shorts in Germany. The terms called for outright sale of the negatives, much to the displeasure of Roy Disney, who strongly preferred the standard rental agreement. By all accounts the Disney shorts had been extremely popular in Germany, but because of tight currency export regulations, neither United Artists nor Disney had been paid for them. The funds were still frozen in Germany, and this was becoming an increasingly aggravating problem for Roy. When he and Walt visited Europe in 1935, they had personally called on one of the German distributors to try to resolve the problem, but without success. Now, in 1938, this impasse further complicated attempts to arrange a German release of *Snow White*. Two separate German distributors negotiated for rights to the feature, but with the film companies in the hands of the government and Germany increasingly isolated from the Allied countries, financial negotiations became impossibly convoluted and finally collapsed altogether. By 1940 the Reichsfilmarchiv had acquired a print of *Snow White*, but the film was not shown theatrically in the Grimms' homeland until long after the end of the war.

Elsewhere, Roy's and Buchanan's efforts were more successful. The newly dubbed editions of *Snow White* began to open across western Europe late in the spring of 1938 and, once again, settled in for long runs: six weeks in Geneva, ten weeks in Brussels, nineteen weeks in Amsterdam. In Prague, where the Czech government had waived the usual exhibition taxes in gratitude to the Disney studio for producing a special Czech version, the film played for three months. Countries without specially dubbed versions ran the English-language prints with superimposed subtitles. In Helsingfors, Finland, two different editions of *Snow White* opened simultaneously at different theaters: the American version at the Capitol, the Swedish at the Adlon. By the fall of 1938, RKO could announce that its European business was triple the amount of the previous year, thanks mainly to the popularity of *Snow White*. And still the film continued to conquer new territories: in January 1939 the Diana Palace theater in Cairo erected a 38-by-26-foot neon sign, described as the first neon display ever used for an Egyptian movie theater, to announce *Snow White* dubbed in Arabic.

Meanwhile, in the fall of 1938, *Snow White* capped a successful run in Italy with special honors at the Venice

International Film Festival. The Great Art Trophy, a huge statuette picturing Biancaneve (Snow White), the dwarfs, and the animals, was a work of art in its own right. In the highly charged political climate of Europe in 1938, however, this honor was actually seen by some observers as a slap in the face. The Anglo-American delegation to the festival, charging that the judging was biased in favor of the Axis countries, had already filed a protest when the Mussolini Cup, the festival's highest honor, was awarded to Leni Riefenstahl's *Olympia*, a visual record of the 1936 Olympic Games in Berlin. They were further incensed when *Snow White*, rather than being awarded top honors, was given a special "camouflaged" award instead, isolated from the rest of the competition in a separate category. (Needless to say, no such furor ensued when both the New York Film Critics and the Academy did the same thing in the United States a few months later.) As *Film Daily* explained: "Critics of the exposition charge that the Disney opus could not be gracefully side-stepped, and that the action of the committee was obviously aimed at a diplomatic way of doing so, and hence a new prize was created so that a political purpose could be achieved."

This controversy notwithstanding, it was clear that *Snow White* had scored as great a success in the international arena as in the United States. It had also set yet another precedent. Foreign editions of future Disney films could now be created with relative ease, thanks to the methods and network of contacts established for the studio's first feature.

In the United States, meanwhile, a special engagement of the French edition, *Blanche Neige et les sept nains*, opened at the Waldorf Theater in New York on Saturday, 8 April 1939. A display of original *Snow White* art adorned the Waldorf lobby. Walt, then in Philadelphia supervising the recording of the special *Fantasia* soundtrack, traveled to New York to make a personal appearance on opening night. The timing of this special booking was not a coincidence; the World's Fair was due to open later the same month, and theater management anticipated a high proportion of European visitors to New York for the occasion. "Incidentally," said the *New York Times*, "the management of the Waldorf announces that French francs will be accepted during the run of *Blanche Neige*."

11

THE DWARFS GO TO WAR

In the excitement surrounding the great success of *Snow White*, one of the questions reporters most frequently asked Walt was whether the Seven Dwarfs would return in new films. The reading public received sharply contradictory answers to this question. To some journalists, Walt flatly declared that a return appearance by the dwarfs was out of the question: "I sincerely believe that it would be an anticlimax to put them in anything other than the production for which they were created." But these outright refusals were interspersed with other statements in which Walt confessed that "We all feel we should start another picture with the dwarfs right away. They're like real people by now. It will be hard to say good-bye to them." Some writers, with or without Walt's encouragement, speculated that Dopey might soon star in a series of his own.

Walt did, in fact, periodically consider an encore appearance by the dwarfs for years after the release of *Snow White*. One possible vehicle was a version of *Hansel and Gretel*, an idea that was under consideration at the studio for several years.[133] The Disney writers considered this story from many angles, and at one point they suggested that Hansel and Gretel might meet the Seven Dwarfs, in guest-starring roles, in the forest. Walt entered enthusiastically into this idea. "This thing is hot," he said at one 1941 conference. "The characters are set, and the public would really go for a repeat on the dwarfs stuff." He discussed the most effective ways to use the characters in the story: "You don't have to have all the seven dwarfs in the scene at the same time, but you don't want to overdo Dopey. He is much funnier when in contrast to the others."

A tentative outline was established: the dwarfs would warn Hansel and Gretel not to enter the enchanted forest, and Dopey would be assigned to escort them back to their parents while the other six dwarfs went to work at the mine. But the children, lured by fantastic tales of the enchanted forest, would escape Dopey's custody and enter anyway. Dopey would alert the rest of the dwarfs to the children's danger at the Witch's hands, and the picture would climax with another furious race to the rescue—hopefully a successful one this time. Walt also suggested an alternate idea: the Witch might capture Hansel, Gretel, *and* Dopey. Otto Englander suggested that the Witch from *Snow White* might also make a return appearance in this story, but Walt didn't think this necessary: "She should be more of a regular witch with her cats and props . . . I see her as an old Hallowe'en witch."

Along with this unproduced idea, we have evidence of another: an out-and-out sequel to *Snow White*. A collection of story sketches, explicitly labeled *Snow White Returns,* was unearthed in the studio's Animation Research Library in 2009 after being forgotten for decades. A quick perusal of these sketches reveals that the "story" was actually a cut-and-paste job, cobbled together from outtakes from the original feature. Clearly intended as a response to the studio's financial straits in the mid-1940s, this project would have resurrected large blocks of animation, painstakingly produced for *Snow White* and then eliminated from the final cut, and stitched them together—with a minimal amount of new interstitial animation—to produce an instant ersatz feature.

As depicted in the sketches, *Snow White Returns*

133 The studio's interest in *Hansel and Gretel* was apparently sparked by a local production of Humperdinck's opera, attended by a Disney studio group in November 1937. After seeing the performance, Ted Sears wrote a memo to Walt suggesting that the studio buy the rights to the opera. Sears's primary concern was the story—he wanted to retain the option of using some story material exclusive to the operatic version—but he also allowed the possibility of incorporating other elements, including the music. This may seem surprising today, but for a studio that was just beginning to explore the dark terrors of *Pinocchio* and the rich classical repertoire of *Fantasia,* Humperdinck's *Hänsel und Gretel* might have been highly appropriate source material. Roy Disney tried to use the studio's frozen German funds to negotiate for rights to the opera, but his efforts were not successful.

would have opened with a familiar sight: the dwarfs marching home from the mine, singing "Heigh-Ho." Lingering closeups of individual dwarfs marching past the camera suggest that Bill Tytla's original scene 3 from sequence 4B—his legendary scene of the marching dwarfs, which had established a benchmark for all the other dwarf animators in the studio—would finally have enjoyed its moment of glory on the screen. The dwarfs' homeward march was to be interrupted by a bird bearing a sheet of paper: an "air mail" delivery of a letter from Snow White. "Dears: I'm coming tomorrow for my annual visit." The dwarfs' joy would be quickly replaced by concern: "We'll hafta give her a surprise!" What kind of gift would it be? This would lead to the Lodge Meeting and Bed-Building sequences, both of which had been at least partially animated at the time of *Snow White*.

Proceeding home, the dwarfs would discover that Snow White had already arrived and had cooked them

another pot of soup. This would set the stage for the Soup sequence, which had been cut from the original feature with such anguish and regret. Now, at last, the dwarfs would receive their etiquette lesson from Snow White. The meal finished, the dwarfs would prepare to present their guest with their homemade gift—only to find that they had neglected to cut loose the four "bedpost" trees, and the bed was still firmly rooted in the forest. While waiting for the dwarfs to return, Snow White would fall asleep.

Little is known about this proposed project, and we have no direct record of Walt's response to the notion of passing off this plate of leftovers as a new Disney feature. In the end, however, neither this nor the planned adaptation of *Hansel and Gretel* was ever produced, nor did the dwarfs appear in any other feature. However tempting the prospect may have been, Walt ultimately decided not to exploit the dwarfs' popularity with another feature-length showcase.

Story sketches for the never-completed *Snow White* sequel, in which the Dwarfs finally would have built a bed for Snow White.

[134] The Academy parade had also included some miscellaneous characters that were, themselves, reworked from yet another parade scene in the 1931 Silly Symphony *Mother Goose Melodies*. In a recycling process that makes for fascinating comparisons today, both the nondescript characters (redrawn each time to conform to current studio style) and the parade music (adapted from Franz Josef Wagner's "Under the Double Eagle") were used in all three films: *Mother Goose Melodies, Parade of the Award Nominees,* and *The Standard Parade.*

[135] According to the original agreement, the trailers were supposed to have an average running time of two minutes. In fact *All Together,* the shortest of the finished films, ran just short of three minutes, while the longest, *The Thrifty Pig,* ran well over four.

THE STANDARD PARADE FOR 1939

In 1939, however, the dwarfs did make a modest return in a short sponsored film. The studio had recently licensed its characters for Standard Oil's current advertising campaign, and one of the results was *The Standard Parade for 1939,* a short trailer designed to be shown at Standard's sales conventions. In *The Standard Parade* familiar Disney characters marched across the screen, carrying banners and signs that declared their support for Standard Oil. The parade animation was loosely based on drawings from a special short, *Parade of the Award Nominees,* that had been shown at the Academy Awards banquet in 1932. In the Academy short, Mickey, Minnie, and other characters had marched at the head of a parade that included caricatures of the current year's acting nominees for Academy Awards.[134] Now the marching action was modified to show the same Disney characters, and some new ones, advertising Standard Oil. Among the new characters were the Seven Dwarfs. Proudly bringing up the rear of the parade, six of the dwarfs carried signs that spelled out S-T-A-N-D-A—after which Dopey appeared, carrying a four-sided sign which (finally rotated into proper position) provided the final *R* and *D.* Riley Thomson, the director of this short trailer, had been one of the junior animators of the dwarfs in *Snow White.*

What's notable here is the source of the dwarf animation. All the animation in *The Standard Parade* was recycled from earlier pictures, and the dwarf action was based on none other than scene 3 from sequence 4B in *Snow White*—that now-legendary Bill Tytla scene of the marching dwarfs. Here, of course, the individual dwarfs' actions are modified for the needs of the short: the drawings are reversed to show the dwarfs marching from screen right to screen left, and the picks over their shoulders are replaced by the signs they carry. *The Standard Parade* is hardly a lost Disney classic, but it did finally allow Tytla's scene to reach the screen in some form, be it ever so humble. Two years later the scene would be modified again for still another use.

THE CANADIAN BOND TRAILERS

In 1941, four years after the opening of *Snow White,* the dwarfs returned to theater screens in a way no one could have anticipated just a few years earlier. The occasion was a major one: World War II.

In the course of the 1940s, the Walt Disney studio would make a tremendous contribution to the Allied war effort, encompassing hundreds of training films, propaganda films, posters, military insignia, and other efforts. The first of these war-related activities began in 1941, before the United States had officially entered the war. In April 1941 the Disney studio hosted a conference for members of the aviation industry, whom Walt hoped to impress with the potential of animation (specifically Disney animation) outside the realm of entertainment: as a medium for education, instruction, and propaganda. One of the conference attendees—simply because he happened to be in town—was John Grierson, the distinguished British documentary filmmaker. In addition to his own filmmaking activities, Grierson was the founder and commissioner of the National Film Board of Canada, and he was indeed impressed with what he saw and heard at the Disney conference. Canada, as a member of the British Empire, *was* already involved in the World War, and Grierson was quick to see the role that Disney animation might play in helping to prosecute the Canadian war effort.

The dialogue between Walt and Grierson continued after the conference, and by late July 1941 the Disney studio had agreed to undertake two projects for the National Film Board. One was a training film on the use of the Boys MK-1 Anti-Tank Rifle, a film completed in two reels in 1942 and titled *Stop That Tank!* The other project was a series of four theatrical shorts, designed to encourage Canadian citizens to buy war savings bonds. These short trailers would appeal to audiences by featuring Disney characters already well known from earlier films. Further, said the agreement between Disney and the NFB, "it is specifically understood that the animation of said scenes will, when feasible, be the same as that already used in Walt Disney short or feature films released in the past—although in such cases different backgrounds will be used."

In the finished Canadian bond trailers, the studio modified more than the backgrounds.[135] Extended animated scenes from familiar films reappeared in these shorts, ingeniously revised to fit the trailers' sales

In this publicity still for *7 Wise Dwarfs,* the Dwarfs prepare to trade in their diamonds for war bonds.

mission and contemporary world events. These revisions, of course, make them doubly fascinating viewing today. *The Thrifty Pig,* the first of the bond trailers, is a good example: it recycles generous helpings of animation from the 1933 Disney hit *Three Little Pigs.* This time, however, the Big Bad Wolf is explicitly redrawn as a Nazi, wearing a hat and armband adorned with swastikas. The Practical Pig, as a loyal Canadian subject, proudly flies the Union Jack from a flagpole in his yard, and the bricks from which he builds his house are revealed in closeup as Canadian savings bonds. For good measure he pelts the Wolf with more of the same "bricks" as the latter, frustrated, beats a retreat.

7 WISE DWARFS

The Seven Dwarfs came in for a somewhat different treatment in the second Canadian bond trailer, *7 Wise Dwarfs.* No overt Nazi imagery this time; *7 Wise Dwarfs* made liberal use of animation from sequences 4A and 4B of *Snow White,* in which the dwarfs were seen working in their mine and then marching home. This time, however, the mine was explicitly located in Canada, and the dwarfs ended their working day by carrying their bags of jewels into the city to trade them in for savings bonds!

The beginning of the short is a virtual replay of the opening scenes in sequence 4A of *Snow White.* Once again the dwarfs sing "Dig Dig Dig," tracked from the original soundtrack and featuring Al Eugster's, Eric Larson's, Bill Roberts's, and Marvin Woodward's unaltered animation. Doc's scenes at the workbench are slightly revised: as he sorts the jewels, he distributes

them in bags marked with the various dwarfs' names. Dopey still sweeps up the rejects, but instead of discarding them he puts them into his own bag.

The real patchwork begins as the dwarfs march out of the mine singing "Heigh-Ho." Here again, original *Snow White* animation of the marching dwarfs is recycled—not from Tytla's scene this time, but from Jimmie Culhane's. Now the scenes are redrawn to show the dwarfs carrying jewel bags over their shoulders in place of the picks and lanterns in the original film. Their lip-sync is faulty, too, because at this point a new soundtrack takes over with revised lyrics. "Heigh-ho, heigh-ho, we're the wisest dwarfs we know," sing the dwarfs. "We'll do our part with all our heart . . . we'll win the war with five for four." ("Five for four" was one of the Canadian government's slogans for selling the war bonds; it referred to a special promotion by which the purchaser could receive five bonds for four dollars. All four of the Disney bond trailers featured the phrase "five for four" in some way.) Here, too, the richly textured original backgrounds are replaced by new ones—bland, less skillfully painted, but appropriate to the subject. Once again the dwarfs march across a fallen log, this time spanning not a chasm but a shallow gully, with the Canadian Parliament buildings visible in the distance.

In the city scenes, animation of the dwarfs becomes an odd hybrid: original animation from the feature is used wherever possible, mixed with new action drawn by less expert hands. As in sequence 4D of *Snow White,* Doc stops, points offscreen, and shouts "Look!" while the other dwarfs pile up behind him like boxcars. But

TRACE BALANCE #95

(16)

IE—

Sleepy marches through three different films, courtesy of repurposed animation by Bill Tytla.

Left: The scene as originally animated for *Snow White.*

Center: The same scene retraced for *The Standard Parade,* with the pick over Sleepy's shoulder replaced by a sign, and his direction reversed.

Right: For *All Together* Sleepy is retraced again and given a new sign (his direction is later reversed by the inkers).

this time he's pointing to a post office, one of the locations where the bonds could be purchased. (In a closeup, Doc points to the post office and stammers excitedly in a voice that is clearly not Roy Atwell's, Atwell presumably being unavailable in 1941. In the earlier singing scenes, the substitution of new voices is less noticeable because the dwarfs as a group sing in a gaggle of non-descript male voices. In this closeup, however, Doc sounds distinctly like Pinto Colvig, who had returned to the studio after a four-year absence.) Anxious to buy their bonds, the dwarfs race into the post office—all except Dopey, who lags behind and has the door slammed in his face. But, to make the point that bonds were also available at banks, he quickly spies a nearby bank that likewise displays the bond poster, and takes his business there instead.

Soon the first six dwarfs emerge from the post office, large bundles of bonds carried under their arms and crammed in their pockets. After a brief glimpse of Doc, marching out of the bank in a scene adapted from his exit from the cottage in sequence 10A of *Snow White,* he and the rest of the dwarfs march past the camera in a new, awkwardly drawn 17-foot closeup. (Bashful, carrying his bonds in his hat, sports an odd nimbus of white hair around his bald dome that makes him practically unrecognizable.) Dopey, leaving the bank with his own bundle of bonds, trips and drops it on the sidewalk. Here again, as Dopey briefly romps along on all fours, we get a quick snippet of Fred Spencer's animation from *Snow White*—inserted in a scene that is otherwise not nearly so well drawn.

As Dopey hurries away to rejoin the others, a few stray bonds fall from his pile, float into closeup, and wrap themselves in a cylindrical formation to become a shell. The shell is promptly loaded into a cannon, and we segue into a montage of scenes of military strength, some of them reused from the closing moments of *The Thrifty Pig.* But whereas the previous sequence had been accompanied by music tracked from the 1936 short *Three Little Wolves,* most of the music in this military montage is taken from sequence 3A of *Snow White,* in which Snow White had fled into the woods. Separated from its original animation and overlaid by the sounds of exploding bombs, Churchill's and Smith's dramatic music provides a stirring foundation for scenes of war and mass-produced armaments. The climactic strains of the music, which had originally led up to Snow White's scream and collapse in the woods, now underscore another kind of climax: the appearance of the "five for four" slogan on screen.

Partly because the Canadian shorts had been given a high priority at the Disney studio, *7 Wise Dwarfs* moved quickly through production. The Technicolor answer print was shipped to Grierson at the NFB on 12 December 1941, eight days ahead of schedule. By this time, of course, Pearl Harbor had been attacked, and the United States had officially joined Canada and the other Allies in the war effort.

ALL TOGETHER

The fourth and last of the Disney bond trailers for the NFB was *All Together,* an appropriately titled short in which a large assortment of characters from previous Disney shorts and features paraded past the Canadian Parliament buildings in Ottawa, carrying banners and balloons promoting the savings bonds.[136] Unlike the other trailers, *All Together* makes no attempt at telling a story; it simply depicts the parade. Pinocchio, Geppetto, Figaro, Donald Duck and his nephews, and Pluto all make appearances, stitched together from walking or marching scenes in their earlier films, but redrawn to show them carrying signs and balloons. For today's Disney enthusiast, much of the enjoyment of *All Together* comes from identifying the sources of those original scenes. For example, the procession includes a large parade float on which Mickey Mouse is seen conducting a band, the scenes taken from the 1935 classic *The Band Concert*. But one of the performers on the float is Goofy, struggling to play a one-man–band contraption in a scene from *Mickey's Amateurs* (1937), and we also see Horace Horsecollar playing the tympani in an original scene animated by Ken Muse—the only original character animation in all of *All Together*.

In this haphazard procession of Disney characters, the Seven Dwarfs bring up the rear. Here again the original source of the animation is Tytla's *Snow White* scene, modified once more. Now the dwarfs' signs from *The Standard Parade* are replaced with new ones promoting Canadian bonds, and a new gag is added for Dopey: he trips and falls, then runs to catch up with the parade. *All Together* was completed and shipped in January 1942.

THE WINGED SCOURGE

Shortly after completion of *All Together*, the dwarfs made one final screen appearance on behalf of the war effort. During 1941 Walt Disney had started to work with the U.S. government on war-related projects, and in particular with the office of the Coordinator of Inter-American Affairs. This connection would lead the studio to produce *Saludos Amigos, The Three Caballeros*, and other films with Latin American themes.

In addition to these theatrical films, Walt was still interested in producing nontheatrical subjects. Early in 1942 he started work on several educational and health-related pictures that were to be distributed on 16mm in Latin America. One of the first subjects the studio tackled was "The Mosquito and Malaria." Malaria was perhaps the deadliest disease facing Latin America, and prevention was mainly a matter of combating the anopheles mosquito, the agent responsible for spreading the disease. Disney's malaria film, produced in 1942, replaced the working title "The Mosquito and Malaria" with the more dramatic *The Winged Scourge*. The first part of the picture was a relatively serious depiction of malaria and its disastrous consequences. Then the narrator asked for "six or seven people in the audience" to help fight the anopheles mosquito, and the Seven Dwarfs volunteered. The rest of the film shifted into a far more lighthearted and encouraging mood, as the dwarfs demonstrated various techniques for protecting themselves and their home from the mosquitoes.

Production of the Canadian bond trailers in 1941 had been done hurriedly, on a tight budget, and the animation in them had quite openly been assembled from leftovers. By contrast, *The Winged Scourge* was one of a group of films specially produced for the Coordinator's office in 1942, as a showcase of what the Disney studio could accomplish in the nontheatrical field. Accordingly, it featured all-new animation. The first part of the picture, showing the mosquito's depredations, was produced simply, in a style that was graphically powerful but made few demands on the animation staff. True character animation was reserved for the second half of the film, featuring the dwarfs, and was the work of Harvey Toombs and two of the original *Snow White* animators, Milt Kahl and Frank Thomas. Two of the junior animators at the time of *Snow White*, both Kahl and Thomas had risen rapidly to become two of the studio's top artists by 1942.

But *The Winged Scourge* was no *Snow White;* its purpose was not to enchant but to instruct. At one story meeting Walt warned his crew against including too many distracting gags: "The only reason to bring in the dwarfs is to add a little interest; when you begin to get into gags and impossible things, you're not accomplishing the job we're supposed to do—show in a simple way how to get rid of mosquitoes . . . [The gags are] nothing they'll laugh at to beat hell, but something to lighten it." The dwarfs as they appear in *The Winged Scourge* are

[136] For the record, the third short in the bond series had been *Donald's Decision,* made up largely of scenes from two 1938 Donald Duck shorts: *Self Control* and, primarily, *Donald's Better Self.*

simply vehicles for the film's educational message. Dopey is still distinct from the others as the "odd man out," but he stands out by way of mild gags, calculated not to distract. In the dwarfs' introductory scene, animated by Kahl, Dopey lags behind the others as they pop into view, then brains himself with a meat cleaver when he tries to salute. As the narrator describes the seriousness of their mosquito-destroying mission, Dopey retains his silly grin—until he looks around, notices the other dwarfs' expressions of grim determination, and quickly adopts a fierce frown of his own.

Thomas, the only artist on this short who had animated the dwarfs in *Snow White,* was assigned the scenes of Dopey inside the cottage. His experience shows: while both Kahl's and Toombs's dwarf animation is somewhat off-model, Thomas, when he chooses, gives us a Dopey who looks and moves like the character in the feature. Just as Dopey had looked under Happy's beard in the bedroom sequence of *Snow White,* and stared in amazement at Sneezy's pulsing throat as the latter yodeled in the entertainment sequence, now he checks underneath Grumpy's beard for an errant mosquito, smacks it with a flyswatter against Grumpy's throat—and gets conked on the head again for his efforts. Later, pursuing another runaway mosquito across the floor, he stomps it repeatedly with a loose, floppy action that looks as if it could be a scene from the feature.

In other scenes, Thomas takes Dopey's personality into his own hands and alters it in surprising ways, almost to the point of reinventing the character. Thomas had distinguished himself in the interim since *Snow White* with a variety of other outstanding scenes, including much of the title character in *Pinocchio,* and some of his closeups in *The Winged Scourge* feature a Dopey who unmistakably suggests Pinocchio. In one remarkable scene, Dopey strolls through the cottage, casually demolishing the mosquitoes with an insecticide spray gun and displaying a cool aplomb far removed from the original Dopey. His cocky self-assurance is similar to that of the unchastened Pinocchio, and his supple, nonchalant moves with the spray gun suggest a championship billiards player showing off for his audience. In another scene, backed up against a wall by a flank of advancing mosquitoes, Dopey seems at the mercy of the enemy—until he whips off his hat, revealing a frog that quickly picks off the mosquitoes with its tongue. Most of Dopey's antics in *Snow White* had seemed to spring from a simple childlike silliness. In scenes like these he displays, instead, a resourceful ingenuity directed toward the purpose at hand—less Harry Langdon, more Harpo Marx.

The Winged Scourge accomplished both of its purposes: it impressed the Coordinator's staff, who eagerly contracted for more Disney shorts, and it proved equally popular—and consequently effective—in nontheatrical distribution, both in the United States and in Latin America (where it was shown in Spanish and Portuguese editions). Russell Pierce of the Coordinator's office, writing to the studio in 1944, called *The Winged Scourge* "one of the most popular films" in the agency's library and reported that it had been shown to more than a million viewers in Latin America. Today, as one of the studio's best-known wartime shorts, it retains its popularity among Disney enthusiasts.

12
THE RETURN
OF SNOW WHITE

In the spring of 1939, after a record-breaking worldwide run of more than a year, *Snow White* made headlines once again when the Disney studio pulled it *off* the market. RKO exchanges were informed that the film would no longer be available for bookings after 29 April. "This unprecedented plan of taking a film out of circulation while it is still making money was announced by Disney today," a syndicated news item explained, "because he does not want the cartoon opera to wind up in the nickel and dime showhouses." In the spring of 1939 *Snow White* was still regarded as a rare and precious jewel, but Walt and Roy knew that, if its exhibition continued indefinitely, it would eventually make its way to the lowly neighborhood theaters. Rather than allow it to be cheapened by overexposure, they elected to retire it—for the time being—while it still retained the cachet of a prime attraction. Vague hints to the press suggested that the film would return to theater screens on some future occasion, but the specific date was never confirmed.

THE "WALT DISNEY FESTIVAL OF HITS"

It arrived far sooner than anyone expected. One year later, in the spring of 1940, the Disney studio's fortunes had changed radically. By now, inspired by *Snow White*'s success, Walt had plunged into an ambitious program of new features. The first, *Pinocchio*, was even more luxurious and elaborately produced than *Snow White*, as well as far more expensive, and Walt and Roy expected that it would meet with another spectacular success. They were in for a rude surprise. Released with great fanfare in February 1940, *Pinocchio* opened to ecstatic reviews—and a tepid box-office response. Not

that it was a box-office disaster; *Pinocchio*'s ticket sales would have been considered quite successful for an ordinary film. But this was no ordinary film; its negative cost exceeded that of *Snow White* by nearly a million dollars, and it soon became clear that it was going to lose money. For *Fantasia*, currently working its way toward completion on a similarly grand scale, this did not bode well. In addition, Walt and his staff had recently completed their move into an expensive new studio in Burbank, partly financed by the success of *Snow White* but, likewise, partly dependent on future successes.

Clearly, it was time for action. For some time the studio had been supplementing its box-office income with a strategy inspired by the all-Disney theater Walt had observed in Paris in 1935. Beginning in 1937 with the *Academy Award Review*, the studio had reissued *packages* of earlier Mickey Mouse and Silly Symphony shorts. These feature-length programs were well received in theaters, and the additional revenues helped bolster the studio's fortunes. Most recently, in March 1940, a group of six one-reel gems had been grouped together for release to theaters in France, Belgium, and Switzerland. Now Roy, RKO, and the resourceful Hal Horne, who by this time had joined Disney's eastern sales force, concocted the ultimate reissue package: the "Walt Disney Festival of Hits." This program consisted of four popular Disney shorts—*Ferdinand the Bull*, *The Practical Pig* (the latest sequel to *Three Little Pigs*), *Donald's Lucky Day*, and the 1938 version of *The Ugly Duckling*—and, as the centerpiece, *Snow White*. This high-profile program was guaranteed maximum attention in theaters, and *Film Daily* announced that

Snow White reopened at this Broadway theater in 1944 and played there for three months, as popular as ever.

"availability [to exhibitors] will be tied to key first-runs, with RKO asking 'A' pix treatment for the show."

Their wish was granted: in New York the "Festival of Hits" opened in late July at Loew's Criterion—a small but prestigious first-run Broadway house—and, as the press reported, "overcame the handicap of unprecedented torrid weather, shattering week-end attendance records of the Criterion." Despite the heavy exposure all five pictures had already received, the program played the Criterion for a solid three weeks, continuing for two more at the Little Carnegie Playhouse. Similar success stories were enacted around the country, as *Snow White* continued to demonstrate its unflagging appeal to audiences. In some areas the "Festival of Hits" was still playing as late as March 1941.

THE 1944 REISSUE

This was undoubtedly both gratifying and financially beneficial, but it was only the beginning. In March 1942, returning by train from a visit to the East Coast, Walt found that one of his fellow passengers was Nathan Blumberg, the president of Universal Pictures. As the train rolled across the continent, the two men conversed at length about their mutual business concerns. Universal was, like Disney, an independent studio, and Blumberg offered a number of comments and business advice

that deeply impressed Walt. Upon his return to the studio, he wrote Roy a long memo on the subject. Among the other topics of conversation, Walt wrote, Blumberg "spoke of how they had gone through their past releases and dug out certain subjects which they put out as reissues. These proved very profitable for them—in fact, they made a lot of money from them. He wondered why we didn't capitalize on what he termed 'the gold' we had in our vaults."

Blumberg knew what he was talking about; in recent years Universal had been actively mining the gold in its own vaults. In 1937 an independent California exhibitor had discovered prints of Universal's two big 1931 hits, *Dracula* and *Frankenstein,* at a local film exchange. Booking them together as a double feature, he enjoyed such unexpected success that the program was held over at his theater for weeks, and other exhibitors around the country began to pick up the idea. Universal, belatedly realizing the potent box-office power of this combination, officially released the *Dracula* and *Frankenstein* double bill across the nation in 1938 and was rewarded with some of the most spectacular business in the studio's history. This was something more than the isolated rebooking of an old picture into a repertory house, or even the widespread release of a program like the "Festival of Hits," which essentially

Coronation of "the new Snow White" at the Cincinnati opening in February 1944.

was still an extension of the film's original success. This was an entirely new release of a "retired" film—one that, by Hollywood's usual reckoning, was assumed to have exhausted its commercial life—with sparkling new prints, a carefully coordinated release strategy, and an advertising and promotional campaign that would normally have been reserved for an up-to-the-minute "A" production. Walt recognized that *Snow White*, with its deliberately timeless quality, was ripe for such a treatment, and he continued to press for a full-fledged reissue. By mid-1943 RKO and the Disney studio were beginning to lay their plans.

As if to test-market the idea, they released the film first in England, where war-weary audiences were especially hungry for light entertainment. *Snow White* opened in time for Christmas 1943 at London's New Gallery cinema, the same theater where it had played for eight months in 1938. Once again it was eagerly welcomed by audiences; the *Times* reported that it "triumphantly proves . . . that time can do little to mar the freshness of the lyrical and humorous inspiration which went to its making."

As the American advertising campaign began to take shape, it was unanimously agreed that the film "should be advertised . . . with no mention of reissue or 'by popular request,' or 'here again,' or, in fact, anything that might tend to suggest to the layman's mind that it is a reissue or an old picture. They [the promotion experts planning the reissue] felt that it has sufficient entertaining qualities and is of such a peculiar character that such phrases would only handicap the possibilities of the picture. They want to play it straight away as a new picture and certainly with no reference that anyone could construe it to be an old one." However this phobia against "old" films may strike us today, it was taken seriously in 1943.

So seriously, indeed, that a major publicity campaign was carefully planned to launch the new release of *Snow White*. Ultimately that campaign would be centered not in New York or in Hollywood, but in Cincinnati, Ohio. Major support for the promotion was provided by Cincinnati radio station WLW, nicknamed "The Nation's Station," which boasted a signal powerful enough to reach four states. A team composed of

publicity specialists from Disney, RKO, and WLW mapped out a massive strategy: *Snow White* would open simultaneously in 50 cities in Ohio, Indiana, Kentucky, and West Virginia in February 1944. (Their program was so successful that, by the time of the opening, it had grown to embrace 60 cities.) Celebrities from the Disney studio, perhaps Walt himself, would make public appearances. Asked to step back into the spotlight, Adriana Caselotti instantly accepted, any former animosity quickly forgotten. Pinto Colvig, Clarence Nash, and junior Disney animator Dick Mitchell were recruited for personal appearances as well. (Nash had provided some incidental voices for *Snow White* and therefore was, like Caselotti and Colvig, a bona fide veteran of the film, but he was best known as the voice of Donald Duck, and it was in this role that he was presented to the public.) The festivities included talent contests to find "the new Snow White," as well as talented young artists.

Promoters of the campaign continued to hold out for an appearance by Walt himself in Cincinnati. As the date approached, even Roy, who had initially rejected any such idea, began to agree that perhaps Walt should make the trip. "Anything we can do to make it more successful promises to be extremely worthwhile," he wrote to his brother. "I'm really amazed at the impetus of this whole exploitation and the enthusiastic support being put forth by RKO." Walt, of course, was consumed with work on his current projects. As late as 22 February, Cincinnati papers promised his appearance at the event; at the last minute it was explained that "cancellation of Los Angeles plane flights, due to weather conditions," prevented his making the trip. But even without Walt, the Snow White event on the 24th was a gala occasion.

The point of all the hoopla, of course, was to promote the film, and in this it was wildly successful. *Snow White* was a smash hit all over again, not only in Cincinnati but in all of the 60 cities covered by the WLW campaign. And this was just the beginning: the momentum launched by the Cincinnati promotion fanned out across the nation, bringing *Snow White* to the attention of a new audience. In April, six weeks after the Cincinnati opening, the film made its appearance in New York—at

Marguerite Clark, whom Walt had seen as Snow White in the Paramount film nearly three decades earlier, visits him at the studio.

Brandt's Manhattan, on Broadway, only a few blocks away from Radio City—and continued there for three months. Once again, long lines at the box office testified to *Snow White*'s enduring appeal. Bosley Crowther, in the *New York Times,* offered a poignant wartime perspective: "Can it be six years since this picture was first taken out of its box, all new and full of wonder and infinite surprise? Can it be six years since we first came to know those incomparable dwarfs? . . . We felt good and sublimely complacent when the dwarfs sang us 'Whistle While You Work.' Who'd have thought that this jovial little ditty was destined to become a war-plant song? What kill-joy dreamed that American draftees would soon be marching to 'Hi-Ho, Hi-Ho'?

"Destiny has its way, regardless of feelings and fairy tales. And now we are in the midst of warfare more deadly than the gravest man conceived. Yet there, at the Manhattan Theatre, the dwarfs are still whistling while they work. Snow White is still dreaming of Prince Charming. And Dopey is still getting underfoot . . . There is evidence in this revival that such a masterwork on the screen has the timeless and universal richness of classic music or lore. Its pleasures are forever diverting; their recapture is a refreshing delight. There is even an elemental premium to be enjoyed at this particular time in seeing the Old Witch destroyed by a fortuitous but inevitable device. And there is more than fictitious satisfaction in the evidence that the Prince finally returns . . . Also, we would like to inform you that it is

deeply encouraging today to hear a theatre full of children laughing as though the world were new."

These were not isolated sentiments; across the country, *Snow White* continued to evoke a delighted response from audiences. The personal appearances by Disney talent continued: three touring units—one featuring Caselotti and Colvig, a second featuring Nash and Mitchell, and a third with another troupe of seven masked "dwarfs"—continued to appear onstage throughout the U.S. and Canada well into June. And *Snow White,* which had opened in Cincinnati in February 1944, continued to play in some American cities as late as October.

Meanwhile, just as in 1938, the film's promotional campaign produced some odd new sidelights on the *Snow White* story. Some could be heard in a new wave of *Snow White*–related radio broadcasts, most of them authorized by the Disney studio. Edgar Bergen, who had "hosted" Snow White and the dwarfs on his own program in December 1937, was himself a guest on the *Screen Guild Players* broadcast in April 1944, where he claimed that he himself had been asked to play the Prince, and proceeded to tell the story of Snow White to Charlie McCarthy. This was a very loose abridgement of the story, allowing plenty of time for Charlie's signature wisecracks. The only member of the film's original voice cast to appear in this broadcast was Billy Gilbert as Sneezy. As a result, Sneezy and Bashful—played by Bergen himself with his Mortimer Snerd voice—were the most prominent dwarfs in this version of the story. Adriana Caselotti, who was making a personal appearance in Pittsburgh, was not available to play Snow White this time; instead the role was played by fourteen-year-old Jane Powell, who had recently appeared in her screen debut, and who made a far more mature-sounding Snow White than Caselotti.[137]

Jane Powell returned a year later to reprise the role in another notable radio version, staged by Orson Welles. On the 27 March 1945 broadcast of his *This Is My Best* program, Welles narrated the story and dedicated it to his daughter on the occasion of her seventh birthday. The script, adapted by Robert Tallman, was a hybrid of the Grimms' text (complete with the opening), the Disney film (complete with dialogue and some of the songs), and some inventions common to neither. Perhaps the most striking departure was the ending, in which the Queen, who had *not* been chased by the dwarfs, returned to her mirror. Learning that Snow White was still alive, she uttered a curse (unheard) that smashed the mirror to pieces, and was herself instantly destroyed, reduced to "only a heap of ashes." Another surprising twist was heard on the *Academy Award* radio adaptation in March 1946: here the dwarfs did chase the Witch but, reversing the situation in the film, killed her by rolling the boulder down on *her*. One of them could even be heard paraphrasing her line: "We'll crush your bones!"

But these variations were nothing compared to the wild departures that were starting to appear in contemporary comic books. In the early 1940s the Disney comic-book publishing program was accelerating, and by 1944 a promotional *Snow White* comic book, retelling the story of the film with art recycled and adapted from the 1937–38 newspaper comic continuity, was a foregone conclusion. But as early as 1943 there was also an intriguing offshoot: *Thumper Meets the Seven Dwarfs*, designed to cross-promote both *Snow White* and the more recent Disney feature *Bambi*. Despite the fact that the two films were set in very different cartoon universes, this comic book united them convincingly as the eponymous baby rabbit, exploring in the forest, fell into a hole and landed in the dwarfs' mine. The dwarfs and Thumper then embarked on an adventure which, for good measure, also included the giant from the 1938

short *Brave Little Tailor*, as well as animals that seemed to come from *The Old Mill* and *The Ugly Duckling*. This was only the beginning; in ensuing years the Disney comic-book universe became a freewheeling environment in which the dwarfs might encounter Donald Duck, Jiminy Cricket, or Dumbo the flying elephant. In subsequent adventures, the dwarfs saved Humpty Dumpty's younger brother from another giant, Willie, who had appeared in *Fun and Fancy Free* (*The Seven Dwarfs and Humpty Dumpty*, 1949); protected the *Bambi* animals from a gun-happy Br'er Bear on a shooting spree (*The Seven Dwarfs*, 1952); and sailed in search of buried treasure (*The Seven Dwarfs and the Pirate*, 1949)!

THE 1950s AND BEYOND

Today, of course, we know that the 1944 reissue of *Snow White* was only the first of many, and that other Disney features followed suit in a rotation of reissues that kept an ever-shifting array of classic animation before audiences. Each new release was carefully coordinated and brought unique circumstances and challenges. *Snow White* next appeared in theaters in 1952. Like its predecessor, this reissue was promoted heavily on radio, but by 1952 another medium had become an important force in American homes: television. This would become the first release of *Snow White* to be publicized extensively on television, as we'll see in a later chapter.

The 1952 reissue was launched not in the Midwest, but in New England, once again with a personal-appearance tour. This time there was no question about Adriana Caselotti's availability; the moment she heard rumors of another *Snow White* reissue, she contacted the studio and eagerly volunteered her services. Clarence Nash, too, was pressed back into service. Studio artists were represented this time by Roy Williams and animator Ken Walker, both with local experience in live "chalk talk" performances. Williams, already a twenty-year veteran of the Disney studio, displayed a natural, winning performance style that made a special hit with young audiences. Within a few years this would lead to his new role as television's "Big Mooseketeer."

Unexpectedly, the 1952 reissue also served to bring another *Snow White* veteran to light. Late in March the studio received a letter from a theatrical promoter in

[137] It's worth noting that Bergen reprised this performance on the same program in December 1946, following more or less the same script, this time with another young singing prodigy, Mary Jane Smith, in the role of Snow White (and with character actor Charles Kemper as Sneezy). It's also worth noting that, earlier in 1946, Bergen and his dummies had filmed their scenes for the Disney feature *Fun and Fancy Free,* which would be released the following year. In those scenes Bergen narrated the story of "Mickey and the Beanstalk," while Charlie McCarthy heckled him with some of the same wisecracks he had used in the *Snow White* broadcast.

Salt Lake City, inquiring about a local performer who billed herself as "Whistling Snow White" and traded heavily on what she claimed was her former connection with the Disney studio. "Whistling Snow White" turned out to be none other than Ruth Magden, who had indeed provided some of the bird whistles in *Snow White* fifteen years earlier. After checking production records, the studio's Joe Reddy was able to confirm that her Disney connection was genuine.

The next reissue of *Snow White* took place in 1958, and once again reflected the changes that had taken place in the intervening six years. Perhaps most notably, the Disney presence on television had increased dramatically during that time and had included the launch of a wildly popular daytime children's program, *The Mickey Mouse Club*. The 1958 campaign began with another personal-appearance tour of New England, but this time the tour featured none of the actual veterans of *Snow White*. Instead moviegoers turned out to see Jimmie Dodd, the adult host of *The Mickey Mouse Club*, and three of the most popular Mouseketeers: Tommy Cole, Annette Funicello, and Doreen Tracey.

Another major change had taken place behind the scenes. In the early 1950s, after distributing its films worldwide through contracts with existing major studios for more than two decades, the Disney studio had formed its own releasing outlet: Buena Vista Film Distribution. The original 1937 main and end titles for *Snow White* had included a distribution credit to RKO Radio; now in 1958, for Buena Vista's first release of the film, new titles were photographed to eliminate that obsolete credit.

And so it went: each new release of the film reflected a changing world. In all, *Snow White* would be given eight major reissues over the course of five decades and would be retired from theatrical showing only after its release on home video in 1994. The studio's reissue program, initially born out of necessity, would become a well-loved Disney tradition. *Snow White* itself did fortify the studio's fortunes during the 1940s as Walt and Roy had hoped, proving again and again that its appeal to audiences was fresh and inexhaustible. And, in fact, this consistent success developed a dark side: Walt soon found that he was struggling to compete with himself. In time the other Disney features would find their audience and would become widely successful in their own right, but in the immediate aftermath of 1938, *Snow White*'s spectacular triumph with audiences and critics became a gold standard that no other film could match. The unflagging success of his first feature became a specter that dogged Walt's steps, mocking his continuing efforts. Always savvy in dealing with the press, Walt seldom mentioned this problem on the record, but in 1956 he confessed to Pete Martin: "The [films] that followed were disappointing in a way . . . Every time I'd make a feature after that, they'd always compare it with *Snow White*, and it wasn't as good as *Snow White*. And I actually got around to the point where I hated *Snow White and the Seven Dwarfs*."

Happily, this was not his last word on the subject. In a 1961 interview, Peter Bogdanovich asked Walt to name his favorite Disney feature. "Oh," Walt answered, "I guess *Snow White*. Maybe because I'm sentimental, and it was our first."

Left: Clarence Nash, Roy Williams, Donald Duck, Adriana Caselotti, and Ken Walker on tour with *Snow White* in 1952.

Right: Williams entertains the crowd in the lobby of the Criterion Theater, New York. "We tied in with a radio station for lobby broadcasts," wrote a publicity man, "and Roy operated in the lobby and on the sidewalk until the cops broke it up."

13

MORE PRINCESSES

As early as 1912, Winthrop Ames had drawn freely on the story of Cinderella in constructing his stage *Snow White*. The stories of the two heroines had meshed well: Snow White's danger at the hands of her murderous stepmother had been enhanced, made more pitiable, by her Cinderella-like forced kitchen labor. Ames's adaptation had had a far-reaching effect. By the time young Walt Disney encountered the 1916 Paramount *Snow White*, the blending of the Snow White and Cinderella stories was accepted and ingrained in American popular culture. Two decades later, when Walt came to produce his own *Snow White*, he had analyzed his material and was well aware of the particulars of the Grimms' story—but even so, in elaborating his own version, he found it natural to include an element of the Cinderella story, just as Ames had done.

Now, in the wake of *Snow White*'s success, the destinies of the two fairy-tale sisters continued to intertwine in an unexpected way. *Snow White* had been produced at the height of the Disney studio's creative powers, and Walt and his team had generated far more story material than they could possibly use in a single film. We've seen how they stripped away the excess material as story development continued, ruthlessly weeding out any ideas that impeded the flow of the story. But some of those ideas were too good to waste, and years later they were resurrected.

In some ways, production of *Cinderella* preceded that of *Snow White* at the Disney studio. In Kansas City, in 1922, Walt had produced a silent *Cinderella* as one of his series of Laugh-O-grams, "modernized fairy tales" that essentially used the familiar stories as frameworks on which to hang a series of slapstick gags and Jazz Age jokes. (The Laugh-O-gram Cinderella is a Cinderella who wears a short flapper skirt and goes to the ball in a Tin Lizzie.)

Late in 1933, even as plans began to form for a feature-length *Snow White, Cinderella* resurfaced at the Disney studio, this time as a proposed Silly Symphony. A story outline circulated in December 1933 suggested that this *Cinderella* would "[follow] the story rather closely as to plot" but would allow opportunities for plenty of gags. Two of the ideas suggested in the outline are especially striking in hindsight. At the beginning of the story, after Cinderella's stepmother and stepsisters have left her at home and departed for the ball, "She might build a dummy Prince out of kitchen props and dance with him and speak to him." Later, at the ball, "the background of the palace will fade away and [the] cloud background dissolve in, giving the effect that the Prince and Cinderella are dancing on clouds, oblivious to all others around them."

A number of gag suggestions were submitted, but this Silly Symphony version was soon abandoned. Today it's not clear whether this was because of the Fleischers' concurrent production of *Poor Cinderella*, or because some of the *Cinderella* story ideas were being appropriated for *Snow White*, or both. What is clear is that a pool of story material was being accumulated, ideas that might be used interchangeably for *either* of the fairy-tale princesses. Most of the artists and writers who submitted gags in response to the December 1933

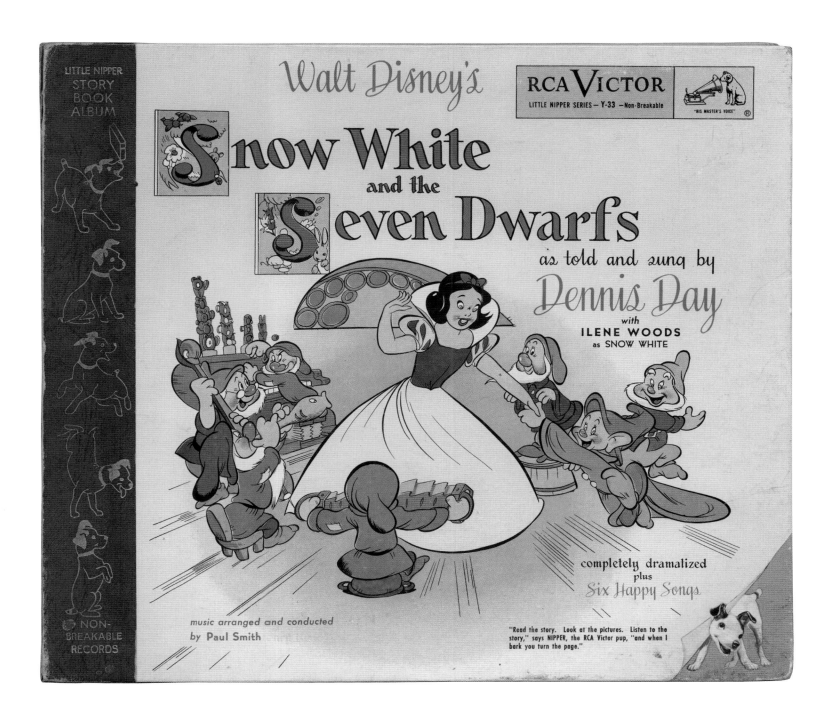

outline were the same artists and writers who would go on to work on *Snow White*. As the story for the feature began to take shape, the "dummy Prince [built] out of kitchen props" was lifted from this outline and became the "Prince Buckethead" episode in *Snow White*. Similarly, the "dancing on clouds" idea was expanded and made far more spectacular as the dream version of "Some Day My Prince Will Come."

However, as we've seen, the story of *Snow White* changed considerably during production. By the time the film was finished in 1937, both Prince Buckethead

and the dancing-in-the-clouds idea had been eliminated. Accordingly, when the studio tackled a feature-length *Cinderella* in the 1940s, these ideas and more were still available for use. There's no record that the Prince Buckethead idea was seriously considered for this new *Cinderella*, but the concept of a dance in a spectacular cloudscape *was* revived and, once again, extensively developed. Larry Morey and Charles Wolcott wrote a new song, "Dancing on a Cloud," for the occasion.

By the time *Cinderella* was finished and released in 1950, the dance in the clouds had been dropped again.

This record album, produced in 1949, underscored the link between *Snow White* and *Cinderella* (see page 274).

Above and opposite: Tom McKimson contributed these story suggestions for the proposed version of *Cinderella* in December 1933.

At the same time, however, another unused story idea from *Snow White was* adapted for the new feature. The earliest outlines for *Snow White* had suggested that the Queen would have the Prince imprisoned in a dungeon, but that he would later escape. According to some of these outlines, his escape would be aided by some friendly birds: "Two of them go out and stage a fake fight to get the guard's attention, while the other three or four are trying to get the keys off his hook—They succeed in getting the keys off, but drop them—The noise attracts the guard's attention, and the birds hide . . ." In the 1950 *Cinderella,* this suspenseful episode was reworked as Cinderella's stepmother locked her in her room to prevent the Prince from seeing her.

The efforts of Cinderella's friends, the mice, to retrieve the key, transport it up the stairs, and release her from her room were developed into a protracted and anxiety-ridden sequence.

(As if to underscore the link between the two stories, RCA Victor issued a new record album of the Disney *Snow White* story and songs in 1949, with Snow White's songs and dialogue provided by Ilene Woods—the voice of Cinderella in the new feature.)

Finally, in 1959, nearly all of the remaining *Snow White* leftovers reached the screen in yet another animated feature: *Sleeping Beauty.* We've already seen that *Snow White* had borrowed from the Grimms' "Briar Rose" the idea of the princess awakened by the kiss of

Handwritten notes on sketches:

IN HURRY TO GET HER OUT OF WAY, STEP-SISTER PUSHES "CINDERELLA" INTO ASHES OF FIREPLACE (NO FIRE)

WHEN "C". COMES OUT TO TRY ON SLIPPER — SHE DOES NOT REAL-IZE HOW DIRTY + RAGGED SHE IS

"C". TURNS INTO SHINING WHITE + COLOR THE INSTANT HER FOOT TOUCHES GLASS SLIPPER

Tom McKimson 113– FOR CINDERELLA

RESPLENDENT!

true love. Now, in 1959, the favor was returned. In *Sleeping Beauty* the Prince Buckethead idea became a sequence in which the forest animals, stealing a hat, cloak, and boots from the nearby Prince, costume themselves collectively as Briar Rose's dream prince and "dance" with her in the forest. For *Snow White* it had been suggested in early meetings that the Prince would confide in his horse "like Tom Mix and Tony—Horse interested in what Prince says—Seems to understand— paws with forefoot, and so on." This idea had soon been dropped from *Snow White,* but here it was resurrected for the new Prince and his horse, Samson. Here, too, the idea of the Prince imprisoned in the dungeon was finally realized, complete with the Queen's (here, Maleficent's)

visit to the dungeon to taunt the Prince with the details of her cruel plan. And, at film's end, Briar Rose and her Prince finally enjoyed the dance in the clouds that had been denied their predecessors. At last, nearly all the major story material that Walt and his writers had devised in the mid-1930s (except the Soup and Bed-Building sequences) had been brought to the screen— but it had taken three feature films to do it.

14

TELEVISION

In the 1950s, and especially with the opening of Disneyland, the Walt Disney studio entered a new period of prosperity. The struggling times at the Hyperion studio, trying to make ends meet long enough to finish *Snow White,* were left far behind; so were the very different struggles of the war years in the 1940s. Now the goodwill that Walt and his films had built up with audiences for several generations was rewarded with a more stable level of success. Television was a new and highly visible facet of Disney activities in the 1950s; Walt plunged into the electronic medium with his characteristic enthusiasm, eager to explore new horizons. But in this fresh venture, *Snow White* was hardly forgotten.

One Hour in Wonderland
25 December 1950, NBC

This special program, broadcast on Christmas Day 1950, was designed to publicize the release of the new Disney feature *Alice in Wonderland* the following summer—but in this, Walt Disney's first foray into television production, Snow White and the dwarfs maintained a presence as well.

The popular ventriloquist Edgar Bergen and his dummies Charlie McCarthy and Mortimer Snerd, continuing their connection with the Disney studio, shared top billing with Walt in *One Hour in Wonderland.* In the program, Bergen and his dummies are invited to a "tea party" at the Disney studio—although the beverage of choice at this "tea party" is actually Coca-Cola, the show's sponsor. Kathryn Beaumont, the voice of Alice, is the party hostess, and the program concludes with a preview of the still-unfinished *Alice in Wonderland,* but

otherwise the hour is rounded out with a generous helping of favorite Disney moments from the past, brought to life by the magic mirror from *Snow White.* Walt introduces the mirror and explains that he recently had the opportunity to buy it and bring it to the studio. The mirror, as seen in this program, is somewhat different from the one seen in the feature; the astrological symbols that had appeared on the Queen's chamber wall, surrounding the mirror, are here worked into the frame of the mirror itself.

Walt summons the slave in the mirror—played here by Hans Conried, who was then recording the voice of Captain Hook for the Disney feature *Peter Pan*—by uttering the same incantation that the Queen had used in *Snow White.* Unlike the Queen, Walt plays the words for comedy, roaring them melodramatically and accompanying them with wild gesticulations. (Not surprisingly, this elicits a wisecrack from Charlie McCarthy. Turning to two lovely young ladies sitting nearby, Charlie scoffs: "How hammy can you get? Do you girls know this character Disney?" "Yes," Sharon answers. "He's our father," adds Diane.)

There follows a series of clips from earlier Disney films, shown by the slave in the mirror in response to requests from the audience. Fittingly, the first request, from Kathryn Beaumont, is for a scene from *Snow White.* The mirror obliges with another party scene: the entertainment sequence from *Snow White,* complete with the dwarfs' performance of the "Silly Song," Snow White's dance with "Dozey," and the calamitous sneeze at the end of the sequence. Elsewhere, too, the program echoes *Snow White* in its musical score: the instrumental

strains of "Whistle While You Work" can be heard in the show's opening music, while "Some Day My Prince Will Come" can be heard at the end. Walt's television debut makes it clear that *Snow White* was not just a relic of the past, but continued to play a vital part in the Disney studio's image.

The Walt Disney Christmas Show
25 DECEMBER 1951, CBS

One Hour in Wonderland was a tremendous success with viewers, and the Disney studio created a second Christmas Day special for the following year. The sponsor of the 1951 program was Johnson & Johnson, and the format was similar to that of the previous year's show—but this time the film being promoted was *Snow White* itself, due for its second major reissue the following February.

Edgar Bergen and his dummies did not return for this program; instead the show opens in the children's ward of a hospital, where the patients are treated to a visit, via television, to another party at the Disney studio. Kathryn Beaumont and Bobby Driscoll, who had appeared in the previous year's show, are on hand again, this time in their capacities as character voices (Wendy and Peter, respectively) in the Disney work-in-progress *Peter Pan*. The magic mirror is back, too, displaying clips from such Disney shorts as *The Band Concert* and *Donald and Pluto*. But the focus is on *Snow White*. This program features an international flavor; the guests at the "party" are children from around the world who request and receive *Snow White* clips in their native languages: English, French, Polish, Swedish, Danish, Dutch, Italian, Spanish, Portuguese, and Czech. Hindustani doesn't seem to be available, so the mirror fills in with a Hindustani clip from *Bambi* instead.[138]

Toast of the Town
8 FEBRUARY 1953, CBS

This episode of Ed Sullivan's early-1950s television series was framed as a tribute to Walt Disney, and was supported by Walt, who appeared on camera in an interview setting with Sullivan. Their scripted reminiscences of Walt's career were liberally illustrated with clips from Disney films. Similar clips had already been seen on Walt's own Christmas specials and would later become a regular feature of his *Disneyland* series, but this broadcast, predating *Disneyland* by a year and a half, was still a notable early appearance of vintage Disney animation on TV. In the program Walt discusses *Snow White* with Sullivan, shows a clip from the feature, and, as a bonus, explains and includes the dwarfs' return appearance in *The Winged Scourge*.

Left: Sharon Disney, Charlie McCarthy, Edgar Bergen, Mickey Mouse, Walt, and Diane Disney with Walt's miniature locomotive, the Lilly Belle, on the set of *One Hour in Wonderland* (1950).

Right: Kathryn Beaumont, in her new role as Wendy in *Peter Pan,* returns for the 1951 Christmas program.

[138] This shrewd bit of showmanship highlights an experiment in which Walt and the studio took special pride. At the end of the war, as the Disney studio sought to reestablish itself in the international market, a special edition of *Bambi* had been prepared for India. Besides offering dialogue dubbed in Hindustani, this version replaced the original musical score with native Indian music. The soundtrack had been recorded in Bombay under Jack Cutting's supervision, and this special edition of the film had earned the studio a special Golden Globe award.

Disneyland: *The Plausible Impossible*

31 October 1956, ABC (reruns: 22 May 1957, 9 October 1960)

The *Disneyland* TV series occasionally offered viewers a look inside the Disney studio and a glimpse of its techniques. One such episode, "The Plausible Impossible," has long been a cult favorite among Disney enthusiasts because of its *Snow White* connection. It was in this television program, nearly two decades after the release of *Snow White,* that sequence 6B—the Soup sequence—was finally shown to the public in the form of pencil animation.

The title "The Plausible Impossible" refers to animation's ability to portray impossible actions in a convincing manner. Walt, speaking directly to his television audience, illustrates this principle by means of a series of clips: condensed versions of the shorts *Thru the Mirror* and *Donald's Cousin Gus,* an assortment of excerpts from *Fantasia,* and some new animated scenes created especially for the episode. The Soup sequence comes at about the midpoint of the show. As Walt explains the history behind the sequence and its exclusion from the feature, there's an almost palpable sense of his pleasure at finally being able to allow this hidden gem its moment of glory. His introduction is straightforward and factual, explaining that "even though we liked the sequence," it wasn't strictly necessary to the telling of the story. "Something had to be left out," he smiles, "and this was it." Preparing for the belated unveiling, he beams with delight—and we sense that, somewhere offscreen, Ward Kimball is beaming too.

The sequence proper is preceded by scenes from the feature that help to establish the context: Snow White's admonition to the dwarfs to wash their hands, Grumpy's defiance, a truncated version of the "Washing Song," and Dopey swallowing the soap. Then comes the Soup sequence itself. Oddly, it begins with Grim Natwick's scene of Snow White calling the dwarfs to supper in sequence 6A—in pencil form, even though the same scene had been fully inked and painted in the feature. This cutaway is apparently inserted to mask what otherwise might have been an awkward transition from the dwarfs in full color, outside the cottage, to their black-and-white images inside.[139]

Despite the show's claims, the Soup sequence as presented here is not photographed from "the animators' original pencil drawings"—and with good reason. Confronting a 1956 television audience with pencil animation was a daring move in itself; to use the animators' original roughs might have rendered "the plausible impossible" downright incomprehensible. Instead, new cleanup drawings were made for the program. "I worked on the TV show," Dick Huemer later told historian Joe Adamson. "We took these old drawings and we cleaned them up and shot them, so it could be used to show people on TV." The result is a sequence which—allowing for the pencil lines that give an intriguing "behind-the-scenes" feel to the proceedings—is otherwise as handsomely produced as the feature itself. Curiously, considering the important role Happy plays in this sequence, his appearance is the one weak element of the presentation. As he sings "Music in Your Soup," Happy is as beautifully drawn as any of the other dwarfs, but in the latter part of the sequence, as he directs the man-handling of Dopey, he's amateurishly drawn by comparison with the others. Whether this has anything to do with Bill Roberts's original animation we may never know. In any case, it's a minor blemish on an otherwise satisfying moment, a moment that gave Disney enthusiasts of 1956 the thrill of seeing a hitherto unknown facet of *Snow White.*

Disneyland: *Tricks of Our Trade*

13 February 1957, ABC (rerun: 3 July 1957)

This episode, another "behind the scenes" glimpse of Disney animation, followed closely on the heels of the first. It concentrates on three aspects of the studio's technique: action analysis, effects animation, and the multiplane camera. Action analysis is featured in the first segment of the episode, a staged scene in which production of *Snow White* seems to be taking place in 1957. A group of "animators" is seen studying live-action film that features, not Eddie Collins or any of the performers that the actual *Snow White* animators had studied twenty years earlier, but contemporary comedian Billy House.[140] As House executes a simple dance, the supposed animators screen the film in slow motion, observing the movement of House's ample body mass,

[139] *Disneyland* was telecast in black and white in 1956, but the studio showed its usual foresight by producing most episodes, including this one, in color.

[140] Although the "animators" in this scene are actually actors *cast* as animators, a generous complement of authentic Disney artists—Josh Meador, Jack Boyd, Dan MacManus, Milt Kahl, Frank Thomas, Ollie Johnston, and Marc Davis, each identified by name—do make onscreen appearances later in the same episode, cast in similarly fanciful scenes depicting the making of *Fantasia.*

Milt Kahl, Frank Thomas, Marc Davis (seated), and Ollie Johnston—four of the junior animators on *Snow White*— appear as seasoned veterans, two decades later, in the behind-the-scenes program *Tricks of Our Trade*.

the principles of squash and stretch, and the follow-through motion of his clothing. These observations are then translated into pencil animation of a dance performed by Happy, which in turn dissolves into a full-color scene of Happy completing his short solo dance in the "Silly Song" sequence from *Snow White*.[141] Happy's dancing action here is based on Bill Tytla's original animation in scene 9 of sequence 8A, but has been reinked and repainted to simplify the scene. Gone are the other characters in the scene; gone, too, are the subtleties of line and color with which Happy was rendered in the feature. In their place, perhaps to present the principles of movement in an uncomplicated fashion, the character is inked with thick outlines and painted in flat, simple colors.

Immediately following this, Walt addresses the camera on the subject of delineation of character through dialogue. To illustrate his point, we see a long excerpt from the bedroom sequence in *Snow White*, beginning as Snow White tries to guess the dwarfs' names, and ending with her promise to cook for them and "Hooray! She stays!"

Snow White and its characters were mentioned, seen, or celebrated in innumerable other television programs. More than a few of these featured Adriana Caselotti, still reminding viewers of her role as the original Snow White. One of her more notable appearances came in 1972 on ABC's *Julie Andrews Hour*. By this time Andrews had made her own mark on Disney culture as the star of *Mary Poppins*, and the two women joined their voices in duets of "I'm Wishing" and "Some Day My Prince Will Come." Caselotti reappeared in 1983 in a syndicated *Snow White* tribute called *Fairest of Them All*, this time reunited with Harry Stockwell, with whom she sang another duet. Other tributes continued to proliferate in the meantime, most of them well intentioned but some treating the film with dubious honor. During Walt Disney's own lifetime, he had discussed *Snow White* on television without ever talking down to his audience; in later years both the film and the audience were treated with less respect. By this time, of course, *Snow White* was safe from debasement, having long since been absorbed into popular culture.

141 This episode of *Disneyland*, too, was filmed in color, although most television viewers did not see it that way in 1957.

15

RED AS THE ROSE, BLACK AS EBONY, WHITE AS SNOW

Like every other aspect of producing *Snow White*, the film's color had received Walt's careful attention. He had been producing cartoons in Technicolor since 1932, and he had very definite ideas about the use of color in his feature. At a December 1936 sweatbox session, he commented: "We want to imagine it as rich as we can without splashing color all over the place." At the movies the night before, he had seen a recent Harman-Ising short, *To Spring*—a cartoon patterned on the Silly Symphonies, with elves awakening after a long winter and pumping color back into the dormant flowers and plants. Walt was unimpressed. "They got colors everywhere and it looks cheap. There is nothing subtle about it at all. It's just poster-like. A lot of people think that's what a cartoon should have. I think we are trying to achieve something different here. We are not going after the comic-supplement coloring. We have to strive for a certain depth and realism, to set these characters in a setting that has depth. We have to get a lot of depth through the use of colors, the subduing of the colors at the right time and for the right effect."

One of the factors that made *Snow White* a perfect story for the feature was that much of the story took place in a forest setting. This meant that long passages of the story were planned with a muted color scheme, staged against dark backgrounds dominated by cool greens and browns. Bright colors were used sparingly and, in other sections such as the entertainment

sequence, stood out the more vividly by contrast. As the film took shape, its color palette was carefully orchestrated, and Phil Dike, the studio's color coordinator, worked closely with Walt to ensure that his ideas for subtle, elegant use of color were carried out.

The critical stage of the process was photography, in which this artistic vision was committed to film. As each finished scene emerged from the lab, Walt and his team studied it minutely, and the camera crew received frequent retake orders when some flaw was found in the negative. When the film was released to theaters, Technicolor release prints were subjected to a similar level of scrutiny. (During the premiere run at the Carthay Circle, the theater was supplied with two separate prints—an "afternoon print" for matinees and an "evening print"— and both were inspected for color balance and regularly monitored for wear.) It was this film, produced with such rigorous attention to detail, that so entranced audiences around the world in 1937–38.

Unfortunately, other audiences over the next half-century would see a somewhat different version of *Snow White,* a version produced to less exacting standards while Walt's attention was concentrated elsewhere. The trouble began as early as the 1944 reissue, when Technicolor, preparing to manufacture a large quantity of release prints, notified the studio that the original camera negative was too brittle and shrunken to proceed. On Technicolor's advice, the studio authorized

The "warm" look of late-1930s Technicolor was well suited to the cottage interiors, illuminated by lanterns and firelight. Frames from an original 1937 release print.

new protective masters and a new dupe negative. The classic three-strip Technicolor process was still in its heyday in 1944 and would continue into the early 1950s, its rich, vivid hues enhancing many a musical or live-action drama. But that propensity toward brilliant color was exaggerated in cartoons, especially when printed from a dupe negative, which produced slightly heightened contrast. Virtually every print of *Snow White* shown in theaters for the next forty years was a descendant of that 1944 negative, and the color balance was pushed inexorably in the direction of the gaudy, "poster-like" colors Walt had sought to avoid.

In 1987, on the occasion of *Snow White*'s fiftieth anniversary, the Disney studio determined to produce a new, improved master positive that might restore the visual luster of the original film. The three-strip color process was a thing of the past by this time, and the Technicolor company was scarcely equipped to undertake a project of this magnitude. Instead the studio contracted with YCM Laboratories, one of the leading companies in the field of historical film restoration (its name derived from the three component color elements in classic Technicolor: yellow, cyan, magenta). Returning to the original camera negative—which was in relatively good condition for restoration work, having been virtually untouched since 1944—YCM technicians examined it with meticulous care. Their inspection addressed both photographic anomalies, such as light leaks, and physical defects in the negative itself, some of them as minute as tiny wood fibers that had been embedded in the surface of the film since 1937 (and which were "surgically removed from the emulsion

with a variety of instruments ranging from razor blade to fingernail"). Having made all these repairs to the fifty-year-old negative, they used it to create their new master positive, striving for optimum contrast, density, and color balance.

Six years later the studio took another giant step to preserve *Snow White* for posterity by undertaking a digital restoration. Having achieved so many "firsts" in its lifetime, *Snow White* in 1993 became a pioneer in the field of film digitization. Cinesite, a Kodak company, scanned each frame of the film to a separate digital file, fine-tuned the image, then "wrote" it back to film. Working with the YCM master positive, the Cinesite technicians not only addressed the clarity and color balance of the image, but also took the opportunity to repair photographic imperfections—in particular, multiplane dust. Despite the Disney studio's best efforts in 1937, it had not been possible to keep the huge, exposed surface areas of the multiplane crane free of dust, and some multiplane scenes had suffered from distracting specks crawling across the image. (When the studio moved into its new Burbank facility in 1939–40, one of the first buildings completed was the new camera department, which boasted advanced humidity and dust controls. Immediately on completion of this building, the camera crew moved in and began photographing the follow-up feature, *Pinocchio. Snow White* was the one Disney feature *not* to benefit from this development.) Now the digital restoration technicians used special software to scan each frame of *Snow White* and remove unwanted specks of dust from the image. It quickly became apparent that this process required

Another warm cottage interior: Snow White, illuminated from below, bids the Dwarfs goodnight.

careful supervision: on the first attempt to scan sequence 2A, when the pigeons appeared in long shot with what appeared as tiny red dots on their faces, the software removed their eyes!

Like their counterparts at YCM, the Cinesite technicians conducted their work with respect for the original. Artists who had worked on the film in the 1930s were invited to view the work in progress, and the restoration team took note of their comments. Ollie Johnston, echoing Walt's words six decades earlier, thought that "the first stuff they showed me had too much contrast. I felt it looked too poster-ish. I wanted to get back to a subtle quality. It looked almost medicinal, it was so clean; the whites were too pure. So they corrected that and showed it to me again. It's very good."

Johnston's words underscore an important point: technicians of each generation have manipulated the film's color *according to the standards of their own time*. Perceptions of the role of color, especially in animation, were very different in the 1980s and '90s than they had been in the 1930s, and the Cinesite technicians had had no intention of distorting the film's color balance; they were simply conforming to what was then accepted practice. This issue was vexing enough in the world of theatrical motion pictures, but the variables increased exponentially when *Snow White* was released to home video shortly afterward. Now the film's color scheme varied, not only according to the vagaries of each new video master, but with those of each separate player and monitor. Since that time the film has been repurposed again and again with each new release to videotape, laserdisc, DVD, and Blu-Ray, its image tweaked again each time. Of the millions of people who have watched *Snow White* in these latter-day incarnations, it's possible that no two have seen precisely the same image.

This raises the question: what *is* the ideal color standard? In a perfect world, how should *Snow White* best be preserved for posterity? For many purists, the answer is simple: we should strive to recapture the original image. The optimum viewing experience of *Snow White* should be the one that most closely re-creates that of the first audiences at the Carthay Circle and Radio City Music Hall. But color preservation is a complex business, and recent editions of the film have their propo-

nents too, those who argue that the "improvements" really are improvements, that Walt's ideas for a subtle color palette have been honored, and that newer versions of the color balance actually approximate his original vision more closely than the 1937 prints. (Ollie Johnston tactfully acknowledged the differences: "*Snow White* was a beautiful picture. It's probably just as good now; maybe better in some ways.") That warm glow that suffused the original Technicolor prints now appears to some viewers as merely an excessive yellow cast; and if we lose the glow, we gain increased clarity and a profusion of visual details that were always latent in the original negative but were lost on the screen. The Queen's robe can now be more clearly distinguished from the dark curtain behind her; objects hidden in the shadows of the dwarfs' cottage can be discerned; brush strokes in those painstakingly rendered watercolor backgrounds are now visible.

A similar controversy has extended even to the digital removal of multiplane dust specks. Critics have argued that that dust was 1937 dust and should have been preserved as part of the historical artifact; proponents have insisted that those crawling objects distracted from the beauty of the whole and that, given a choice, Walt would surely have removed them himself.

In the end, perhaps the answer is that this film, like other timeless works of art, is many things to many people. As with a great symphony or play, perhaps there is no one definitive performance. The very fact of these debates over the image, so many decades after the film's release, is evidence of the respect and love that *Snow White and the Seven Dwarfs* still inspires in its devotees. As Snow White, awakened by her Prince, lives on into the 21st century and beyond, we can be sure that history will continue to pay her tribute—striving to recapture and preserve, by any means at hand, the elusive but enduring beauty of Walt Disney's original vision.

PART FOUR

RESOURCES

APPENDIX A: PRODUCTION CREDITS

This list is an attempt to compile the most complete possible list of production credits for the film. Information is drawn from production documents in the Walt Disney Archives and Animation Research Library, and in the collection of the Walt Disney Family Museum. The principal documents consulted were the *drafts* (animation assignment sheets, generally showing which animators were originally assigned to individual scenes) and *exposure sheets* (maintained throughout production, often reflecting changes made in casting or footage during the making of a scene). These were supplemented by other studio papers, including sweatbox notes and cutting records, as well as the personal work records maintained by Grim Natwick, Ward Kimball, and effects animator Sanford (Sandy) Strother. It's hoped that this will be a useful tool for future researchers and, in addition, will honor the many dedicated artists who contributed their talents to the film.

SNOW WHITE AND THE SEVEN DWARFS

Copyright © 21 December 1937 by Walt Disney Productions, Ltd. (LP7689)
Los Angeles opening: 21 December 1937–24 April 1938, Carthay Circle
New York opening: 13 January–16 February 1938, Radio City Music Hall

Producer: Walt Disney
Supervising director: Dave Hand
Character design: Albert Hurter, Joe Grant
Story adaptation: Ted Sears, Dick Creedon, Otto Englander, Dick Rickard, Earl Hurd, Merrill de Maris, Dorothy Ann Blank, Webb Smith
[uncredited:]
  Harry Bailey, Homer Brightman, Kathleen Millay, Harry Reeves, George Stallings, Leo Thiele, Roy Williams

[Joe Grant, Larry Morey, and others whose names appear elsewhere in this list also made substantial contributions to the story.]

Layout: Charles Philippi, Ken Anderson, Tom Codrick, McLaren Stewart, Hugh Hennesy, Ken O'Connor, Gustaf Tenggren, Harold Miles, Terrell Stapp, Hazel Sewell
[uncredited:]
  John Hubley, Bob Kuwahara, Jack Miller, Ernest Nordli, Charles Payzant, Thor Putnam
Backgrounds: Sam Armstrong, Phil Dike, Mique Nelson, Ray Lockrem, Merle Cox, Maurice Noble, Claude Coats

VOICE TALENTS

Snow White: Adriana Caselotti
Supplemental voices: Thelma Hubbard, Virginia Davis; Esther Campbell whistles for Snow White in "Whistle While You Work"
Prince: Harry Stockwell
Queen/Witch: Lucille LaVerne
Slave in the Magic Mirror: Moroni Olsen
Huntsman: Stuart Buchanan
Doc: Roy Atwell
Grumpy: Pinto Colvig
Happy: Otis Harlan
Sleepy: Pinto Colvig
Bashful: Scotty Mattraw
Sneezy: Billy Gilbert [Gilbert also doubles for sneezing squirrels and chipmunk in housecleaning sequences]
Miscellaneous dwarf voices: Jim Macdonald, Clarence Nash, Hal Rees, Lem Wright
Dwarf singing voices: Freeman High, Bill Cowles, Sonny Dawson, Harry Stanton
Dwarf yodeling chorus on "Silly Song": Jad Dees, Zeke Clements, Wes Tuttle, Les Miller, Sonny Dawson
Bird calls: Esther Campbell, Anne Darlington, Marion Darlington, Peggy Downey, Ruth Magden, Louise Meyers, Clarence Nash, Ruby Ray
Songs: Larry Morey (lyrics), Frank Churchill (music)
Incidental music score: Frank Churchill, Leigh Harline, Paul J. Smith

SEQUENCE 1A: CREDITS AND STORYBOOK

Title and storybook lettering: Gordon Legg

SEQUENCE 1B: FIRST QUEEN AND MIRROR SEQUENCE

Director: Bill Cottrell
Animation: Art Babbitt (Queen)
Woolie Reitherman (Slave in the mirror)
  assistant: Charles Nichols
Efx animation: Cy Young (shadows and DX shadow masks; wind efx and blowing drapery; lightning)
John McManus (smoke efx in mirror)
  assistant: Dan MacManus
Stan Quackenbush
  [Quackenbush's assignment in this sequence is not clear from production papers, but he may have animated the flames that are seen in the mirror before the slave and the smoke appear.]
Shadowgraph: Lee Payne
Assistant directors: Hal Adelquist, Jerry Prosk

SEQUENCE 2A: SNOW WHITE AND THE PRINCE IN THE GARDEN

Director: Perce Pearce
Animation: Jack Campbell (Snow White scrubs steps, approaches well and sings "I'm Wishing"; Prince climbs over wall; Snow White closes curtains at end of his song)
  assistants: Clair Weeks, Hugh Fraser, Amby Paliwoda
Clair Weeks (Prince on horseback approaches castle)
Hugh Fraser (Snow White at well reaches for rope)
Eric Larson (pigeons around wishing well)
  assistant: Don Lusk
Milt Kahl (pigeons in CU at well's edge; pigeons surround Prince and Snow White's meeting and Snow White on balcony; Prince sings "One Song"; pigeon conveys Snow White's kiss to the Prince; Prince with pigeon at end of song)
  assistant: Murray McClellan
Ham Luske (reflections of Snow White and Prince in well; Snow White closes curtains at end of Prince's song)
Paul Busch (reflections of Snow White and Prince in well)
Grim Natwick (Prince and Snow White's meeting at the well; Snow White runs into castle; Prince sings "One Song"; Snow White listens from room and balcony; Prince with pigeon at end of song)
  assistant: Marc Davis
Art Babbitt (angry Queen)
[Larson animated most of the pigeons in this sequence through the end of "I'm Wishing." Kahl animated the first CU of the pigeons at well's edge as Snow White begins her song, and all of the pigeon action that followed it: the birds fluttering around Snow White and the Prince at their first meeting, and the pigeon that conveys Snow White's kiss to the Prince. This was Kahl's original assignment as part of the animal unit, but in the course of production he also became a cleanup artist on the Prince and worked with Natwick on animation of the Prince's singing scenes and at the close of the sequence. Campbell worked with both Natwick and Luske on this sequence, but he and his assistants (including Weeks and Fraser, each of whom animated a key solo scene) were all part of Luske's unit; and Luske worked with them on several of their scenes, in particular with Busch on the reflections in the wishing well. (*Snow White* contained many scenes that were the combined work of two or more animators.

Throughout this list, such scenes are listed under all applicable names, accounting for the overlapping credits in some sequences.) The closing Snow White scene, originally assigned to Natwick, was reassigned to Luske's unit.]

Efx animation: Sandy Strother (shadows; rope, bucket, pulley, and water in wishing well; Queen's curtain)

Assistant director: Carl Fallberg

SEQUENCE 2B: QUEEN ORDERS SNOW WHITE'S DEATH

Director: Bill Cottrell
Animation: Art Babbitt (Queen)
Errol Gray (Huntsman)
Efx animation: Cy Young (highlights on Queen's robe; shadows and DX shadow masks; Queen's box)
Assistant director: Hal Adelquist

SEQUENCE 3A: SNOW WHITE AND HUNTSMAN; SNOW WHITE INTO WOODS

Directors: Perce Pearce, Ham Luske
Animation: Grim Natwick (Snow White sings, talks to bird and to Huntsman)
   assistants: Marc Davis, Les Novros
Ham Luske (Huntsman; Snow White backs away from Huntsman and runs into woods; Snow White goes through bushes and vines; Snow White frightened by owl and bats; branch "hands" clutch at Snow White; Snow White frightened by hideous face on tree trunk; Snow White runs toward camera; Snow White trips over branches; Snow White's fall into pit and into the water; Snow White frightened by alligators; Snow White runs away from and toward camera; montage: trees, Snow White turns and whirls, glaring eyes; and Snow White's final scream and collapse)
   assistant: Harry Hamsel
Errol Gray (Huntsman; Snow White trips over branches)
Eric Larson (baby bird; owl in tree; bats; Snow White runs toward camera)
   assistants: Don Lusk, Jack Bradbury
Jack Campbell (Snow White backs away from Huntsman and runs into woods; Snow White goes through bushes and vines; Snow White frightened by branch "hands"; Snow White runs toward camera; Snow White trips over branches; Snow White frightened by alligators)
Tony Rivera (Snow White backs away from Huntsman and runs into woods; Snow White

goes through bushes and vines; Snow White frightened by bats; branch "hands" clutch at Snow White; Snow White's fall into pit and into the water; Snow White escapes from alligators onto land and is menaced by another clutching tree)
Milt Kahl (log/alligators)
   [Gray, Campbell and Rivera were all part of Ham Luske's unit; Luske supervised all their scenes and collaborated on some of them. (For example, Luske, Campbell and Rivera all worked together on the scenes of Snow White fleeing from the Huntsman into the woods.) The log/alligators, originally assigned to Larson, were reassigned to Kahl. Luske animated all of the closing montage, with assists from Campbell and Larson on some of the scenes involving Snow White. Some scenes animated for the montage, including a second fall into the water, were eliminated before the final cut.]
Efx animation: Sandy Strother (shadows; flashes on the knife; logs, falling rocks, and water efx)
Reuben Timmons (blowing leaves)
Assistant director: Hal Adelquist

SEQUENCE 3B: SNOW WHITE MEETS ANIMALS

Directors: Perce Pearce, Ham Luske
Animation: Ham Luske (Snow White sobs on ground; chipmunk and squirrel peek at Snow White; surprised Snow White frightens animals; bunny hides in log, birds in nest; Snow White talks to animals; bunny and chipmunk peek out; parent birds land on branch; Snow White sings "With a Smile and a Song" and talks to animals; animals nod in response to Snow White's dialogue; Snow White with quail; Snow White on her way to the dwarfs' cottage; Snow White looks through parted branches)
   assistants: Errol Gray, Don Lusk
Jack Campbell (Snow White sobs on ground; Snow White sings "With a Smile and a Song" and talks to animals; Snow White on her way to the dwarfs' cottage; Snow White looks through parted branches)
Jim Algar (animals come out of shadows; raccoons and turtle listen to Snow White's song; quail; chipmunks and squirrels applaud; animals nod in response to Snow White's dialogue)
   assistant: Murray McClellan
Eric Larson (chipmunk and squirrel peek at Snow White; animals approach Snow White and run away again; squirrels hide in trunk and peek

out; baby and parent birds; birds on deer's antlers; birds cheer Snow White's song; birds pull Snow White away; animals follow Snow White to the path; animals lead Snow White past the water; animals part branches)
   assistants: Jack Bradbury, Don Lusk
Milt Kahl (first bunny approaches Snow White; chipmunk, fawn and bunny approach Snow White as she sings; animals surround Snow White as she finishes song; animals listen to Snow White)
   assistants: Murray McClellan, Jack Bradbury
Bernard Garbutt (deer and other animals jump into bushes and peer over log; deer and birds listen to Snow White's song; animals approach her as she sings; deer runs to the path; animals lead Snow White over rise and to clearing)
   assistant: Lynn Karp
Tony Rivera (Snow White sings "With a Smile and a Song" and talks to animals; Snow White on her way to the dwarfs' cottage; Snow White looks through parted branches)
Grim Natwick (Snow White asks "Will you take me there?" and is pulled away by birds)
   assistant: Marc Davis
   [Aside from Natwick's single scene, all the Snow White animation in this sequence was the work of Luske's unit. (In Natwick's scene, Kahl animated the animals listening to Snow White at the beginning of the scene; Larson animated the birds that pull her away by the edges of her cloak.) Luske, Campbell and Rivera worked jointly on most of Snow White's scenes during and after the song. Inconclusive evidence suggests that Ward Kimball may also have worked with Luske on some of his Snow White scenes in this sequence. Most of the bird animation (including some of the birds perched on deer's antlers) was by Larson, but Luske animated them hiding in their nest early in the sequence and worked with Larson on the scene of the parent birds landing on the branch beside their baby. For one CU of a deer listening to Snow White's song, Garbutt was assisted by an artist believed to be John Sewall.]
Efx animation: Sandy Strother (shadows; bush)
Assistant director: Hal Adelquist

SEQUENCE 3C: SNOW WHITE DISCOVERS DWARFS' HOUSE

Directors: Perce Pearce, Ham Luske
Animation: Ham Luske (Snow White looks through branches; Snow White runs to the

dwarfs' house; Snow White looks through window, knocks and enters door; sees and sits in chair; Snow White looks at table; Snow White at table; birds on pickaxe handle; Snow White at the fireplace, blows dust from fireplace; animals at fireplace, on mantel and at sink; animals and cobwebs; bunnies and quail beside broom; Snow White: "Maybe they have no mother"; Snow White decides to clean house and assigns cleaning tasks; discouraged animals get cleaning assignments; Snow White picks up the broom)

    assistant: Bill Weaver

Eric Larson (animals look with Snow White through branches; animals look through window and enter with Snow White; animals run out door, knocking down turtle; birds on pickaxe handle; animals at fireplace; animals on mantel and at sink; birds take Snow White's cloak)

    assistants: Don Lusk, Jack Bradbury

Milt Kahl (animals look with Snow White through branches; animals accompany Snow White to the house; discouraged animals get their cleaning assignments)

Bernard Garbutt (animals look with Snow White through branches; animals accompany Snow White to the house and enter with her; animals and cobwebs; bunnies and quail beside broom)

Jack Campbell (Snow White looks through window, knocks and enters door, sees and sits in chair, looks at table and sits at table, blows dust from fireplace; Snow White: "Maybe they have no mother"; Snow White hands cloak to birds, assigns cleaning tasks and picks up the broom)

Tony Rivera (Snow White sits in chair; Snow White: "Maybe they have no mother"; Snow White hands cloak to birds, assigns cleaning tasks and picks up the broom)

Jim Algar (animals cautiously reenter house and peek out; animals on table; doe and fawn; animals with Snow White as she takes the broom)

    assistant: Murray McClellan

Eddie Strickland (Snow White at table; Snow White picks up the broom)

Grim Natwick (Snow White at the fireplace)

    assistant: Marc Davis

    [Luske, as co-director of the sequence and supervisor of the unit assigned most of the animation, worked with other artists on many of the scenes assigned to them. Natwick, not a member of the unit, was assigned the medium

shot of Snow White at the fireplace, but Luske also worked on the scene with him. Some evidence suggests that Luske, Campbell, and Rivera worked together on the scene of Snow White saying "Maybe they have no mother," but that Luske later reanimated the scene alone after filming new live action for it.]

Efx animation: Cy Young and Paul Satterfield (opening scene: butterflies and flowing water)

Cy Young (shadows; cobwebs)

Assistant directors: Jerry Prosk, Hal Adelquist

SEQUENCE 3D: SNOW WHITE AND ANIMALS CLEAN HOUSE

Directors: Perce Pearce, Ham Luske

Animation: Eric Larson (birds and animals at start of song; animals carry dishes; animals wipe and wash dishes; squirrels dust music box; squirrel beats dust out of tail and sneezes; chipmunk and spider; birds arrange flowers; deer carries clothes on antlers; birds wring and hang shirt; bird on Snow White's finger; animals in closing scene)

    assistants: Don Lusk, Jack Bradbury

Ham Luske (animals carry dishes; Snow White cleans and sings "Whistle While You Work"; rabbit and deer dust chair; Snow White tells animals to put the dishes in the tub; squirrel winds cobweb in rafters; chipmunk winds cobweb and falls in sock; raccoons and deer at stream)

Jim Algar (animals carry dishes; animals sweep; animals pull clothes on pan; deer carries clothes on antlers; animals in closing scene)

Louie Schmitt (animals carry dishes; rabbit and deer dust chair; animals pull clothes on pan)

Grim Natwick (Snow White cleans and sings "Whistle While You Work")

    assistants: Jack Campbell, Marc Davis

Milt Kahl (rabbit and deer dust chair; squirrels sweep dust, mouse protests; animals help Snow White dust; chipmunk winds cobweb and falls in sock; raccoons and deer at stream; animals in closing scene)

Jack Campbell (Snow White tells animals to put dishes in the tub)

Leonard Sebring (squirrel winds cobweb in rafters; chipmunk winds cobweb and falls in sock; chipmunk, turtle and birds at stream)

    [Grim Natwick was the principal Snow White animator in this sequence, but Luske, co-director of the sequence, worked jointly with Natwick on many of her scenes. Luske also

worked with Campbell on the one Snow White scene in this sequence *not* animated by Natwick: Snow White telling the animals to put the dishes in the tub. For the two pan shots, scenes 2 and 12, the character animators were Luske, Larson, Schmitt, and Algar (sc 2) and Schmitt and Algar (sc 12); if any additional efx animators worked on the moving floorboards and props, their names were not recorded. The scene of the chipmunk, turtle, and birds at the stream, originally assigned to Kahl, was reassigned to Sebring. Conversely, the scene of the squirrels sweeping dust into the mouse's hole, whereupon he angrily kicks it back out again, was first assigned to Sebring and then reassigned to Kahl.]

Efx animation: Cornett Wood (dust; cobwebs)

Stan Quackenbush (cobwebs)

Cy Young (water; cobwebs; dust; flowers)

Josh Meador (shirt dripping with water)

Sandy Strother (shirt dripping with water)

Assistant directors: Jerry Prosk, Hal Adelquist

SEQUENCE 4A: DWARFS AT MINE

Director: Perce Pearce

Animation: Al Eugster (dwarfs dig in opening scene)

    assistant: Bob Youngquist

Eric Larson (Sleepy, mine car, and deer in opening scene; deer pulls mine car)

    assistant: Don Lusk

Bill Roberts (Happy and Grumpy sing "Dig Dig Dig" in CUs)

    assistant: John Elliotte

Marvin Woodward (Bashful and Sneezy sing "Dig Dig Dig" in CUs; dwarfs listen to echo)

    assistant: Herb Johnson

Les Clark (Sleepy drives the mine car)

Art Babbitt (Doc sorts diamonds)

Fred Moore (Dopey sweeps up jewels; Dopey and Doc at the workbench; Doc and Dopey throw their sacks into the vault and Dopey hangs up the key)

    assistant: Ollie Johnston

Frank Thomas (Doc and Dopey hear clock striking, Doc starts to sing "Heigh-Ho")

    assistant: Art Elliott

Jimmie Culhane (dwarfs start to sing "Heigh-Ho" and exit mine)

    assistant: Nick de Tolly

    [Larson animated Sleepy, the mine car, and the deer in the opening scene, while Eugster animated all the other dwarfs digging in the mine.

In Sleepy's two later scenes, Clark animated Sleepy; the deer was still animated by Larson.]

Efx animation: Cy Young and Andy Engman (clock strikes five), Paul Satterfield, Ed Aardal, Sandy Strother (all efx animators: jewels and sparkle efx)

Assistant director: Carl Fallberg

SEQUENCE 4B: DWARFS MARCH HOME FROM THE MINE

Director: Ben Sharpsteen
Animation: Jimmie Culhane (dwarfs march around bend, across log and into distance)
  assistant: Nick de Tolly
Assistant director: Lou Debney

SEQUENCE 4C: SNOW WHITE DISCOVERS BEDROOM

Directors: Perce Pearce, Ham Luske
Animation: Ham Luske (Snow White downstairs; Snow White walks upstairs and looks at beds; animals read names on beds; Snow White yawns; bunny family; bird puts out candle; deer asleep in bed and awakened by song; turtle climbs stairs, reaches top, knocked over by returning rush of animals and falls downstairs)
  assistant: Jack Campbell
Jack Campbell (Snow White downstairs)
Eric Larson (animals with Snow White downstairs and going up the stairs; animals with Snow White as she yawns and lies down; birds watch Snow White sleeping and one puts out candle; animals hear dwarfs' song, look out window and exit bedroom)
  assistant: Don Lusk
Louie Schmitt (turtle starts to follow Snow White and other animals upstairs)
Grim Natwick (Snow White walks upstairs, enters room and looks at beds; Snow White yawns and lies down)
  assistant: Jack Campbell
Milt Kahl (animals enter room with Snow White; animals with her as she looks at beds; bunny family; deer asleep in bed and awakened by song; turtle climbs stairs, reaches top, knocked over by returning rush of animals and falls downstairs)
  assistant: Murray McClellan
Jim Algar (animals read names on beds)
  assistant: Murray McClellan
Bernard Garbutt (animals run out of front door, take cover and peek out)
  assistant: Lynn Karp

[Snow White animation in this sequence was more or less evenly divided between Luske and Natwick; each had isolated scenes, but the two worked together on most of the Snow White scenes (with a strong contribution from Campbell). In the scene of the birds covering Snow White with the sheet, Snow White herself was represented by a single still drawing by Marc Davis.]
Assistant directors: Carl Fallberg, Hal Adelquist

SEQUENCE 4D: SPOOKS

Director: Perce Pearce
Animation: Bill Roberts (marching dwarfs see light in house and stop; dwarfs blown across room and against wall by force of sneeze)
  assistant: John Elliotte
Dick Lundy (dwarfs peek from behind trees; individual dwarfs discover cleanup; Happy, Dopey, and Grumpy by the soup pot)
  assistant: Berk Anthony
Bill Tytla (Grumpy predicts trouble; dwarfs decide to sneak up on house; Doc instructs and leads dwarfs sneaking through house; Doc and Grumpy react to cleanup; dwarfs at foot of stairs)
  assistant: Bill Shull
Bob Wickersham (dwarfs at door; dwarfs sneak in house in LS)
Art Babbitt (dwarfs sneak in door; Dopey slams door and others react; dwarf dialogue after bird noises; dwarfs send Dopey upstairs; Dopey enters bedroom and is frightened by Snow White)
  assistants: Jack Larsen, Robert Leffingwell, Murray Griffin
Eric Larson (birds in house; Snow White stretches and yawns on bed)
  assistant: Don Lusk
Bernard Garbutt (animals at window)
Fred Moore (Sneezy's sneezing fit; other dwarfs try to stifle him)
Ham Luske (birds tap and screech; Snow White stretches and yawns on bed)
Fred Spencer (dwarfs frightened by bird sounds, dive for cover and peek out; dwarfs down stairs and outdoors, Dopey trapped at door and covered with pots and pans, dwarfs attack Dopey; Dopey's pantomime; dwarfs decide to reenter house and attack monster)
  assistant: Volus Jones
Jack Campbell (Snow White stretches and yawns on bed)

[Except for one scene of Doc and Grumpy, animated by Tytla, all the scenes of the individual dwarfs reacting to their newly cleaned-up house were animated by Lundy. Larson animated the first scene of the birds high in the rafters; for the later scenes of their tapping and screeching to frighten the dwarfs, Larson worked with Luske. Dopey's frightening adventure upstairs was essentially divided between Babbitt, who animated the dwarfs' downstairs conference and Dopey sneaking upstairs, through his fright at seeing the supposed monster; and Spencer, who animated Dopey's terrified flight downstairs, his ambush by the dwarfs outside the house, and all the rest of the action through the end of the sequence. During Babbitt's part of this passage, Tytla animated the dwarfs at the foot of the stairs, and Luske, Campbell, and Larson collaborated on the "monster" that frightened Dopey—actually Snow White, stretching underneath the bedsheet. Wickersham's assistant, identified on the exposure sheets as "Steve," was probably Stephen Bosustow.]
Efx animation: Ugo D'Orsi (smoking chimney, flowing stream)
  assistant: Harry Hamsel
Josh Meador (steam from soup pot)
Bob Martsch (shadows)
Sandy Strother (Dopey's candle and shadow upstairs; dust when dwarfs beat up Dopey)
Assistant director: Carl Fallberg

SEQUENCE 5A: BEDROOM

Director: Perce Pearce
Animation: Frank Thomas (dwarfs sneak into room and pull sheet off Snow White)
  assistant: Art Elliott
Ham Luske (Snow White through her promise to cook for them; Snow White: "Stop!"; Snow White thanks dwarfs, then sniffs soup)
  assistant: Bill Weaver
Jack Campbell (Snow White asleep; Snow White yawns and sits up; Snow White looks at Sneezy; Snow White: "Stop!")
Fred Moore (dwarfs)
  assistants: Frank Thomas, Ollie Johnston
Tony Rivera (Snow White yawns and sits up)
Grim Natwick (Snow White listens to dwarfs discuss Queen; Snow White starting with "Hooray! She stays!")
  assistants: Jack Campbell, Tony Rivera, Marc Davis
[This was the sequence on which Moore did pre-

liminary work in 1936, and during that time Thomas graduated to the position of full animator, his place as Moore's assistant taken by Johnston. Consequently, with the exception of Thomas's opening scenes (in which the dwarfs sneak into the room to kill the "monster" and raise the sheet), all the dwarf animation in this sequence was done by Moore, assisted first by Thomas and later by Johnston. Luske, sometimes working with Campbell and/or Rivera, animated almost all of the Snow White action that remains in the finished version of this sequence. Natwick animated the two one-quarter rear views of Snow White, in group scenes with the dwarfs; but his principal Snow White scenes came at the end of the fight between Doc and Grumpy, which was eliminated from the picture. (This cut also meant that a large chunk of Moore's dwarf animation, along with an isolated Snow White scene by Luske and Campbell, was likewise dropped from the finished film.)]

Efx animation: Cy Young (quilt)
Paul Satterfield (soup pot boils in fireplace)
Assistant directors: Mike Holoboff, Hal Adelquist

SEQUENCE 5B: SNOW WHITE TELLS DWARFS TO WASH

Director: Perce Pearce
Animation: Jack Campbell (Snow White rushes downstairs to soup kettle)
Frank Thomas (dwarfs at top of stairs; dwarfs react to the idea of washing and in dialogue with Snow White)
    assistant: Art Elliott
Fred Spencer (dwarfs at bottom of stairs and crowding around table)
    assistant: Volus Jones
Grim Natwick (Snow White tells dwarfs to wash; Snow White questions dwarfs and examines their hands)
    assistant: Marc Davis
Bill Tytla (Grumpy defies Snow White)
    assistant: Bill Shull
[With the exception of Spencer's scenes of the dwarfs reaching the bottom of the stairs and scrambling around the table, and Tytla's solo Grumpy scenes, all the dwarf animation in this sequence was done by Thomas. Similarly, apart from Campbell's opening scene, Natwick animated all of the Snow White action in this sequence, but many of his scenes were later

worked over by Ham Luske. Although Thomas's usual assistant was Art Elliott, an artist tentatively identified as Charles Menges assisted him on the long pan of the dwarfs reluctantly showing their hands.]
Efx animation: Cy Young (steam from pot; soup drips from spoon)
Sandy Strother (shadows)
Assistant director: Mike Holoboff

SEQUENCE 6A: DWARFS AT TUB WASHING

Director: Perce Pearce
Animation: Bill Tytla (dwarfs)
    assistant: Bill Shull
Riley Thomson (fly on soap)
Fred Spencer (Dopey and the soap)
    assistant: Volus Jones
Grim Natwick (Snow White calls dwarfs to supper)
    assistant: Marc Davis
[The scenes of Dopey with the soap, originally animated by Fred Moore, were reanimated by Fred Spencer. Aside from this passage, and the single scenes contributed by Thomson and Natwick (the latter, again, worked over by Ham Luske), this sequence was animated in its entirety by Bill Tytla.]
Efx animation: Art Palmer (highlights and reflections in still water)
John Reed (splashes, ripples, and reflections as dwarfs begin to stir water)
George Rowley (highlights in still water; splash as Grumpy is dropped in tub)
Stan Quackenbush (splashes, lather, and ripples in agitated water; splashes and suds as dwarfs wash Grumpy; water dripping from Grumpy at end)
    assistant: Sandy Strother
Ugo D'Orsi (bubbles and suds on soap as fly washes himself)
    assistant: Harry Hamsel
Josh Meador (water and drops as Doc sings in CU; suds and bubbles as Dopey chases and swallows soap)
    assistant: Sandy Strother
Cornett Wood (lather and water in Happy's beard; splashes and suds as dwarfs wash and submerge Grumpy)
Cy Young (flames under soup pot and vapor rising from pot)
Assistant director: Hal Adelquist

[SEQUENCE 6B: SOUP SEQUENCE]

Director: Perce Pearce
Animation: Fred Spencer (dwarfs rush in to table and start eating)
Grim Natwick (Snow White)
Ward Kimball (Happy sings "Music in Your Soup," dwarfs eat; dwarfs interrupted by Snow White; dwarfs imitate Snow White's etiquette lesson; Dopey swallows his spoon)
    assistant: Claude Smith
Bill Tytla (Grumpy)
Marvin Woodward (Bashful and Happy respond to Snow White's question)
Dick Lundy (group shots of dwarfs responding to Snow White; Sneezy and Doc slurp soup after her lesson)
Les Clark (Happy and Bashful notice Dopey's problem)
Bill Roberts (Dopey hiccups; other dwarfs manhandle him and deliver the kick that gets out the soap and spoon)
[Kimball animated the bulk of this sequence, with short passages contributed by others: Spencer's two opening scenes; Natwick's Snow White animation; Tytla's CUs of Grumpy (including Grumpy nudged by Sleepy); the extended closing episode animated by Roberts, and miscellaneous dwarf scenes by Woodward, Lundy, and Clark.]
Assistant director: Hal Adelquist

SEQUENCE 7A: QUEEN LEAVES MIRROR, PREPARES DISGUISE

Director: Bill Cottrell
Animation: Bob Stokes (Queen questions mirror, descends steps to laboratory, goes to bookshelf; Queen's hand selects book, moves across page, turns wick and spigot; Queen at window)
    assistants: Sam Dawson, Bill Weaver, Campbell Grant
Sam Dawson (Queen descends steps to laboratory; Queen's hand selects book)
Woolie Reitherman (Slave in the mirror)
    assistants: Charles Nichols, Dan MacManus
Jim Algar (rats around staircase)
Norm Ferguson (raven; Witch after transformation)
    assistant: John Lounsbery
Tony Rivera (Witch's hand traces words in book)
Art Babbitt (Queen turns pages of book, recites spell, mixes chemicals; Queen's hands hold glass; Queen's reflection in glass; Queen drinks potion and during montage)

assistant: Murray Griffin

Campbell Grant (Queen with hair blowing as it changes to white)

Eric Larson (Queen's hands changing to Witch's; Witch shadow on wall)

[Animation of the Queen was unevenly divided between Stokes, who animated all of the character until she reaches the dungeon, and Babbitt, whose scenes were interspersed with Stokes's thereafter. Dawson, one of Stokes's assistants, worked with him as a full animator on two scenes; and Grant, another assistant, animated a solo scene of his own (working with efx animator Stan Quackenbush). After the "transformation" montage, Ferguson took over the character, who was now the Witch. Rivera worked with Ferguson on one scene of the Witch's hand tracing the words in the book.]

Efx animation: Cy Young (Queen's box; Queen's book; reflections from lightning; Witch's shadow)

John McManus (smoke efx in mirror)
assistant: Dan MacManus

Cornett Wood (shadows)

Stan Quackenbush (candle flames and smoke; bubbles, steam, ghost vapor screams in fright; Queen's hair blows in wind as it changes color)

Josh Meador (flames; bubbles, steam, lightning, "octopus")

Sandy Strother (bubbles and spark efx in glass)

George Rowley (candle flame and smoke; cobwebs; raven's shadow; whirlpool, bubbles, lightning; Witch's shadow)

Bob Martsch (steam; shadows; candle flame at end of sequence)

[Young and Rowley worked with Larson on the Witch's shadow on the wall, immediately after the transformation. McManus's smoke effects, animated for the mirror in sequence 1B, were repeated for the mirror scenes in this sequence.]

Shadowgraph: Lee Payne
Assistant director: Hal Adelquist

SEQUENCE 8A: ENTERTAINMENT

Director: Wilfred Jackson
Animation: Ham Luske (animals outside window; Snow White)

Jim Algar (animals outside window)
assistant: Murray McClellan

Paul Busch (Snow White watches dwarfs dance and claps her hands at start of sequence)

Bill Tytla (dwarfs dance and yodel at opening; Happy's verse of the "Silly Song"; Happy dances while other dwarfs play and sing chorus; other dwarfs play and clap during first part of "Dozey's" dance with Snow White)
assistant: Bill Shull

Fred Moore (yodeling dwarfs in CU; all of "Dozey" until he clicks his heels)
assistant: Ollie Johnston

Dick Lundy (Grumpy at the organ; Dopey gets Snow White to kick cymbal, Dopey and Happy dance; Happy yodels to Snow White; Doc, Bashful, and Sneezy take turns dancing with Snow White while Happy plays swanette; Bashful, Sleepy, and Grumpy after sneeze)
assistant: Berk Anthony

Les Clark (Sneezy's verse; Sleepy plays fish horn, yawns and swats at fly; Dopey hands cymbal to him and he smashes himself; Doc and Happy dance with Snow White; Doc plays duckette; Doc and Happy run from impending sneeze; Doc and Happy emerge from behind pillar as Dopey slides down)
assistant: Phil Duncan

Fred Spencer (Dopey on drums; Bashful plays concertina; Doc plays swanette; "Dozey" clicks heels and snaps fingers as dwarfs play instruments; Sneezy's buildup; Grumpy, Sleepy, Bashful and Dopey anticipate sneeze; Sneezy's sneeze; Dopey blown out of scene and sitting on rafter)
assistant: Volus Jones

Marvin Woodward (Happy and Sneezy push Bashful forward; Bashful's verse; Bashful dances with Snow White)
assistant: Herb Johnson

Grim Natwick (Snow White sings in CU; Snow White during middle part of her dance with "Dozey"; second CU of Snow White clapping hands; Snow White anticipates sneeze and laughs afterward)
assistants: Marc Davis, Les Novros, J.S. Escalante

Jack Campbell (Snow White dances with Doc, Bashful and Sneezy; Snow White laughs and curtseys to "Dozey" and starts to dance)
assistants: Clair Weeks, Hugh Fraser

Marc Davis (Snow White dances with Doc and Happy)

Errol Gray (Snow White dances with Bashful)

Amby Paliwoda (Snow White laughs and curtseys to "Dozey"; Snow White during latter part of dance with "Dozey")

Frank Thomas (other dwarfs play and clap during latter part of Snow White's dance with

"Dozey")
assistant: Art Elliott

Riley Thomson (Happy on drums; hands clap; Sleepy gets hot on the fish horn; Sneezy dances and peeks out of coat during montage)

[Luske animated most of the Snow White scenes in this sequence, sometimes working with Busch, Campbell, Davis, Gray, and Paliwoda. Clark's scene of Sneezy singing a verse of the "Silly Song" was cut from the finished picture. Moore animated all of "Dozey" until the montage of musical instruments, after which Spencer's and Thomson's scenes appeared. For one scene of Bashful playing the concertina, Spencer was assisted not by Jones but by an artist identified as "Steve," possibly Stephen Bosustow. Thomson's scenes were all concentrated in the second part of the montage, toward the end of the song. His assistant, referred to on the exposure sheets as "Roberts," has not been identified. Tytla's assistant throughout the film was Bill Shull, but for the scene of Happy singing his verse Tytla was assisted by an artist identified as "Moore." This was surely not Fred Moore but may have been Jim Moore.]

Efx animation: Ed Aardal (vibrating strings)
Andy Engman (organ pipes)
Cornett Wood (crashing and vibrating cymbal)
Cy Young (dust)
Assistant director: Ford Beebe

SEQUENCE 8B: STORY TELLING

Director: Wilfred Jackson
Animation: Ham Luske (Snow White laughs after end of dance; dwarfs gather around Snow White as she starts to sing "Someday My Prince Will Come"; birds and animals listen to Snow White's song)

Jack Campbell (Snow White laughs after end of dance)
assistant: Hugh Fraser

Dick Lundy (Happy and Bashful before song; Sneezy's first question; Happy's question; Grumpy in corner)
assistant: Berk Anthony

Grim Natwick (Snow White talks to dwarfs and sings "Someday My Prince Will Come")
assistants: Marc Davis, Les Novros

Les Clark (Sleepy before song; Doc's questions and Sneezy's second question; dwarfs gather around Snow White as she starts to sing "Someday My Prince Will Come"; pan shot of dwarfs listening to Snow White; Sleepy awak-

ened by high note)
    assistant: Phil Duncan
Marvin Woodward (Bashful's question)
    assistant: Herb Johnson
Jim Algar (birds and animals listen to Snow
    White's song)
    assistant: Don Lusk
[Except for the opening scene of Snow White
    laughing (a continuation of sequence 8A), all of
    Snow White in this sequence was animated by
    Grim Natwick. The draft claims that Luske
    worked with Natwick on many of his scenes,
    but the exposure sheets, Natwick's work diary,
    and the evidence on screen suggest otherwise.
    Luske did redraw Snow White's face in one
    scene (sc 26, Snow White sings last line of the
    song) for a retake after the Natwick crew had
    finished with it.]
Assistant director: Ford Beebe

SEQUENCE 8C: GOING TO BED

Director: Wilfred Jackson
Animation: Marvin Woodward (dwarfs sigh,
    interrupted by clock; Doc, Sneezy, Dopey,
    Sleepy, and Sleepy's fly go to sleep)
    assistants: Herb Johnson, Ray Patin
Grim Natwick (Snow White notices the time and
    "herds" dwarfs from room and toward stairs;
    Snow White talks to dwarfs and climbs the
    stairs; Snow White enters the bedroom)
    assistants: Marc Davis, Les Novros
Riley Thomson (dwarfs start toward stairs,
    stopped by Doc)
Les Clark (Doc makes his announcement,
    Grumpy heckles him; dwarfs reassure Snow
    White the first time and watch her start to
    climb the stairs)
    assistant: Phil Duncan
Fred Spencer (Dopey claims the pillow; dwarfs
    reassure Snow White the second time; dwarfs
    fight over the pillow, Dopey left with one
    feather)
    assistant: Volus Jones
Ham Luske (Snow White enters the bedroom;
    Snow White's prayer)
Errol Gray (Snow White's prayer)
Dick Lundy (Grumpy tries to sleep in soup pot)
    assistant: Berk Anthony
[As in sequence 8B, the draft suggests that Luske
    and Natwick worked together on most of the
    Snow White animation. Production documents
    and the finished scenes indicate, instead, that
    Luske's Snow White animation began only after

she reached the top of the stairs. As in sequence
    8A, Thomson was assisted by an artist named
    "Roberts" who has not been identified.]
Efx animation: Andy Engman (clock)
    assistant: Dick McDermott
John Reed (feathers)
Sandy Strother (shadows)
[Strother also did the cleanup work on Reed's ani-
    mation of the feathers.]
Cy Young (fireplace efx)
Assistant director: Ford Beebe

SEQUENCE 9A: WITCH AT CAULDRON, PREPARES APPLE

Director: Bill Cottrell
Animation: Norm Ferguson (Witch, raven, skel-
    eton, spider)
    assistant: Chester Cobb
Tony Rivera (Witch consults book for antidote
    and slams book shut; Witch walks through bul-
    rushes and over hill)
    assistant: Norm Tate
John Lounsbery (Witch exits down trap door;
    Witch gets into boat and rows it)
Chester Cobb (Witch's feet pause before skeleton)
[In addition to the raven, skeleton, and spider,
    Ferguson animated all scenes of the Witch,
    sometimes working with Cobb, Rivera, and
    Lounsbery. Lounsbery claimed in later years
    that Ferguson had given him the scene of the
    Witch exiting down the trap door to animate by
    himself, though this is not clear from produc-
    tion papers.]
Efx animation: George Rowley (liquid and
    bubbles in retort; steam from cauldron)
Stan Quackenbush (steam from cauldron)
Paul Satterfield (liquid in test tube and cauldron;
    steam)
Reuben Timmons (steam)
Art Palmer (liquid dripping down apple's surface)
Bob Martsch (shadows)
Cy Young (reeds)
[Much of Rowley's, Satterfield's, and Timmons's
    efx animation was in the opening scenes of the
    sequence (Witch: "Boil, cauldron, boil," and so
    on) which were later eliminated from the final
    cut.]
Assistant directors: Mike Holoboff, Hal
    Adelquist

SEQUENCE 10A: DWARFS LEAVE FOR MINE
Director: Perce Pearce
Animation: Eric Larson (animals outside door)

Fred Moore (Doc, Sneezy, Dopey, Sleepy)
    assistant: Ollie Johnston
Jack Campbell (Snow White with Doc, Bashful,
    Sneezy, and Dopey the first time)
    assistants: Hugh Fraser, Amby Paliwoda
Ham Luske (Snow White kisses Doc, Sneezy, and
    Dopey)
Frank Thomas (Bashful)
Bill Tytla (Grumpy)
    assistant: Bill Shull
Grim Natwick (Snow White with Sleepy, Dopey
    the second and third times, and Grumpy)
    assistants: Marc Davis, Les Novros, J.S.
    Escalante
[Animation of Snow White was divided between
    Campbell, in the first part of this sequence, and
    Natwick in the last part. Luske worked with
    Campbell on the scenes of Snow White planting
    kisses on Doc, Sneezy, and Dopey, and he may
    have worked with Natwick on the similar scene
    with Grumpy. Several cuts were made in this
    sequence before it reached its finished version
    in the film; among the scenes eliminated was
    Snow White's farewell to Happy, animated by
    Campbell, Thomas, and Moore.]
Efx animation: Sandy Strother (shadows)
Assistant director: Carl Fallberg

SEQUENCE 10B: QUEEN ON WAY TO DWARFS' HOUSE

Director: Ben Sharpsteen
Animation: Norm Ferguson (Witch)
Tony Rivera (Witch)
    assistant: Norm Tate
Ward Kimball (vultures)
    assistant: Claude Smith
[As in some scenes in sequence 9A, Ferguson
    worked with Rivera on both scenes of the Witch
    in this sequence.]
Efx animation: Harry Hamsel (waterfall)
Cy Young, Ed Aardal (shadows)
Assistant director: Lou Debney

[SEQUENCE 11A: LODGE MEETING]

Director: Ben Sharpsteen
Animation: Ward Kimball (group shots of
    dwarfs; Doc, Bashful, Sneezy, Happy, and
    Dopey ponder in CU; Happy's suggestion;
    Bashful's suggestion; Sneezy sneezes; individual
    dwarfs react to Sleepy's idea)
    assistant: Claude Smith
Dick Lundy (Grumpy)
Les Clark (Sleepy; Doc's suggestion)

[Like sequence 6B, this sequence was mainly Kimball's work. The exceptions: Clark animated all of Sleepy's scenes, and Lundy animated all of Grumpy's scenes. Clark also was assigned one scene in which Doc suggested his idea. This and sequence 11B were abandoned before some scenes were fully animated.]

Assistant director: Lou Debney

[SEQUENCE 11B: BED BUILDING]

Director: Ben Sharpsteen
Animation: Al Eugster (opening scene: Doc with plans, group shot of dwarfs at work)
  assistant: Bob Youngquist
Dick Huemer (Happy chops and saws; Dopey chops; Sneezy and Sleepy chisel)
Bernard Garbutt (deer carries tools for Happy)
Eric Larson (Grumpy with beavers and wood-peckers; beavers and birds)
Marvin Woodward (Bashful; Bashful and bird)
Bob Wickersham (Happy sews)
Jim Algar (birds help Happy with sewing)
Woolie Reitherman (Dopey steals other dwarfs' shirttails, gathers dandelions)
Milt Kahl (birds gather dandelions and give feathers; Sneezy stuffs mattress; bunnies give fur)
Dick Lundy (Dopey shakes dandelions at Sneezy; Sneezy sneezes)
  assistant: Berk Anthony
[Ham Luske worked with Eugster and Algar on their scenes. Reitherman, in animating the scenes of Dopey's mischief, also animated the other characters who interact with Dopey in those scenes: Happy, Bashful, Doc, and the squirrel who watches Bashful working on the bed frame. This and sequence 11A were abandoned before some scenes were fully animated.]

Assistant director: Lou Debney

SEQUENCE 13A: SNOW WHITE MAKING PIES, WITCH ENTERS HOUSE

Director: Bill Cottrell
Animation: Eric Larson (animals and birds watch and help as Snow White bakes pie; birds anxiously watch vultures and Witch; birds attack Witch and are chased away by Snow White; birds and animals watch as Snow White takes Witch inside house; animals start through woods to summon dwarfs)
  assistants: Don Lusk, Jack Bradbury
Bob Stokes (Snow White)
  assistants: Bill Weaver, Sam Dawson
Norm Ferguson (Witch)

Nick George (Witch seen through the window)
  assistant: William de la Torre
Milt Kahl (animals peek around corner of house, look through window)
Tony Rivera (Witch in two-shots with Snow White)
  assistant: Norm Tate
Ward Kimball (vultures)
  assistant: Claude Smith
Chester Cobb (Witch, inside house, sits in chair)
Bernard Garbutt (deer start through woods to summon dwarfs)
  assistant: Lynn Karp
[Stokes animated all of Snow White in this sequence. Similarly, Ferguson worked on all of the Witch's scenes, but worked variously with Nick George (his former assistant), Rivera, and Cobb. Except for two isolated scenes by Kahl, and Garbutt's animation of the running deer in the last scene, all the animal and bird animation in this sequence was Larson's work.]
Efx animation: Paul Satterfield (Witch's shadow at window)
Sandy Strother (Witch's shadow after she leaves window; water from pump)
Assistant director: Hal Adelquist

SEQUENCE 14B: DWARFS AT MINE, ANIMALS WARN THEM

Director: Ben Sharpsteen
Animation: Bernard Garbutt (animals run through woods, out of woods, down bank and through stream; deer pushes Doc; Bashful, deer and birds)
  assistant: Lynn Karp
Jimmie Culhane (dwarfs march and sing "Heigh-Ho")
  assistant: Nick de Tolly
Eric Larson (animals run out of woods, down bank and through stream; animals and birds arrive at mine and start to tug at dwarfs)
  assistant: Don Lusk
Bill Roberts (dwarfs pull mine car; Doc sees animals approaching and stops line of dwarfs; Grumpy fights birds; Doc pushed by deer; Sneezy sneezes birds and animals away)
  assistant: John Elliotte
Jim Algar (birds harass Grumpy and Dopey; birds and animals blown away by sneeze, birds fly back)
Al Eugster (Dopey fights birds, dragged along)
  assistant: Bob Youngquist
[Larson worked with Garbutt on the scene of the

animals emerging from the forest and crossing the stream, and added the birds in the scene of the deer pushing Doc. Culhane's animation of the marching dwarfs was reversed from one of his scenes in sequence 4B.]
Assistant director: Lou Debney

SEQUENCE 14C: WITCH URGES SNOW WHITE TO MAKE WISH

Director: Bill Cottrell
Animation: Norm Ferguson (Witch)
Frank Kelling (Witch)
  assistant: Bob Cormack
Bob Stokes (Snow White)
  assistant: Sam Dawson
[Ferguson worked with Kelling on the Witch animation in this sequence.]
Assistant director: Hal Adelquist

SEQUENCE 14E: DWARFS START FOR HOUSE TO RESCUE SNOW WHITE, MEET TURTLE

Director: Ben Sharpsteen
Animation: Bill Roberts (dwarfs pulled by animals; group and solo scenes of dwarfs)
  assistant: John Elliotte
Bernard Garbutt (animals in group shots; deer under Grumpy)
  assistant: Jack Bradbury
Les Clark (Sleepy suggests Queen has Snow White)
Eric Larson (Bashful and Sneezy leap on deer; Happy starts to fall off deer and is pulled back into place by birds; deer under Doc; Dopey hangs onto deer's tail; turtle meets stampede of dwarfs and animals and spins)
  assistants: Jack Bradbury, Dan Noonan, Don Lusk
Jim Algar (dwarfs and animals ride past camera, down hill and off in perspective)
[Except for Clark's single scene of Sleepy (adapted from a scene in the abandoned sequence 11A), Roberts animated all of the dwarfs in this sequence through Grumpy leaping onto the deer's back. Production papers suggest that Ham Luske worked with Larson and Algar on the last two scenes in the sequence, depicting the stampede of the animals and dwarfs through the woods and their encounter with the turtle. An assistant identified as "Ozzie" also worked on the last scene; this may have been Osmund Evans.]
Assistant director: Lou Debney

SEQUENCE 14F: SNOW WHITE STARTS WISH

Director: Bill Cottrell
Animation: Norm Ferguson (Witch)
Bob Stokes (Snow White)
    assistant: Bill Weaver
Assistant director: Hal Adelquist

SEQUENCE 14G: DWARFS ON WAY TO HOUSE

Director: Ben Sharpsteen
Animation: Bernard Garbutt (dwarfs ride deer over log, down cliff, through forest)
    assistant: Lynn Karp
[This short sequence was animated in its entirety by Garbutt, but production papers suggest that Ham Luske worked on it with him. One of Garbutt's scenes from sequence 14B, showing the animals running through the forest, was extended and reused in this sequence, with the action reversed and the dwarfs inserted on the deer's backs.]
Assistant director: Lou Debney

SEQUENCE 14H: SNOW WHITE DIES

Director: Bill Cottrell
Animation: Ham Luske (Snow White makes her wish and starts to bite the apple)
Jack Campbell (Snow White makes her wish and starts to bite the apple)
    assistant: Amby Paliwoda
Norm Ferguson (Witch)
Eric Larson (cutaway to dwarfs riding deer)
    assistant: Don Lusk
Bob Stokes (Snow White's hand and apple)
    assistant: Bill Weaver
Nick George (Witch exults over her victory)
    assistant: William de la Torre
[Luske and Campbell worked together on most of the Snow White animation in this sequence. Ferguson animated all of the Witch, collaborating with George on the last scene in the sequence.]
Efx animation: Cy Young (lightning and rain)
Assistant director: Hal Adelquist

SEQUENCE 14J: DWARFS CHASE THE QUEEN

Director: Ben Sharpsteen
Animation: Norm Ferguson (Witch exits house and runs; Witch trapped on slope; Witch tries to pry boulder loose and is struck by lightning)
Frank Kelling (Witch exits house and runs)
    assistant: Bob Cormack
Jim Algar (dwarfs ride through forest)
Bernard Garbutt (dwarfs ride animals to doorway and pursue Witch through woods)
    assistant: Lynn Karp
Bill Roberts (Grumpy at the cottage doorway; Witch runs through woods and climbs rocky slope; dwarfs close in on Witch and threatened by boulder; dwarfs look over precipice)
    assistants: John Elliotte, Bob Cormack
Ward Kimball (vultures)
    assistant: Claude Smith
Eric Larson (dwarfs reach rocks, dismount, and start up slope)
    assistant: Don Lusk
John Lounsbery (Witch tries to pry boulder loose)
[The Witch's action scenes, running through the woods and climbing the slope, were animated by Roberts. All the rest of the Witch was animated by Ferguson, working with Kelling in the early scenes and with Lounsbery in the later ones. Cormack worked as an assistant to both Ferguson/Kelling and Roberts on their Witch scenes. Garbutt animated the dwarfs riding the animals to the cottage and then pursuing the Witch, but Grumpy's action on arriving at the doorway was animated by Roberts, and the dwarfs in one scene (after they pass the cottage) are believed to have been cleaned up by Richard Blundell. The first part of the dwarfs' climb up the mountain after the Witch was animated by Larson, the second part by Roberts.]
Efx animation: Art Palmer (rain)
Cornett Wood (rain; shadows)
Bob Martsch (lightning)
Josh Meador (rain, boulder, and lever [second and third scenes]; lightning strikes rock; clouds)
Sandy Strother (boulder and lever [first scene])
Cy Young (boulder and lever)
Assistant director: Lou Debney

SEQUENCE 15A: SNOW WHITE DEAD

Director: Wilfred Jackson
Animation: Frank Thomas (dwarfs)
    assistant: Art Elliott
Milt Kahl (animals)
    assistant: Murray McClellan
[Thomas later identified Bob McCrea as the in-betweener who helped achieve the dwarfs' slow movements in this sequence.]
Efx animation: Ed Aardal (tallow on candle)
Cy Young, Cornett Wood (rain)
Assistant director: Ford Beebe

SEQUENCE 15B: TITLES

Director: Wilfred Jackson
Efx animation: Cy Young, Jim Will (falling leaves, snowflakes, blossoms)
[No director was actually credited for this short sequence, but it was regarded as a transition between sequences 15A and 16A, both directed by Jackson; and it was Jackson who reviewed the effects animation with Walt in sweatbox.]

SEQUENCE 16A: SNOW WHITE IN COFFIN, BACK TO LIFE, AWAY WITH PRINCE

Director: Wilfred Jackson
Animation: Frank Thomas (dwarfs mourn, then see Snow White start to move; dwarfs surround Prince as he places Snow White on horse; dwarfs kissed good-bye by Snow White and waving good-bye)
    assistant: Art Elliott
Jim Algar (animals and birds mourn, see Snow White start to move; animals watch Prince lead horse away)
Grim Natwick (Prince sings and kisses Snow White; Snow White comes to life and sits up)
    assistants: Milt Kahl, Marc Davis
Jack Campbell (Prince picks up Snow White and carries her, places her on horse; Snow White kisses dwarfs good-bye; Prince leads horse along stream; Prince leads horse to top of hill)
    assistants: Hugh Fraser, Clair Weeks, Amby Paliwoda
Dick Lundy (dwarfs wild with joy)
    assistant: Berk Anthony
Bernard Garbutt (animals wild with joy; animals surrounding Prince's horse)
Fred Spencer (dwarfs surround Prince as he carries Snow White)
Ham Luske (Prince leads horse away carrying Snow White; Prince leads horse along stream; Prince leads horse to top of hill)
Hugh Fraser (Prince leads horse along stream)
Clair Weeks (Prince leads horse to top of hill)
[Natwick animated the Prince and Snow White until she comes to life, after which both characters were taken over by Ham Luske's unit. Kahl, in addition to assisting Natwick with some of his original animation, may have reanimated some of the Prince's key scenes after the premiere. Luske and Campbell worked together on some of the closing scenes in the sequence, and Fraser and Weeks, two of Campbell's assistants, also collaborated as full animators on some of these scenes. An artist tentatively identified as Charles Menges, who had assisted Thomas on one scene in sequence 5B, likewise assisted him on the scene of the mourning dwarfs stepping aside as the Prince approached Snow White. Thomas's regular assistant, Art Elliott, worked on the rest of his scenes. One of the closing scenes, showing the Prince leading Snow White on horseback beside a stream, was eliminated from the final cut.]
Efx animation: Jim Will (falling blossoms)
Stan Quackenbush (flowing stream)
Assistant director: Ford Beebe

APPENDIX B: LATER SHORTS FEATURING THE SEVEN DWARFS

This appendix documents the four short subjects in which the Seven Dwarfs made return appearances in 1939–43, as described in chapter 11. Credits in this appendix are, like those in Appendix A, compiled primarily from the drafts and exposure sheets for these shorts, although production papers for the Canadian bond trailers are sometimes inconsistent and lead to inconclusive results. The first three shorts in this list were largely assembled from stock animation from *Snow White* and other films, and the credit lists are designed to reflect both the animators of the original scenes and those responsible for the new animation. None of the films in this list were shown commercially in U.S. theaters; printing, shipping, and copyright dates are included here in lieu of the usual opening and release dates.

THE STANDARD PARADE FOR 1939
2602

Copyright 8 May 1939 by Walt Disney Productions: MU9350

Director: Riley Thomson
Layout: Jim Carmichael
Reworked animation:
 Sam Cobean (Mickey, Minnie, trumpeters; Sleepy)
 Rex Cox (drummers)
 Ozzie Evans (bass drummer and helpers)
 Amby Paliwoda (sweepers)
 Scott Whitaker (rug roller; Sneezy)
 Bob Carlson (Doc, Grumpy, Bashful)
 Art Elliott (Happy)
 Volus Jones (Dopey)
 Ken Peterson (Toby Tortoise)
 Based on original scenes animated by:
 Ben Sharpsteen (miscellaneous characters in opening procession, from *Mother Goose Melodies*)
 Rudy Zamora (Mickey and Minnie, from *Parade of the Award Nominees*)
 Dick Lundy (Toby Tortoise, from *The Tortoise and the Hare*)
 Bill Tytla (Seven Dwarfs, from *Snow White and the Seven Dwarfs*)
 [Al Bertino also worked over Sharpsteen's original animation of Clarabelle Cow from *Mother Goose Melodies,* but this was cut from the finished version of *The Standard Parade.*]
 Original animation:
 Johnny Cannon (Donald Duck)
 Nick De Tolly (Pluto, Big Bad Wolf)
 Eddie Strickland (Goofy)

Claude Smith (Three Little Pigs)
Music supervised by: Charles Wolcott
Assistant director: Jack Bruner

7 WISE DWARFS
2607 [Sequence 2]

Directors: Ford Beebe, Ub Iwerks
Animation reused from *Snow White*:
 Al Eugster (dwarfs dig in opening scene)
 Eric Larson (Sleepy, mine car, and deer in opening scene)
 Bill Roberts (Happy and Grumpy sing in CU)
 Marvin Woodward (Bashful and Sneezy sing in CU; dwarfs listen to echo)
 Art Babbitt (Doc sorts diamonds)
Animation reworked from *Snow White*:
 Les Clark, Ford Beebe, Ub Iwerks, based on original scenes animated by:
 Fred Moore (Dopey sweeps up rejected gems; Doc comes out of doorway)
 Jimmie Culhane (dwarfs march out of mine, across log and into CU, and away into distance)
 Bill Roberts (Doc stops dwarfs)
Original character animation:
 Ken Muse (Doc in CU; Dopey in LS on sidewalk; six dwarfs file out of post office; Dopey comes out of bank)
 Ford Beebe, Ub Iwerks (dwarfs streak into post office, Dopey slams into door; Dopey enters bank)
Original efx animation:
 Josh Meador (jewels fall into bags; closing montage of shells, anti-aircraft guns, planes, shrapnel, assembly lines, and bonds)
 [Surviving production records for this short are inconsistent, but do seem to indicate that Beebe and Iwerks, the co-directors, also contributed some of the new animation. Muse's last scene of Dopey coming out of the bank incorporates some of Fred Spencer's Dopey animation from sequences 5B and 6A of *Snow White*.]
Assistant director: Richard Lyford
 Shipped to National Film Board of Canada: 12 December 1941

ALL TOGETHER
2607 [Sequence 4]

Directors: Ford Beebe, Ub Iwerks
Reworked animation:
 Josh Meador, Ford Beebe, Ub Iwerks, based on original scenes animated by:
 Frank Thomas (Geppetto and Figaro, from *Pinocchio*)

Milt Kahl (Pinocchio, from *Pinocchio*)
Paul Allen (Donald Duck and nephews, from *Good Scouts*)
Ken Muse (Pluto, from *Canine Caddy*)
Ray Patterson (Pluto, from *Bone Trouble*)
Gilles "Frenchy" de Trémaudan (Mickey Mouse and band, from *The Band Concert*)
Gerry Geronimi (Clarabelle Cow, from *The Band Concert*)
Art Babbitt (Goofy, from *Mickey's Amateurs*)
Bill Tytla (Seven Dwarfs, from *Snow White and the Seven Dwarfs*)
Original character animation:
 Ken Muse (LS marching band; Horace Horsecollar)
Original efx animation:
 Josh Meador (balloons and placards; montage of planes, guns, coins and bonds)
 Release prints authorized: 12 January 1942

THE WINGED SCOURGE
2732

Copyright 11 January 1943 by Walt Disney Productions: MP13619

Director: Bill Roberts
Layout: Hugh Hennesy
Animation: John McManus (mosquitoes and larva; fish eat larva; wigglers in dipper and sardine can)
 Milt Kahl (introduction of dwarfs; Doc and Sneezy in boat; Happy sprays oil; Dopey with dipper and oilcan; Bashful and birds apply Paris green; Sleepy and mole dig ditches; Grumpy chops stump; dwarfs with deer and cart; Doc with cans in wheelbarrow; Grumpy and woodpecker)
 Frank Thomas (Dopey and mosquitoes sequence, with Grumpy)
 Harvey Toombs (Happy covers rain barrel; dwarfs and birds hang screens; Sleepy and birds with netting; dwarfs in bed snoring)
Efx animation: Josh Meador (parasites taken out of bloodstream; sprayed oil)
 Andy Engman (parasites injected into bloodstream)
 Ed Aardal (Paris green; dirt shoveled into water)
 George Rowley (dust shoots from chimney)
Assistant director: Mike Holoboff

NOTES

CHAPTER 1. THE BIRTH OF THE TALE

12 *La schiavottella* "The Young Slave" was published in English in 1893, but is widely known by the more accessible 1932 translation. Today's reader can find the 1893 translation in Heidi Anne Heiner (ed.), *Sleeping Beauties,* pp. 112–15, and the 1932 translation, with helpful annotations, in Maria Tatar (ed.), *The Classic Fairy Tales* [Norton], pp. 80–83. "La schiavottella" is the story's Neapolitan title; Basile's (1575–1632) collection of stories was first published posthumously in Neapolitan as *Lo cunto de li cunti overo Lo trattenemiento dé peccerille.* Today the collection is usually identified by its Italian title *Il Pentamerone.* Special thanks to Piera Patat for this additional information.

12 *Like many traditional fairy tales* It's worth noting that many folklorists resist the term "fairy tale" as an inaccurate description of stories like "Snow White," preferring such terms as "magic tale" instead. See Ashliman, *Folk and Fairy Tales,* pp. 31-32.

12 *long-standing oral tradition* This is a highly simplified account of a folkloric tradition that covered several centuries and has been studied in depth by a community of scholars. Most folklorists agree that "Snow White" and other tales have their roots in oral tradition, but most also acknowledge a complex connection between oral and literary traditions, and some go farther than that. Ruth B. Bottigheimer, in her books *Fairy Godfather: Straparola, Venice, and the Fairy Tale Tradition* (2002) and *Fairy Tales: A New History* (2009), suggested a specific 16th-century Italian author as the actual originator of many of our best-known fairy tales. Bottigheimer's claim was roundly challenged by her peers; see the *Journal of American Folklore,* which devoted its entire Fall 2010 issue (vol. 123, no. 490) to the controversy.

12 Note: *Sneewittchen/Schneeweißchen* See D.L. Ashliman's excellent "Folktexts" website.

13 *"Sneewittchen" . . . successive editions* For those seeking an authentic translation of the Grimms' story, numerous versions are available. One of the best is Maria Tatar's translation of the 1857 edition, published both in *The Classic Fairy Tales* [Norton], pp. 83–89, and in *The Annotated Brothers Grimm,* pp. 240–49. For more information on the Grimms themselves, see Tatar's "The Brothers Grimm: Biographical Essay" in *The Annotated Brothers Grimm,* pp. 385–96; see also Ruth B. Bottigheimer's "Jacob Grimm" (pp. 100–107) and "Wilhelm Grimm" (pp. 108–113), *Dictionary of Literary Biography,* vol. 90.

13 *"Snow-Drop"* See Iona and Peter Opie (ed.), *The Classic Fairy Tales* [Oxford], pp. 175–182.

13 *[British] "Snow-White"* See Katherine M. Briggs (ed.), *A Dictionary of British Folk-Tales in the English Language,* pp. 494–95.

13 *In Italy, whose folklore* Some of these stories appear in Italo Calvino, *Italian Folktales:* "Bella Venezia" on pp. 395–98, "Giricoccola" on pp. 154–56. "Maria, the Wicked Stepmother, and the Seven Robbers," published in German in *Sicilianische Märchen, aus dem Volksmund gesammelt* (Leipzig: Verlig von Wilhelm Engelmann, 1870), vol. 1 no. 2, pp. 4–7, is translated in English in Heidi Anne Heiner, *Sleeping Beauties,* pp. 124–26, and on D. L. Ashliman's website. "The Crystal Casket," published in English in Thomas Frederick Crane, *Italian Popular Tales* (Boston and New York: Houghton Mifflin, 1885), no. 21, pp. 326–331, likewise appears in Heiner, pp. 116–20, and on Ashliman's site. "A Tuscan Snow-White," published in English in Isabella Mary Anderton, *Tuscan Folk-lore and Sketches* (London: Arnold Fairbairns, 1905) and "The Beautiful Anna," published in German in *Sicilianische Märchen,* can also be found in Heiner's anthology (pp. 121–23 and 127–30, respectively).

13 *Death of the Seven Dwarfs* Ernst Ludwig Rochholz, *Schweizersagen aus dem Aargau,* vol. 1 (Aargau: Druck und Verlag von H.R. Sauerländer, 1856), no. 222, p. 312; English translation on D.L. Ashliman's website.

13 *"Gold-Tree and Silver-Tree"* This story, published in Joseph Jacobs, *Celtic Fairy Tales* (London: David Nutt, 1892), no. 11, pp. 88–92, appears in Heiner, *Sleeping Beauties,* pp. 192–94, and on Ashliman's website.

13 *"Myrsina, or Myrtle"* See Georgios A. Megas (ed.), *Folktales of Greece,* pp. 106–113.

13 *"Lasair Gheug"* See Tatar (ed.), *The Classic Fairy Tales* [Norton], pp. 90–96.

13 *one of our most powerful cultural stories* Maria Tatar (ed.), *The Annotated Brothers Grimm,* p. 243.

13 *Aarne-Thompson-Uther index* See Uther, *The Types of International Folktales,* pp. 383–84. Antti Aarne's *Verzeichnis der Märchentypen,* published in Finnish in 1910, was translated into English and expanded by Stith Thompson in 1928. It was designed as a scientific classification system to categorize the thousands of variations on individual themes in world folklore. In 1961 it was still further expanded; then, in 2004, a full revision was published by Hans-Jörg Uther. Some elements, including the numbering system, remained unchanged in Uther's version. Special thanks to Maria Tatar and to Holly Hutchison for my introduction to this aspect of folklore history.

CHAPTER 2. "SNOW WHITE" ON STAGE AND SCREEN

14 *Introduction* For her pioneering research into the theatrical antecedents of Disney's *Snow White,* I am particularly indebted to Karen Merritt, whose two important articles on the subject are cited in the Bibliography.

14–15 *Sneewittchen und die Zwerge (Görner)* I am indebted to Helmut Färber for locating a rare published edition of Görner's script and making it available to me, as well as providing a digest of its contents in English.

15–17 *Snow-White (Merington)* This account of Merington's script is based on an original promptbook in the Billy Rose Theatre Collection of the New York Public Library (hereinafter identified as "NYPL"). Throughout this promptbook the heroine's name is spelled "SnowWhite." However, in a later published account by A. Minnie Herts, founder of the Children's Educational Theatre (see below), the play is consistently referred to as *Snow-White.* Accordingly, that spelling is used here for both the title and the character.

16 *lofty ideals of the Children's Educational Theatre* See A. Minnie Herts, "The Children's Educational Theatre," pp. 798–99. For more about this see Karen Merritt, "The Little Girl/Little Mother Transformation," pp. 106–07.

17 *I like Snow-White because* A. Minnie Herts, "The Children's Educational Theatre," p. 802.

17 *the stage* Wizard of Oz . . . *so slanted toward an adult audience* An extraordinary 2-CD set of vintage recordings, compiled by David Maxine in 2003 for the Hungry Tiger Press, reconstructs this long-forgotten version of *The*

Wizard of Oz for modern ears. Supplemented by a thorough historical text that places the recordings and the play in context, this collection is highly recommended. Also highly recommended is John Canemaker's account of the *Little Nemo* stage production (chapter 7, pp. 118–127) in *Winsor McCay: His Life and Art.*

18 Note: *I think your ideas* Letter, Merington to Ames, 10 August 1912 (Shubert Archive, hereinafter identified as "SA").

19 *"Cinderella" is being combined with the story of Snow White* This point has been made previously by Robin Allan (*Walt Disney and Europe,* p. 38) and Karen Merritt ("The Little Girl/Little Mother Transformation," p. 109).

19 *these two persecuted heroines . . . may well have been blended* Maria Tatar to author, 21 May 2010.

20 *standing with reluctant feet* This quote from Longfellow's "Maidenhood" was applied to Mary Pickford's career by Edward Wagenknecht in *The Movies in the Age of Innocence,* p. 156.

20 *She did not look in the least Snow White* review, *New York Dramatic Mirror,* 15 November 1912 (NYPL).

20 *her legs look a lot more than seven* Charles Darnton, *Snow White* review, *Evening Worker,* 8 November 1912 (NYPL).

20 *other changes were made* The script was published in book form by Dodd, Mead and Co. in 1913, with illustrations by Charles B. Falls. Still later, in 1925, the Samuel French company published an edition for the amateur theatrical market, which is still in print at this writing. (For both of these editions, see Bibliography.) The Samuel French version differs considerably from the earlier edition and, in general, reflects the many changes made in the play during and after its 1912–13 run, including the removal of the original Scene VI. Quotes from the dialogue in these pages are taken from the Dodd, Mead edition which, in most respects, is much closer to Ames's original presentation.

20 Note: *two of the Cats may be omitted* "Notes to the Producer," *Snow White* (Ames) script [Samuel French edition], p. 91.

20 *some cities' child-labor laws* "Marguerite Clark Ends Tour and Starts on Hunt for Play," *New York Telegraph,* 29 March 1913 (NYPL).

21 *Grown people will enjoy this play* George N.

Shorey, *Snow White* review, *Motion Picture News,* 6 January 1917, p. 113 (Margaret Herrick Library, Academy of Motion Picture Arts and Sciences, hereinafter identified as "AMPAS").

21 *Snow White is a remarkable picture* George Blaisdell, *Snow White* review, *Moving Picture World,* 6 January 1917, p. 97 (AMPAS).

22 THEY CAME IN THOUSANDS *Kansas City Star,* 28 January 1917, p. 1A.

22 *a combined audience of 67,000* "'Snow White' Set Record," *Kansas City Times* (morning edition of *Kansas City Star*), 29 January 1917, p. 1. A month later, a story in *Moving Picture World* set the figure at 75,000 ("How 'Snow White' Was Put On," *Moving Picture World,* 24 February 1917, p. 1189, AMPAS).

22 *one of the most astonishing* Letter, Kevin Brownlow to author, 3 November 2005.

22 *My impression of the picture* Letter, Walt to Frank Newman, 21 February 1938. Courtesy Katherine and Richard Greene. Walt's letter was written in response to a letter Newman had written to him, congratulating him on his own *Snow White* film and reminding him of the 1917 exhibition.

23 *full of American spunk* Merritt, "Marguerite Clark as America's Snow White," *Griffithiana* 64, p. 5.

24 Note: *probably one of my first big feature pictures* Walt to journalist Pete Martin, 1956. This was one of a series of interviews that led to a publication of Walt's life story in *The Saturday Evening Post.*

24 *Lubin had advertised a version* Ad, *New York Clipper,* 5 July 1902, p. 424 (Library of Congress, hereinafter identified as "LoC").

24 *La petite Blancheneige (Pathé)* Special thanks to Catherine A. Surowiec for researching the surviving European elements of this film for me. Many thanks, too, to Bryony Dixon of the British Film Institute for her special efforts to make the fragments available for viewing.

25 *This picturization of Grimm's fairy tale* Peter Milne, *Snow White* (Educational, 1916) review, *Motion Picture News,* 9 December 1916, p. 3672 (AMPAS).

25 *it will be interesting to note* "Cleveland to Judge Two 'Snow Whites'," *Motion Picture News,* 6 January 1917, p. 103 (AMPAS).

26 *big field* George Blaisdell, *Snow White*

(Powers) review, *Moving Picture World,* 8 February 1913, p. 582 (AMPAS).

CHAPTER 3. A NEW CHALLENGE

31 *As far as I can say* Walt Disney quoted in "Why I Chose *Snow White,*" *Photoplay Studies,* p. 8.

31 *Alice in Wonderland (unrealized Pickford version, 1933)* For this writer's fuller account of the unrealized *Alice* project, as well as the Disney sequences for two 1934 features that *were* completed—MGM's *Hollywood Party* and Fox's *Servants' Entrance*—see Kaufman, "Before Snow White."

31 *Disney has plans worked out* "Cartoon Comedy Feature Contemplated by Disney," *Film Daily,* 25 July 1933, p. 1 (AMPAS).

31 *didn't call his staff together and announce* "World-Wide Appeal in Disney's 'Snow White'," undated Disney press release (Walt Disney Archives, hereinafter identified as "WDA.") This press release was adapted in various newspaper stories in the fall of 1937; see, for example, "Walt Disney Spends Four Years and $1,000,000 on 'Snow White'," *Washington Post,* 31 October 1937, p. F2.

31 *We're definitely going ahead* Letter, Babbitt to Tytla, postmarked 27 November 1933, quoted by Michael Barrier in *Hollywood Cartoons,* p. 587, note 28. This letter and the Horvath letter (24 May 1933, translated from the Hungarian by Tissa David) are both in the John Canemaker collection at New York University (hereinafter identified as "JC/NYU").

32 *El apóstol (Cristiani, 1917)* See Giannalberto Bendazzi, *Cartoons,* pp. 49–50.

32 Note: *Walt is growing cold on 'Bambi'* Letter to Roy Disney (in New York), 21 October 1933 (WDA). The carbon copy of this letter preserved at the Disney Archives is unsigned, but it was likely written by studio attorney Gunther Lessing.

32 *Snow White . . . is known and beloved* Walt, "Why I Chose *Snow White,*" pp. 7–8.

32 *And won't that be a welcome event* Edwin Schallert, "'Snow White' Legend to Be Made in Color," *Los Angeles Times,* 4 July 1934, p. 6.

33 *We were spellbound* Anderson quoted by Robin Allan in "The fairest film of all: *Snow White* reassessed," *Animator,* October–December 1987, p. 18.

33 *I think I probably heard* Grant to Richard Greene, 2000, interview for *Walt: The Man Behind the Myth.*

33 *We are now working* Letter, Walt to Edd J. Haas, manager, Miller Theater, Wichita, Kansas, 11 October 1934 (WDA).

33 *"The Goddess of Spring" . . . is a preliminary study* The Goddess of Spring review, *Christian Science Monitor,* 10 November 1934, p. 10.

34 *With the best men* Dick Huemer to Joe Adamson. This was one of a series of six Huemer interviews, recorded by Adamson in 1968–69 for the UCLA Oral History of the Motion Picture in America Project, funded by the American Film Institute and the National Endowment for the Humanities. This particular quote has been published in Michael Barrier's *Funnyworld* 17, p. 39, and Didier Ghez (ed.), *Walt's People,* Vol. 4, p. 62.

34–36 *putting five or six of these things/I made up my mind* Walt to Pete Martin, 1956.

34 Note: *New York's Bijou Theatre* See Frank S. Nugent, "Semi-Annual Report on the Cartoon Theatre," *New York Times,* 7 April 1935, IX:3:3.

36 *We never tried [a feature] before* Walt quoted by Eileen Creelman, "Picture Plays and Players," *New York Sun,* 5 August 1935 (NYPL).

36 *very fascinating illustrations* Memo, Walt to Ted Sears and the Story Dept., 23 December 1935 (WDA).

36 *Albert [is] to be the supervisor* Hand in Background Meeting with Layout Men, 23 November 1936 (WDA). See John Canemaker, *Before the Animation Begins,* chapter 2.

36 *Gustaf Tenggren* See Canemaker, *Before the Animation Begins,* chapter 4.

36 *because he delegates* Hand in Conference of Assistant Directors on Feature Procedure, 3 February 1937 (WDA).

36 *She's got to be doing/Her dress here* Walt in story conferences on sequence 2A, 5 April 1937 and 4 May 1937 (both WDA).

36 *So many people remember* Walt in story conference on sequence 7A, 10 March 1937 (WDA).

CHAPTER 4. CHARACTER DESIGN

39 Note: *Earl Hurd* See Canemaker, *Paper Dreams,* pp. 109–114.

40 *The rotoscope* The complete rotoscope patent is reproduced, with an excellent introduction by Mark Langer, in *Animation Journal,* Spring 1993 (vol. 1 no. 2), pp. 66–78. Also see Fleischer, *Out of the Inkwell,* pp. 15–21.

40 *smooth and graceful/walks, dances and leaps* "The Inkwell Man," *New York Times,* 22 February 1920, III:9:1.

41 Note: *Having just completed 'The Pied Piper'* Sears quoted by I. Klein in "At the Walt Disney Studio in the 1930's," *Cartoonist Profiles,* September 1974, p. 14.

41 *viewers and critics were greatly impressed* After the picture's New York opening at Radio City Music Hall, Hal Sloane of United Artists (then Disney's distributor) wrote Roy Disney a glowing letter that described *The Goddess of Spring* as a highlight of the Disney output. "I . . . experienced a genuine thrill as I stood in a side aisle watching the picture unfold on the screen and listening to the comments of the audience." (Letter, Sloane to Roy, 2 November 1934, WDA). Reviewers, too, lavished special praise on the short; see the rave review in *The Christian Science Monitor,* 10 November 1934, p. 10.

42 *From now on, Ham Luske is definitely assigned* Memo, Walt to Paul Hopkins, Roy Disney, Bill Garity, Harry Bailey, 25 November 1935, subject: Production Notes on Snow White (WDA).

42 *whose charm would be largely comic* Frank Thomas and Ollie Johnston, *Disney Animation,* p. 113. This passage is illustrated with one of Luske's drawings based on this concept.

42 Note: *Stage settings/the building of the* Snow White *sets* Harry Bailey, "Routine Procedure on Feature Production," undated; memo, Roy to Walt, 16 August 1935 (both WDA).

43–45 *you're in there eight hours a day* O'Connor to author, 30 October 1989.

45 *They showed me storyboards/It was heavy, it was hot/they hung a rope* Marge Champion to John Canemaker, filmed and recorded by Ted Thomas, New York, 3 October 2006.

46 *So I drove over after work* Natwick to author, 1 February 1981.

47 *Michael Barrier has offered a useful analysis* Barrier, *Hollywood Cartoons,* pp. 197–200.

47 Note: *To help speed Ham up* Memo, Walt to Paul Hopkins, Roy Disney, Bill Garity, Harry Bailey, 25 November 1935, subject: Production Notes on Snow White (WDA).

48 *She is getting on my nerves* Luske at Dwarfs Personality Meeting, 29 December 1936 (WDA).

48 *I do think the singing* Walt in Dialogue Conference, 9 February 1937 (WDA).

48 Note: *a voice like a chime of bells* "Mouse & Man," *Time,* 27 December 1937, p. 19.

48 *are symbolic expressions* Ashliman, *Folk and Fairy Tales,* p. 49.

49 *Most illustrations for the story* Tatar (ed.), *The Annotated Brothers Grimm,* p. 244.

51 *taking each one of those dwarfs* Huemer to Adamson, 1968–69, UCLA Oral History Project. This particular quote has been published in *Funnyworld* 17, p. 38, and Didier Ghez (ed.), *Walt's People,* Vol. 4, p. 57.

51 CALL THEM SEVEN LITTLE MEN Conference, Suggestions and Notes on "Snow White," 3 October 1934 (WDA).

51 Note: *I think a duck* Hand in conference, Personalities of the Seven Dwarfs, 10 November 1936 (WDA).

52 *one of these characters* Walt in conference, Characteristics and Personalities of the Seven Dwarfs, 15 December 1936 (WDA).

52 *Whenever he hears a noise* "Manuscript" outline, 9 August 1934 (WDA). As we've seen, this early document—comprising a brief outline of the story and many isolated suggestions for scenes, songs and characters—seems to have been written by Dick Creedon. Walt ultimately rejected most of the ideas in this outline but accepted a few of them. On his own copy, Jumpy/Hoppy is one of the characters marked "OK."

52–53 JUMPY *leaps high into the air* Outline, "The Dwarfs Find Snow White," typed 22 October 1934 (WDA).

53 *a fat little red-nosed dwarf* "Songs" memo (WDA). This document, suggesting both song ideas and characters, is undated but written very early, possibly pre-August 1934.

53 *a pompous, oily tongued/Eddie Holden* "Manuscript," 9 August 1934 (WDA).

54 *steals and drinks and is very dirty* Ibid.

54 *He has a peg leg* Early "Songs" memo (WDA).

54 *Always behind or last* Suggestions and Notes on "Snow White," conference, 9 October 1934 (WDA).

54 *cherub-faced/determined, but futile* Outline,

"The Dwarfs Find Snow White," typed 22 October 1934 (WDA).

54 *You know the type* Brief Outline for Gag Suggestions, typed 6 November 1934 (WDA). This document was probably written by Dick Creedon.

55 *A horn was suggested* Story Notes on Snow White, Dwarfs Washing and Eating Sequence, 14 December 1935 (WDA).

55 *misinterprets other people's attitude* Walt, Description of the Seven Dwarfs as I See Them at the Present Time, undated but ca. early December 1935 (WDA).

55 *With Deafy gone* Barrier, *Hollywood Cartoons,* p. 201.

58 Note: *most of the artists who worked with him* Stories about Morkovin circulated for years afterward among the Disney artists who encountered him. For a published example (with the name misspelled "Markoven"), see Shamus Culhane, *Talking Animals and Other People,* pp. 141–42. After the release of *Snow White,* Morkovin published an appreciation of it in his self-edited journal: "Coöperative Imagination," *Cinema Progress,* May–June 1938 (vol. 3, no. 2), pp. 14–15. (Special thanks to Ned Comstock for bringing this to my attention.)

58 *Doc's stethoscope tangles up* Suggestions and Notes on "Snow White," conference, 9 October 1934 (WDA).

58 *The wise man of the family* Early "Songs" memo (WDA).

58 *The Leader and Spokesman* "Cast of Characters," undated but ca. October 1934 (WDA).

58 Note: *talk as W.C. Fields would speak* Suggestions and Notes at Sound Stage Meeting, 16 November 1934 (WDA).

59 Note: *Joe Twerp . . . as the voice of Mickey Mouse* See Keith Scott, "Mickey Mouse, Radio Star," p. 20.

59 *[Doc] is the pompous guy* Moore in conference, Discussion of Dwarfs' Personalities & Characteristics, 8 December 1936 (WDA).

59 *sort of a French Provincial Mayor's attitude* Tytla in conference, Discussion on Personalities of Dwarfs, 17 November 1936 (WDA).

59 *Doc is upset by the least little thing* Walt in conference, Characteristics and Personalities of the Seven Dwarfs, 15 December 1936 (WDA).

59 *When Doc corrects himself* Sweatbox note on

sequence 4D, Walt to Babbitt, 1 April 1937 (WDA).

60 *the easiest character* Hand in Discussion on Personalities of Dwarfs, 17 November 1936 (WDA).

60 *One skeptical & pessimistic dwarf* Walt's handwritten note on the early "Songs" memo (WDA).

60 *Typical Dyspeptic and Grouch* "Cast of Characters," undated but ca. October 1934 (WDA).

60 *a hold-out* Suggestions and Notes on "Snow-White," conference, 15 October 1934 (WDA).

60 *Grumpy has sort of a Mickey body* Moore in Dwarf Meeting, I.B.T. [Inbetweeners'] Annex, 1 June 1937 (WDA). This meeting was called expressly so that Moore could explain the fine points of the dwarfs to the inbetweeners who would be working on their scenes. (One of these artists was future comics legend Walt Kelly.)

60 *only Grumpy was an obvious vehicle* Barrier in *Hollywood Cartoons,* p. 203.

60 *We shouldn't have Grumpy fall for her* Walt in story conference on sequence 8C, typed 10 December 1936 (WDA).

61 *It's a gag license* Walt in story conference on sequence 6B, undated but December 1936 (WDA).

61 *Watch Grumpy's nose* Walt in story conference on sequence 5A, 14 July 1936 (WDA).

62 *a little skinny fellow/a twinkle in his eye* Early "Songs" memo (WDA).

62 *Professor Diddleton D. Wurtle/It is funny to the eye* "Manuscript" outline, 9 August 1934 (WDA).

62 *Happy is a cartoon of Otis Harlan* Moore in Discussion on Personalities of Dwarfs, 17 November 1936 (WDA).

62 *Walt had a particular walk* Moore in Discussion of Seven Dwarfs' Personalities, 24 November 1936 (WDA).

63 *You will find* Walt in story conference on sequence 8A, 31 March 1937 (WDA).

63 *I never heard of that angle* Hand in story conference on sequence 8C, typed 10 December 1936 (WDA). As we'll see, the gag in question was the "woodpile gag" which, again, was cut from the picture.

64 *Holloway's melodious and screwy singing voice* "Manuscript" outline, 9 August 1934 (WDA).

64 *long, lanky type* Suggestions and Notes on

"Snow White," conference, 9 October 1934 (WDA).

64 *He drags along* Babbitt in Discussion of Dwarfs' Personalities & Characteristics, 8 December 1936 (WDA).

65 *after Snow White has been taken out* Early "Songs" memo (WDA).

65 *You can't use the fly* Pearce in Discussion on Personalities of Dwarfs, 17 November 1936 (WDA).

65 *the fly might fly into Sleepy's mouth* As described by Larry Morey in story conference on sequence 8A, 31 March 1937 (WDA).

65 *Walt created this character* Pearce in Discussion on Personalities of Dwarfs, 17 November 1936 (WDA).

65 *Sleepy isn't sleepy all the time* Walt in story conference on sequences 14B, 14E and 14G, 2 March 1937 (WDA).

66 *He is bashful* Early "Songs" memo (WDA).

66 *Bashful Baldy* Conference, Suggestions and Notes on "Snow White," 9 October 1934 (WDA).

66 *Funny shaped head* Early "Songs" memo (WDA).

66 *the dwarf with the pyramid-like skull* "Manuscript" outline, 9 August 1934 (WDA).

66 *He is not a sissy/when he looks at anything* Pearce in Discussion on Personalities of Dwarfs, 17 November 1936 (WDA).

66 *he would have music in his soul* Walt in conference, Characteristics and Personalities of the Seven Dwarfs, 15 December 1936 (WDA).

66 *blushing, hesitating, squirmy, giggly* This phrase was applied to the formative Bashful in "Cast of Characters," undated but ca. October 1934 (WDA).

68 *Always sneezing/Dapper—quick movements* "Manuscript" outline, 9 August 1934 (WDA).

68 *a topic inclined to incite a smile* *Harper's Weekly,* 24 March 1894, p. 280. *Fred Ott's Sneeze* was also known as *Edison Kinetoscopic Record of a Sneeze,* January 7, 1894. See Musser, *Edison Motion Pictures,* pp. 87–88.

68 *Sneezy has a funny voice* Walt in story conference on sequence 8A, 6 January 1936 (WDA).

69 *People remember me* Billy Gilbert obituary, *Los Angeles Times,* 24 September 1971 (AMPAS).

69 *In . . .* Maid in Hollywood Special thanks to film-comedy scholar Ben Urish for bringing this film to my attention.

69 *Everybody seems to get a kick* Walt in dialogue conference, 21 January 1937 (WDA).

69 *There is more to him* Pearce in Discussion on Personalities of Dwarfs, 17 November 1936 (WDA).

69 *He looks over the top of his nose* Moore in Dwarf Meeting for inbetweeners, 1 June 1937 (WDA).

69 *Sneezy carries that nose/As though he had* Pearce and Thomas in Discussion on Personalities of Dwarfs, 17 November 1936 (WDA).

69 *We kind of pair Sneezy and Bashful* Walt in story conference on sequence 11A, 11 December 1936 (WDA).

70 *the baby and the goat/It's always me!* Outline, "The Dwarfs Find Snow White," typed 22 October 1934 (WDA).

70 *in November 1934, in another outline* Outline, "The Dwarfs Discover Snow White," 16 November 1934 (WDA).

70 *He is not an imbecile* Pearce in conference, Personalities of the Seven Dwarfs, 3 November 1936 (WDA).

70 *I see Dopey* Walt in conference, Characteristics and Personalities of the Seven Dwarfs, 15 December 1936 (WDA).

70 *At times there is great violence* Pearce in conference, Personalities of the Seven Dwarfs, 3 November 1936 (WDA).

70 *He is unable to talk* Walt, "Dwarfs' Personalities/Description of the Seven Dwarfs As I See Them at the Present Time" (WDA). This document is itself undated, but the date 3 December 1935 has been suggested for it (see Barrier, *Hollywood Cartoons*, p. 589, note 89). In any case, since the document describes Deafy and never mentions Sneezy, it's safe to assume that it was written no later than January 1936.

72 *He can't talk but he can yodel* Paul Buchanan in story conference on sequence 8A, 18 January 1936 (WDA).

72 *The explanation is* Walt to Dick Rickard in Dwarfs Personality Meeting, 22 December 1936 (WDA).

72 *conceived . . . as a "bucktoothed imp"* Barrier, *Hollywood Cartoons*, pp. 202-03.

73 *Les Clark and I went down there* Babbitt to author, 3 February 1981.

73 *ran the Collins film* Thomas and Johnston, *Disney Animation*, p. 320.

73 Note: *Roy Scott had interviewed several comedi- ans* Memo, Scott to Walt, 29 August 1935, subject: Pantomime (WDA).

73 Note: *his announcements to the trade press* "'Dopey' Is Grounded," *Hollywood Reporter*, 13 June 1938, p. 3 (AMPAS).

73 Note: *His obituary . . . credited Walt* Collins obituary, *Los Angeles Times*, 4 September 1940, p. A1.

73 *Thomas enjoyed telling the story* See Canemaker, *Walt Disney's Nine Old Men*, p. 178. Thomas also told this story in a television interview on *Disney Family Album*, the Disney Channel, April 1985.

73 Note: *I see Dopey going around* Walt in story conference on sequences 11A and 11B, 23 February 1937 (WDA).

73 Note: *Try for effect of Dopey* Walt in story conference on sequence 11B, 2 April 1937 (WDA).

73 *Dopey is waiting for the last* Walt in story conference on sequence 4A, 2 October 1936 (WDA).

73–74 *Dopey is kind of pounding those steps* Stallings in story conference on sequences 4A and 4B, 2 November 1936 (WDA).

74 *this game of his* Jackson in Discussion of Seven Dwarfs' Personalities, 24 November 1936 (WDA).

74 *a series of Walt's notes to Bill Tytla* Sweatbox notes, Walt to Tytla, 28 September 1936; 4 February 1937; 10 and 16 July 1937 (WDA).

74 *Fred Spencer got almost all* Natwick to author, 1 February 1981. At the time I thought he simply had his Freds mixed.

77 *romantic sap/giving him a masculine sounding name* "Manuscript" outline, 9 August 1934 (WDA). All of this is marked "OK" on Walt's copy of the outline.

77 *Get a decent pose/the Prince ought to be amused* Walt in story conference on sequence 2A, 12 June 1937 (WDA).

77 *I have in mind* Memo, Walt to Paul Hopkins, Roy Disney, Bill Garity, Harry Bailey, 25 November 1935, subject: Production Notes on Snow White (WDA).

77 *Part of it, at least* Natwick to author, 4 January 1981.

78 *The Queen is stately* "Manuscript" outline, 9 August 1934 (WDA).

78 *a mixture of Lady Macbeth* "Cast of Characters," undated but ca. October 1934 (WDA).

78 *Queen to be tried out* Suggestions and Notes on "Snow White," meeting on sound stage, 30 October 1934 (WDA).

78 Note: *a fat bulging old woman peddler* Suggestions and Notes on "Snow White," conference, 9 October 1934 (WDA).

78 *Some . . . enthusiasts have long believed* See Behlmer, *America's Favorite Movies: Behind the Scenes*, pp. 49–51.

78 *Joe [Grant] says it was* Story conference on sequence 7A, 20 March 1937 (WDA).

78 Note: *something like Theda Bara* Frederick C. Othman, syndicated story published as "Movie Folk Say Disney's Super Cartoon Is 'Hit,'" *Fresno Bee*, 22 December 1937, and as "Disney's Full Length Movie is Acclaimed," *Modesto Bee*, 23 December 1937.

79 Note: *Fergy's handling of her face* Thomas and Johnston, *Disney Animation*, p. 105.

79 *It was the age of the voice* Hand in Layout Meeting on Snow White, 3 May 1937 (WDA).

79–80 *She was just marvelous to work with* Cottrell to author, 18 November 1985.

80 *All the dialogue sounded bad* Walt in story conference on sequence 14C (but discussing sequence 13A), 5 January 1937 (WDA).

83 *stalks after her about the room* "Manuscript" outline, 9 August 1934 (WDA).

83 *predicts that within a week/The mirror's laughs multiply* Walt, Skeleton Continuity, typed 26 December 1934 (WDA).

83 *I like the idea* Walt in story conference on sequences 1B, 2A, 2B, and 7A, 26 September 1936 (WDA).

83 *He is a motionless type* Walt in story conference on sequence 7A, 20 March 1937 (WDA).

83 *Make him more poetic* Walt in story conference on sequence 7A, 10 March 1937 (WDA).

83 *Are you going to try/Yes, just like he looks* Morey and Walt in story conference on sequence 7A, 20 March 1937 (WDA).

83 *to have Olsen speak into a long, hollow tube* This method was described in the cutting record for sequence 7A, 18 May 1937 (WDA).

83 *an article in* Photoplay Kirtley Baskette, "The Amazing Inside Story of How They Made 'Snow White,'" *Photoplay*, April 1938. See especially p. 68.

83 *Olsen inserted his head* Andrew R. Boone, *"Snow White and the Seven Dwarfs," Popular Science Monthly*, January 1938. See especially pp. 52 and 131.

84 *We won't let the Huntsman weaken* Walt in story conference on sequence 3A (but discussing sequence 2B), 27 June 1936 (WDA).

84 *No one seems to like that name* Morey in story conference on sequence 3A, 3 July 1936 (WDA).

84 Note: *Buchanan's dialogue was recorded outdoors* Cutting record for sequence 3A, 20 July 1937 (WDA).

85 *As Karen Merritt has pointed out* See Merritt, "The Little Girl/Little Mother Transformation," p. 115.

85 *Animals will not talk* Brief Outline for Gag Suggestions, typed 6 November 1934 (WDA).

85 *We have taken the characters* Walt in Dwarfs' Personality Meeting, 22 December 1936 (WDA).

85 *You could hardly call them deer/When we got to Bambi* Larson quoted in Canemaker, *Walt Disney's Nine Old Men*, p. 63. Quote attributed to interview by Barrier. Larson made a similar comment on the *Disney Family Album* program, Disney Channel, January 1985.

85 *Don't have the deer too real* Sweatbox note on sequence 3C, Walt to Garbutt, 28 March 1936 (WDA).

CHAPTER 5. PRODUCTION

87 Note: *In an interview with Didier Ghez* See Ghez (ed.), *Walt's People*, vol. 11, p. 22.

87 *Certain transparent tones may be added* Bob Martsch, Supplement to Lecture on Effects, 15 June 1938 (WDA).

88 *Some time ago* "Hollywood Inside" column, *Daily Variety*, 25 February 1936, p. 2 (AMPAS).

88 *We were all put into* Weeks to author, 27 May 1995.

89 *We used to meet at lunch* Walt to Pete Martin, 1956.

90 *To have Frank play anything* Jackson to Care, quoted in Care, "Symphonists for the Sillies," pp. 43–44.

90 Note: *testifying in an (unsuccessful) plagiarism suit* Case summary, Allen v. Walt Disney Productions Ltd., 27 June 1941. Special thanks to Charles Wixson and Phyllis Berenson for researching this and other lawsuits.

90 *Really, we should set a new pattern* Walt in story conference on sequence 8A, 16 February 1937 (WDA).

93 Note: *Frank had an idea* Walt in story conference on sequence 6A, 23 June 1936 (WDA).

93 *I now have to write additional* Harline quoted in R. Vernon Steele, "Fairyland Goes Hollywood: An Interview with Leigh Harline," *Pacific Coast Musician*, 20 November 1937, p. 10.

94 *First frame was shot* Broughton to author, 25 August 1991.

95 *I would like to bring up something* Hand in Layout Conference on Snow White, 14 December 1936 (WDA).

95 *We had many triple exposures* C.W. Batchelder, Multiplane Camera Lecture for Assistant Directors, undated but late 1938 (WDA).

96 *but with longer scenes* Bob Martsch, Supplement to Lecture on Effects, 15 June 1938 (WDA).

96 *This mirror is draped with curtains* Walt in Dwarfs' Personality Meeting, 22 December 1936 (WDA).

96 *swing on vines* Conference, Suggestions and Notes on "SnowWhite," 3 October 1934 (WDA).

96 *the waterfall hid the entrance* Walt in Skeleton Continuity, typed 26 December 1934 (WDA).

CHAPTER 6. THE FILM

99 *Walt said, 'Make sure/So we went to Technicolor* Legg to author, 2 May 1999.

99–100 *The Mirror could say* Walt in story conference on sequence 7A, 20 March 1937 (WDA).

100 *Then Snow White would be* Walt in story conference on sequence 2A, 5 April 1937 (WDA).

100 *That was tough/I did that thing over* Woolie Reitherman interviewed for *Disney Family Album*, the Disney Channel, March 1985.

100 Note: *John Canemaker . . .reports that Reitherman* Canemaker, *Walt Disney's Nine Old Men*, p. 35.

100 *serving his apprenticeship as an inbetweener* By the mid-1930s, there was a hierarchy of animators at the Disney studio. The top artists, in animating a scene, would generally make only the "key" or "pose" drawings that defined the action. The drawings that came in between, filling the gaps and producing smooth action on the screen, were broken down and delegated through a chain of assistants. The artists at the bottom of this chain were called "inbetweeners," and newly hired candidates for the anima-

tion staff usually started their employment by working in the inbetween department.

100 *They just brought scenes over/[The dwarfs] were more fun* Justice to author, 26 March 1994.

106 Note: *the echoes were recorded* Kirtley Baskette, "The Amazing Inside Story of How They Made 'Snow White,'" *Photoplay*, April 1938. See p. 68.

106 *The girl does a good cadenza* Morey in story conference on sequence 2A, 5 April 1937 (WDA).

107 *I think we have to figure out* Walt in story conference on sequence 2A, 4 May 1937 (WDA).

108 *She is not getting/A little saucy* Walt in story conference on sequence 2A, 12 June 1937 (WDA).

110 Note: *the similarity of eyes* Ham Luske in story conference on sequences 1B, 2B, and 7A, 19 October 1936 (WDA).

114 *sings a gay hunting song/rising proudly* "Manuscript" outline, 9 August 1934 (WDA).

114 *has become a favorite example* See Finch, *The Art of Walt Disney*, pp. 182, 187; Thomas and Johnston, *Disney Animation*, pp. 380–86; Canemaker, *Paper Dreams*, pp. 38–43, 67–68.

114 *which gives you a swell position/Even [for] actors* Walt in story conference on sequence 3A, 27 June 1936 (WDA).

114 *If you build up the Huntsman* Cottrell, ibid.

115 *seemed a little clownish* Natwick, Group Reactions & Comments on Nine Snow White Reels, 17 March 1937 (WDA). Dick Creedon had expressed a similar opinion in notes submitted the previous week.

115 *That sequence . . . is all* Hand in response to a question from Charlie Philippi, Layout Meeting on Snow White, 3 May 1937 (WDA).

116 *the rise of expressionism in cinema* See David Robinson, *Das Cabinet des Dr. Caligari*, especially pp. 33–41.

116 *When she hits the branches* Walt in story conference on sequence 3A, 23 October 1936 (WDA).

116 *They are all short, fast blends* Walt in story conference on sequence 3A, 12 October 1936 (WDA).

116 *The montage I want to shoot* Walt in Luncheon Meeting, Production F-1, 18 February 1937 (WDA).

116–17 *Some of the sequences/Originally Larry*

prepared the story Holoboff and Adelquist in Meeting of Assistant Directors, 9 March 1937 (WDA).

117 *I think it all has to be dark* Walt in story conference on sequence 3A, 12 October 1936 (WDA).

120 *The way you have straightened this out* Sears in story conference on sequence 3B, 3 July 1936 (WDA).

120 *It has what I was/I wonder/I try to say to myself* Luske and Walt, ibid.

120 *We are just getting* Cottrell, ibid.

122 *shy but sniffing forward* Otis Ferguson in "Walt Disney's Grimm Reality" (*Snow White* review), *New Republic,* 26 January 1938, p. 339.

123 *I introduced the turtle* Natwick to author, 1 February 1981.

123 *Natwick made his suggestion* Natwick in story conference, cleaning sequence, 17 January 1936 (WDA).

123 *the turtle's head* Walt in story conference on sequence 3B, 27 June 1936 (WDA).

123 *he claimed more than once* See Canemaker, *Walt Disney's Nine Old Men,* p. 101; Ghez (ed.), *Walt's People,* Vol. 3, p. 41.

123 *he suggested that tin might be used* Walt in story conferences on sequence 2A, respectively, 3 June and 12 June 1937 (WDA).

126 *I cannot make this girl frown/If we could get a line* Luske and Walt in Discussion of Snow White's Personality, 11 November 1936 (WDA).

126 *bubbling quality/we asked Ed Plumb* Thomas and Johnston, *Disney Animation,* p. 286.

126 Note: *little work song* Skeleton Continuity, typed 26 December 1934 (WDA).

127 *Get the gag folder* Walt in story conference on sequence 11B, 14 January 1937 (WDA).

127 *I didn't realize* Eric Larson interviewed on *Disney Family Album,* The Disney Channel, January 1985.

127 *I don't like the bunny* Sweatbox note, Walt to Schmitt, 21 April 1936 (WDA).

127 *Personality touch: Last bird* Sweatbox note, Walt to Larson, 6 March 1936 (WDA).

128 Note: *Anderson later claimed* Anderson, interviewed for *Disney Family Album,* The Disney Channel, November 1984.

128–29 *In my youth/Because you could take a 6H pencil* Natwick to author, 4 January 1981.

129 Note: *A similar account* Garity, "Latest Tricks of the Animated Film Makers," *Popular Mechanics,* May 1938. See especially p. 114A.

129 Note: *drawings on second cel [level]* Exposure sheet for scene 18A in sequence 3D (Walt Disney Animation Research Library, hereinafter identified as "ARL").

132 *introducing the characters . . . by way of a roll call* Walt in story conference, 17 January 1936 (WDA). This conference was nominally devoted to sequences 3C and 3D.

132 *Funny if they had/The old owl is perched up there* Walt in story conference on sequence 4A, 2 October 1936 (WDA).

132 *Make little miners of them* Pearce in story conference on sequences 4A and 4B, 28 October 1936 (WDA). Walt was not present at this conference.

134 *Cut all mine stuff/What does it matter* Walt in story conference on sequences 4A and 4B, 2 November 1936 (WDA).

136 *to be sung by the dwarfs* Undated "Songs" memo, ca. mid-1934 (WDA).

136 *their marching song/We're seven men of the woods* Skeleton Continuity, 26 December 1934 (WDA).

136 *They do this every day* Stallings in meeting, Discussion of Seven Dwarfs' Personalities, 24 November 1936 (WDA).

136 *as though he were putting* Wilfred Jackson, ibid.

136 *Grumpy, by contrast* Bill Tytla, ibid.

136 *Walt has mentioned two or three times* Stallings, ibid.

139 Note: *change the root on the tree/prepare a new rough* Sweatbox note, Sharpsteen to Culhane, 20 August 1937 (WDA).

139 *It took me almost six months/My whole goddamn sequence* Culhane, *Talking Animals and Other People,* pp. 178–79.

140 *It is not necessary* Memo, Bee [Selck] to Perce/Hal, 16 July 1937, subject: Seq. 4C, Scenes 2 and 13A (WDA). When the sweatbox notes sometimes failed to catch Walt's miscellaneous comments, secretary Bee Selck conveyed them later in memos. This particular concern was repeated in a sweatbox note a couple of weeks later: "Scene 2: Turtle crunch sound is still in." Unidentified sweatbox note, typed 29 July 1937 (WDA).

140 *I always have the feeling* Creedon quoted in

Group Reactions & Comments on Nine Snow White Reels, 17 March 1937 (WDA).

140 *He worked out a musical pattern* Kahl quoted by Canemaker in *Walt Disney's Nine Old Men,* p. 137.

144 *Brothers, there must be Robbers* Jessie Braham White (Winthrop Ames), *Snow White and the Seven Dwarfs* (1912). This passage appears on pp. 106–108 of the 1913 Dodd, Mead edition of the script, and on pp. 50–51 of the 1925 Samuel French edition.

144 *Some scoundrel lurks within* Treatment, "The Dwarfs Find Snow White," typed 22 October 1934 (WDA), p. 2.

144 *a simpler gag* Skeleton Continuity, typed 26 December 1934 (WDA). This action appeared twice in the continuity, on pp. 10 and 11.

146 Note: *a story conference in May 1936* Story conference on sequence 4D, 21 May 1936 (WDA).

146 Note: *If you used something like* Babbitt in story conference on sequence 4D, 7 October 1936 (WDA).

147 *There was much discussion* Notes on story conference on sequence 4D, 7 October 1936 (WDA).

147 *At times there is great violence* Pearce in conference, Personalities of the Seven Dwarfs, 3 November 1936 (WDA).

148 *What we have to keep in mind* Walt in story conference on sequence 5A, 14 July 1936 (WDA).

148 *Ward Kimball received a bonus* Kimball to author, 15 March 1981.

148 Note: *This dialogue exchange had been suggested* Outline, "The Dwarfs Find Snow-white," typed 22 October 1934 (WDA).

149 *almost as though he had* Sweatbox notes, Walt and Dave to Moore, 2 March 1937 (WDA).

149 *It sounds like he was doing it/It doesn't sound funny enough* Anderson and Walt in story conference on sequence 5A, 14 July 1936 (WDA).

149 Note: *two generations of master Disney animators* Thomas and Johnston, from their position as eyewitnesses, have also left us two amusing anecdotes about Moore's work on the sequence; see their book *Disney Animation,* pp. 127–28 and 230–31.

149–52 *animated the group of dwarfs as a single mass* Thomas and Johnston elaborate on this effect, and illustrate it, in *Disney Animation,* p.

365.

152 *a song about gooseberry pie* Walt in story conference on sequence 5A, 14 July 1936 (WDA).

152 *We want to make use/Get the tweak of the nose* Ibid.

152 *I expected to see them* Natwick in Group Reactions & Comments on Nine Snow White Reels, 17 March 1937 (WDA).

152–53 *Her line "I don't want* Philippi, ibid.

153 *Mary made this comment* Pearce in Dialogue Conference, 9 February 1937 (WDA). It's not clear who "Mary" was, but she may have been Mary Lennox, the stenographer who transcribed some of these production meetings.

154 *Doc would sort of slip* Walt in story conference on sequence 5B, 25 September 1936 (WDA).

154–55 *Everything is okay* Sweatbox note, Walt to Thomas, 11 June 1937 (WDA).

158 Note: *action of catching soap/one blindly reaching* Suggestions and Notes on "Snow-White," conference, 15 October 1934 (WDA).

158 *dwarfs are driven by Grumpy's sarcasm* Walt in story conference on sequence 6A, 14 December 1935 (WDA).

158 *joining the others* Ibid.

158 *2' 4 frames blank film* Recording notes, 2 March 1936 (WDA).

158 *Have bubbles come up* Sweatbox notes, Walt to Stan Quackenbush, 10 July 1937 (WDA).

158 *The [dwarfs'] hands are on the side* Tytla in Action Analysis lecture, 8 June 1937 (WDA).

159 *There are very definite attitudes* Tytla in Discussion of Dwarfs' Personalities & Characteristics, 8 December 1936 (WDA). The live-action footage, filmed "a year ago now" (ca. December 1935), was being screened alongside Tytla's finished animation to demonstrate to the other dwarf animators how to use the process to maximum effect.

160 *Tytla had completely mastered* Barrier, *Hollywood Cartoons,* p. 208.

160 *Your characters of Grumpy* Sweatbox notes, Walt to Moore and Tytla, 16 April 1936 (WDA).

161 *It would be funny* Sweatbox notes, Walt to Tytla, 6 June 1936 (WDA).

161 *Have Bashful open his eyes* Sweatbox notes, Walt to Tytla, 4 February 1937 (WDA).

162 *to clean up the water* Summary of Effects in Sequence 6A (Washing), 5 April 1937 (WDA).

162 *Don't have so many suds/Have a bigger splash* Sweatbox notes, Walt to Wood, 30 July 1937 (WDA).

162 *If she called in the direction* Codrick in Layout Conference on Snow White, 14 December 1936 (WDA).

164 *Soup Symphony/Funny business of the gang* Skeleton Continuity, typed 26 December 1934 (WDA). This was before the washing sequence, with Dopey swallowing the soap, had been developed.

164 *drink countless thick malted milks* This press release was published as "Dwarfs Tough On Sound Men," *New York Telegram,* 4 October 1937 (WDA).

164 *Make the sounds rhythmic* Walt in story conference on sequence 6B, 2 March 1936 (WDA).

164 *The kick that they give Dopey* Walt in story conference on sequence 6B (WDA). This transcript was not dated, but the meeting seems to have taken place in December 1936.

164 *Yes, Harlan sings better* Walt in story conference on sequence 6B, 9 December 1936 (WDA).

164–66 *If you see [Doc]/Perce, tell the other reason* Pearce and Moore in Dwarfs' Personality Meeting, 29 December 1936 (WDA).

166 *I was trying to think* Pearce in story conference on sequence 6B, 30 November 1936 (WDA).

166 *I think the way Grumpy peeks* Walt in story conference on sequence 6B, 9 December 1936 (WDA).

167 *Everybody thought it was a great sequence* Kimball to author, 15 March 1981.

168 Note: *Would he tantalize her* Walt in story conference on sequences 1B, 2A, 2B, 7A, 26 September 1936 (WDA).

168 Note: *a meeting in February 1937* Luncheon Meeting on Production F-1, 18 February 1937 (WDA).

168 Note: *You have lost your biggest punch* Luske in story conference on sequence 7A, 20 March 1937 (WDA).

168 *I'd like to see her come down those steps* Walt in story conference, November 1936 (WDA). (The exact date is unclear; this and other comments on sequence 7A were apparently made on 25 November, but were combined with the transcript of a conference on sequence 9A on 24 November.)

168 *Get them all working together* Ibid.

168–69 *Hugh Hennesy . . . pointed out* Hennesy in Layout Meeting on Snow White, 3 May 1937 (WDA).

173 *a Jekyll and Hyde* Walt used this term to describe the transformation as early as November 1935 (memo, Walt to Hopkins, Roy, Garity and Bailey, 25 November 1935, subject: Production Notes on Snow White, WDA), and repeated it in other written memos and in story meetings.

173 *I felt terrifically disappointed* Walt in story conference on sequence 7A, 10 March 1937 (WDA).

173 *the shadow of a giant bat* Several references to the bat's shadow were made in Layout Meeting on Snow White, 3 May 1937 (WDA).

173 *I wanted to get away/you can't tell* Walt in sweatbox session on sequence 7A, 20 August 1937 (WDA).

174 *Snow White dances* Walt's handwritten note on undated "Songs" memo (WDA).

174 *he announced the two animators* Memo, Walt to Paul Hopkins, Roy Disney, Bill Garity and Harry Bailey, 25 November 1935, subject: Production Notes on Snow White (WDA).

174 *Ted [Sears] and Pinto can help* Walt in story conference on sequence 8A, 6 January 1936 (WDA).

174 *a song called "Funny Little Bunnies"* Undated "Songs" memo (WDA).

175 *each dwarf sings a jingle* Brief Outline for Gag Suggestions, typed 6 November 1934 (WDA).

175 *Now there's 'Grumpy' Gus* Philippi, story suggestions submitted 16 November 1934 (WDA).

175 *Dwarfs sing their special little song* Walt in Skeleton Continuity, typed 26 December 1934 (WDA).

176 *Now when the moon came up at night* "Lady in the Moon" lead sheet preserved in the Walt Disney Music Department.

176 *Walt liked this song* Story conference, "Dwarfs Entertaining Snowwhite [sic] Sequence," 13 December 1935 (WDA).

176 *A big hoot owl* Ibid.

176 *because of a woman* Ibid.

177 *Anybody could do the yodel* Walt in story conference on sequence 8A, 6 January 1936 (WDA).

177 *I had never yodeled* Macdonald quoted by

Thomas and Johnston in *Disney Animation*, p. 298.

177–78 *It's like each guy sits there* Walt in story conference on sequence 8A, 18 January 1936 (WDA).

178 *Their instruments have got to be/I don't want a flute* Walt in story conference on sequence 8A, 16 February 1937 (WDA).

178 *If you use clarinets* Walt in story conference on sequence 8A, 6 January 1936 (WDA).

178 Note: *Walt suggested a gag* Walt in story conference on sequence 8A, 9 April 1937 (WDA).

179 *As early as 1934* Brief Outline for Gag Suggestions, typed 6 November 1934 (WDA), mentions the organ in the course of prompting studio personnel for more suggestions on the interior of the cottage.

179 *The smaller pipes would be carved* Walt in story conference on sequence 8A, 6 January 1936 (WDA).

179–80 *We cut to a C.U.* Larry Morey reading continuity in story conference on sequence 8A, 31 March 1937 (WDA).

180 *I think you ought to figure/You're not going to use/We might use an organ* Walt and Buchanan in story conference on sequence 8A, 16 February 1937 (WDA).

180 *Use a few legitimate instruments* Walt in story conference on sequence 8A, 16 February 1937 (WDA).

180 Note: *Hurd specifically claimed credit* See Canemaker, *Paper Dreams*, pp. 110–12.

181 *It's kind of cold* Walt in story conference on sequence 8A, 16 February 1937 (WDA).

181 Note: *you got that and afterwards we couldn't make it over* Ibid.

181 *Ted Sears even suggested* Sears had expressed this sentiment privately a full year earlier, and seemed embarrassed when Dick Rickard brought it to the group's attention at the 18 January 1936 story conference (WDA).

184 *go right on out of the scene* Sweatbox notes, Walt and Jackson to Lundy and Luske, 1 September 1937 (WDA).

184 *Sneezy was to . . . sing* The scene was okayed for inkers in Wilfred Jackson's sweatbox notes of 29 October 1937 (WDA).

184 *more like the original layout sketches* Sweatbox notes, Walt to Lundy, 7 August 1937 (WDA).

184 *Doc takes quite an important part* Walt in story conference on sequence 8A, 18 January

1936 (WDA).

185 *Snow White does not come in actual contact* Unattributed comment, conference on Personalities of the Seven Dwarfs, 10 November 1936 (WDA).

186 *teach them a dance of the court* Brief Outline for Gag Suggestions, typed 6 November 1934 (WDA).

186 *I felt this sequence* Walt at story conference on sequence 8B, 8 December 1936 (WDA).

188 *I thought somehow I wandered in the sky* Ibid.

188 *I see myself all in the loveliest gown* Cutting records for sequence 8B (WDA). Caselotti recorded the verse three times, on 2 February, 24 March, and 11 May 1937, and the cutting records for the last two sessions reproduce the text identically as it appears here.

188 *Ham, how do you feel/The way you talked it* Walt and Luske in story conference on sequence 8B, 14 January 1937 (WDA).

188 *There is Jaxon's dream sequence* Hand in Layout Meeting, 22 February 1937 (WDA).

189 *I see that we have yet/I am glad to know* Walt and Hand in story conference on sequence 8C, typed 10 December 1936 (WDA).

190 *She was sitting in a chair/When you take a nose* Natwick to author, 4 January 1981.

190 *Les Novros did a beautiful job* Natwick to author, 1 February 1981.

190 Note: *Ken Anderson had suggested . . . Walt had pushed for individual cuts* Comments by Dave Hand during layout meeting, 25 January 1937 (WDA).

190 Note: *When Walt told me* Jackson in story conference on sequence 8C, typed 23 November 1936 (WDA). Walt was not present at this meeting.

191 *I feel in Snow White we should have had* Walt in story conference on *Clair de Lune (Fantasia)*, 8 December 1938 (WDA).

192 *in later years . . . Lounsbery would recall* See Canemaker, *Walt Disney's Nine Old Men*, p. 246.

194 THIS IS NOW THE FIRST SCENE Cottrell, retake order to camera department, 18 November 1937 (ARL).

194 *My reason for disliking that shot* Memo, Perkins to Walt, 3 January 1938, subject: Herewith (WDA).

194-95 *Arrange a dissolve for safety's sake* Sweatbox notes, Walt to Cottrell, 16 July 1937

(WDA).

195 Sidebar: *Scott MacQueen has pointed it out* MacQueen to author, March 2008.

195 Sidebar: *dozens of little people* "Manuscript" outline, 9 August 1934 (WDA).

196 Note: *SnowWhite, in the early morning light* Suggestions and Notes on "SnowWhite," conference, 9 October 1934 (WDA).

196 *It was not until we had* Thomas and Johnston, *Disney Animation*, pp. 496-97.

196 *Grumpy still has sort of a sourpuss expression* Walt in story meeting, Characteristics and Personalities of the Seven Dwarfs, 15 December 1936 (WDA).

197 *It confines you so much/the objection was* Tom Codrick in Layout Meeting on Snow White, 22 March 1937 (WDA).

198 Note: *The huntsman is very sad* Skeleton Outline, typed 26 December 1934 (WDA).

198 *In the take-off* Sweatbox notes, Sharpsteen to Kimball, 8 September 1937 (WDA).

198 *Extend the head and neck* Sweatbox notes, Walt and Sharpsteen to Young, 17 September 1937 (WDA).

198 *Do not show cast shadows* Ibid., Walt and Sharpsteen to Stewart.

202 *one [dwarf] gets up on a stump* Suggestions and Notes on "SnowWhite," conference, 9 October 1934 (WDA).

202 *The meeting at which they decide* Brief Outline for Gag Suggestions, typed 6 November 1934 (WDA).

202 *The best way to come back* Walt in story conference, 7 December 1936 (WDA). This meeting was nominally devoted to sequence 11A, but also wandered into other parts of the picture including sequence 11B.

205 *We show the mine entrance/I see these guys* Walt in story conference on sequence 11B, 14 January 1937 (WDA).

205 *They have carved these trees* Walt in story conference on sequences 11A and 11B, 23 February 1937 (WDA).

207 *That was kind of a tragic period* Kimball to author, 15 March 1981.

207 *Big angels or little angels?/Both* This was the dialogue as suggested by Walt in story conference on sequence 11A, 7 December 1936 (WDA).

207 *That's why I wonder* Hand in story conference on sequence 11A, 27 November 1936 (WDA).

208 *have that oven* Walt in story conference on sequence 13A, 16 December 1936 (WDA).

208 *I wouldn't like that in a picture* Blank, ibid.

208 Note: *That wouldn't disturb me* Tytla in Dwarfs Personality Meeting, 29 December 1936 (WDA).

208 *The smile should be more Lionel Barrymore* Sweatbox note, Walt to Ferguson, 20 August 1937 (WDA).

208 *You are to get* Sweatbox note, Walt to Ferguson, 23 September 1937 (WDA).

213 *After a new layout has been given* Sweatbox note, Ben Sharpsteen to Larson, 12 July 1937 (WDA).

214 *a reason for Snow White/I believe any fairy tale* Walt in story conference on sequence 13A, 15 December 1936 (WDA).

215 *You know a chase in the rain* Ibid.

215 *climactic action at the top of the rocky crag* A generous selection of story sketches from this sequence can be seen in John Canemaker, *Paper Dreams,* pp. 48–55. See also Canemaker's observations on the sequence on pp. 46–48.

215 *this thing isn't working out* Memo, "Sweatbox notes - Toby" to Ben Sharpsteen and Ward Kimball, 13 September 1937, subject: Seq. 14-J (WDA). "Toby" was studio stenotypist Eloise Tobelman.

216 *As late as November 1936* Discussion on Personalities of Dwarfs, 17 November 1936 (WDA), includes comments that suggest this concept is still current.

216 *Is there more value/I don't think so/I think we can handle* Anderson and Walt in story conference on sequences 15A and 16A, 6 May 1937 (WDA).

216 *You know what happened* Walt, ibid.

216 *It just felt like/There was an unexpected bonus* Thomas and Johnston, *Disney Animation,* pp. 475–78.

216 *you have to pick an inbetweener* Thomas quoted by Canemaker in *Walt Disney's Nine Old Men,* p. 179. Several of Thomas's drawings from the sequence also appear on this page, including one of the unused Dopey drawings.

217 *Ham [Luske] thought perhaps* Sweatbox note, Walt to Thomas, 18 August 1937 (WDA).

217 *Get more roundness in the tears* Sweatbox note, Walt and Jaxon to Efx Department, 4 October 1937 (WDA).

217 *Walt commended the mourning animals* Walt

in story conference on sequences 15A and 16A, 6 May 1937 (WDA).

217 *Suppose you left out the titles* Walt in story conference on sequences 15A and 16A, 6 May 1937 (WDA).

218 Note: *They refuse to let him approach* Brief Outline for Gag Suggestions, 6 November 1934 (WDA).

218 *Lifting her up seems important/I think the coffin should be* Walt in story conference on sequences 15A and 16A, 6 May 1937 (WDA).

CHAPTER 7. FINISH THE PICTURE!

222 *In some cases* Hand in Conference with Dwarf Animators, 8 June 1937 (WDA).

222 *Do they know anything* Moore, ibid.

223 *And the room was on an angle* Noble to author, 8 July 1993.

223 *production of the Silly Symphony* Merbabies For more information on this see Merritt and Kaufman, *Walt Disney's Silly Symphonies,* pp. 198–201.

224 *When the Queen gulped down her potion* Diane Disney Miller to author (e-mail), 25 April 2010.

224 *She hated it* Walt quoted by Dorothy Ducas, "The Father of Snow White," *This Week, Los Angeles Times,* 19 June 1938, p. 7 (AMPAS).

224 *Now, he says, he doesn't think* Eileen Creelman, "Picture Plays and Players," *New York Sun,* 6 February 1940 (NYPL).

224 *Mr. Disney's attorneys say* Letter, Ames to Frank J. Sheil (Samuel French, Inc.), 24 October 1936 (SA).

224 *We were alarmed* Memo, Lessing to Walt, 7 April 1937, subject: Ames version Snow White (WDA).

225 *Roy didn't show up/He talked about everything* Walt to Pete Martin, 1956.

225 Sidebar: *Giannini brothers* See Barbara L. Ciccarelli, "A.H. Giannini."

225 Sidebar: *the AMPA awarded him its Sam Harris cup* "To Honor Giannini At Amity Dinner Tonight," *Film Daily,* 20 November 1928, pp. 1, 7; "Internationalism Stressed at Giannini Dinner," *Motion Picture News,* 24 November 1928, p. 1581 (both AMPAS).

225 Sidebar: *The Doc's been more than a banker* Walt quoted in Frank J. Taylor, "He's No Angel," *Saturday Evening Post,* 14 January

1939, p. 23 (Cinema-Television Library, University of Southern California, hereinafter identified as "USC"). Special thanks to Ned Comstock for bringing this article to my attention. The title of the article was of course a takeoff on the Mae West film title, as well as a reference to Giannini's claim that his loans to stage and film producers were simply good business.

CHAPTER 8. THE OPENING

226 Note: *Mickey Mouse birthday week* Memo, Roy to Walt, 9 September 1936 (WDA).

226 *Al Perkins . . . wanted me to come over* Kinney to author, 13 August 1988.

226 Note: *as early as December 1937* "Mouse & Man," *Time,* 27 December 1937. See especially p. 19.

226–28 *Brevity is the secret/For the present, at least* Leon Schlesinger quoted in "Cartooning Stirs Speculation," *Box Office,* 19 June 1937 (WDA).

228 *I have talked with Tom/What help we could give* Memo, Dike to Walt, 9 July 1937 (WDA).

228–29 *the Good Housekeeping pages* The *Good Housekeeping* serialization of *Snow White* appeared in the issues of November 1937 (pp. 35–38 and 221–226) and December 1937 (pp. 35–38 and 162–168). For a reprinting of this material see Gerstein (ed.), *Walt Disney's Mickey and the Gang,* pp. 140–153. While this anthology reproduces facsimiles of the previous *Good Housekeeping* pages, the *Snow White* feature is represented by a seamless transcription of the Dorothy Blank text. Tenggren's illustrations, sometimes greatly enlarged, are supplemented in the anthology by other images. For the record, the original November installment of the story ends with Doc's line "Yes, bless my soul, that's what it is—a girl!" The December text picks up the story with: "The Seven Dwarfs stood on tiptoe, staring wide-eyed at the sleeping Princess."

229 *will be released Good Housekeeping,* November 1937, p. 35.

230 *New York—especially the younger generation* Irene Thirer, "Theatres Line Up Films As Yuletide Draws Near," *New York Post,* 14 December 1937 (WDA).

230 Note: *It was figured by RKO* "Disney 'Dwarfs' For Regular Release," *Hollywood*

Reporter, 12 August 1937, p. 6 (AMPAS). For more trade-press coverage of RKO's vacillating announcements, see "RKO Won't Roadshow Disney 'Snow White,'" *Motion Picture Daily,* 12 August 1937, p. 2; "No Roadshow for Disney," *Motion Picture Herald,* 28 August 1937, p. 114; "Disney Feature To Be Sold Separately," *Motion Picture Herald,* 4 September 1937, p. 58; "'Snow White' Won't Be Sold Until Tested In Key Cities," *Hollywood Reporter,* 30 November 1937, p. 5 (all AMPAS).

230 *Don't make the children any promises* Mary Wynn, "Don't Make the Kids Any Disney Promise," *Fort Worth Star-Telegram,* 5 January 1938 (WDA).

230 *But how they enjoyed it* "Important Preview Here," *(Pomona) Progress-Bulletin,* 7 December 1937 (WDA).

230 CROWDED HOUSE GAVE PICTURE EXCELLENT RECEPTION Telegram, Depinet to Jules Levy (RKO), 7 December 1937, reproduced in "Sneak Preview Audience Incited To 'Snow White' Ovation," *Radio Flash,* 11 December 1937, p. 1 (WDA).

232 *several hundred Disney artists* "Disney Staff Pay to See Own Product," *Los Angeles Times,* 18 December 1937, p. A7.

232 *Laughter was induced at will* William R. Weaver, *Snow White* review, *Motion Picture Herald,* 25 December 1937, p. 36 (AMPAS).

232 *Everybody in the audience* Ward Kimball to Jim Korkis, 24 April 1996, reprinted in Ghez (ed.), *Walt's People,* Vol. 2, pp. 82–83.

232 *the Hollywood intelligentsia stood around* W.E. Oliver, "'Snow White and 7 Dwarfs' Outdraws Jupiter Pluvius," *Los Angeles Herald & Express,* 28 December 1937 (WDA).

232 *Men, women and children* *Snow White* review, *Motion Picture Daily,* 23 December 1937, p. 3 (AMPAS).

232 *Walt Disney has so perfectly captured* Louella Parsons, *Snow White* review, *Los Angeles Examiner,* 22 December 1937 (USC).

232–33 *It is a masterpiece of entertainment* *Snow White* review, *Hollywood Reporter,* 22 December 1937, p. 3 (AMPAS).

233 *'Snow White' is the genius of craftsmanship* *Snow White* review, *Daily Variety,* 22 December 1937, p. 3 (AMPAS).

236 *one of the year's worst headache nights* W.E. Oliver, "'Snow White and 7 Dwarfs' Outdraws Jupiter Pluvius," *Los Angeles Herald & Express,* 28 December 1937 (WDA).

236 *Tournament of Roses Parade* "Spectacle of Flowers Thrills Vast Throng," *Los Angeles Times,* 2 January 1938, pp. 5–6.

236 Note: *Walt had hoped to commission* "Disney Seeks Sarg Balloons," *Los Angeles News,* 14 December 1937 (WDA).

236 *Harpo Marx . . . Mary Pickford . . . Chaplin* "'Snow White' Lauded By Screen Notables," *Hollywood Citizen-News,* 10 January 1938 (WDA); "Mary Pickford Has Praise for 'Snow White,'" *Los Angeles Times,* 12 January 1938, p. A10; "Chaplin Lauds Dwarf Dopey as Great Comic," *Los Angeles Times,* 14 January 1938, p. 11.

236 Note: *compared Dopey's pantomime to Chaplin's gag* "Dopey Succeeds in Variation of Chaplin 'Gag,'" *Los Angeles Times,* 28 June 1938, p. 8.

236 *The Los Angeles Public Library* "'Snow White' Popular Reading at Library," *Los Angeles Times,* 7 February 1938, p. A14.

236 *even then the theater reported* "'Snow White' Nears End of Record Run," *Los Angeles Examiner,* 20 April 1938 (WDA).

236 *Sheer fantasy* Frank S. Nugent, *Snow White* review, *New York Times,* 14 January 1938, 21:1.

236–37 *once again, business actually increased* "'Snow White' Grosses Half of Production Cost at Music Hall," *Motion Picture Herald,* 12 February 1938, pp. 13–16, 18 (AMPAS).

237 *By hearing, rather than seeing* Thomas M. Pryor, "Movies for the Blind," *New York Times,* 10 April 1938, X:4:3.

238 *As he walked down the path* Roy to Richard Hubler, 20 February 1968 (Collection of the Walt Disney Family Museum, hereinafter identified as "WDFM").

238 Note: *if I hadn't been so damn tight* Ibid.

238 *even after the film was running in New York* Miriam Stillwell, "The Story Behind Snow White's $10,000,000 Surprise Party," *Liberty,* 9 April 1938.

238 *smash biz* "'Snow White' Big in Miami," *Film Daily,* 14 January 1938, p. 2 (AMPAS).

239 *one of the noted Miami Beach bathing beauties* Picture caption, *Miami Daily News,* 18 January 1938 (WDA).

239 *You can say for me* "Midgets Disguised in Masks Here to Boom Fairy Tale Film," *Washington Star,* 20 January 1938 (WDA).

239 *my former associates at the Disney Studios* See John Canemaker, *Paper Dreams,* pp. 84–85.

239 *Miss Caselotti will warble* "'Snow White' Voice Doublers Form Act," *Variety,* 26 January 1938, p. 1 (AMPAS).

239 *It appears that, as usual* Memo, Dickson to Walt, 27 January 1938 (WDA).

239 *It was his voice* Grace Kingsley, "Bright Vaudeville Bill Presented at Orpheum," *Los Angeles Times,* 22 September 1938, p. 19.

239 Note: *a cutie who comes through* "Cohen," *Seeing Stars* review, *Variety,* 31 January 1940, p. 20 (AMPAS).

240 *cartoon is getting practically no bookings* "Philly Exhibs Tacitly Agree Not to Pay 50% to RKO for 'Snow White,'" *Variety,* 12 January 1938, p. 5 (LoC).

240 *it is among the genuine artistic achievements* Otis Ferguson, "Walt Disney's Grimm Reality" (*Snow White* review), *New Republic,* 26 January 1938, p. 339.

240 *We're businessmen* Schlesinger quoted in "Mouse & Man," *Time,* 27 December 1937, p. 19.

240 *It is astonishing* James Shelley Hamilton, *Snow White* review, *National Board of Review Magazine,* January 1938, quoted in *From Quasimodo to Scarlett O'Hara,* p. 274.

240 *the happiest thing that has happened* Westbrook Pegler, syndicated *Snow White* review, *Washington Post,* 17 January 1938, p. 7.

240 Note: *remarked that he was beside himself* Letter, Horne to Walt, 15 January 1938 (WDA).

240 *Disney gives credit to his directors* Ferguson, *Snow White* review, *New Republic,* 26 January 1938, p. 340.

240 Note: *the average to be given each [employee]* "Disney's 800G Melon to Employees," *Variety,* 29 June 1938, pp. 1, 52 (AMPAS). Distribution of the bonuses had started by spring 1938; the WDFM has in its collection Walt's memo to Ward Kimball, 3 May 1938, subject: Snow White Adjustment Compensation, which accompanied the first installment of his payment. See also "Why Hollywood Loves

Disney," *Motion Picture,* October 1938, p. 46 (AMPAS).

240 Note: *Walt never did that again!* Huemer to Adamson, 1968–69, UCLA Oral History Project. This particular quote has been published in Ghez (ed.), *Walt's People,* Vol. 4, p. 63.

240 *We have been told* "Walt Disney Puts Soap in the Movies," *Soap,* December 1937, p. 34 (WDA).

241 *Dopey was the clear winner* "Here Are the Lucky Winners!", *Hollywood,* August 1938, pp. 54–55 (USC).

241 *I am completely at a loss* Winsten, "More Minority Report on 'Snow White,'" *New York Post,* 18 January 1938 (WDA).

241 *an anatomic automaton/I merely wish to point out* Hirschfeld, "An Artist Contests Mr. Disney," *New York Times,* 30 January 1938, X:4:1.

242 *there were only 5,000 copies/Orders for more than 50,000 copies* "Snow White and the Seven Dwarfs," *Publishers' Weekly,* 5 February 1938, pp. 721–22.

242 *dead, maimed and disfigured* The Famous Movie Story of Walt Disney's Snow White and the Seven Dwarfs (New York: K.K. Publications, 1938), p. 14 (WDA).

245 *none of us look like dwarfs* Jack Benny broadcast, NBC, 24 April 1938. Special thanks to Ben Urish.

245 *Mickey Mouse Theatre of the Air* See Keith Scott, "Mickey Mouse, Radio Star." Special thanks to Keith Scott for this and other radio research.

248 *Fleischer intends to sue us* Memo, Walt to Bill Garity, 1 September 1937 (WDA).

249 *The [Caselotti] case was decided* Case summary, Caselotti v. Walt Disney Productions, 17 November 1939–14 November 1941. Special thanks to Charles Wixson and Phyllis Berenson for researching the case summaries of this and the other *Snow White* lawsuits.

249 *Was the Prince a Yale man?* "Snow White Accused of Pirating Yale Song; Publishers of 'Old Eli March' Ask Damages," *New York Times,* 16 October 1938, 34:2.

249 *There's a plague* Lessing quoted by Frederick C. Othman, "Walt Disney Victor in 10 Million Suit," *New York World-Telegram,* 29 June 1940 (NYPL).

249 *fear of universal warfare* "Whole World Held Taking Up Fantasy," *New York Times,* 28 June 1938, 20:2.

249 *who are certainly not much agitated/These are all avenues* "Snow White and Escape from Reality," *The Christian Century,* 20 July 1938, p. 886.

249 *after enthusiastic reception* "45th Film Case Filed With NLRB," *Daily Variety,* 31 December 1937, p. 20 (AMPAS).

249 *a great historical figure* "Disney Joins the Masters in Metropolitan; Museum to Show 'Snow White' Watercolor," *New York Times,* 24 January 1939, 21:3; "Museum Accepts Disney Painting," *New York Sun,* 24 January 1939 (NYPL); "'Snow White' Now In Metropolitan Museum," *Motion Picture Herald,* 28 January 1939, p. 18 (AMPAS); "Honored," *Newsweek,* 6 February 1939, p. 6.

250 *All I can say* "Screen Winners Get Awards of Critics Here; Formal Presentations Made at Broadcast," *New York Times,* 9 January 1939, 10:2.

250 *because of its unique character* "Film Critics Here Vote Year's 'Bests,'" *New York Times,* 3 January 1939, 18:5.

250 *I thought you might like* Memo, Walt to Bill Cottrell, 4 February 1939 (WDFM).

250 Note: *Up to the time Jack died* Roy to Richard Hubler, 18 June 1968 (WDFM).

250 *No grownup could have been* "Hedda Hopper's Hollywood," *Los Angeles Times,* 25 February 1939, p. A9.

250 Note: *going Disney one better/Lantz says that he will* Douglas W. Churchill, "Late Summer In Hollywood," *New York Times,* 4 September 1938, X:3:6.

250 *he would produce four animated features* "Walter Lantz Planning Four Feature Cartoons," *Film Daily,* 7 September 1938, p. 2 (AMPAS).

251 *Hugh Harman . . . finally left MGM* "Harmon [sic] Quits MGM To Produce Feature," *Hollywood Reporter,* 7 August 1941, pp. 1–2 (AMPAS).

251 *The trail blazed by 'Snow White'* "Ingenuity And Efficiency Speed Up Cartoon Prod'n," *Hollywood Reporter,* 20 October 1942, p. 6 (AMPAS). This article also revealed the title of Hugh Harman's feature project: "Knights of the Round Table."

251 Sidebar: *a prominent Los Angeles builder/designer* Steve Vaught to author (e-mail), 22 April 2007.

CHAPTER 10. SNOW WHITE IN OTHER LANDS

252 *more easily upset by fairy stories* "British Fear 'Snow White' Will Cause Nightmares," *New York Times,* 6 February 1938, 37:6.

252 *all fairy stories are wildly unsuitable* "Fairy Tales A and U," *Times* (London), 9 February 1938, p. 13.

252 *cutting the offending scenes* "British Fear 'Snow White' Will Cause Nightmares."

252 *shown with a "U" certificate* "'Snow White and the Seven Dwarfs'/'U' Film in London, Essex, and Middlesex," *Times* (London), 19 February 1938, p. 10.

252 *By virtue of the fact* "'Snow White' Okay In British Counties," *Hollywood Reporter,* 26 April 1938, p. 5 (AMPAS).

255 *The Spanish version has certain flaws/Disney's creation has lost* Salvador Baguez, "'Snow White' In Spanish Given At Carthay Circle," *Los Angeles Times,* 2 March 1938, p. 11.

255 *The French government . . . waived this regulation* "France Breaks Its Synchronizing Law For Disney Picture," *Hollywood Reporter,* 19 October 1937, pp. 1, 3 (AMPAS).

255 *was quite a gala affair* Letter, Buchanan (in Amsterdam) to Hand, 10 May 1938 (WDA).

255 *We have definitely decided* Ibid.

256 *showing the film in Germany* A much more detailed account of the Disneys' fortunes in Germany has been published in *Wie Micky unter die Nazis fiel,* by Carsten Laqua. I am indebted to Ulrich Ruedel for bringing this book to my attention and for summarizing the *Snow White* information for me in English.

256 *its European business was triple* "RKO Radio's European Biz Trebled -- Reisman," *Film Daily,* 19 September 1938, pp. 1, 9 (AMPAS).

257 *Critics of the exposition* "Venice Exposition Awards To American Films, Stars," *Film Daily,* 7 September 1938, pp. 1, 6 (AMPAS).

257 *the management of the Waldorf* "Screen News Here and in Hollywood," *New York Times,* 8 April 1939, 19:4.

CHAPTER 11. THE DWARFS GO TO WAR

258 *I sincerely believe* Walt quoted in "Creators Seek Lasting Fame For 7 Dwarfs," *Syracuse*

Post-Standard, 19 September 1937 (WDA).

258 *We all feel we should start another picture* Walt quoted in Eileen Creelman, "Picture Plays and Players," *New York Sun,* 30 August 1937 (NYPL).

258 Note: *Ted Sears wrote a memo to Walt* Sears, "Hansel and Gretel: Comments on Subject," 29 November 1937 (WDFM).

258 *This thing is hot/You don't have to have* Walt in story conference, "Babes in the Woods," 7 May 1941 (WDFM). *Babes in the Woods,* the current working title of this story, had also been the title of a 1932 Silly Symphony partially based on *Hansel and Gretel.*

258 *She should be more of a regular witch* Ibid.

260 Note: *reworked from yet another parade scene* See Merritt and Kaufman, *Walt Disney's Silly Symphonies,* p. 87.

260 *it is specifically understood* Memo, Robert Spencer Carr to Roy Disney, 28 July 1941 (WDA). The purpose of this memo was to provide "raw material" (Carr's phrase) for the Disney-NFB letter of agreement.

263 *The only reason to bring in* Walt in "Malaria & Mosquito" story meeting, 14 May 1942. A partial transcript of this story meeting was reprinted in "Walt Disney: Great Teacher," *Fortune,* August 1942. This quote appeared on p. 91.

264 *one of the most popular films* Letter, Russell Pierce (CIAA) to Jack Cutting (Walt Disney Productions), 15 May 1944 (National Archives and Records Administration).

CHAPTER 12. THE RETURN OF SNOW WHITE

266 *This unprecedented plan* "Disney to Stop U.S. Showings of 'Snow White'" (UP, dateline 4 February 1939), *South Bend (Indiana) Tribune,* 5 February 1939 (WDA).

267 *availability [to exhibitors] will be tied* "No National Release Date For Walt Disney Festival," *Film Daily,* 11 July 1940, p. 2 (AMPAS).

267 *overcame the handicap of unprecedented torrid weather* "Its Timeless Appeal Makes Snow White Difficult to 'Date,'" *New York Herald-Tribune,* 4 August 1940 (NYPL).

267 *spoke of how they had gone through* Memo, Walt to Roy, 16 March 1942 (WDA).

267 *an independent California exhibitor* The theater was the Regina in Beverly Hills. For a more complete account of the 1937–38 reissue

of *Dracula* and *Frankenstein,* see Turner, *The Cinema of Adventure, Romance & Terror,* p. 99.

268 *triumphantly proves . . . that time can do little* "The Christmas Films," *Times* (London), 24 December 1943, p. 6E.

268 *should be advertised . . . with no mention* Tentative Plans for WLW Area Campaign on Walt Disney's Snow White & 7 Dwarfs (WDA). This document, written by RKO publicity man Terry Turner, is undated but was written sometime between 9 and 20 December 1943.

268 *Anything we can do* Memo, Roy to Walt, 11 February 1944 (WDA).

268 *cancellation of Los Angeles plane flights* E.B. Radcliffe, "Out in Front," *Cincinnati Enquirer,* 24 February 1944, p. 8.

269 *Can it be six years* Bosley Crowther, *Snow White* review, *New York Times,* 9 April 1944, II:3:1.

269–70 *Screen Guild Players/This Is My Best* Here again I am indebted to Keith Scott and to Ben Urish for information on *Snow White*-related radio broadcasts.

270 *contemporary comic books* For a comprehensive introduction to Disney comic books, my debt is to David Gerstein.

271 *"Whistling Snow White"* Letter, John D. Klebe (Salt Lake City) to Walt Disney Productions, 26 March 1952; letter, Joe Reddy to Klebe, 28 March 1952 (both WDA).

271 *The [films] that followed* Walt to Martin, 1956.

271 *Oh, I guess Snow White* Walt quoted by Bogdanovich, *Pieces of Time,* p. 38.

CHAPTER 13. MORE PRINCESSES

272 *[follow] the story rather closely/She might build a dummy Prince* Cinderella story outline, undated (but giving 14 December 1933 as a deadline for submission of gags) (WDA).

274 *Two of them go out and stage a fake fight* Snow White Skeleton Continuity, typed 26 December 1934 (WDA).

275 *like Tom Mix and Tony* Suggestions and Notes on "Snow White," conference, 9 October 1934 (WDA).

CHAPTER 14. TELEVISION

277 Note: *a special edition of* Bambi *. . . prepared for India* See "Disney Expands Dubbing Program," *Hollywood Reporter,* 2 June 1947,

p. 4; "Rambling Reporter," *Hollywood Reporter,* 24 November 1947, p. 2; "Disney Setting Up Holland Dub Plant," *Hollywood Reporter,* 5 December 1947, p. 6 (all AMPAS).

278 *I worked on the TV show* Huemer to Adamson, 1968–69, UCLA Oral History Project. This passage was quoted in *Funnyworld* 17 (Fall 1977), p. 37, and Ghez (ed.), *Walt's People,* vol. 4, pp. 62–63.

CHAPTER 15. RED AS THE ROSE, BLACK AS EBONY, WHITE AS SNOW

280 *We want to imagine/They got colors everywhere* Walt in sweatbox session, Effects on Sequences 3C and 3D, 1 December 1936 (WDA).

280 *a somewhat different version of* Snow White This survey of the later color mutations of *Snow White* owes much to conversations with Scott MacQueen and to his article, "*Snow White and the Seven Dwarfs:* Epic Animation Restored," cited in the bibliography.

281 *surgically removed from the emulsion* Memo, YCM Laboratories to "Snow White" file, 1 April 1987, subject: Restoration from original nitrate negative (WDA).

281 *a digital restoration* See Bob Fisher, "Off to Work We Go: The Digital Restoration of *Snow White,*" *American Cinematographer,* September 1993, pp. 48–54. This article begins with a flawed historical survey of *Snow White,* but then proceeds to a valuable account of the digital restoration process.

282 *the first stuff they showed me* Johnston quoted in sidebar, MacQueen, "Epic Animation Restored," p. 31.

282 Snow White *was a beautiful picture* Ibid.

BIBLIOGRAPHY

ARTICLES

Andrew R. Boone, "Snow White and the Seven Dwarfs," *Popular Science Monthly,* January 1938, pp. 50–52, 131–132

Ruth B. Bottigheimer, "Jacob Grimm," *Dictionary of Literary Biography,* Vol. 90, pp. 100–107

——————, "Wilhelm Grimm," *Dictionary of Literary Biography,* Vol. 90, pp. 108–113

DeWitt Bodeen, "Marguerite Clark," *Films in Review,* December 1964, pp. 611-625

Ross Care, "Symphonists for the Sillies," *Funnyworld* 18 (summer 1978), pp. 38-48

Fred Carstensen, "A.P. Giannini," John A. Garraty and Mark C. Carnes, eds., *American National Biography* (New York: Oxford, 1999), Vol. 8, pp. 898-899

Barbara L. Ciccarelli, "A.H. Giannini," John A. Garraty and Mark C. Carnes, eds., *American National Biography* (New York: Oxford, 1999), Vol. 8, pp. 899-900

Walt Disney, "Why I Chose *Snow White,*" *Photoplay Studies,* Vol. III, no. 10 (1937), pp. 7-9

A. Minnie Herts, "The Children's Educational Theatre," *Atlantic Monthly,* December 1907, pp. 798-806

J.B. Kaufman, "Before Snow White," *Film History,* Vol. 5 (1993), pp. 158–175

Scott MacQueen, "*Snow White and the Seven Dwarfs:* Epic Animation Restored," *The Perfect Vision,* July 1994, pp. 26–31

Karen Merritt, "Da bambina a piccola madre: la transformazione americana di *Biancaneve e i sette nani,*" *Griffithiana* 31 (dicembre 1987), pp. 23–38; English translation: "The Little Girl/Little Mother Transformation: The American Evolution of 'Snow White and the Seven Dwarfs,'" pp. 105–121 in John Canemaker (ed.), *Storytelling in Animation: The Art of the Animated Image,* Vol. 2 (Los Angeles: American Film Institute, 1988)

——————, "Marguerite Clark as America's Snow White: The Resourceful Orphan Who Inspired Walt Disney," *Griffithiana* 64 (ottobre 1998), pp. 4–25 (includes parallel Italian translation)

Keith Scott, "Mickey Mouse, Radio Star," *Animato!* 39 (spring 1998), pp. 18–21

BOOKS

Robin Allan, *Walt Disney and Europe* (London: John Libbey, 1999)

D.L. Ashliman, *Folk and Fairy Tales: A Handbook* (Westport CT, London: Greenwood, 2004)

Michael Barrier, *Hollywood Cartoons: American Animation in Its Golden Age* (New York, Oxford: Oxford, 1999)

Rudy Behlmer, *America's Favorite Movies: Behind the Scenes* (New York: Ungar, 1982)

Giannalberto Bendazzi, *Cartoons: One Hundred Years of Cinema Animation* [English translation] (London: John Libbey, 1994)

Peter Bogdanovich, *Pieces of Time* (New York: Arbor House/Esquire, 1973)

Katherine M. Briggs (ed.), *A Dictionary of British Folk-Tales in the English Language* (London: Routledge and Kegan Paul, 1970, 1971)

Italo Calvino (George Martin, trans.), *Italian Folktales* (New York and London: Harcourt Brace Jovanovich, 1980)

John Canemaker, *Winsor McCay: His Life and Art* (New York: Abbeville, 1987)

——————, *Before the Animation Begins: The Art and Lives of Disney Inspirational Sketch Artists* (New York: Hyperion, 1996)

——————, *Paper Dreams: The Art & Artists of Disney Storyboards* (New York: Hyperion, 1999)

——————, *Walt Disney's Nine Old Men & The Art of Animation* (New York: Disney Editions, 2001)

Shamus Culhane, *Talking Animals and Other People* (New York: St. Martin's Press, 1986)

Christopher Finch, *The Art of Walt Disney: From Mickey Mouse to the Magic Kingdoms* (New York: Abrams, 1973)

Richard Fleischer, *Out of the Inkwell: Max Fleischer and the Animation Revolution* (Lexington, KY: University Press of Kentucky, 2005)

David Gerstein (ed.), *Walt Disney's Mickey and the Gang: Classic Stories in Verse* (Timonium, MD: Gemstone, 2005)

Didier Ghez (ed.), *Walt's People,* Vol. 2 (XLibris Corporation, 2006)

——————, *Walt's People,* Vol. 3 (XLibris Corporation, 2006)

——————, *Walt's People,* Vol. 4 (XLibris Corporation, 2007)

——————, *Walt's People,* Vol. 11 (XLibris Corporation, 2011)

Heidi Anne Heiner, *Sleeping Beauties: Sleeping Beauty and Snow White Tales From Around the World* (Nashville, TN: SurLaLune Press, 2010)

Stanley Hochman (ed.), *From Quasimodo to Scarlett O'Hara: A National Board of Review Anthology* (New York: Ungar, 1982)

Carsten Laqua, *Wie Micky unter die Nazis fiel: Walt Disney und Deutschland* (Reinbek bei Hamburg: Rowohlt Taschenbuch Verlag GmbH, 1992)

Georgios A. Megas (ed.), Helen Colaclides (trans.), *Folktales of Greece* (Chicago: University of Chicago Press, 1970)

Russell Merritt and J.B. Kaufman, *Walt Disney's Silly Symphonies: A Companion to the Classic Cartoon Series* (Gemona [Udine], Italy: La Cineteca del Friuli, 2006)

Charles Musser, *Edison Motion Pictures, 1890-1900* (Gemona: Le Giornate del Cinema Muto/Washington: Smithsonian Institution Press, 1997)

Iona and Peter Opie (ed.), *The Classic Fairy Tales* (New York: Oxford University Press, 1974)

David Robinson, *Das Cabinet des Dr. Caligari* (London: British Film Institute, 1997)

Maria Tatar (ed.), *The Classic Fairy Tales: Texts, Criticism* (New York, London: Norton, 1999)

——————, *The Annotated Brothers Grimm* (New York, London: Norton, 2004)

Frank Thomas and Ollie Johnston, *Disney Animation: The Illusion of Life* (New York: Abbeville Press, 1981)

George E. Turner (ed.), *The Cinema of Adventure, Romance & Terror* (Hollywood: ASC Press, 1989)

Hans-Jörg Uther, *The Types of International Folktales: A Classification and Bibliography, Based on the System of Antti Aarne and Stith Thompson* (Helsinki: Suomalainen Tiedeakatemia, Academia Scientiarum Fennica, 2004)

Edward Wagenknecht, *The Movies in the Age of Innocence* (Norman, OK: University of Oklahoma Press, 1962)

Orson Welles and Peter Bogdanovich, *This is Orson Welles* (New York: Da Capo-Perseus, 1992)

Jessie Braham White [Winthrop Ames], *Snow White and the Seven Dwarfs* [play script] (New York: Dodd, Mead, 1913)

Jessie Braham White [Winthrop Ames], *Snow White and the Seven Dwarfs* [play script] (New York: Samuel French, Inc., 1925)

INDEX

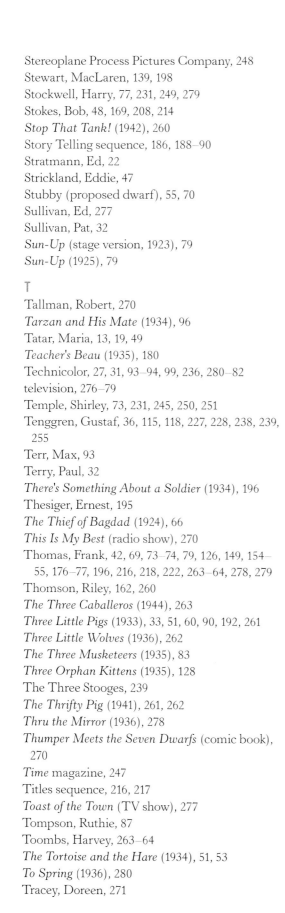

IMAGES COURTESY OF

IMAGES COURTESY THE WALT DISNEY ANIMATION RESEARCH LIBRARY AND THE WALT DISNEY ARCHIVES © DISNEY WITH THE EXCEPTION OF THE FOLLOWING:

WALT DISNEY FAMILY FOUNDATION
© Disney: 30, 35, 38, 44, 45, 46-47, 56-57, 58, 61, 63, 64, 67, 68, 71, 76, 80, 85, 86, 91, 92, 97 (bottom), 115, 116 (left), 117, 122, 124-125, 129, 160, 167, 169, 175, 176-177, 187, 195, 199, 227, 232 (left), 238-239, 240-241, 242-243, 244-245, 246-247, 249, 250, 251 (top), 253-256, 257, 259, 269, 283
© Radio City Music Hall: 239
© Time, Inc.: 247
© Sony: 273

DISNEY PHOTO LIBRARY
© Disney: 34, 49, 59-60, 93, 95, 223, 224, 231, 232 (right), 237, 248, 268, 271, 277, 279

THE AUTHOR'S COLLECTION
© Disney: 40-41, 88, 273

ACADEMY FILM ARCHIVE
© Disney: 87, 281, 282

ACADEMY OF MOTION PICTURE ARTS AND SCIENCES
26

ALAMY
12, 13, 33

BANK OF AMERICA HERITAGE AND ARCHIVES
225

JERRY BECK
© King Features Syndicate: 27
©2002 - 2010 King Features Syndicate, Inc. / Fleischer Studios, Inc. TM Hearst Holdings, Inc. / Fleischer Studios, Inc.

BILLY IRELAND CARTOON LIBRARY, OHIO STATE UNIVERSITY
74

DEREK BOOTHROYD
18

BRITISH FILM INSTITUTE
25

CORBIS
78

GEORGE EASTMAN HOUSE
21,22

MIKE GLAD
© Disney: 54, 109, 141, 142, 172, 203

HATHI TRUST
20: Winthrop Ames, from *Modern Theatre Construction* © 2011 by Edward Bernard Kinsila, published by Dutt Press.

TONY HOFFARTH
251 (bottom)

STEVE ISON
© Disney: 38, 101

NEW YORK PUBLIC LIBRARY
14, 16, 19
p. 14: Print Collection, Miriam and Ira D. Wallach Division of Art, Prints, and Photographs, The New York Public Library, Astor, Lenox, and Tilden Foundations
pp. 16, 19: Billy Rose Theatre Division, The New York Library for the Performing Arts, Astor, Lenox, and Tilden Foundations

WIKIMEDIA COMMONS
15, 17, 24, 69, 96

ACKNOWLEDGMENTS

FROM THE AUTHOR

The opportunity to research the background of *Snow White and the Seven Dwarfs*—to get inside this beautiful film and explore it in depth—has been one of the great blessings of my life, and I can never adequately thank those who made it possible. Above all, I owe an incalculable debt to The Walt Disney Family Foundation, and especially to its founder, Diane Disney Miller, who not only supported the idea of this book from the beginning, but fought for the integrity of the project against sometimes daunting odds.

A book of this kind can never be written without great quantities of help, and I am humbled to realize how many kind and talented individuals have helped me with this one. Several of them in the Collections department of the Walt Disney Family Museum have become good friends as well as colleagues, in particular Michael Labrie, Mark Gibson, Issey Honton, Brenda Litzinger, Tonja Morris, Anel Muller, Harvey Newman, Ben Peters, Martín Salazar, and Lynn Zook. Thanks to their help, I've drawn liberally on the Museum's collection for unique research material as well as extremely rare illustrations.

Needless to say, the cooperation of the Walt Disney Company has also been indispensable to the writing of this book. In particular, I'm grateful to Howard Green, Vice President of Studio Communications at the company, to Margaret Adamic in the Corporate Legal office, to Booker White and Leslie Smith in the studio music department, and to Dave Smith, Robert Tieman, and Rebecca Cline of the Walt Disney Archives—as well as the other kind and (extraordinarily) patient Archivists who included, during my work on this book, Edward Ovalle, Michael Buckhoff, Alesha Reyes, Collette Espino, and Brian Hoffman. Similarly, the Walt Disney Animation Research Library has also been both an important site for research and an extremely pleasant place to visit, thanks especially to Lella Smith, Vivian Procopio, Ann Hansen, Fox Carney, Doug Engalla, Marisa Leonardi, Kristen McCormick, Jackie Vasquez, Darryl Vontoure, Mary Walsh, and Patrick White.

At other institutions, too, I have benefited from the help of dedicated and generous individuals. At the Special Collections Department of Margaret Herrick Library, Academy of Motion Picture Arts and Sciences, Barbara Hall, Jenny Romero, and Howard Prouty have gone out of their way to find and make available the historical materials I needed. At George Eastman House in Rochester, New York, Nancy Kauffman, Ed Stratmann, and Jared Case have done the same, as have Pat Loughney, Caroline Yeager, Dan Wagner and, in the Eastman House library, Rachel Stuhlman. At the Library of Congress, I'm particularly grateful to Mike Mashon, Madeline Matz, Rosemary Hanes, and Josie Walters-Johnston. At the Academy, Laura Lee McKay, a skilled historian in her own right, went far beyond the usual role of a research assistant, turning up rare information previously unknown to me. Ned Comstock, of the Cinema-Television Library, University of Southern California, a tireless and resourceful benefactor of so many film historians, has made an unusually great contribution to this book. Maryann Chach of New York's Shubert Archive, Christine Karatnytsky (Billy Rose Theatre Collection, Lincoln Center branch) and Cynthia Rosado (Special Collections) of the New York Public Library, Ann E. Butler of New York University, Pamela Madsen of the Harvard Theatre Collection, and Sandra Joy Lee Aguilar and Taylor Nygaard of the Warner Bros. Archives (USC) have yielded rare treasures from their respective collections which have cast new light on the story of *Snow White*. So has Bryony Dixon of the British Film Institute, whose special efforts made rare fragments of film available for viewing.

All of us owe a tremendous debt to the extraordinary artists who created *Snow White and the Seven Dwarfs* in the 1930s. I am especially indebted to several who shared with me their memories of the film: Art Babbitt, Bob Broughton, Bill Cottrell, Bill Justice, Ward Kimball, Gordon Legg, Grim Natwick, Kendall O'Connor, and Clair Weeks. Marge Champion, the original Snow White, graciously recalled her experiences for John Canemaker and Ted Thomas, an interview I've been privileged to share.

The richly varied illustrations in this book, a source of special pride, have drawn voraciously on the collections of the Walt Disney Family Foundation and the Walt Disney Animation Research Library, whose staffs have previously been mentioned. Special mention should be made of the Walt Disney Photo Library, which has also provided a wealth of precious visuals, thanks to the help of Ed Squair, Andrea Carbone, Rick Lorentz, LaToya Morgan, and Michael Buckhoff. And some of the rarest and most exciting illustrations appear thanks to the kindness of Michael Pogorzelski and May Haduong (Academy Film Archive, Los Angeles), Marilyn Scott and Jenny Robb (Billy Ireland Cartoon Library and Museum, Ohio State University), David Mendoza (Bank of America Heritage and Archives, San Francisco), the aforementioned Bryony Dixon (British Film Institute), and several private collectors and suppliers of original animation art: Howard Lowery, Pete Merolo, and Mike Glad. Any mention of private collectors must necessarily single out Stephen H. Ison, whose legendary private collection of *Snow White* production art, now in the possession of the ARL, has had the effect of returning to the Disney company a vital and invaluable part of its legacy.

Fellow Disney historians, whom I'm proud to call friends as well as colleagues, have also given generously for the betterment of this book. Among these are Michael Barrier, John Canemaker, Paul F. Anderson, Robin Allan, Joe Campana, Bill Cotter, David Gerstein, Didier Ghez, Bruce Gordon, Katherine and Richard Greene, Russell and Karen Merritt, Don Peri, and Keith Scott. Other, less Disney-centric historians have provided indispensable help too: Catherine A. Surowiec and Geoff Brown, Jerry Beck, Rudy and Stacey Behlmer, Tim Engels, David Mayer, Scott Phillips, David Robinson, Ben Urish, and Steve Vaught. The multitalented Scott MacQueen has kindly offered the benefit of his unique experience and insights, an offer of which I've taken shameless advantage. Folklore specialist Maria Tatar has benefited my knowledge of Snow White's literary background enormously, not only through her own writing but through her patient assistance to a novice in the field. Helmut Färber and Ulrich Reudel, separately, have translated extremely rare German documents for me; Piera Patat has done the same with Italian. Charles Wixson and Phyllis Berenson have lent their legal expertise to researching the various *Snow White* lawsuits. Many of the above have also read all or part of the manuscript and offered helpful comments, as have Bodie Weiss and Cathy Biggs.

Special thanks are also due to two individuals at the Wichita Public Library: Michelle Enke (history collections) and Gavin Thomas (interlibrary loan). Nan Myers, government documents librarian at Wichita State University, guided me through the maze of Disney copyrights, trademarks, and patents of the 1930s, including the Shadowgraph patent. And for miscellaneous help of various kinds, it's a pleasure to thank Tracey, Jim, Molly and Sam Doyle; Jo Ann Briseño; Bill and Ellie Klein; and, for their sterling technical support, the fine folks at Concergent.

Publication of this book marks an important milestone for The Walt Disney Family Foundation Press, and we are delighted to acknowledge the crucial role played by our silent partner, Weldon Owen, of San Francisco, as well as project manager Ani Chamichian. A large and able contingent of Weldon Owen's staff, led by Roger Shaw, Mariah Bear, and Kelly Booth, has made an indispensable contribution to this book. Mariah and the rest of the editorial staff, in particular Elizabeth Dougherty, Katharine Moore, and Emelie Griffin, responded to my sometimes less than diplomatic demands with unfailing courtesy and grace, as well as professionalism. And I am eternally grateful to art director Marisa Kwek and designer Michel Gadwa for working their visual wizardry on the design of the book.

Margaret and Chris Kaufman have patiently borne with my long-term focus on *Snow White,* and have also contributed assistance and insights of their own. Little Ali and Layla showed their support for the project by remaining, respectively, grumpy and happy at all times. And to bring these acknowledgments full circle, I must close with my sincere gratitude for the moral and practical support of the Walt Disney Family Foundation, in particular Diane and Ron Miller and Walter Elias Disney Miller. I'm as thankful for their help as I am to be able to call them friends—and that's very thankful.

J.B. Kaufman

April 2012

FROM WELDON OWEN

Special thanks to John Owen and Ani Chamichian, and to Charmaine Zoe for image assistance. Invaluable editorial help came from Ian Cannon, Ken DellaPenta, Gail Nelson-Bonebrake, Kim Oswell, Cathleen Small, and Katie Schlossberg, and expert design assistance from Sarah Edelstein and Katie Cavenee. Color proofing by Tamara Khalaf at the Walt Disney Animation Research Library.

First published in Great Britain 2012
by Aurum Press Ltd
7 Greenland Street
London NW1 0ND
www.aurumpress.co.uk

Published by arrangement with Weldon Owen Inc, 415 Jackson Street,
San Francisco, California 94111, United States of America

A catalogue record for this book is available from the British Library.

ISBN 978 1 78131 025 0

10 9 8 7 6 5 4 3 2 1

2016 2015 2014 2013 2012

Printed in China by Toppan-Leefung

weldon**owen**

President, CEO Terry Newell
VP, Sales and New Business Development
Amy Kaneko
VP, Publisher Roger Shaw
Executive Editor Mariah Bear
Project Editor Elizabeth Dougherty, Emelie Griffin
Editor Katharine Moore
Creative Director Kelly Booth
Art Director Marisa Kwek
Designer Michel Gadwa
Production Director Chris Hemesath
Production Manager Michelle Duggan
Weldon Owen is a division of **BONNIER**
www.weldonowen.com